# Revenue Sources of Local Governments



With limited fiscal capabilities, effective and efficient budgeting is a necessity for local governments in the United States. Acknowledging the critical (but often overlooked) part that raising enough revenue to fund desirable and mandatory programs plays in the budgetary process, this book offers an exclusive and comprehensive examination of the revenue side of the budget. It provides much-needed and wide-ranging context for examining and understanding local government revenues and local government revenue policy.

Author J. Edwin Benton presents a comprehensive overview of the revenue structure for local governments, in general, and for counties, municipalities, townships, special districts, and school districts, in particular. The bulk of this book meticulously examines the historical patterns and trends in revenue usage by local governments and provides explanations for variations among different units of government, states, and regions of the country. This book enhances our understanding of the most relevant research and aids in refining theories that seek to explain why local governments (or different types of local governments) rely more on certain kinds of revenues. It also offers immediately applicable real-world case studies on revenue-raising capabilities, practicalities, and experiences of local governments around the country. It will be of enormous interest to public budgeting practitioners, students, and scholars.

**J. Edwin Benton** is a Professor of Political Science and Public Administration at the University of South Florida. He has written extensively about county government, state-local relations, urban government and politics, intergovernmental fiscal behavior, and city-county consolidation. His articles have appeared in top-ranking journals, and he is the author or co-author of nearly 40 technical/grant reports/white papers for state and local governments, local government associations, and non-profit organizations.

"This book is a timely and important treatise on the oft-overlooked revenue side of local government ledgers. J. Edwin Benton's discussion and analysis of the various resources available to local governments, as well as those proscribed to them, enhance our understanding of budgeting and provide insight into what might be considered by elected and appointed city officials. A must read."

**Michael A. Pagano**, *Dean Emeritus & Professor Emeritus, University of Illinois Chicago, USA*

"J. Edwin Benton's study of local government revenue sources provides an extensive analysis of the complex world of taxation, fees, intergovernmental transfers, and borrowed funds. Through engaging description and meticulous evaluation of various revenue streams, this volume builds a solid foundation for scholars and students alike."

**Ann O'M. Bowman**, *Professor and Hazel Davis and Robert Kennedy Endowed Chair, Texas A&M University, USA*

"This book helps the reader understand the fundamentals of the revenue streams of local governments while also providing guidance on opportunities for revenue improvements. It will be useful to practitioners and students in the classroom, and it is certain to be a classic in the field."

**Bruce D. McDonald, III**, *Professor, North Carolina State University, USA*

# Revenue Sources of Local Governments

## Persisting Challenges and Emerging Opportunities

**J. Edwin Benton**

Routledge
Taylor & Francis Group
NEW YORK AND LONDON

Designed cover image: Shutterstock

First published 2024
by Routledge
605 Third Avenue, New York, NY 10158

and by Routledge
4 Park Square, Milton Park, Abingdon, Oxon, OX14 4RN

*Routledge is an imprint of the Taylor & Francis Group, an informa business*



*Library of Congress Cataloging-in-Publication Data*
Names: Benton, J. Edwin, 1950- author.
Title: Revenue sources of local governments : persisting challenges and emerging opportunities / J. Edwin Benton.
Description: New York, NY : Routledge, 2024. | Includes bibliographical references and index.
Identifiers: LCCN 2023033856 (print) | LCCN 2023033857 (ebook) | ISBN 9781032640372 (hardback) | ISBN 9781032640365 (paperback) | ISBN 9781032640389 (ebook)
Subjects: LCSH: Local finance--United States. | Local government--United States.
Classification: LCC HJ9145 .B46 2024 (print) | LCC HJ9145 (ebook) | DDC 336/.01473--dc23/eng/20230929
LC record available at https://lccn.loc.gov/2023033856
LC ebook record available at https://lccn.loc.gov/2023033857

ISBN: 978-1-032-64037-2 (hbk)
ISBN: 978-1-032-64036-5 (pbk)
ISBN: 978-1-032-64038-9 (ebk)

DOI: 10.4324/9781032640389

Typeset in Times New Roman
by KnowledgeWorks Global Ltd.

**Dedicated to**

**my wife**

**Teresa Thomas Benton**

# Contents

# Foreword

Local governments are the engine of American government. They provide or coordinate many of the services we care about most in our daily lives: streets, public safety, education, drinking water, sewer service, electricity, and emergency medical services. Strong communities also need good buildings for schools, universities, libraries, hospitals, parks, and sports arenas. Without revenue, the services will stop, and the facilities will quickly close. It is frightening to imagine where things would be without well-funded local services—it is no exaggeration to say that without sufficient revenue for local governments, chaos would ensue.

Revenues need to be sufficient to fund services, but this is not enough. We expect the tax burden to be fair and predictable, and for public money to be well managed. We want a fiscal policy to contribute to economic growth and a better environment. Charges and fees need to be fair and productive. We want to build new public facilities that will enhance local wealth with a manageable plan of payments. In short, a prosperous, growing, equitable, and sustainable community relies on a good revenue policy.

Government policy does not happen overnight; it has deep roots that explain and constrain the present and the future. Protests about tax policy go back to the founding of the U.S. The notorious Boston Tea Party led to the American Revolution, and the Whiskey Rebellion during President George Washington's term imposed a practical constraint on government tax policy. In 1978, the Proposition 13 tax rebellion in California changed the property tax forever in that state and many others. Understanding the historical evolution of tax policy is critical to knowing what is and is not possible in the current day.

Professor J. Edwin Benton has assembled an impressive book that explains these issues to the reader. It details how local governments are funded, and the recurring issues facing communities. It uses long-term data so the reader can see the evolution of tax policy. It covers in depth the perennial issues of fairness, efficiency, and economic growth. Moreover, this book breaks this analysis down both by type of revenue source and by type of local government. Schools, for example, are funded much differently than cities, and one needs to understand this to know why one tax is higher than another and the distribution of the tax burden on the community.

Benton also identifies some of the pressing challenges that we will face in the future: the explosion of information sharing and technology, pressing security threats beginning on September 11, 2001 that continue to test us, and the challenge of worldwide public health crises such as COVID-19. These present troubling issues for local governments that will assuredly require new sustainable revenue sources. Benton identifies several new or growing revenue sources that offer opportunities and will be on the agenda for local governments. Therefore, this book foreshadows future developments in local government.

Local government is particularly earthy, as the issues affect our property, neighborhoods, and businesses. A new stoplight at a nearby intersection or changes in a nearby park can be very emotional issues for some because they are so local and personal. As Benton points out, political and social issues are often more intense at the local level. These issues then affect the consideration of financing local services, making these issues much more interesting and multilayered with a variety of considerations affecting the decision.

Practitioners, students, and researchers will all find this book to be very valuable. Those who are not experts in government finance will find that this book gets them up to speed quickly and foreshadows the issues to come. It will be a book you keep handy and come back to often.

John R. Bartle
Dean, College of Public Affairs and Community Service
Professor of Public Administration
University of Nebraska at Omaha

# Preface

Local governments (i.e., counties, municipalities, townships, special districts, and school districts) are without a doubt the bedrock of the American system of democratic government and governance. Some would even go so far as to say that it is at the local level of government "where the rubber meets the road" and people at some point are most likely to connect with a local government of some kind, while people are also more likely to look to local government for the provision of the most basic kinds of services that affect a person's quality of life (i.e., ranging from collecting and disposing of their garbage, providing health and welfare services, fire and police protection, and amenities like libraries, street lighting, sidewalks, parks and recreational facilities, and a host of utilities like potable water, sewage, electric power, and natural gas, in addition to offering K12 and post-high school educational opportunities. Moreover, public opinion polls over the years have consistently informed us that Americans are more likely to trust and respect their local government officials than the federal government or their state governments. Yet, all of this seems somewhat odd because the U.S. Constitution does not even mention—even once—local governments. But, within a very short period of time, these seemingly unmentioned, nameless, and perhaps forgotten or ignored governmental entities emerged as major players on the governmental scene. So fast-forward and welcome to the local government world of the third decade of the 21st century, where it often seems that these omnipresent fixtures take center stage even if they do not have all the answers or ready-made solutions to their citizens' questions and concerns.

Given the central role that local governments frequently play in our lives and the faith, confidence, and hope we place in them, it is important for the public to both understand and appreciate the fiscal challenges, constraints from their constituents and higher levels of government, and social, economic, and political pitfalls associated with the awesome task of raising a sufficiently large amount of monetary resources while being ever mindful of how their decisions affect the local and state (and perhaps national and global) economy, as well as the poor, needy, overlooked, and sometimes shunned people in their jurisdictions. How will the revenue-raising options they chose to use to amass enough money to run their governments affect the pocketbooks of their citizens? Then, there are always social and racial equity and justice issues to consider when raising huge sums of revenue for the public good. These are enormous concerns and considerations when formulating a budget designed to provide the long menu of staple services they do, as well as an ever-expanding wish list of more services and programs. It is as though the public has never seen a service that it does not like or want. Therefore, the purpose for writing this book is two-fold. First, it hopefully will serve to enlighten the governed (that is, local government citizens) as to the awesome and demanding job of crafting a balanced budget that will please most of the people in their county, municipality, township, or special or school district, and guide for local government practitioners who seek to learn from the past successes and failures when it comes to the raising of the necessary revenues to provide the most good for their community with the least amount of money. In addition to learning from history, it is hoped that local practitioners will dare to be bold with a willingness to try some of the innovative ideas mentioned in this book for raising sufficient money to run their county, city, township, special district or school district, as well as developing additional "out-of-the-box" strategies and notions along these lines.

Furthermore, it is my earnest hope that scholars reading this book will be encouraged to test some of the assumptions and implied hypotheses mentioned herein. If so, we could expand our knowledge base to test the accuracy of old theories about local government decision-making in the areas of government finances and budgeting, as well as formulate new or revised theories. Additionally, the data analysis presented here should provide local government officials with "food for thought" and a desire to learn more from the current tumultuous and uncertain economic and political environment within which they must function and conduct the public's business at the local grassroots level of our system of government. Truly, local governments and local government officials, and the public they serve are living in and trying to navigate through "uncharted waters." This is why a follow-up to this book is planned so as to analyze revenue data for 2021 and beyond when it becomes available in order to learn more about the impact that the COVID-19 pandemic and the unusually high rate of inflation have had and is likely to continue to have on the revenue-raising capabilities of local governments and the elected and appointed officials who lead them presently and in the uncertain future that lies ahead.

# Acknowledgments

It goes without saying that there seem to be an infinite number of people to thank for what they have contributed, individually and collectively, to my ability and tenacity to write this book, as my journey began almost 12 years ago. If I fail to acknowledge anyone who deserves mentioning, I truly apologize in advance since it was an unintentional oversight for someone whose age is quietly catching up with him as he endeavors to complete an ambitious research agenda that he set for himself about ten years ago.

First, let me thank two of the most wonderful staff members of the School of Interdisciplinary Global Studies at the University of South Florida. Ms. Jamie Lane was always gracious with her time in printing off figures included in my book from the school's color printer which facilitated greatly my ability to analyze a tremendous amount of data. Moreover, she assisted me with things such as helping me assemble and upload my annual evaluation report (as she does for many of our faculty) which allowed me to spend precious time making my final edits on this book. Jamie was also instrumental in having a new computer installed in my campus office which permitted me to work from there when I needed to be in the office and was able to print draft copies of chapters for editing purposes. Like, Ms. Lane, Ms. Kimberly Jones was another person who was gracious with her time in answering questions and explaining some new tricks in how to navigate through and employ some relatively new technologically advanced desktop publishing tasks and routines. Her knowledge of these kinds of things was nothing short of amazing! In addition, she also assisted me in getting my new computer up and running so that I would be able to print material for my book for final proofing and editing.

Trusted, loyal, highly valued, and encouraging colleagues John Bartle (University of Nebraska-Omaha), Michael Pagano (University of Illinois, Chicago), John Kincaid (Lafayette College), Bruce McDonald (North Carolina State University), David Berman (Arizona State University), and Michael Sccicitano (University of Florida) read several draft chapters of my manuscript and provided me with excellent and inspiring feedback and suggestions for improving the quality of the manuscript and its readability, as did several blind reviewers used by the publisher (Routledge). John Bartle was especially helpful in that he and some of his colleagues assembled and made available to me and other scholars data contained in the 2017 *Compendium of Local Government Finances* which I vitally needed to complete this book with the most recent data on local government revenues. This source of official local government financial data is normally published every five years (in years ending in "2" and "7"). When I started this book, I had only 2012 data and was adamant that I would not publish the book without being able to include data from 2017. Unfortunately, the collection and publication of these data for general consumption were delayed for an extraordinarily long time because of the COVID-19 health pandemic. In the past, these data were available every 2–3 years after being collected. However, John and others had been successful in getting this data released, so I would be able to use it in the book. John was also gracious in agreeing to write the Foreword for the book. A special "thank you" goes out to Bruce McDonald for being willing to write an endorsement for the book, while I am very appreciative of my long-time friend and colleague Ann Bowman (Texas A&M University) for also writing an endorsement for the book. In addition to being the co-author (with Richard Kearney) of one of the leading state and local government textbooks, Ann has been an inspirational professional role model to me and other colleagues who conduct research in our particular area of study; it also helps that, like me, she is a former University of South Carolina Gamecock but now is an A&M Aggie! I am also greatly appreciative of the support and encouragement of my friend and greatly trusted colleague, Mike Sccicitanno (former Editor-in-Chief of the *State and Local Government Review*), with whom I closely worked for ten years (2011–2021 as the Managing Editor of *SLGR*). Knowing about the all-encompassing time it took me to perform my duties for the journal, he always supported and encouraged me to keep plugging away at my writing. When I would get discouraged and overloaded, he would give me a pep talk and back to work I went! Thank you, Mike, for your support and cheering me on!

But, my greatest "thank you' goes to my devoted wife, Terry, and my daughter, Brittany. They have both made my life easier, more enjoyable, and less stressful by being just the great people they are—immediate family but, most importantly, friends. As those of you in academia know, life in the academy can be lonely and is filled with ups and downs and great expectations from many people (fellow faculty, administrators, students, media, and the public). Both my wife and daughter have truly been the "day in and day out" supporters, encouragers, confidents, and inspirers to lean on during times of discouragement, challenges, and burnout. I couldn't ask for better people to be around me! When I suffered a mild stroke in April 2022, they assumed more of the responsibilities of the home and helped in myriad other ways to lighten the load for me so I could turn my complete attention to writing. Terry and Brittany, I could not do what I do and accomplish what I have if it weren't for the two of you! Terry has read draft after draft and proofread the manuscript more times than I can count and never said "no" when I knew she was tired of seeing another draft. She never complained but only offered encouragement and good advice. At this point, I would be remiss if I forget to mention the love and support of our two cats in Tampa—Cassie Mae and Tigger—and the four in Georgetown—Daisy, Allie, Baby Kitty, and Moma Kitty, for they are stress releasers as well as adorable and loveable kitties.

Aside form the encouragement and support given to me by those people mentioned above, it is important that I share perhaps the greatest incentive for me to complete the book. For the last few years, I have had an insatiable passion to push the book to ultimate publication as a result of what I saw happening around the country with not one but three recessions (dot com recession at the beginning of the 21st century, the Great Recession, and the COVID-induced recession). Then, what was happening in my hometown of Georgetown, South Carolina, was particularly gut-wrenching to watch. I have witnessed the struggle that Georgetown City officials had with making ends meet in an area where the effects of the Great Recession lingered for a longer period of time after economists claimed that the recession had ended in 2009 and are currently struggling to keep their heads above water with the wave of rapid inflation continuing to wreak havoc with not only the local economy but with efforts of the City to raise sufficient revenue to pay for the provision of even basic services. Therefore, I earnestly hope and pray that my book, in some small way, will offer a modicum of encouragement to local government officials everywhere that there is "light at the end of the tunnel" and you can make it to solid solvent ground if you continue your efforts and stay committed to your government and the people you serve. I say this with all humility because I have always regarded myself as a "blue collar scholar" and a "pracacademic" who consciously and often leaves the mythical "Ivy Tower" to mix, interact, and work side by side with the folks who live, work, and serve "where the rubber meets the road."

J. Edwin Benton
May 1, 2023

# 1 Revenue Side of the Local Government Budget

## The Money to Match Expenditures

On a cold, snowy Tuesday evening in early February 2023, the city manager, budget/finance director, 17 department heads, mayor, and six members of the city council of a suburban fringe city of approximately 22,000 persons in the Philadelphia metropolitan area attend the first of what will be a series of five budget workshops that will be held over the next three months. Their job is to begin the process of hammering out the details of the proposed city budget for the next fiscal year. Prior to this initial workshop, staff from the city's line departments and agencies and staff from the city's budget/finance office have had multiple meetings and traded countless communiques over the last several months in a very time-consuming effort to craft a proposed budget document that will be examined at this Tuesday evening meeting. In the weeks after the conclusion of the last workshop, the city's elected officials (i.e., the council and mayor) will continue the due diligent exercise of analyzing, discussing, and debating the merits and demerits of the content of the continually evolving proposed budget document in one or more public council meetings (with possible input from the general public, businesses, and citizen groups) before ultimately voting to adopt, amend, or even reject the final product. Their deadline to make a final decision on the adoption of a budget (as it still is in many local jurisdictions that operate on a July 1–June 30 fiscal year) is the last day of the month of June since this day marks the end of the current fiscal year.

Joining the public officials mentioned above at this first budget workshop are 12 citizens, representatives from five civic groups, three employee unions and three city regulatory boards, two vendors who have contracts with the city, and one local television and two newspaper reporters who have braved the cold weather to watch the night's proceedings from the audience gallery. Just two weeks before this meeting, the manager had unveiled to the mayor, members of city council, press, and public a proposed budget document after having received budget requests from department heads and revenue estimates from the city's budget/finance office.

At tonight's meeting, city department heads undoubtedly will be asked to explain and justify the need and the reasons behind their proposed departmental

DOI: 10.4324/9781032640389-1

operating costs, personnel requests, and capital expenditure projects. Moreover, the staff of the city's budget/finance office is likely to face questioning about the accuracy of their revenue projections. After tonight's meeting, several public hearings are also scheduled so that interested residents and civic and community groups can provide input to those persons who are charged with the responsibility of finalizing and adopting the budget. Others will also provide input and perspective in the weeks ahead. For instance, a representative from the state revenue department will provide estimates of the amount of state aid and shared revenue the city can expect to receive from the State of Pennsylvania, while the city's budget/finance office will inform the council, mayor, and manager as to the likelihood of receiving funding from pending federal grant applications, other federal government sources, and private sector donations or in-kind assistance. In addition, an economist from the Fels Institute of Government at the University of Pennsylvania will provide an assessment of the state of the national, state, and local economies and what these projections could mean for the revenue collections of the city. This representative will also provide an update on the municipal bond market; in the event, the city is contemplating borrowing money through the sale of bonds to balance this year's budget and finance capital improvements. All in all, a significant amount of time and effort is likely to be devoted to debate and consider the wisdom and necessity of proposed expenditures, to determine how much money should be allocated to carry out the myriad functions of the city and to provide a long menu of city services, and to determine the best way to raise the necessary revenue to accomplish these purposes.

Suffice it to say that other local governments in the area (i.e., large-, small-, and medium-sized cities, Bucks County, several townships, and a number of special service districts/authorities and school districts) will be going through a similar process in the upcoming months in an attempt to strike a balance between the service needs of their respective jurisdictions and the pocketbooks of local residents, businesses, and industries. Moreover, this process is repeated many times on an annual basis in the Nation's over 19,000 municipalities, 3,032 counties (or parishes in Louisiana and boroughs in Alaska), approximately 16,500 towns and townships, nearly 13,500 school districts, and roughly 35,000 special service districts, as local officials, in the words of political scientist Harold Lasswell (1936), endeavor to define and identify "who gets what, when, and how." This means that around 87,000 local governments across the United States annually prepare a budget document that identifies how much money from a variety of sources will be raised (revenues) and ultimately spent (expenditures) for thousands of services and programs.

Simply stated, budgeting becomes a necessity for every type of government since there is a limited amount of resources (i.e., money) that can be reasonably extracted from individuals and businesses.[1] As such, "budgeting is a process of allocating resources to prevent the waste of scarce resources, setting the size of the public sector, and deciding what government activities are supported from that pool of public resources" (Mikesell 2018, 26). Even if governments had infinite resources to draw upon, they would still have to be involved in fashioning a budget (for instance, to check for efficiencies and effectiveness or guard against waste or corruption), but the budgeting process would certainly be made easier and thereby less agonizing. Governments, therefore, would merely determine how much they wished to spend in the upcoming fiscal year to provide services and programs expected or demanded of their citizens and then draw down a sum of money from an unlimited pool. But, of course, this is not reality. Throughout his classic book *City Limits*, Peterson (1981) constantly emphasizes the inherent limited fiscal capabilities of local governments. Limitations range from state constitutional and/or statutory provisions regarding revenue options and debt restrictions to the states' willingness to share some of its revenue to economic realities of local communities to citizens' attitudes and views toward government and taxing and spending generally. Therefore, since local governments must live within a limited amount of money available to them, this clearly implies that projected expenditures are inextricably related to and indeed dependent on the government's ability to raise an adequate amount of revenue. Consequently, the ability of every government to amass enough money to fund desirable services and programs becomes an issue of paramount importance and ultimately determines how much money can be spent.

Given the critical part that raising revenues plays in the budgetary process, it seems appropriate that an exclusive and comprehensive examination of the revenue side of the budget as conducted in this book would be useful to both scholars and state and local government practitioners. For scholars, it would enhance the knowledge base in this area of research and aid in refining theories that seek to explain why local governments (or different types of local governments) rely more on certain kinds of revenues as opposed to other revenue alternatives. For practitioners, it would provide them with important information on revenue-raising capabilities, practicalities, and experiences of local governments in other states or in other local governments in their own state. Moreover, for reasons discussed further below in this chapter, this book will focus exclusively on the revenue-raising efforts of local governments (i.e., counties, municipalities, townships, special districts, and school districts) in the United States.

## Public budgets and budgeting

As anyone knows, government spending must be financed. As explained by Mikesell (2018, 56), "receiving the benefits of a good or service is linked in the private sector to you paying for it (you have to buy it before you can use it), while in the public sector what the government provides does not determine how its operations will be financed." Thus, public finance is divided into two distinct parts: the expenditure planning side and the revenue planning side. The expenditure side of budgeting "sets the size of the public sector, establishing what is provided, how it is provided, and who gets it, while the revenue side determines whose real income will be reduced to finance the provision of budgeted services" (Mikesell 2018, 56). Any thorough study such as the one conducted in this volume that examines the how's, why's, and what's of raising local government revenues and provides viable explanations and motivations for these governments' revenue choices logically needs to start with a basic description and discussion of the nature of public budgets and budgeting.

### *Public budgets*

As noted above, public budgets describe what governments do by recording how governments raise and spend money. A budget connects tasks to be performed with the amount of resources necessary to accomplish those tasks, thereby guaranteeing that money will be available to provide police and fire protection and health care and welfare services; construct and operate recreational facilities, schools, libraries, and jails; build and maintain streets and sidewalks; conduct elections; collect and dispose of sewage and solid waste; illuminate streets and roads; and so forth. Budgets limit expenditures to the revenues available so as to ensure balance and avoid overspending. Most of the work in devising a budget is technical—for example, estimating how much it will cost to inoculate 2,000 school-aged children against childhood diseases or how much revenue will be produced from a 1 mill levy on residential and commercial properties. Public budgets, however, are not simply technical managerial documents but rather they are, in the words of Irene Rubin (1993, 1), "inherently and profoundly political" documents. In a similar vein, Harold Lasswell (1936) refers to the public budget as the single, most important political document that a government will adopt. The case for a public budget being "political" gains added credence, when one considers the following salient points made by Rubin (1993, 1–2):

- Budgets reflect choices about what governments will and will not do; that is, they reflect general public consensus about what kinds of services governments should provide and what citizens are entitled to as members of society.
- Budgets show priorities—between emergency medical services and storm water drainage, parks and economic development, libraries and solid waste collection and disposal, and the eastern versus the northern part of the county. Simply put, the budget process referees between individuals and groups who want different things from government and determines who gets what.
- Budgets reflect the virtual proportion of decisions made for local and constituency objectives and for efficiency, effectiveness, and broader public goals. In short, budgets reflect the degree of importance local legislators place on pleasing their constituents and legislators' willingness to listen to interest group demands.

- Budgets provide a powerful tool of accountability to citizens who want to know how the government is spending their money and if government has basically followed their preferences; in this way, budgeting connects citizen preferences and governmental outcomes.
- Budgets reveal citizens' preferences for different forms of taxation and different levels of taxation as well as the ability of specific groups of taxpayers to shift tax burdens to others; likewise, budgets can signal citizens' preferences for shifting the burdens of providing services and their costs to users instead of taxpayers.
- Budgets of local governments influence local economies and subsequently affect the level of employment in the community and region.
- Budgets reveal the relative power of different individuals and organizations to influence budget outcomes. More specifically, budgetary decision-making provides a glimpse into the relative influence of budget actors within and between branches of government as well as the importance of citizens in general and specific interest groups.

In all of these ways, public budgeting is quite political. While budgeting is not typical of other political processes, it is nonetheless an important and distinctive arena in politics. It is important because of the precise policy issues revealed in the budget—that is, the scope of government, the allocation of wealth, the openness of government to interest groups, and the accountability of government to the public it serves (Rubin 1993). It is distinctive because these decisions have to occur in the context of budgeting, with its need for balance, its openness to the environment, and its requirement for timely decisions so that governments continue to operate without interruption.

In his seminal work on budgeting entitled *The Politics of the Budgetary Process*, Aaron Wildavsky (1966) also asserts that politics is a significant attribute of budgets and that budgets are strongly influenced by political forces since those people who control the executive and legislative branches are in a strategic position to determine who pays (revenues) and who receives (expenditures). But Wildavsky does not stop here in his characterization of budgets and the budget process, as he identifies three additional important features of both.

First, budgets, for the most part, are conservative entities. That is, they usually preserve the status quo, generally, do not reconsider or evaluate the merits or value of existing programs, and change incrementally from year to the next. Stated differently, budgets change very little from year to year, and the budget in a given year typically is nothing more than last year's revenue and expenditure figures with a small increment added (or deleted). The exception to this typical pattern is when local governments experience the infusion of large new sources of funds (e.g., federal revenue-sharing funds from the early 1970s through the mid-1980s and American Rescue Plan Act money in 2002–24). In such instances, budgets can experience significant change.

Second, budgets are fundamentally fragmented documents. This owes to the fact that innumerable people—members of Congress, state legislators, city/county councils and commissions, township-governing boards, school boards, special districts, those who serve on congressional and state legislative and local government legislative bodies' committees and sub-committees, presidents, governors, mayors, city managers, county administrators, staffs of budget offices, interest groups, members of civic associations, and concerned citizens—have a hand in the preparation of budgets. Simply stated, no single individual or small group of people have a monopoly over the construction of budgets.

Finally, budgets historically have usually been non-programmatic in the sense that they rarely include performance standards that agencies and programs must achieve in order to merit the allocation of resources for another fiscal year. However, with the introduction of the planning-programing budgeting system into the federal budgeting process in the early 1960s, more and more local and state governments also began to adopt this new mode of budgeting or some variant of it.

### *Public budgeting*

In its simplest terms, budgeting is the deliberate process that any organization—private or public—undertakes to identify and allocate limited resources for the purpose of providing sundry goods and services to a designated clientele or constituency. With respect to the public sector, the budget process is a formalized routine process that involves the legislative and executive branches of government. According to Mikesell (2018, 25), "the [budgetary] process fulfills tasks similar to those of an economic market because it determines what government services will be provided and how they will be financed." As the opening story of a medium-sized city in suburban Philadelphia suggests, governments have some method for making financial decisions, although the amount of formality varies widely. For the most part (with the exception being the small number of town-meeting and referendum decisions), elected representatives ratify the decisions of the nonelected budget making personal. In budget preparation and implementation, nonelected public employees (i.e., bureaucrats) make many vital decisions. While these employees typically have job security and may be less responsive to public demands for service than elected officials, the logic of representative government posits that bureaucrats can be made to respond to executive and legislative orders emanating from the citizenry.

In public budgeting, the expenditure and revenue sides of the budget are like hand and glove and are inseparable since the document that is produced must balance. This is due to the fact that every state, either through its constitution or by statute, mandates that the budgets of all local governments—as well as the budget of the state government—be balanced. Balance means only that spending (expenditures) is matched or exceeded by income (revenues). In those cases where projected expenditures exceed projected revenues, a budget may technically be balanced by borrowing. The borrowing, of course, has to be paid off over time; thus, borrowing means spending more now and paying more in the future in order to maintain balance.

With that said, public budgeting however cannot proceed without some kind of decision-making process. Even in the most rudimentary scenarios of public budgeting, there must be some limit set to spending, some order of decision-making, some way to structure comparisons among alternatives, and some way to compare expenditure and revenue choices (see Rubin 1993). Furthermore, public budget processes must control the flow of decisions so that they are made in a well-timed manner (Rubin 1993; Lee, Johnson, and Joyce 2020).

While it is often useful to compare public budgeting and other types of budgeting (individual and organizational), public budgeting is different in five major ways. First, public budgeting is characterized by a multiplicity of budgetary actors who often have different priorities and different levels of influence over budget outcomes. These actors have to be controlled and coordinated by the budget process. Second, in government, there is a difference between those who pay taxes and those who determine that how money will be spent—citizens and the elected politicians. Public officials can compel citizens to pay taxes for expenditures they do not desire, but citizens can vote politicians out of office. Third, the budget document is important as a way to ensure public accountability in both elected and appointed officials. Fourth, public budgets are very susceptible to influences from the environment—to the economy, to changes in public opinion, to elections, and to local contingencies such as natural disasters like hurricanes and earthquakes or political disasters like rioting and insurrections. Fifth, budgets are extremely constrained. In spite of the built-in necessity to make budgets adaptable to unforeseen events and emergencies, there are many aspects of public budgets that are outside the direct control of those who devise budgets.

In addition to these characterizations and descriptions of public budgets and the public budgeting process, government officials at all levels usually have added their own descriptions. For instance, they often refer to the budgetary process as a ubiquitous experience that never seems to end or that it seems like they must start the process all over again for the next fiscal year almost immediately after they have "put to bed" the newly crafted and adopted budget. Moreover, government officials are constantly reminded of the important responsibility that they have in raising and spending the community's scarce resources and that they were elected to be good stewards of the public's money. Others have likened the experience of preparing and executing their government's budget to the ultimate "high wire act," as they meticulously try to appease as many people as makes sense and offend as few as possible. In spite of the best and most noble intentions of elected officials, however, some would conclude that the end result of the budgeting exercise is akin to the old adage of "you are damned if you do and damned if you don't." Perhaps, Charles Lindblom's portrayal of the budgetary process as one in which political actors engage in the art of "satisficing" sums up what seems like an endless array of compromises that must take place in the exasperating effort to try to please everyone (Lindbloom 1959).

While it may be said of all government officials, it seems that local officials may have more to agonize over or debate as to how they spend what always seems to be insufficient money available to them or the lack of authority to consider additional revenue options.[2] They perhaps struggle and deliberate more about how to raise the revenue required to doing all of the things that their governments must do, are expected to do, and are presently doing. Should they rely most heavily on the owners of commercial and residential property (i.e., real estate and structures located on it) in their community to finance the operations of the government? Or, should they broaden the revenue base of the government to include all wage earners—that is, both those who own and those that do not own any real estate? Or, should the government seek to identify specific users of their jurisdiction's services and thereby employ user fees or special assessments? How much should they depend on or expect from their state or the federal government to provide outside money in the form of grants-in-aid or shared revenue? How much revenue should they estimate will be generated from fines and property and/or money forfeited to the government. Finally, will all of the above revenue sources produce enough money to pay for projected expenditures or will it be necessary to borrow money to balance the budget? Each of these revenue sources has its pros and cons and economic and political implications. And, those combinations that worked best in the past may not be available, appropriate, or feasible in the future. Moreover, what works for one government may not work for another government. In short, the art of determining the best mix and degree of reliance on various streams of revenue is not an exact science, and at times, must seem like having to "shoot at a moving target" for local government officials.

## Why the focus on local governments?

Two principal motivations can be offered for the selection of local governments (and consequently the revenue streams they tap to provide a long list of services) as the focus of this book. One motivation has historical roots that are grounded in Americans' philosophical and ideological view of government and its relationship to the governed (i.e., a historical high regard for and faith and trust in local government). A second motivation is directly and inextricably related to the practical, everyday importance of local governments in the lives of the citizens they serve and the sheer volume of services they provide, what it costs to provide these services, and how these services are paid for.

***High regard and citizenry preference for local governments***

Historically, local governments in the United States (i.e., full-service governments like counties and municipalities and limited-service entities like townships, special districts, and school districts) have been viewed by the public as the preferred "governments of choice" to deliver the most basic, staple services instead of the national (federal) or state governments. This is in spite of the fact that there is some degree of comingling of service financing, production, and even provision at times. Several reasons seem to account for the citizenry's first preference for local governments.

First, Americans have always had a clear preference for decentralized government, believing that this type of governmental arrangement is a logical safeguard against tyranny and authoritarianism. Closely related to this widespread citizenry perception is the belief that dispersal of power in a political system that accompanies decentralization is a further protection from the possibility of government abuse and oppression. Generally speaking, Americans, while preferring the least amount of government intervention possible, tend to be more trusting of their local governments which are viewed as being closest to them than their state governments or the national government. This is supported by innumerable public opinion polls conducted by survey research institutes at major U.S. colleges and universities such as the much-heralded Survey Research Center (SRC) at the University of Michigan, notable media outlets (e.g., *The New York Times*, *The Washington Post*, *Miami Herald*, *USA Today*), many state and local governments, private polling companies such as Gallop, Roper, Nielson, PEW, and until the early 1990s, the U.S. Advisory Commission on Intergovernmental Relations (ACIR).

Second, there is the belief that local government officials who are closer to the people will behave more responsibly and be more responsive to citizenry expectations, opinions, and needs. That is, it is believed that local officials, who for the most part are more accessible and easier to monitor, will be more accountable, attentive, and willing to take guidance from their constituents, fearing retribution in future elections or could face the possibility of a recall in between elections. In short, it permits citizens to keep their public officials on a proverbial "short leash."

Third, there is the presumption that local governments are better able to insure greater efficiency in government operations, more effectively utilize resources at their disposal, and are more likely to tailor programs and services to the needs, preferences, and affordability of its citizens. Simply put, it is believed—rightly or wrongly—that many specific services can be better managed and delivered by a local government. For the typical citizen, it is not only logical but preferred that a government at the most local level determines what days of the week that solid waste (i.e., garbage) is collected, streets are swept and cleared of snow, and parks, recreation facilities, and libraries are open, what type of police cars and firefighting apparatus (and the kinds of equipment on them) should be purchased, where traffic lights should be erected and if they should be synchronized, decide on landscaping and housing/business setback distances, reasonable speed limits, location of fire stations, establish land use designations, and so forth.

Fourth, local officials, because they live and work among their constituents, are likely to be more mindful of and take into account the philosophical views of constituents and the unique political culture (traditionalistic, individualistic, or moralistic)[3] of the community. In fact, there is something to be said for remaining immersed in one's community while serving as a public servant, as opposed to spending a lot of time as an elected official in the distant state capitol or Washington, DC. Affirming this point, Perlman (2016, 189) writes: "In designing, and delivering [local] services, there is a ground assumption that the choices made for the amount, level, or emphasis of services are the expression of local preferences, community mores, and homegrown values."

Consider these two scenarios. On the one hand, it is logical to expect that an elected official who resides in an area characterized by a blend of a traditionalistic and an individualistic culture would be sensitive and responsive to the belief that government activity should be minimized and that government should resist the temptation to interfere with the natural workings of the market place and free enterprise. Moreover, local governments in this type of setting and also exhibiting a private-regarding perspective would typically keep taxing and spending relatively low. On the other hand, one would anticipate that an elected official from an area that can be best described as having a moralistic culture would be more inclined to envision a more activist role for local government in the provision of services. Likewise, communities marked by a moralistic culture and a public-regarding ethos, with an inordinate amount of revenues, may well spend more money on the "niceties" (e.g., swimming pool, libraries, and parks) rather than simply the necessities (education, police, fire protection, EMS) of community well-being. Furthermore, it is reasonable to speculate that nonelected government officials (bureaucracy) would take their cues from the elected officials as well as their own awareness of the predominant political culture.

In addition, local officials are thought to be more sensitive to the demographic characteristics of their community and constituents and less likely to embrace the "one size fits all" approach to service delivery. Local officials typically are very familiar with the needs and service preferences of their community they represent and what the citizens living there can afford to pay in the way of taxes and fees by virtue of their awareness of the racial/ethnic composition of the community, variability in the income and education levels, and age and religious affiliation of the citizenry. Local officials can also take things into consideration like population growth rate and population density of the community as well as the level of urbanization and political culture.

***Practical importance of local governments***

The second motivation for choosing to focus on local governments in this book centers around the undeniable, ubiquitous, and huge presence and importance of local governments, given the wide range of services they provide on a daily basis. Without question, local governments in the United States profoundly and frequently touch the lives of all Americans. For most Americans, local governments are the entities that provide protective inspections (e.g., safety, building, health), fire, police, and consumer protection, a variety of health care services (including hospitals and mosquito abatement), welfare assistance, EMS services, parks and recreation facilities and programs, and potable water and water for other purposes (bathing, cleaning, washing clothes, sprinkling lawns and shrubbery). In addition, they are expected to establish and operate court systems to adjudicate civil disputes and criminal matters, corrections facilities, cemeteries, museums, stadiums, sports arenas, marinas, water transportation facilities, libraries, and education services (including K-12 schools and community colleges). If that is not enough, local governments are responsible for immunization against diseases, construction and maintenance of roads and bridges, operating airports and mass transit systems, keeping vital statistics (e. g., births and deaths), conserving national resources, establishing and operating the machinery for elections, promoting economic development, engaging in redevelopment and revitalization of blighted areas, just to name a few. Suffice it to say that there is more that local governments do, but there is not enough space here to list them.

This abridged listing of the countless number and variety of local government services only scratches the surface of the many ways in which counties, municipalities, townships, special districts, and school districts impact and improve the quality of life for those residents who live within these jurisdictions through the provision of vital services and associated programs. Moreover, the number, diversity, and complexity of local government services have grown exponentially over the years. This has been so in spite of early American thinking that characterized government—even democratic types—as a "necessary evil" that had to be established and tolerated while yet closely monitored and policed to protect the citizenry from oppression, tyranny, and corruption. Suspicion of and cynicism toward government in early America (although somewhat less so for local governments than for the national government and state governments) was commonplace in colonial America as well as in the new Republic well into the early 20th century. It should be remembered that it was the revered Thomas Jefferson, who, speaking for most Americans of his time, passionately insisted that "government which governs least, governs best." Throughout the 19th century and into the first three decades of the 20th century, Americans strongly embraced the basic precepts of laissez-faire and Social Darwinism. This period of time, but especially the period of roughly 1870–1930, was also marked by massive waves of immigration and the rise of powerful political party machines (e.g., Tammany Hall in New York City headed by the likes of William "Boss" Tweed, Charles Murphy, "Big Tim" Sullivan, and Jimmy Walker, Curley machine in Boston, Hague machine in Jersey City, Magee machine in Philadelphia, and Pendergast machine in Kansas City) that led to the expansion of the service role of cities and counties. Expansion continued under an era of reformism push-back that resulted in the adoption of new forms of local government (e.g., commission and council-manager types). Over time, therefore, Americans would become increasingly accepting of a more active, public-regarding, and progressive form of governance and an enlarged role for government (including greatly enhanced service roles for local governments) in keeping with the basic tenets of the New Deal and Great Society periods. Governments, at all levels during these two epic periods, were given greater latitude to breathe new life into the lofty platitude contained in the U.S. Constitution pertaining to the expectation that government ought to vigorously "promote the general welfare" through the power to tax and spend.

Quite often today, people take local government services for granted and do not necessarily make the connection between what they pay in the way of taxes, fees, levies, assessments, and so forth and the provision of sundry services that are readily available to them. It is as though people believe that they have an inalienable right to expect a vast array of local government services that in their totality are intended to produce the "good life" for all Americans. Americans' thinking in this regard is closely akin to children's belief in a benevolent Santa Claus with unlimited resources who joyfully dispenses toys, clothing, candies and other goodies, and other things to everyone without regard to race, creed, color, religion, or income. Accordingly, everyone should be entitled to a minimum level of health care services, a decent place to live, food to eat, a job (and if needed, job training), welfare assistance and social services in hard times, a quality and meaningful educational experience, protection from criminal elements, predators in the business sector, natural events (fires, hurricanes, floods, etc.), potable water and safe disposal of sewage and solid and hazardous waste, parks and recreational facilities, social events (e.g., county fairs, parades, and exhibitions) and amenities (including but not limited to museums, sports stadiums and arenas, and marinas), libraries, promotion of economic development, airports and seaports, conservation of natural resources and well-planned and maintained communities, roads, streets, sidewalks, street lighting, traffic control, agricultural advice, cable television, and many, many other things. Sometimes, it appears as though local government citizens have not seen a service that they do not like or would not want to have. Furthermore, when asked in the many surveys that are conducted by and for local governments annually, those who live within the jurisdictions of the Nation's counties, municipalities townships, special districts, and school districts overwhelmingly indicate a desire to either enlarge the scope of existing services or add to the current menu of services, while rarely expressing a wish to reduce the number and scope of local government services.

In undertaking the huge responsibility to provide so many varied services, local governments in many ways resemble and operate like large private sector firms and corporations. That is, they employ lots of workers and provide them with wages and fringe benefits, deal with the same kinds of personnel issues and abide by relevant labor laws, purchase raw materials and goods necessary to produce services, interact with consumers (citizens both in and outside of their jurisdiction) who use their services and other entities (other governments) that may produce similar products or services, can be affected by both a sluggish and booming economy, and can declare bankruptcy and go into receivership (e.g., the cities of Detroit, Michigan and Stockton, California and San Bernardino and Orange Counties in California). An additional and sometimes overlooked similarity is that local governments tend to be major players and stimulants in the local economy, as they can employ thousands of workers and be a major purchaser of materials and products from private sector firms in their area. The only difference, it seems, between local governments and private sector companies is that local governments (like any government) typically are not driven by the profit motive, but even if that is not always true as there are increasing incidences of local government agencies being abolished, reorganized, or reinvented when they have been inefficient, wasteful, outmoded, corrupt, or unpopular.

Like their counterparts in the private sector, local governments spend lots of money to produce and dispense products (or services). Moreover, like private sector companies, local governments must generate large sums of money to sustain themselves and provide a plethora of services. Sometimes, this money is generated by selling services (i.e., by implementing a system of charges for services or user fees). But, most of the time, the money necessary to carry on the operations of local government is extracted from the consumers of government services (i.e., citizens under the government's jurisdiction) through the levying of taxes, fees, and assessments. Additional revenue comes from grants-in-aid, loans, shared revenues from the federal and their state government, sale of bonds (or borrowing), and a variety of miscellaneous sources of revenues (e.g., fines and forfeitures, interest income, dividends, sale of property, liquor store sales, rents, royalties, and donations from private sources).

According to the latest expenditure data available from the U.S. Bureau of the Census's *Census of Governments* series, the cost of providing this enormous assortment of local government services in 2020 was a staggering \$2.147 trillion in total expenditures or \$6,515 per capita (see Table 1.1).[4] By comparison, total expenditures done by state governments were \$2.705 trillion or approximately \$400 billion more than that for local governments or \$8,210 per capita. This perspective on expenditures, however, changes as the focus shifts to an

*Table 1.1* Total, Direct, and Per Capita Expenditures of Local Governments, 2020

| | *Total Expenditures* | | *Direct Expenditures* | |
|---|---|---|---|---|
| | *Expenditures** | *Per Capita* | *Expenditures** | *Per Capita* |
| Local | $2.147 | $6,515 | $2.129 | $6,462 |
| State | $2.705 | $8,210 | $2.098 | $6,368 |

* In trillions of dollars.

*Source:* U.S. Bureau of the Census. 2017 Census of Governments. Compendium of Government Finances (Washington, DC: Government Printing Office), Table 4.2.2. Available at: https://federalism.us/significantfeatures. Accessed on June 13, 2021.

inspection of direct expenditures for both governments. Here, it can be seen that local governments were responsible for a *larger amount* of expenditures in terms of both dollars spent ($2.129 trillion versus $2.098 trillion) and per capita spending ($6,462 versus $6,368). This finding is hardly surprising since states routinely redirect a sizable amount of the revenue they collect to their local governments via grants-in-aid and revenue-sharing agreements that show up as direct expenditures of local governments rather than direct expenditures of states.

In order for local governments to be able to spend these huge sums of money and provide an enormous array of services and thereby satisfy the rising expectations of their citizens, local governments must also raise large sums of money—indeed, trillions of dollars on an annual basis. It is important to remember that local governments in all 50 states are either statutorily or constitutionally required to have a balanced budget. Therefore, this means that their revenue collections must be at least equal to or exceed their expenditures or financial outlays.

In 2020, total revenue collections from all sources for all local governments (i.e., counties, municipalities, townships, special districts, and school districts) amounted to $1.917 trillion (or $5,818 per capita), while around $1.25 trillion of that sum or $3,799 per capita was in the form of own source revenue (see Table 1.2).[5] By comparison, state governments amassed a considerably larger sum of money—$2.305 trillion in total revenue or $7,001 per capita—with

*Table 1.2* Total, Own Source, and, Per Capita Revenue of Local Governments, 2020

| | *Total Revenue* | | *Own Source* | |
|---|---|---|---|---|
| | *Revenue** | *Per Capita* | *Revenue** | *Per Capita* |
| Local | $1.917 | $5,818 | $1.252 | $3,799 |
| State | $2,307 | $7,001 | $1,461 | $4,435 |

* In trillions of dollars.

*Source:* U.S. Bureau of the Census. 2017 Census of Governments. Compendium of Government Finances (Washington, DC: Government Printing Office), Table 4.3.2. Available at: https://federalism.us/significantfeatures. Accessed on June 13, 2021.

$1.461 trillion or $4,435 per capita of this amount being derived from own source revenues. Although state governments collected roughly $400 billion more in general revenue than their local governments, a comparison of total and direct expenditures in Table 1.1 indicates that state governments did not directly spend at least $600 billion of the revenue they collected. A large part of this $600 billion was distributed to local governments through various grant-in-aid programs or through a number of revenue-sharing arrangements. This means, therefore, that local governments have much more money available to pay for service provision than their revenue derived from own sources would indicate.

This second perspective of local governments that clearly portrays them as pivotal providers of innumerable staple and much-sought-after services by the public is perhaps the most compelling motivation for conducting a detailed study of local governments and subsequently the revenue streams they depend on to provide these services in a book-length treatment such as this volume. More credence is given to this argument since the amount of money that local officials can legally spend is ultimately determined by how much money they can or are willing to raise, given state constitutional or statutory balanced-budget provisions. Therefore, it is not difficult to imagine that the chief focus in the budgetary process quickly becomes one of wrangling over what are the most politically expedient and palatable ways to raise an amount of money to pay for an acceptable or mandated level of services. And, as those people who are close to the budgetary process readily know, raising revenue is far from a value-free exercise but is one that frequently involves political calculations and risks, economic, cultural, and social considerations, and ideological and value-laden perspectives and concerns.

### *Other motivations for focus on local governments*

Beyond the historical and practical reasons discussed above for examining local government budgets and their unique budgetary processes, there are other important incentives for a special focus at the local level.

First, even a cursory examination of textbooks on local government and politics reveals that they do not devote much attention to budgets and the budgeting process. While these books will typically cover the basics of what budgets are, describe the features of different types of budgets, identify major categories of expenditures and revenue sources, and walk the reader through the various steps in the budgetary process, they usually dedicate little, if any, coverage to revenue trends over time or variations in revenue sources within and among all five types of local governments. What is routinely presented is, at best, a snapshot in time of the most current total revenue figures or revenue numbers disaggregated by major categories (e.g., taxes, fines and forfeitures, charges for services, intergovernmental, and miscellaneous) for cities and sometimes counties but rarely for townships, special districts, and school districts.[6]

Second, greater attention needs to be devoted to the local governmental budgetary process in this new "informational age" (also frequently referred to as the "computer age" or "digital age"), since the new technology it makes available has revolutionized how all governments—and not just local governments—both devise and implement their budgets. The ability to collect, store, and manipulate huge amounts of information permits government officials to simulate new and innovative programs and revenue-raising schemes, conduct intricate cost-benefit, cost-effective, and cost-efficiency analyses, and compare themselves with other governments. In short, the face of budgeting has changed forever and cannot be understood or be carried out without first comprehending and knowing how to use the new "toolkit" of the "information age." Moreover, the advent of the "information age" would naturally entail the necessity of local government budgets allocating more financial resources for education.

Third, more attention should be given to the local governmental budgetary process because of the increasing security problems confronting local governments in the aftermath of 9/11. At one time, the military and defense systems operated by the national government were the Nation's bulwark against our enemies. Given the new realities of threats to terrorism from without as well as from within—as well as meddling on the part of our foreign adversaries like Russia and the People's Republic of China—the responsibility for America's security is no longer the exclusive responsibility of the national government. It is now a responsibility that must be shared by state and local governments. This means that local government must now allocate more resources not only to the obvious kinds of services (e.g., those associated with "first responders" like police, fire control, EMS) but also to health care, water supply, basic infrastructure (roads, bridges, public buildings), and civil defense.

Likewise, more attention needs to be paid to local government budgeting, given the Nation's eye-opening experiences gained from the havoc created by COVID-19. More to the point, Americans were given a valuable lesson about the important—indeed, indispensable—role played by counties through their health departments in helping to curb the debilitating effects of COVID-19 and later variants of it. If the truth be told, county health departments, which are prime examples of administrative arms of their states, were clearly "upfront and center" in the country's battle to slow down the spread of this disease, educate the public, and provide assistance to hospitals and other medical facilities. The funds needed to wage a war against COVID-19, while provided primarily by the national government and the states, were utilized judicially, efficiently, and effectively by these invaluable county departments. In fact, the role played by county governments and their health departments was the epitome of a trend that Reeves (1981) and Glendening and Reeves (1984, 186–87) referred to as the increasing "galloping intergovernmentalization" of many public service. So along with homeland security, now add health care to a growing list of services that local governments provide that have catapulted them into the national spotlight.

Finally, a focus on the local governmental budgetary process is highly relevant for yet another practical reason. Simply put, the local budgeting process provides, in many instances, a "training ground" for both elected officials and bureaucrats who later serve in higher levels (state and federal) of government. The experience in the budgeting process gained at the local level means that these people, for the most part, can "hit the ground running" in their new position.

## Organization of the remainder of this book

Chapter 2 provides a wide-ranging context for examining and understanding local government revenues and local government revenue policy. To that end, a search of state constitutions and statutes, government studies, and the scholarly literature will be conducted as a means of identifying local government revenue patterns as well as likely explanations for the choices or mix of revenue choices that local governments rely on to balance the cost of providing a long list of programs and services. In addition, Chapter 2 lays out the methodological plan (time frame of study, units of analysis, definitions of key terms and data, and statistical techniques) that will be used in conducting both descriptive and inferential analyses described in Chapters 4–9 of this book.

Then, Chapter 3 presents a comprehensive overview of the revenue structure for local governments, in general, and for counties, municipalities, townships, special districts, and school districts, in particular. Being essentially "creatures of their states" and not legally independent governmental entities makes local governments unique in their ability to raise revenue and thereby poses challenges as well as opportunities when compared to the national government and the state governments. This chapter will also include some initial general observations and thoughts about revenue trends and patterns as a prelude to the more in-depth analysis to follow in the next six chapters.

Chapters 4–9 serve as the focal point of this book, in that each chapter will meticulously examine the historical patterns and trends in revenue usage of counties, municipalities, townships, special districts, and school districts, as well as provide explanations for variations among these units of government and variations among the states or regions of the country. Chapters 4 and 5 take an in-depth look at tax revenues, with the first of these two chapters being devoted exclusively to property taxes, while the latter chapter is dedicated to the analysis of sales, income, and a variety of miscellaneous taxes. Chapter 6 examines local government usage of charges for services (sometimes referred to as user charges and fees). Chapter 7 directs attention to a number of miscellaneous sources of general revenue, including but not limited to special assessments, fines and forfeitures, sale of property, proceeds from the operation of liquor stores, rents, royalties, donations, and interest earnings. Then, Chapter 8 focuses on intergovernmental revenue from the federal, state, and other local governments, while

Chapter 9 explores the local government reliance on borrowing money primarily but not exclusively through the sale of bonds.

The final chapter of this book (Chapter 10) offers some perspective on the road ahead for local governments in their quest to continually raise sufficient revenues to finance the cost of providing an increasing menu of services whose price tag has grown exponentially over the years. The daunting challenges confronting local governments are numerous, but none no more important than remaining fiscally solvent during downturns in the economy, willing to "think and plan outside the box," practicing efficiencies, and staying one step ahead of their citizens in efforts to satisfy what appears to be an insatiable appetite for new services and the expansion of existing ones. The New Normal[7] for raising revenues and balancing budgets is not a sporadic aberration like what was experienced during the Great Recession or the most recent recession brought on by the COVID-19 health pandemic but will present an enduring, persistent, and critical long-term challenge as to whether local officials and their governments have the capacity to adapt successfully.

## Notes

1 First and foremost, it must be understood that "the public sector exists [and subsequently government financing and the budgeting of government resources] to provide valued services when the market [the private sector] fails to provide them appropriately, including services needed" (Mikesell 2018, 4–5). When thrust into this situation, governments must be ever-wary to budget its resources judicially.

2 An edited volume (Bartle 2001) and an applied monograph (Bartle, Hildreth, and Marlowe 2012) provide some provocative and insightful essays and thoughts on the budgetary and financial management challenges posed to local government officials in what some have referred to as "budgeting in a new age."

3 See Elazar (1984) for a thorough description and discussion of three political subcultures in the United States that he identified as traditional, individualistic, and moralistic.

4 See Table A1.1 in the Appendix for a breakdown of total and direct expenditures by the type of local government in the last year that these figures were available (2017).

5 See Table A1.2 in the Appendix for a breakdown of general and own source revenue by the type of local government in the last year that these figures were available (2017).

6 One exception to this type of very limited review of local government finances and some tentative analysis of the impact of the Great Recession is an article by Bartle, Kriz, and Morozov (2011). In addition, this article provides some useful recommendations for local governments regarding their revenue structure.

7 The term "new normal" was coined by Roger McNamee (2004) in his book of the same name. While McNamee was writing about the business sector, the "new normal" has entered the lexicon of government, in general (Davis 2009; Martin, Levey, and Cawley 2012), and local government, in particular (Miller 2011; Miller and Link 2009; Martin, Levey, and Cawley 2012; Mathers 2010; Hoene and Pagano 2011). The "new normal" perspective is predicated on the contention that the Great Recession of 2008–11 represented a break point for local governments, with implications that would likely last long after the onset of any subsequent economic recovery. As a result, government observers (Martin, Levey, and Cawley 2012) predicted that local governments would be characterized by fewer resources, smaller workforces, and new ways of delivering services. To date, many of these expectations have been realized.

## References


Bartle, John R. (Ed.). 2001. *Evolving Theories of Budgeting*. New York: Amsterdam Press.

———. Kenneth A. Kriz, and Boris Morozov. 2011. "Local Government Revenue Structure: Trends and Challenges," *Journal of Public Budgeting, Accounting, and Financial Management*, 23(Summer): 268–87.

———. W. Bartley Hildreth, and Justin Marlowe. 2012. *Management Policies in Local Government Finance*. Washington, DC: International City/County Management Association.

Davis, Isaac. 2009. "*The New Normal*." The McKinsey Quarterly. http://www.mckinseyquarterly.com/The_new_rormal.2336. Accessed June 13, 2021.

Elazar, Daniel J. 1984. *American Federalism. A View from the States*. New York: Harper and Row.

Glendening, Parris and Mavis Mann Reeves. 1984. *Pragmatic Federalism: An Intergovernmental View of American Government*. 2nd ed. Pacific Palisades, CA: Palisades Publishers.

Hoene, Christopher, and Michael A Pagano. 2011. *National League of Cities: Research Briefs on America's Cities*. Washington, DC: National League of Cities.

Lasswell, Harold D. 1936. *Politics: Who Gets What, When, How*. New York: McGraw-Hill.

Lee, Robert E. Jr, Ronald W. Johnson, and Phillip G. Joyce. 2020. *Public Budgeting Systems*. 10th ed. Burlington, MA: Jones & Bartlett Learning LLC.

Lindblom, Charles E. 1959. "The Science of 'Muddling Through'," *Public Administration Review*, 19(Spring): 79–88.

Martin, Lawrence, L. Richard Levey, and Jenna Cawley. 2012. "The 'New Normal' for Local Government," *State and Local Government Review*, 44(Supplement 1): 17S–29S.

Mathers, Edwin. 2010. "Commentary on Moderating the 'New Normal' in Local Government," *PM Magazine*, 92: 1–3.

McNamee, Roger. 2004. *The New Normal: Great Opportunities in a Time of Risk*. New York: Penguin Books.

———. 2018. "*Fiscal Administration: Analysis and Application for the Public Sector*." 8th ed. Boston: Cengage.

Miller, Gerald J. 2011. "Six Rules for the New Normal." *Governing*. December. 48.

Miller, Gerald J., and James Link. 2009. "'New Normal' Retirement Plan Design," *Government Finance Review*, 25: 126–36.

Perlman, Bruce J. 2016. "The Illusion of Local Control: The Paradox of Local Government Home Rule," *State and Local Government Review*, 48(September): 189–93.

Peterson, Paul E. 1981. *City Limits*. Chicago: University of Chicago Press.

Reeves, Mavis Mann. 1981. "Galloping Intergovernmentalization as a Factor in State Management," *State Government*, 54(3): 102–07.

Rubin, Irene S. 1993. *The Politics of Public Budgeting*. 2nd ed. Chatham, NJ: Chatham House Publishing.

Wildavsky, Aaron. 1966. *The Politics of the Budgetary Process*. Boston: Little Brown, and Company.

## Appendix

*Table A1.1* Total and Direct Expenditures of Local Governments by Type, 2017

| | *(in thousands of dollars)* | | | | |
|---|---|---|---|---|---|
| | *County Governments* | *Municipal Governments* | *Townships* | *Special Districts* | *School Districts* |
| Total | $431.6 | $626.5 | $57.2 | $245.3 | $580.5 |
| Direct | $416.5 | $609.9 | $54.4 | $238.2 | $577.4 |

*Source:* U.S. Bureau of the Census. 2017 Census of Governments. Compendium of Government Finances (Washington, DC: Government Printing Office), Table 4.2.9. Available at: https://federalism.us/significantfeatures. Accessed on June 13, 2021.

*Table A1.2* General and Own Source Revenue of Local Governments by Type, 2017

| | *(in thousands of dollars)* | | | | |
|---|---|---|---|---|---|
| | *County Governments* | *Municipal Governments* | *Townships* | *Special Districts* | *School Districts* |
| General | $880.9 | $985.3 | $51.2 | $729.2 | $859.1 |
| Own Source | $278.9 | $383.3 | $45.0 | $127.2 | $257.0 |

*Source:* U.S. Bureau of the Census. 2017 Census of Governments. Compendium of Government Finances (Washington, DC: Government Printing Office), Table 4.3.8. Available at: https://federalism.us/significantfeatures. Accessed on June 13, 2021.

# 2 Context for Understanding/Explaining and Studying Local Government Revenues

To conduct the kind of thorough examination of local government revenues as proposed in this book, it is essential to lay out a reasonable and appropriate methodology that consists of two parts. First, a careful and exhaustive review of the extant scholarly literature and relevant government reports and documents needs to be conducted to identify plausible causes of and explanations for revenue trends and variations. Second, it is necessary to identify the study's parameters (time frame, units of analysis, description and sources of data, definition of key terms and concepts).

## Theorizing about revenue trends and variations

Previous efforts intended to assist us in understanding and explaining the trends observed in the revenue collections of counties, municipalities, townships, special districts, and school districts over time as well as variations in or mix of revenue choices of these governments are impressionistic or fragmented at best. They range from thoughtful but non-empirical anecdotal speculations proffered by local government officials and the media to academic/scholarly and governmental studies analyzing data reported by these governments to an entity like the U.S. Bureau of the Census at regular intervals. Most academic studies, however, tend to focus on only one or sometimes two units of local government (e.g., counties and municipalities and may be even school districts). Therefore, we do not know if findings derived from a study of counties, for example, are applicable or transferrable to municipalities or even townships, special districts, or school districts. Moreover, since most of these studies are time-bound, subsequent analyses cannot address any changes in trends and patterns over time that may have occurred.

Therefore, it is important to conduct a sweeping examination of what we do know about local government revenues so as to be able to develop a comprehensive and reliable theory. In this chapter, we begin this task by considering what we know from anecdotal descriptions and observations and thoroughly combing the scholarly literature. From this search, we have been able to identify at least seven broad subject areas that warrant careful scrutiny. They are as follows: state constitutions and statutes, political culture and citizen attitudes/opinions, population

DOI: 10.4324/9781032640389-2

shifts and other changing demographics, intergovernmental transfers, tax revolts and taxing and spending limitation movements, citizen expectations and views on government and government officials, and cycles or changes in the national, state, local, and international economies. Additional subject areas that merit our consideration and will be examined are the outdated and troublesome way in which local governments historically have and continue to formulate their budgets (incrementalism), changes in national laws (but especially the federal tax code), and the impact of federal- and state-unfunded mandates.

### *State constitutions and statutes*

The effect that state constitutions and statutes have on the ability of local governments to raise revenue is derived from the fact that these governments are established by their states who have unilateral authority to grant them any and all powers and likewise have the authority to rescind these same powers. The U.S. Constitution, contrary to popular belief, does not even address the concept of local government, much less establish or recognize local governments as sovereign entities as is the case for the national and state governments. Instead, the chief focus of the U.S. Constitution was on granting 18 (specifically delegated) powers to the national government, leaving to the states those (reserved or residual) powers neither given to the national government nor denied to the states or their people, and identifying several (shared) powers that belong to both the national government and the states. But again, it needs to be emphasized that the U.S. Constitution was conspicuously silent on the subject of local governments, and if local governments were to ever exist in the United States, the states, at their discretion, could create (and if need be) dismantle them.

To further understand the relationship between local governments and their states and hence the state's total control over local government revenues, an understanding of Dillon's Rule is also necessary. Dillon's Rule (articulated by an Iowa state judge in 1868) holds that local governments are creatures of the state and as such receive their authority from the state rather than directly from the people. This sets local governments apart from states in the context of the U.S. Constitution, which does not mention local governments. Under Dillon's Rule, the authority of local governments is confined to powers *explicitly* and *expressly* granted to them by the state, or implied in the explicitly granted power, or powers essential to meeting their "declared objectives and responsibility" as local governments.

So why did states create local governments? There is no simple answer to this question or one universal reason that applies to all five types of local government. County governments and municipal governments, however, do share one common feature that sets them apart from townships, special districts, and school districts—states envisioned them being general-purpose or full-service local governments that would provide a long list of services to their residents. Nevertheless, the purposes behind their service roles differ. On the one hand, counties were intended to be administrative appendages or political subdivisions of the state that would assist the state in providing and managing a number of essential state-level services or activities of statewide concern more efficiently, economically, and more effectively at the local level.[1] Simply put, counties were designed to serve as "satellite offices" or "branch offices" of the state (see Benton 2002a) that would implement or manage a variety of state programs (many of them mandated) in areas such as welfare, health care, roads and bridges, elections, courts and the legal system, among others.[2] On the other hand, municipalities, while to some degree are also expected to assist the state in the implementation of some state policies and programs, were created to assist the state in providing services they or county governments were neither equipped nor desired to provide (around-the-clock fire departments staffed by professionals, water and sewer services, street lights, sidewalks, a higher level law enforcement beyond what sheriffs would normally provide, mosquito abatement, animal control, solid waste collection, recreational facilities, traffic control and signalization, planning and zoning, to name a few). More specifically, states, acceding to the request (via a petition) from residents of an area (usually densely populated) in a county for incorporation, grant a charter that gives the residents and their new municipality the legal authority to elect officials, collect various types of revenue, and provide services. Therefore, municipalities typically have greater decision-making authority and discretion than do counties.

Special districts and school districts also have a common characteristic—they provide a very limited number of services—that distinguishes them from counties, municipalities, and townships. School districts always provide only one service (education). Special districts, if state legislation permits, can provide more than one service but typically do not. It is not inconsequential that most special districts are referred to as "single-purpose" governmental entities in that they are usually limited to providing only one service (fire, water, sewer, and library districts are quite common). That is where the similarity between school districts and special districts ends.

Although free, public education did not become widespread in the United States until after the Civil War, it has always been a core societal value that has been deeply held by most Americans. Beginning in 1647, when English Calvinists enacted a law in the Massachusetts Bay Colony mandating all townships to establish public schools funded by local property taxes, and then spreading throughout the country in the 19th century, "the concept of free-of-charge and universal public education has long been a hallmark of the U.S." (Donovan, Mooney, and Smith 2011, 593). In fact, for many, public education is often viewed as an integral component of the American ethos because it is believed to be a logical pathway to a better life for people who were not born into money or privilege. And, for all students, free public education provides them with the knowledge and skills necessary to find a job or pursue their education and training in college or technical schools. Other side effects include economic development for everyone in a community and the inculcation of students with civic responsibility. Today, public education is regarded by many Americans as a fundamental right, in spite of the U.S. Supreme Court ruling to the contrary.[3]

Because of the value historically attached to education, a lot of thought went into how public education systems would be financed and run. One primary objective was to remove as much partisan politics as possible from both the funding side of education and the day-to-day operation of schools. This concern led the states, who had claimed the power to establish and regulate the provision of educational services as one of their reserved powers, to create a separate and independent unit of government specifically dedicated to the sole purpose of education.[4] A second concern was that public education (i.e., schools) would have to compete with other programmatic concerns (e.g., public safety, health care, public works, housing, transportation, welfare, recreation, community development, environmental protection, and so forth) and the powerful interests that support them for limited financial resources if education were a service responsibility of either counties or municipalities. In short, it was believed that public education needed to be funded and operated by a government that had a singular focus—education.

The establishment of special districts was spurred by somewhat different but interrelated reasons. It has been said that "special districts are supposed to do what other local governments cannot or will not do" (Bowman and Kearney 2008, 279). Ergo, special districts are established to meet unmet service needs in a particular area and thereby are looked upon as the provider of last resort.

Several scenarios will serve to illustrate why and how special districts fill the void when the two principal general-purpose local governments (counties and municipalities) are asked by unincorporated area residents to provide certain services (e.g., water, sewer, and fire protection) but decline to do so. Counties, for instance, may be approached by residents of a sparsely populated part of the unincorporated area about providing one of these services only to be told that economies of scale or cost-efficiencies could not be realized or the cost would be prohibitive for users. These same citizens could also ask a nearby city in the county to provide this service on a specifically structured fee basis and be turned down for the same reason. Municipalities encounter other obstacles such as state constitutions or statutes that prohibit them from extending their service districts beyond their boundaries. Furthermore, appeals for additional services from county and municipal residents that exceed a jurisdiction's revenue-raising ceiling or lead to the assumption of excessive debt make it impossible for these governments to respond positively. Moreover, the service problem to be addressed may not fit neatly within a single jurisdiction. Another problem for counties is that some states prohibit the jurisdictional co-venturing that would permit counties to offer services jointly with other counties.

In addition to the technical and financial deficiencies of general-purpose governments, there are also political considerations. For one thing, restrictive state annexation laws and county governments with limited authority to provide a wide range of services (usually counties without a home rule charter) are political facts of life that encourage the creation of special districts. In fact, for residents of an urban fringe area, a public service district (which may provide more than one service) may be the only alternative. Additionally, residents of unincorporated areas of counties who have no desire to become part of a city may opt for the establishment of special districts when a city attempts to use political blackmail to force them to be annexed into the city as the only means to secure a desired service from that city.

Considering the obstacles and deficiencies mentioned above, special districts may be a best option for addressing the dilemma of unmet service needs. For one thing, special district boundaries can encompass only those areas that desire and are willing to pay for a service not offered by either a municipality or a county. By utilizing special districts, existing counties and municipalities can circumvent the debt and tax ceilings. Special districts are also better suited than general-purpose governments for service charges or user fee financing, whereby the cost of the service can be directly apportioned to the consumer (as with water and sewer charges). Another advantage of opting for a special district is that their governing boards are dedicated to the provision of one specific service, meaning that these boards unlike members of municipal and county legislative bodies are not trying to partial out limited resources to many competing interests and policy areas.

A fifth type of local government—township—is situated somewhere between counties and municipalities on the one end of a continuum and special districts and school districts on the other end when measured by the scope of services that they provide. Most townships, which are geographic and political subdivisions of the county government in 20 states, are unincorporated, meaning that they do not have charters from state governments guaranteeing their political independence or authorizing them to provide many municipal-type services. While county governments were created to assist the state in the administration or management of state programs, townships were established to augment the service role of counties in selected areas within the county. In fact, political scientists have long regarded townships as "mere outlets for the administration or distribution of county government" (Grant and Nixon 1982). The most common service responsibilities of townships include road maintenance, tax and election administration, land use planning, trash collection, and some judicial matters; however, townships in four states (Ohio, Michigan, New Jersey, and Pennsylvania) also provide fire and police protection, similar to what an incorporated city would provide. In spite of predictions about their demise, more than 55 million people, or one-fifth of the U.S. population, still live under township government (Bowman and Kearney 2008, 2022).

The fact that states created all five types of local governments coupled with the legal significance of Dillon's Rule clearly implies that a superior-inferior relationship exists between the state and its local governments. In fact, there has always been a presumption that the state must serve in a role like that of a "watchdog' or "parent" over "children-like" local governments that need constant supervision and scrutiny when it comes to most matters of governance, but especially finances.[5] This is clearly evident in the realm of the types of revenue options available to local governments.[6] The ability and conditions under which local governments can levy taxes and special assessments, collect fees, impose charges for services, assess fines, receive state grants-in-aid and participate in state revenue sharing, invest money to earn interest income, and even borrow money through conventional means or through the sale of bonds are controlled or restricted by the state.[7]

Let's consider several of the more important and onerous revenue restrictions that are placed on local governments by their states, beginning with the property tax. All states limit allowable tax rates to a certain number of mills of the full value of property, although the number of mills may vary among types of local government. States may also permit property to be assessed at artificially low values (i.e., below full market value) and limit annual property assessment increases and/or allow reassessment only on a periodic basis (in some states, every ten years) or when the property is sold. In addition, states can place limits on annual increases in the amount of property taxes paid as did California, Massachusetts, Michigan, and some other states in the wake of rapidly increasing home and real estate values during the late 1970s and 1980s. More recently (2009), one state (Florida) mandated that local governments roll back millage rates to 2007 levels (Benton, Aikins, and Miller 2009). Furthermore, the state and/or citizens through referenda can adopt legal measures that exempt certain kinds of property from taxation or permit it to be taxed at a discounted rate. Quite common are homestead and agricultural exemptions, as well as exemptions for low-income households, widows/widowers, disabled persons, veterans, religious, nonprofit, and charitable organizations, and the elderly. While well-intended and reflecting a state's values, exemptions frequently result in a significant loss of potential revenue for local governments over time and thus put a permanent strain on their revenue-raising capability. In spite of the persistent challenges posed to local governments in exercising their authority to tax property, encouraging progress has been made in recent years in convincing legislatures in some states to grant them more latitude in fiscal home rule (see Bowman and Kearney 2008; Dye and MacManus 2015; Larson and McDonald 2023).

Besides placing various kinds of limits on the most important source of tax revenue (the property tax) for most local governments, states also restrict or even prohibit the use of other kinds of taxes like general and selective sales (e.g., motor fuel, alcohol beverage, tobacco products, public utilities, and telecommunications) and income. Unlike their state government, local governments do not have the unfettered authority to use a variety of optional forms of taxation as a means to diversify their sources of revenue. While states are increasingly allowing local governments to adopt what is referred to as a local option sales tax that is piggy-backed on the state sales tax levy, it is not unusual for its usage to be restricted to only one type of local government (i.e., counties or municipalities)[8] and rarely to school and special districts and townships. Moreover, authorization to levy a local option sales tax typically comes with strings attached to it. For example, there are frequently stipulations that require the local government to reduce property tax revenues dollar-for-dollar with money generated by a sales tax. In addition, it is not uncommon for enabling state legislation to require that sales tax revenues be earmarked for specific purposes (roads and bridges, indigent health care, parks and recreation, sports stadiums and arenas, museums, libraries, etc.) and that voter approval (with a fixed time period for its usage) via a referendum is required. And, of course, local option sales taxes are also subject to the same types of exemptions and restrictions placed on the state sales tax. The limits on all types of sales taxes are probably motivated by three concerns: competition for these revenues; overburdening local residents with more taxes; and misuse.

States have also been more willing to grant municipalities and counties permission to levy both personal and corporate income taxes in the past several decades (but particularly for the former).[9] On the one hand, there is the growing acknowledgment that an income may be a better yardstick to measure wealth (and hence ability to pay taxes) than is property ownership. On the other hand, there is increasing support for the fairness argument that individuals and businesses who earn a salary or operate a business in one local government jurisdiction but live in another (i.e., commuters) ought to help pay for the cost of services (police protection, EMS, drinking water, streets and sidewalks, sports stadiums and arenas, traffic signalization, museums, etc.) provided by the government where they work or seek recreational or cultural opportunities. However, restrictions as to their usage also apply to these types of taxes in the form of lower maximum rates (usually 6 percent or less) and deductions that individual or corporate taxpayers can claim.

While there is less opposition to local government utilization of charges for services or user fees, state permission through enabling legislation is typically required. And, as in other areas of local government finances, states assert the authority to monitor the usage of this type of revenue source to insure that local residents and businesses who pay these fees are charged a reasonable rate and are not being taken advantage of in other ways.

Another area in which the state supervises local government finances has to do with these governments' ability to incur debt, whether through loans from a conventional lending institution or through the sale of bonds. There are a number of restrictions on local governments' ability to borrow money, including how much money can be borrowed, what the money can be used for, and the procedures for approving new debt. In many instances, explicit rules govern the amount a local government can borrow. For example, the amount borrowed through full faith and credit (also called general obligation) bonds is restricted to a certain fixed percentage of the value of all taxable real estate in the jurisdiction or a fixed percentage of the jurisdiction's tax revenue for the preceding fiscal year(s). Almost always, general obligation bonds must be repaid with revenue generated from a tax (usually property) increase. In addition, general obligation bonds can only be issued with the permission of voters (in some instances, a super-majority may be required). Furthermore, local governments cannot borrow money for their operating budget, but rather only for long-term infrastructure and land, i.e., capital improvements). Finally, while local governments can circumvent the need for voter approval to borrow money by issuing revenue bonds, these types of bonds are restricted in the sense that they must be repaid with revenues (fees or charges) generated by the project funded (e.g., sports stadium or arena, water or sewage treatment plant, parking garages, toll road or bridge, electric generating facility, convention center, and marina).

While more and more states are granting home rule to their counties and municipalities and providing more latitude to all local governments in the area of fiscal policy, the bottom line is that local governments are still at the mercy of the state when it comes to revenue-raising options. Punctuating this point, two noted students of local government have concluded that "even with their gradual empowerment…local governments continue to chafe at the traditionally tight reins of state government control" (Bowman and Kearney 2008, 263).

In spite of persisting complaints by local officials about the excessive restrictiveness of state constitutions and statutes, some states have adopted progressive home rule legislation and amended their constitutions. The result has been a noticeable tendency to loosen up revenue limitations and to expand revenue options in recent years. Evidence of the positive impact of these changes can be found in the findings of studies that have investigated the relationship between form of city and county government and revenue collections (Morgan and Peliserro 1980; Park 1996; Benton 2002b, 2003; Zhang and Nguyen-Hoang 2023). More specifically, these studies report that county and municipal finances, generally, and revenue collections, specifically, were positively impacted as a result of cities and counties being permitted to adopt reformed structures of government more conducive to expanding home rule authority as it pertains to determining the appropriate mix of revenue sources to tap to finance the operations of their respective governments.

### *Political culture and citizen attitudes/opinions*

Quite often, the limitations that state constitutions and statutes place on the ability of local governments to raise revenue can be traced back to the political culture of a state and the subsequent attitudes/opinions its citizens hold about government. Support for this assertion can be inferred from Daniel Elazar's (1984) thoughtful study of political culture in the United States. Defining political culture as "the particular pattern of orientation to political action in which each political system is embedded," Elazar (1984, 109–10) reasons that it [political culture] is especially significant as the "historical source of differences in habits, perspectives, and attitudes that influence the political life" observed in the 50 states. As such, political culture, like any culture, is engrained in the cumulative historical experiences and happenings of certain groups of people. Indeed, the origin or "the makings" of a particular political culture seems to occur in a seamless and unnoticed way and is frequently "lost in the proverbial mist of time" (Elazar 1984, 112). While acknowledging that little is known about the exact ways in which political culture is influential, Elazar, nonetheless, concludes that the three distinctive political cultures (individualistic, moralistic, and traditionalistic) found across the United States were "influential in shaping the basic structure and operations of the state political systems" (Elazar 1984, 112).[10] Therefore, is it not logical by extension that the political culture of a state would also shape the structure and operation of local governments therein?

Each of the three "political subcultures," as Elazar called them, evokes a contrasting or different perspective of the role that state government is expected or ought to play in each of the 50 states.[11] These differing perspectives would be expected to influence whether or not states establish a level(s) of government below the state level, and perhaps more importantly, what powers and authority should be given to these inferior units of government, as well as how these governments should be structured and supervised. Therefore, it is reasonable to expect that one would find different perspectives on the degree of or latitude that local governments should be granted in various matters of governance, including revenue options available to them.

Based on the predominant features that define the traditionalistic, individualistic, and moralistic subcultures, we can reasonably speculate as to how each type of subculture could influence the way that a state may superintend local government finances, generally, and revenue options available to them, specifically. For reasons discussed below, it is expected that states with a traditionalistic subculture will impose the most restrictions on local governments' ability to raise revenue to fund the services they offer, while states having a moralistic subculture will have the least amount of restrictions. Then, states that are characterized by an individualistic political subculture will impose more revenue-raising limitations than states with a moralistic subculture but less limitations than states with a traditionalistic subculture.

In the traditionalistic culture, while government is viewed as an actor with a positive role, it is believed that government's role should be limited to maintaining the existing social, political, and economic power structure. In the words of Elazar (1984, 118), the traditionalistic political subculture "reflects an older, pre-commercial attitude that accepts a substantially hierarchical society as part of the ordered nature of things, authorizing and expecting those at the top of the social structure to take a special and dominant role in government." This is an elitist orientation in which government initiates only those policies that are intended to promote the interests of the governmental and economic elite. "Good government" in this subculture "involves the maintenance and reinforcement of traditional patterns," with minimal modifications to it occurring only when absolutely necessary due to changing circumstances (Elazar 1984, 119). As would be expected, political and government officials play conservative and safeguarding instead of initiatory roles unless they are confronted with strong outside pressures. The end result is that politics is viewed negatively and participation is a privilege rather than a right.

This description of the traditionalistic subculture and the history that surrounds it leads to the prediction that states with such a subculture will enact the most stringent kinds of both spending and revenue-raising limitations not only for state government but also for their local governments. In short, local governments would need to raise less revenue since their service provision role (like that of the state) is quite limited compared to governments that are given much more responsibility for the provision of sundry services and expected to be more proactive in providing new services.

With its emphasis on the democratic order as a marketplace, the individualistic political subculture foreshadows a somewhat limited or specialized role for government. In fact, the driving force or motive behind the establishment of government is distinctly utilitarian. Thus, governments operating in an individualistic culture do not take an activist stance in the sense that they do not seize the initiative to propose policy; instead, government provides only those services that are expected by the people it was created to service and then waits for significant public demands before providing any additional services. The individualistic culture also emphasizes the supremacy of private concerns and directs very little attention to the common good unless it is designed to enhance some common conception of the good society devised outside the political arena. Simply stated, the goal of the political system is to clear the way for individuals to pursue their own self-interest and have widespread access to the marketplace. As a result, the individualistic culture "places a premium on limiting community intervention—whether governmental or nongovernmental—into private activities to the minimum necessary to keep the marketplace in proper working order" (Elazar 1984, 115). In this sense, the individualistic culture has always been linked to the notion of laissez faire.

Given this characterization, it is plausible to conjecture that states exhibiting this type of political culture would most likely impose a fair amount of restrictions on local governments' ability to raise revenue, since their service responsibilities would be limited by the state as noted above. But these restrictions would not be as extensive as would be the case in a traditionalistic subculture. Therefore, it would be logical that there would be less need to raise large amounts of revenue.

In a moralistic political culture, government is seen as a positive force and as a means of promoting the general welfare and achieving the "good society." Most of the time, this goal has to be accomplished through direct government action, although definitions of what government's positive function should be may vary from time to time. As Elazar (1984, 117) describes it, "individualism is tempered [in the moralistic culture] by a general commitment to utilizing communal—preferably nongovernmental, but governmental if necessary—power to intervene in the sphere of private activities when it is considered necessary to do so for the public good or well-being of the community." This implies that issues have a significant place in this subculture and thereby sets the tone for political concern. Indeed, political parties compete for office on the basis of issues at election time. In fact, it is not uncommon for public officials to initiate new government activities in an attempt to address issues and problems that are not a current focus of concern for a majority of the general public. While the moralistic political subculture involves a greater commitment to active government involvement in the economic and social life of a community, the strong commitment to the communitarianism feature of this subculture tends to channel the interest in government intervention into highly local-oriented directions.

It comes as no surprise, therefore, that in states where the moralistic culture is dominant, there would be fewer restrictions on local government revenue-raising and spending authority than in states with either a dominant traditionalistic or individualistic culture. In fact, local governments would be expected to be proactive in the provision of a wide array of services. Consequently, it would be reasonable for local governments to be given wider latitude in the choices for raising the amount of revenue needed to pay for a larger menu of services designed to ensure the good society.

The influence that an area's political subculture has on both government structure and operations can be manifested in other ways. For instance, one would expect that the political subculture would set the tone for the political and policy views of citizens or the opinions the public holds about various issues, including government finances. During the 1970s and 1980s, there were a series of anti-tax and anti-spending movements across the country in states like California, Massachusetts, Michigan, and Florida that were driven by intense citizen views regarding what was seen as local government overspending, wastefulness, inefficiencies, and excessive taxation. One of the more notable such movements occurred in California where citizens approved a referenda item known as Proposition 13 in 1979 that imposed a limit on how much property taxes could increase from year to year. A few years later, Michigan voters adopted a similar referenda proposal referred to as Proportion 2 ½, which also imposed a limit on property tax increases. More recently, Florida voters approved an initiative ballot item that required counties, municipalities, special districts, and school districts to roll back property tax millage rates to 2007 levels (Benton, Aikins and Miller 2009).

These anti-spending and anti-tax movements were also fueled by a growing sense of alienation and cynicism and a decline in political efficacy among the general public that became noticeable by the mid-1960s and continues to the present day, with the general public more likely to believe the following: (1) public officials paying little attention to and do not care about the issues or concerns faced by the average person; (2) public officials taking bribes and using their office to make money in other illegal ways; (3) public officials and impersonal bureaucracies are incapable of operating in an efficient and effective manner; (4) they (the public) have a less important voice in or input into government decisions, and (5) there is a lack of accountability and transparency in government. While these views were initially directed at the federal and state governments and their officials, they increasingly have been applied to local governments and their officials as well, especially when incidences of corruption, wastefulness, and inefficacies are exposed.

### *Population and area demographics*

Another set of factors that are likely to affect both the size of local government revenues and local government revenue policies are the characteristics of the citizens of an area and the physical features of the locale, which are usually referred to as demographics. During the 1960s, a number of significant studies were published that demonstrated the importance of examining the part that the environments of state and local governments—more specifically, socio-economic factors—play in determining their revenue-raising and spending policies. Sometimes referred to as the "policy determination" literature, the findings of many of these studies showed that more developed states and their communities were able to raise more revenues and spend more money—everything else being equal such as state constitutional and statutory restrictions—on a variety of services than was the case for less developed areas. In particular, it was found that a sizable proportion of the explained variance in the revenues and expenditures of state and local governments was attributable to factors such as citizen income and education, racial composition of the population, and levels of urbanization and industrialization.

Thomas R. Dye's *Politics, Economics and the Public* (1966) is particularly noteworthy and still considered path-breaking, given the impact it had on research and theorizing in the field at that time.[12] The most potent and consistent variable that significantly affects the size of state and local government budgets is personal income. Simply put, local governments that contain a disproportionately higher number of affluent households often are expected to provide more and better service. Yet, more affluent citizens normally are also quite willing to pay the costs (typically taxes but also charges for services or user fees) associated with larger service menus. Therefore, wealthier local governments have the luxury of having a greater tax base to tap while usually being able to keep tax burdens relatively low. Moreover, more complex economies are usually found in more affluent areas and create demands for rules and regulations, which wealthier local governments can afford.

By contrast, poorer local governments do not have the same kind of resource base to tap. These local governments may contain citizens who also may desire more and better services, but these expectations are unrealistic. That is, local officials are constrained in their ability to raise the necessary amounts of money to pay for these requests, as lower-income people cannot afford to pay higher taxes or charges for additional services than they are currently paying. The economic reality of not being able to extract additional revenue for poorer residents wins out. In addition, poorer communities typically do not have a strong economic base with diversified businesses and industries that can be tapped for additional tax or other kinds of revenue.

Besides highlighting the important influence of personal income in explaining variations in local government taxing and spending policies, the policy determination literature pointed out the importance of other demographic attributes of local communities. First, education was positively correlated with local government taxing and spending policies. More specifically, higher levels of education were associated with higher revenue yields and greater spending. From this, it can be inferred that people with more education expect more and better services and are also willing to pay more in the form of taxes, user fees, charges for services, etc., to pay for these services. The opposite was the case for people with lower levels of educational achievement. However, it is also important to note that education is highly and positively correlated with income (i.e., income increases with rising levels of education), meaning that those with higher levels of education also have the ability and willingness to pay for expanded services.

Second, race/ethnicity (usually measured as percent Black) was negatively associated with revenue collections. Simply stated, smaller revenue collections (typically, taxes) were quite common among jurisdictions that contained a larger percentage of Black residents, while a smaller proportion of Blacks and hence a larger proportion of whites translated into higher revenue yields. Here again, it is noteworthy that race/ethnicity was also highly correlated with both income and education.

Third, the level of industrialization is another factor that was once correlated with taxing and expenditure policies of local governments. Higher levels of industrialization are an asset to a community in terms of providing jobs to area residents but industries can be taxed like homes and businesses and would be required to pay business license and impact fees and could even be a purchaser of utilities like water, electricity, or natural gas. However, in today's economy that has shifted away from a labor-intensive, smoke stack industry model to a highly digital, high-tech model, level of industrialization does not influence revenue collections as much as it did several decades ago. In fact, many large industrial giants in fields like steel and auto have had to scale back operations in light of stiff international competition. In addition, there is less variability in the level of industrialization that still exists due to decisions of companies to build new plants outside of the Northeast and Midwest or relocate old plants to areas like the South to take advantage of cheaper labor costs and lower taxes.

Two additional factors—urbanization and age distribution—also have been shown to influence the local government revenue collections. Given that residents of more urbanized communities tend to place greater expectations on their local governments than do people who live in less urbanized or rural areas, their local governments, of necessity, must raise more revenue. Then, communities with a large percentage of senior citizens who typically live on a fixed income will usually demand less in the way of services and also be less willing to pay higher taxes or fees than communities with smaller senior citizen residents.

In their seminal study of 87 city councils and nearly 500 councilpersons in the San Francisco Bay region, Heinz Eulau and Kenneth Prewitt (1973) reaffirmed the findings of the policy determination literature of the 1960s. Specifically, they found strong relationships between a community's socio-economic environment, the perceptions and attitudes of its council members, and the public policies that are adopted. They reasoned that, due to the fact that city council members have deep roots in their communities (numerous social contacts and group memberships, shared socio-economic, ethnic, racial, and religious characteristics with their constituents), they are likely to reflect these in their policy making, whether they are consciously aware of these constituency influences or not. Hence, the effects of shared community life may be substantially influential in shaping decision-making in small, homogeneous communities, where uniformity of outlook may amount to the feeling that they must acquiesce to the wishes and desires of their constituents. In short, although electoral accountability may have little direct influence over council members, belief sharing may still assure some congruence between the views of community members and the views of their council members.

While the Eulau and Prewitt's study focused on several types of expenditure decisions, it is reasonable to infer that council members' policy "maps" (their perceptions of conditions and goals for the future) were also congruent with revenue-raising decisions. That is, relationships between community environment, council members' attitudes, and revenue decisions must undoubtedly exist. Therefore, council members' attitudes seldom stray far from the constraints placed upon them by their communities' populations, needs, and resources.

While most researchers who have been identified with the policy determination literature often downplayed the importance of political factors of a community's environment, several studies published since the 1970s have argued that there is the potential that "politics matters" (see Dye, 1984). The scenario for this to plausibly happen centers around political parties representing sharply different constituencies. Stated differently, the likelihood that political party competition will produce policy differences is contingent on two things: (1) there is a bimodal distribution of voters' preferences in a state and (2) the parties have strong organization and ideologically motivated activists (see Dye and MacManus 2015, 143). In this type of political setting, the Democratic Party would represent central city, low-income, ethnic, and racial constituencies, while the Republican Party would represent middle-class, suburban, small-town, and rural constituencies (Dye and MacManus 2015, 143). In these states, the Democratic and Republican Parties would disagree over taxation and spending policies much like what is seen at the national level, thus making it easier for candidates to target a party's key, core constituents (see Brown 1995). The same political tendencies would also be present at the local level, as each party would likely target their respective constituencies at election time.

The invocation of these political tendencies should produce two predictable outcomes. First, the Democratic Party at both the state and local levels would push for greater spending in a number of areas including but not limited to welfare, health care, education, infrastructure, public and affordable housing, urban renewal, parks and recreation, and economic development, while the state and local Republican Parties would prefer less spending on these same service areas. Second, one would expect that the state and local Democratic Parties would be more amenable to the relaxation of revenue limitations and permitting a wider range of revenue options for local governments so as to make sufficient revenues available to pay for the costs associated with the types of services mentioned above. Conversely, it would be reasonable to speculate that the state and local Republican Parties would likely oppose any changes in revenue restrictions in order to minimize expenditures in these same programmatic areas. In sum, we would expect to see that state and local political parties there are mimicking their national counterparts (see Brown 1995).

### *Intergovernmental transfers*

Another thing that helps to explain how much revenue local governments have at their disposal at budget time is intergovernmental transfers. Local governments are often the beneficiaries of outside or external money or revenue that is not derived from their own or some internally generated sources. Commonly referred to as intergovernmental transfers—that is, the movement of money or other resources from one level of government to another—such money comes in the form of grants-in-aid, shared revenue, payments in lieu of taxes, or reimbursements for government services. Intergovernmental transfers (hereafter referenced as intergovernmental revenue) come from three primary sources—state government, federal government, or other local governments.

One of the principal benefits of outside money or intergovernmental revenue is that it provides local governments with the opportunity to deliver a higher level or wider variety of services to their citizens than would normally be possible, given their own limited resources. On the one hand, local governments are constantly being inundated with myriad service requests (e.g., replacing or repairing deteriorating infrastructures like streets, bridges, sidewalks, and buildings, expanding or building more water, sewer, library, and recreational facilities, installing more traffic signals and street lights, and hiring more police officers, firefighters, and school teachers). On the other hand, the growing costs of these service requests and expectations far exceed the resources available to local government officials. Therefore, the availability of intergovernmental revenue can sometimes be viewed as a windfall and certainly can ease the fiscal pressures that local governments face day in and day out.

But the opportunity to be the recipient of outside money or intergovernmental revenue brings additional benefits. Specifically, local officials can circumvent the onerous responsibility and burden of having to raise this additional revenue from their citizens directly and thereby can avoid most political costs that may be connected with the revenue-extracting function. Political costs, to the extent they exist, are typically borne by the donor government. Moreover, the recipient government (i.e., local governments) gets any political benefits associated with service delivery. In sum, local government officials are in the enviable position to receive praise for being able to provide services that the public believes it did not pay for, while the federal and state officials are loathed for being the unpopular revenue collector.

Owing to the fact that local governments are administrative subdivisions and creatures of the states, state governments have a vested interest in the success and welfare of their local governments and their citizens. After all, local citizens are also citizens of the state within which they reside and pay state taxes. Therefore, it is logical for state governments to assist their local governments in funding local programs and services (but especially, roads and highways, health care and hospitals, welfare, protective inspections, and law enforcement, corrections, and courts) since many of them are in reality *state* programs and services that are either partially or wholly provided by local governments. In this sense, local governments are acting as implementing agents or administrative arms of their state governments. In fact, states routinely mandate that local governments deliver many of the services mentioned above.

#### *State government sources*

One method by which funds are transferred by the states to their local governments is through shared revenue programs. State-shared revenue programs empower a state to distribute a part of a state-collected tax to certain designated local governments based on eligibility. State law determines how much of a particular state tax or fee is shared with local governments and for what purpose. Most state-shared revenues are allotted to counties and municipalities, but, depending on the state, can also be shared with townships and school districts and occasionally with special-purpose districts.

Some of the more common types of shared revenues that states share with their counties and municipalities include state taxes on tobacco products, alcoholic beverages; insurance premiums; beverage licenses; gas, fuel, and road taxes; general sales taxes and user fees; insurance licenses; intangible taxes; mobile home license taxes; petroleum, natural gas, coal, silver, gold, phosphate, sulfur, and other mineral or natural resources taxes (better known as severance taxes); wireless enhanced 911 fee. It is not unusual for funds coming from some of these sources to be specifically earmarked for specific purposes or services. For example, in Florida, gas, fuel, and road usage taxes are earmarked for roads and transportation, while the documentary stamp tax shared monies must be spent for affordable housing and purchasing endangered land. States that have lotteries, legalized gambling, and casinos often share a part of the proceeds of these activities with their local governments (sometimes school districts).

States, like the federal government, provide a variety of direct broad-based grants-in-aid to local governments. Many of the state grants-in-aid provided to counties and municipalities are similar to categorical grants of the federal government, in that they are usually needs-based, are for specifically defined purposes, are awarded on a competitive basis, typically require a monetary match on the part of the recipient government, and can be accompanied by a number of conditions (i.e., the proverbial "strings attached"). Welfare, health care, highway, economic development, historical preservation, and cultural amenities grants-in-aid tend to be some of the largest in terms of monetary allocations, although there are myriad and lesser-known functional areas that are eligible for state assistance. Aid for these programs is commonly handed out based on some type of formula (welfare and health care programs, for example, are often per-client reimbursement programs).

As we shall see in the analytical chapters to follow, state grants-in-aid to school districts account for much larger sums of money than that provided to counties and municipalities, and even townships and special districts. The manner by which states distribute financial assistance to school districts is not without some controversy. States use a formula for distributing funds. Historically, known as "foundation plans," such formulas are intended "to guarantee a minimum amount of educational expenditures either per pupil or per classroom" (Lee, Johnson, and Joyce 2013, 562). The word "foundation" implies equality of educational opportunity, meaning that every student should have a minimum level of education. Under this plan, poorer school districts receive a proportionately larger share of state funds than wealthier districts; yet, inter-district variation remains, although funding for poorer districts has increased. Wealthier districts merely use the state guarantee as a foundation on which to increase their own resources, while poorer school districts continue to operate with less money. Consequently, states struggle to come up with new, innovative, and more equitable financial arrangements like substituting sales tax and other revenues like lottery proceeds for local property tax revenues.

Payments in lieu of taxes constitute another form of intergovernmental transfers. County governments, but especially municipalities, are expected to provide a number of services to the state government when it has facilities and personnel within the borders of a county or city. A case in point is the location of the state capital. The capital city is in the unenviable position of having to provide services like police, fire, EMS, building permitting and inspections, solid waste and sewer collection and disposal, water, and so forth but is not legally permitted to levy a property or other type of tax on the state to recoup costs. To rectify this situation, most state governments have been amenable to paying a negotiated amount of money (payment in lieu of taxes) to minimally cover the cost of providing services to the state. Most of the time, the payment is barely enough to cover the costs incurred by cities and counties in providing services, while some cities and counties, on occasion, may be able to realize a modest "profit" that can augment the general revenue fund.

*Federal government sources*

Besides receiving financial assistance from their states, local governments also receive substantial amounts of money (although not nearly as much as from their states) via a host of federal grant-in-aid programs. Since the late 1950s, federal grants-in-aid money increasingly has been available on a competitive and demonstrated needs basis for a multitude of services or programs like urban renewal and community redevelopment, law enforcement, water and sewer projects, public housing and housing rehabilitation, public welfare, health care, homeland security, mass transit, air and water transportation, infrastructure, environmental protection and conservation, planning, and so forth. Historically, most of the federal funding for these types of policy areas and programs have been filtered primarily through the states. That is, the federal government usually allocates grant monies directly to the states who, in turn, may or may not reallocate this money to their local government unless the condition for the recipient of these monies as written in the language of the congressional legislation directs otherwise. As one would imagine, state legislatures and governors early on were in a position to reallocate federal money in a partisan, capacious, and irrational manner. More specifically, prior to the U.S. Supreme Court handing down a series of decisions mandating reapportionment in both state legislatures and the U.S. House of Representatives (e.g., *Baker* v. *Carr* in 1962, *Gray* v. *Sanders* in 1963, and *Westberry* v *Sanders* and *Reynolds* v. *Sims* in 1964), state legislatures had a clear tendency to bestow more money to rural areas with fewer critical service problems while giving much less money to urban areas with greater service needs.

Given these patterns of irresponsible reallocation of federal funds by state officials, the Congress began to target grant-in-aid money specifically for local governments during the Kennedy and Johnson administrations of the 1960s. This meant that, contrary to previous patterns of federal grant-in-aid directives, much more fiscal assistance was disbursed directly to local governments and no longer passed through the states. Such an approach was consistent with the basic tenets of President Johnson's desire to attack the most serious problems in the nation's urban areas and assist in building what he referred to as the "Great Society." The short-lived efforts to redirect larger amounts of federal aid to local government ended with the election of Richard Nixon as the President in 1968, as the Nixon administration (under his New Federalism agenda) sought to restore states to what he believed to be their rightful place in the federal system which meant having most federal aid flow through them (see Benton 1986a, 1986b). While state legislatures and governors were less apt to play "politics" with federal aid in the ensuing years and reallocate federal funds in a more rational and fair manner to local governments, local governments had lost their direct pipeline to Washington and greater chance for a larger part of the federal fiscal aid pie.

In spite of the loss of direct federal funds that local governments experienced during the Nixon era, local governments for the next 18 years were able to benefit from a new form of federal fiscal assistance (general revenue sharing) that was part and parcel of the Nixon New Federalism legacy and philosophy. The revenue-sharing program provided funds, with no strings attached, to both state and general-purpose local governments (cities, counties, towns, and townships). It was terminated in 1986, prinicipally because of the mounting national budget deficit and Congress's desire to exert greater control over, and take more credit for, how federal monies were spent.

*Local government sources*

For many years, local governments have been in the business of providing a number of services (e.g., water supply and sewage disposal, fire, EMS, police protection, garbage and solid waste management, libraries, building inspections, housing prisoners, mosquito abatement, just to name a few) to neighboring local governments. One of the most well-known examples is the Lakewood Plan, whereby communities have been able to contract with Los Angeles County for virtually all city services. Other examples include a number of counties in Florida where a number of small cities contract with the Pinellas County Sheriff to provide 24/7 police services, while a growing number of other small cities contract with their county government (e.g., Pinellas and Pasco) to provide fire/rescue services. Also, there are several large cities in Florida and elsewhere that provide services to small cities on a contractual basis, like where the City of Tampa provides sewer disposal services to a neighboring suburban city (Temple Terrace) in Hillsborough County. Furthermore, it is not uncommon for school districts to contact with the county or a city for the provision of school resource officers. These and other cities and counties around the country have come to realize that they cannot provide these kinds of service in-house on a cost/efficient basis. While these smaller governments realize a cost saving that permits them to redirect scarce resources to other services that are provided in-house, larger cities and counties are able to augment their own scarce fiscal resources with "income" earned from the provision of services to their neighboring jurisdictions.

Finally, there are a growing number of local governments that lease office, parking, and warehouse space or sell water, unused office equipment, unneeded buildings, used vehicles, and other surplus materials to other local government as a money-making venture.

In spite of the fact, that intergovernmental transfers are a stable source of revenue for local governments, the growing uncertainty of outside money—but especially fiscal assistance from the federal and state governments—is an issue of mounting concern for local governments.

***Citizen expectations and views on government and government officials***

While state constitutions and statutes set the parameters for local government revenue options and policies, local government officials must be ever-conscious of the ephemeral, fickle, and even contradictory expectations and mindset of their constituents.

Unlike local government officials, the citizens they serve do not always clearly see or fully appreciate the balancing act that is required when crafting a jurisdiction's budget. All too often, local citizens tend to focus more on what they are receiving in the form of services from their local government(s) than how to raise the money to pay for them. Simply stated, it is commonplace for most local citizens to take for granted that the provision of services by their city, county, township, special service district, or school districts occurs in an orderly (even seamless) and matter-of-fact way on a daily basis. More to the point, garbage is picked up twice a week, water flows from the faucet when turned on, traffic lights are operable and streets are passable to facilitate the flow of traffic, police officers, firefighters, and EMS personnel respond quickly when summoned in emergency situations, sewage and solid waste are disposed of, government-operated hospitals treat patients non-stop, while county health department inoculate school-aged children for the prevention of serious diseases, commercial structures and homes under construction are inspected to ensure compliance with building and safety codes, books are available for checkout from the library, and public schools educate our children Monday thru Friday for about nine months a year, and so forth. It is only when the quality of these services falls below a level of unacceptability or local leaders propose to raise the prospect of having to increase taxes and/or fees to address declining service quality or expand existing services or add new ones that the public begins to pay close attention to service costs and the need for additional revenue and where it will come from.

The long and the short of it are that the consuming public often has conflicting (even contradictory) views about the services they receive from their local governments and what they pay for them. Simply put, they want more and better services but are not always willing to pay more to receive them and even think that they are currently paying too much. Some scholars (see Benton and Daly 1992) who have studied this phenomenon have coined the expression "the paradox of the contradictory local government citizen," since their mode of thinking defies the logic that their services cannot be expanded or improved without a subsequent tax or fee hike. It is as though that they do not accept the reality of the world of economics whereby one normally must pay more if one wants more (of anything) but do not want to pay more. Part and parcel of this mindset is the notion that local governments must inevitably be mismanaged, inept, and wasteful. Over time, this perspective was accompanied by a decline in public trust of local officials, a decrease in political efficacy, and a sharp increase in cynicism. Herein lies the makings of what has been termed "tax revolts" among local citizens which poses a severe problem for local government officials who see no way out to satisfy their constituents who adamantly oppose tax and/or fee increases that are required to expand current service levels or provide wholly new services.

### *Tax revolts and taxing and spending limitations*

The growing instance of tax revolts and citizens' movements focused on taxing and spending limits of local governments generated a significant amount of attention from political science and public administration scholars and a massive research literature that was devoted to these subjects during the 1970s, 1980s, and 1990s. The most widely known revolt occurred in the late 1970s in California, as taxpayer resentment of property taxes and changes in assessment practices and the general belief that government was too big, too costly, and too wasteful led to voters approving what was known as Proposition 13. Similar movements occurred in Massachusetts and Michigan and were followed by the adoption of the Taxpayer's Bill of Rights (known a TABOR) by voters in Colorado.

While taxpayer revolts may come and go today, "their legacy, however, remain enormously important" (Bowman, Kearney, and Scavo 2022, 379; see also Martell and Teste 2007) and thereby serve to restrict the discretion of local official in their revenue options. For instance, watchdog organizations like Americans for Tax Reform still demand that candidates for local elective office sign a "no tax" pledge, meaning that these officials "must work hard to justify tax/fee increases; otherwise they risk a voter uprising and perhaps political death" (Bowman, Kearney, and Scavo 2022, 379). Currently, there are 46 states that have some type of taxation and expenditure limitations that local officials must be ever mindful of.[13]

In spite of the fluctuations in local government revenues that can be attributable to local citizens' sometimes contradictory service and funding expectations and shifting attitudes toward government, generally, and local government, specifically, there is still a striking degree of relative stability and evenness in revenue collections that can be understood in terms of the phenomenon of incrementalism which also has its problems.

### *Archaic/repetitive budgetary customs and traditions—Incrementalism*

The budgeting process has never changed and represents a significant stumbling block for local officials (indeed, officials at all governmental levels). It has never moved beyond the "horse and buggy" age. In short, the day for progressive, enlightened, and forward-thinking budgeting has never arrived. Instead of being a positive force, incrementalism is the epitome of "kicking the old can down the road year after year for most local governments. While being a very good descriptor of how a budget is formulated and assembled, it nonetheless does nothing in the way of constructive planning for the future or minimizing, underutilizing, or even wasting finite precious resources; incrementalism represents the worst-case scenario for revenue and expenditure decisions. The shortcoming and drawbacks of incrementalism are endless and will not be discussed here."[14]

***Changes in national laws and national, local, and international economies***

Local government finances, in general, and revenues, in particular, are affected by the activities of the national government. For example, when the federal government alters the tax code, it can create problems directly and indirectly for local governments in those states where they levy a state and/or local income tax that is closely linked to the federal tax code.[15] In a direct sense, state and local officials may be more willing to raise the rates of their own income taxes to generate additional own-source revenue, knowing that their citizens can claim a deduction against their federal income taxes for income taxes paid to their state and local governments. Over the years, state and local governments have benefited from this feature of the federal code. If it were to be taken away, it would make it more difficult for local governments to raise more of their own revenue. Moreover, the elimination of this deduction could also hurt local governments in an indirect way. That is, state governments may no longer be in a financial position to share part of revenue they collect from their income tax with local governments because of the likely negative effect of the federal government eliminating the deduction for payment of state income taxes. In short, a change in the federal tax code could result in a double whammy loss of revenue for local governments. Most recently, the Tax Cuts and Jobs Act (ICIA) in 2017 made some revisions to the federal tax code that have already resulted in revenue losses for some local governments (see Hufer, Iselin, Sammartino, and Weiner 2019).

Another possible negative effect could result from the unwillingness of the federal government to exempt interest income earned by private citizens and other investors who buy local government bonds. State and local governments have always counted on borrowing money at below conventional commercial rates to finance massive infrastructure projects. The loss of this source of "cheap" money would undoubtedly put a crimp in local government budgets. In fact, it is estimated that this loss would result in local governments having to borrow money at much higher interest rates and subsequently having to pay more to borrow.

Besides changing the federal tax code, the federal government can take other actions that can affect the U.S. economy as well as the economies of state and local governments. For instance, when the Federal Reserve Board raises or lowers the prime interest rate or changes reserve requirements of banks and other lending institutions, it can send strong shock waves through the economy which can ultimately directly or indirectly negatively affect local government revenues. Additional shock waves could hit local and their state governments if the federal were to ever default on its debt, with this almost happening in early June 2023.

Furthermore, there is always the possibility that unexpected occurrences in the global economy could potentially wreak havoc with the U.S. economy and eventually filter down to local governments. Examples include the devaluation of the U.S. dollar against other world currencies and balance of trade swings,[16] but especially significant trade deficits between the United States and its global trade partners.[17]

Then, of course, by 2019, the outbreak of COVID-19 was beginning to negatively impact the national, state, and local economies. As state governors ordered businesses like restaurants and bars to close or curtail their hours of operation, practice social distancing, and take other health precautions, as well as limit other types of activities where people gather in large numbers, the U.S. economy came close to all but shutting down completely. Understandably, this led to revenue losses not only for business owners but also for local governments. Although the economy seems to be in a recovery mode currently and the Congress has provided a generous amount of aid through the ARPA, however, the longer-range implications of reductions in local option sales and income tax revenue, money derived from fees and charges for services, and even property tax losses are still unclear.

#### *Burdensome federal and state mandates*

Local officials frequently complain that mandates (sometimes part and parcel of requirements for the receipt of federal or state grants-in-aid or direct, outright orders to do something), but particularly unfunded ones, can "devastate" or "wreak havoc" with their budgets. Federal and state mandates, although typically well-intended to make sure that vital activities are performed and desirable goals are achieved, oftentimes skew local government budget spending priorities. The bottom line is that local governments must scramble to make ends meet with vital and limited OSR having to be shifted in their budgets to cover the cost required from "orders received from on high" (i.e., the federal government or their state government).

When either the federal or state governments mandate that local governments do something and provide little or no money with which to do it, local governments usually have to redirect already-committed money in their jurisdiction's budget to cover the costs of unexpected mandates. Seen as "costly intrusions into local matters," mandates often force local government to spend their internally derived money (OSR) on goals and priorities of federal and state officials (e.g., making public facilities handicapped accessible, using additional chemicals to safely dispose of sewage, implementing new voter registration procedures, or ensuring reasonable overtime pay to local government employees) and not on services and programs that are long-standing service and program priorities for locally elected officials and their constituents. Obviously, this rankles locally elected officials and the people they serve, with the local officials frequently being blamed for not delivering on promises to their constituents. This can place local officials in the exasperating position of having to find additional OSR by raising taxes and charges for services or levying special assessments to keep their commitment to satisfy public expectations and needs to hire vitally needed additional firefighters, police officers, planning and zoning personnel, and sanitation workers, construct sidewalks in residential areas, expand existing recreational programs and parks, add new street lights, or repave streets beset with potholes. Worse still is the possibility that these locally determined service priorities may have to be eliminated from the budget for the lack of funds once money is siphoned off to cover the cost of federal- and state-unfunded mandates. While the number and cost magnitude of unfunded mandates surged in the 1970s and 1980s (see MacManus 1991), they still abound today and their costs have risen and constitute a larger part of local government expenditures (Benton 1996; Grossback 2002; Bowman and Kearney 2011).

## Study methodology

The purpose of this book is to provide a reasonable picture and analysis of revenue trends and practices of local governments in the United States that would be of interest to and useful for both scholars and practitioners. While it might be desirable to provide a moving picture from the inception of the United States until the present, such a lofty ambition is neither beneficial nor practical. First, there is the limitation of data availability. Comprehensive and comparable data on local government finances, including revenues, simply does not exist as far back as 1789. An examination of data collected by the U.S. Bureau of the Census reveals that the reliable data needed for this study goes back only as far as 1962. Yet, that provides us with a time frame of over 50 years with 13 data points, which is certainly sufficient for our purposes in this book. Second, there is the expectation that the data and subsequent analysis must be relevant to the world in which we currently live, satisfy the needs of theory building of scholars, and applicable to the practical consumption and use of and relevancy to practitioners.

Given these considerations and parameters, it was decided to utilize revenue information reported every five years (i.e., those years ending in "2" and "7") by the U.S. Bureau of the Census in what is referred to as the Census of Governments, *Compendium of Government Finances* as our primary source of data. Therefore, the study's beginning point is 1962 and the endpoint is 2017, the most recent for which these data are available. This time frame will be used whenever the analysis focuses on one or more specific types of local governments (i.e., counties, municipalities, townships, special districts, and school districts). These issues of the *Compendium of Government Finances* provide us with 13 data points and cover a 55-year period. Just as importantly, each of these reports contains complete data on all five types of local government (counties, municipalities, townships, special districts, and school districts) and a comprehensive accounting of all revenues by source and type. Whenever possible, these data will be augmented with data from the 2018, 2019, and 2020 Annual Surveys of State and Local Government Finances to provide for more recent financial data on aggregated local government revenue figures (specifically, the time line for analysis will extend to 2020).

Additional data for this book will be derived from other reports in the Census of Governments series specific to individual local governments (i.e., *Finances of County Governments*, *Finances of Municipal and Township Governments*, *Finances of Special Districts*, and *Finances of School Districts*), the U.S. Bureau of the Census, *Census of the General Population*, as well as other entities including but not limited to individual state and National League of Cities (NLC), National Association of Counties (NACo), local government publications, International City/County Association (ICCMA) reports and publications, reports of the National Association of State Budget Officers, and Government Finance Officers Association (GFOA), and indices developed by the authors of several scholarly studies. It is the intention of the author to produce an updated version or a new edition of this book whenever the 2022 *Compendium of Government Finances* is released by the U.S. Bureau of the Census.

Through the remainder of this book, but especially in the analytical chapters, reference will be made to several important terms and concepts that are integral to an understanding of the presentation of massive amounts of financial data and their subsequent interpretations. These terms and concepts and a brief definition/description of each are as follows:

**Own-Source Revenue (OSR)**—money received by local governments from internally derived sources like taxes, funds in lieu of taxes, fines, forfeitures, fees, charges for services, special assessments, donations, gifts, sale of surplus property, and an assortment of miscellaneous revenues.

**Intergovernmental Revenue (IR)**—money received from the national (federal), state, or other local governments.

**Total General Revenue (TR)**—own-source revenue plus intergovernmental revenue (i.e., OSR plus IR).

**Total Tax Revenue (TTR)**—sum total of al revenue obtained from all types of taxes—property, sales, income, and a number of other or miscellaneous kinds of taxes.

**Property Tax Revenue (PTR)**—total amount of money received from taxes on real estate and homes, buildings, and other structures located on it. Sometimes, it is referred to as ad valorem tax revenue.

**Fiscal Year (FY)**—is the 12-month period that governments uses to track its annual finances. Since 1974, the federal government has used a fiscal year that begins on October 1 and ends on September 30 of the next year. While a number of local governments have adopted the federal model, most of them still use the standard type fiscal year—July1–June 30 (like their states). In addition, a handful of local governments still use a traditional private sector calendar-year model (i.e., January 1–December 31). The name given to a fiscal year is the year in which the budget ends (e.g., a budget that begins on July 1, 2022 and ends on June 30, 2023 would be referred to as the budget for FY 2023).

Statistical analyses of the data collected for this study will range from descriptive to inferential, depending on the nature of the data and purposes for illustrating a point or concept or suggesting a trend. On the descriptive side, data may be presented in either tabular or graphic form. That is, data could be arranged in a table or a series of tables (tabular) or depicted in bar graphs, pie charts, or line graphs (graphic).

## What's ahead?

While total revenues of all governments (national, state, and local) have increased appreciably since 1962, this has been particularly the case for all five types of local governments. This massive increase in revenue collected by local governments, notwithstanding, it is also important to identify how and why revenues patterns have changed from 1962 to the present time. To assist in cataloging and describing these changes requires that some thought be given to what may have been responsible for the unique patterns characterizing each of the five types of local governments and changes in them that may have occurred over time. To provide the framework for this analysis and a context for explaining and differentiating between changes in revenue patterns within and across counties, municipalities, townships, special districts, and school districts from 1962–2017 (i.e., my effort at theorizing), the first part of this chapter presented a synthesis of the political science and public administration scholarly literature, government documents and reports, practitioner observations, and anecdotal evidence and information.

## Notes

1 While counties were initially created in all 50 states, only 48 states still had these units of government or their equivalent (parishes in Louisiana and boroughs in Alaska) as of 2023. Rhode Island and Connecticut abolished organized county governments in 1842 and 1958, respectively. Moreover, since 1997, Massachusetts has systematically eliminated nine of its original 14 counties, leaving only Barnstable, Bristol, Dukes, Norfolk, and Plymouth.

2 More recently, a significant number of urban counties with large and diverse populations and under pressure to modernize have been granted home rule charters by their states that permit them to provide a larger array of services that closely resemble the menu of services that municipalities have traditionally provided. These groups of services have been labeled by Benton (2002a) as "municipal-type" (e.g., fire protection, libraries, utilities like water, gas, and electricity, solid waste and sewage collection, and protective inspections) and "urban-type" or "regional type" (e.g., solid waste and sewage disposal, parks and recreational services, natural resource conservation and environmental protection, housing, urban development, airports, transit, water transportation and terminals, and parking). Even in medium- and small-sized counties, county governments without charters or ones benefiting from relaxed state constitutional and statutory language are providing a larger number of optional services that are not mandated by the state but rather are demanded or expected by county residents (e.g., pollution control, homes for the aged, emergency medical services, 911 emergency call centers, mental health and mental retardation programs, day care services, juvenile

courts, job training, emergency financial assistance, hospitals, animal control, alcohol/ drug abuse programs, consumer protection, among others).

3 See Petronicolos and New 1999.

4 There are three states (Maryland, Tennessee, and North Carolina) that have not established independent school districts but mandated their county governments to run K-12 schools, in addition to providing those services that counties normally provide. In addition, a number of large cities (most notably, Buffalo, New York, Rochester, Syracuse, and Yonkers in New York, Chicago in Illinois, Detroit in Michigan, and Philadelphia and Pittsburgh in Pennsylvania) are permitted to operate their own schools, while school districts exist in other parts of these states.

5 In the last decade or so with many U.S. local governments having been unable to cope with the financial pressures of ongoing economic disinvestment and the subsequent Great Recession, some states have declared some of their local governments—particularly municipalities but also counties and school districts—as being in a fiscal crisis and have subsequently placed them in state-led receivership and handed over most local processes to a state-appointed manager. This procedure, usually referred to as a "takeover," effectively removes authority from locally elected officials. Some of the more notable examples are Stockton and San Bernardino, California, Detroit and Benton Harbor, Michigan, East St. Louis, Illinois, Chelsea, Massachusetts, Camden, New Jersey, and Orange County, California. For an excellent discussion of this issue and how it relates to local government home rule, see Nichols (2016).

6 One of the principal criticisms of what is viewed as the overly zealous state oversight and supervision of local governments by home rule proponents is the tight rein the state exercises in the area of fiscal policy. The limits placed on local governments in the area, as well as in policy and program management, are believed to impede the "governing capacity" of these governments in two dimensions: the ability to meet requirements of the state and do what is expected of them by their residents (see Gargan 1997). "Governing capacity" refers to the ability of a government to design and implement collective choices. Thus, any discussion of the capacity of local governments presumes some measure of independence from superior layers of government (Krane, Rigos, and Hill 2001).

7 For a thorough examination and discussion of the constitutional underpinnings of local government finance and subsequent implications in the United States, see Kincaid (2012) and Vaillacourt and Dafflon (2012).

8 In Florida, for instance, while only county governments are permitted to levy a local option sales tax, they are however allowed to share their proceeds with cities and school and special districts.

9 See Wallace (2012) for an in-depth discussion and analysis of the "architecture" and logic behind local government usage of various sources of revenue.

10 While there are no studies that have directly linked Elazar's political culture scheme to levels of spending and revenue policy, there are, however, studies (see Monroe 1977; Savage and Gallagher 1977; Peters and Welsh 1977; Kincaid 1980, 1982; Lieske 1990) that have used the scheme to make indirect inferences to quality of life. A case in point would be the following: Moralistic Minnesota scores very high on quality of life despite its cold climate. Quality of life is surely, to a significant degree, a reflection of the effectiveness of spending and taxing policies, which is, in turn, a reflection of political culture.

11 All three of the political subcultures are of nationwide proportions and have spread over time throughout the United States, from the Atlantic to the Pacific Oceans and from the Canadian to the Mexican borders. At the same time, each subculture is strongly tied to specific sections of the country, thus reflecting the various streams

and currents of migration that have carried people of different ethnic and racial origins and backgrounds across the continent in more or less orderly patterns.

12 Dye's findings were either preceded or affirmed by a numbers of other scholars. For instance, see Dawson and Robinson 1963; Hofferbert 1966; Cnuddle and McCrone 1969; Fry and Winters 1970.

13 For more details and implications, see Bowman, Kearney, and Scavo 2022, 379–80 and Lee, Johnson, and Joyce 2020, 158+. For additional evidence and analysis of the impact and constraints placed on local governments, see also Mullins and Joyce 1996; O'Sullivan 2001; Bae, Moon, and Jung 2012; Chapman and Gorina 2012; Kioko and Martell 2012; Maher and Deller 2013; Sun 2014; Jimenez 2017; Stallman, Maher, Deller, and Park 2017; Park, Park, and Maher 2018; Eliason and Lutz 2018; Shumberger Sumberger and Singla 2022.

14 The interested reader should consult several excellent sources (Simon 1955; Lindbloom 1959; Wildavsky 1964) on the problems and deficiencies as a model to follow in budgeting. Some additional discussion of the drawbacks to incrementalism is also found in Chapter 10 of this book (pp. 11–13).

15 For an excellent discussion of the negative impact of the Tax Reform Act of 1986 on local government finances, see Pagano (1988). According to Pagano, the Act, while advertised as being neutral-free, actually resulted in a significant restructuring of the balance of power in state-federal-local relations. In particular, new restrictions on the tax-exempt bond authority of state and local governments have required significant shifts in traditional local debt policy. Furthermore, the Supreme Court's 1986 decision in *South Carolina* v. *Baker* created additional concerns about the status of state and local tax-exempt bonds. In fact, Pagano (1988, 50) went so far as to say that "the nature of future relations between the federal government and local governments is likely to be molded more by the federal code and by the erosion of state authority over fiscal matters than by federal grant-in-aid programs of the kind that has characterized the past quarter century of intergovernmental relations."

16 See Segal, Kelly, and Logan (2021) for some scenarios how this can potentially affect local government revenues.

17 See McBride and Chatzky (2019) for an explanation of possible implications for local government revenues.

## References


Bae, Suho, Seong-gin Moon, and Changhoon Jung. 2012. "Economic Effects of State-Level Tax and Expenditures," *Public Administration Review*, 72(September/October): 649–58.

Benton, J. Edwin. 2002a. *Counties as Service Delivery Agents: Changing Expectations and Roles*. Westport, CT: Praeger.

———. 2002b. "County Service Delivery: Does Structure Matter?" *Public Administration Review*, 62: 423–31.

———. 2003. "County Government Structure and County Revenue Policy: What's the Connection?" *State and Local Government Review*, 35(Spring): 78–89.

———. 1996. "Intergovernmental Aid and the Mandate Issue: The County Experience." In Menzel, Donald C. (ed.), *The American County: Frontiers of Knowledge*. University, AL: University of Alabama Press: 149–65.

———. 1993. "Providing Services in an Era of Declining Fiscal Fortunes: The Dilemma Confronting Local Governments during the 1990s," *The Florida Political Chronicle*, 5(1): 10–16.

———. 1986a. "Federal Grant-in-Aid Cut-Backs and State and Local Government Spending Policies." In Benton, J. Edwin, and David R. Morgan (eds.), *Intergovernmental Relations and Public Policy*. Westport, CT: Greenwood Press: 1–34.

———. 1986b. "Federalism's 'First Principles' and Reagan's New Federalism Policies," *Policy Studies Journal*, 13(March): 568–75.

———. Stephen Aikins, and Michael Miller. 2009. *Coping with Dwindling Property Tax Revenues: The Tale of Municipalities and Counties in Florida* (Working Paper # 1). Report prepared for the Florida City/County Management Association, Florida League of Cities, Florida Association of Counties, and the Florida Government Finance Officers' Association), August 24.

———. and John L. Daly. 1992. "The Paradox of Citizen Service Evaluations and Tax Preferences: The Case of Two Small Cities," *American Review of Public Administration*, 22: 271–87.

Bowman, Ann O'M, and Richard C. Kearney. 2008. *State and Local Government*. 7th ed. Boston: Houghton Mifflin Company.

———. 2011. "Second-Order Devolution: Data and Doubt," *Publius: The Journal of Federlism*, 41(Fall): 563–85.

———. and Carmine P.F. Scavo. 2022. *State and Local Government*. 11th ed. Boston: Cengage.

Brown, Robert D. 1995. "Party Cleavages and Welfare Effort in the American States," *American Journal of Political Science*, 89: 23–33.

Chapman, Jeffrey, and Eugenia Gorina. 2012. "Effects of the Form of Government and Property Tax Limits on Local Finance in the Context of Revenue and Expenditure Simultaneity," *Public Budgeting & Finance*, 32(Winter): 19–45.

Cnuddle, Charles S., and Donald J. McCrone. 1969. "Party Competition and Welfare Policies in the American States," *American Political Science Review*, 63: 858–66.

Dawson, Richard E., and James A. Robinson. 1963. "Interparty Competition, Economic Variables, and Welfare Policies in the American States," *Journal of Politics*, 25: 265–89.

Donovan, Todd, Christopher Z. Mooney, and Daniel A. Smith. 2011. *State and Local Politics: Institutions and Reform*. 2nd ed. Boston: Wadsworth.

Dye, Thomas R. 1966. *Politics, Economics and the Public*. Chicago: Rand McNally.

———. 1984. "Party and Policy in the States," *Journal of Politics*, 46: 1097–116.

———. and Susan MacManus. 2015. *Politics in States and Communities*. 15th ed. Upper Saddle River, NJ: Pearson.

Elazar, Daniel J. 1984. *American Federalism: A View from the States*. New York: Harper and Row.

Eliason, Paul, and Byron Lutz. 2018. "Can Fiscal Rules Constrain the Size of Government? An Analysis of the 'Crown Jewel' of Tax and Expenditure Limitations," *Journal of Public Economics*, 166: 115–44.

Eulau, Heinz, and Kenneth Prewitt. 1973. *The Labyrinths of Democracy*. Indianapolis: Bobbs-Merrill Company, Inc.

Fry, Brian R., and Richard Winters. 1970. "The Politics of Redistribution," *American Political Science Review*, 64(June): 508–22.

Gargan, John J. 1997. "Local Government Governing Capacity: Challenges for the New Century." In John J. Gargan (ed.), *Handbook of Local Government Administration*. New York: Marcel Dekkar: 520–5.

Grossback, Lawrence J. 2002. "The Problem of State-Imposed Mandates: Lessons from Minnesotta's Local Governments," *State and Local Government Review*, 34(Fall): 183–97.

Grant, Daniel R., and H.C. Nixon. 1982. *State and Local Government in America*. 4th ed. Boston: Allyn and Bacon, Inc.

Hofferbert, Richard I. 1966. "The Relationship between Public Policy and Some Structural and Environmental Variables in the American States," *American Political Science Review*, 60: 73–82.

Hufer, Erin, John Iselin, Frank Sammartino, and David Weiner. 2019. "Effects of the Tax Cuts and Jobs Act on State Individual Income Taxes," *Washington University Journal of Law and Policy*, 38: 205–29.

———. 1969. "Dimensions of State Policies, Economics, and Public Policy," *American Political Science Review*, 63(September): 867–79.

Jimenez, Benedict S. 2017. "Institutional Constraints, Rule Following, and Circumvention: Tax and Expenditure Limits and Choice of Fiscal Tools during a Budget Crisis," *Public Budgeting & Finance*, 37(Summer): 5–34.

Kioko, Sharon N., and Christine R. Martell. 2012. "Impact of State-Level Tax and Expenditure (TELs) Limits on Government Revenues and Aid to Local Governments," *Public Finance Review*, 40(6): 736–66.

Kincaid, John. 2012. "The Constitutional Frameworks of State and Local Governments." In Robert E. Ebel and John E Petersen (eds.), *The Oxford Handbook of State and Local Government Finance*. New York: Oxford University Press: 45–82.

———. 1982. "*Political Culture, Public Policy and the American States*." Philadelphia: ISHI.

———. 1980. "Political Culture and the Quality of Urban Life," *Publius: The Journal of Federalism*, 10(Spring): 89–110.

Krane, Dale, Platon N. Rigos, and Melvin B. Hill Jr. 2001. *Home Rule in America: A Fifty-State Handbook*. Washington, DC: CQ Press.

Larson, Sarah E., and Bruce D. McDonald. 2023. "Taxation and Citizen Choice: The Effect of County Charter on Property Taxes," *Public Budgeting & Finance*, 43(Spring): 64–84.

Lee, Robert E. Jr, Ronald W. Johnson, and Phillip G. Joyce, 2020. *Public Budgeting Systems*. 10th ed. Burlington, MA; Jones & Bartlett Learning LLC.

Lieske, Joel. 1990. "The Correlates of Life Quality in U.S. Metropolitan Areas," *Publius: The Journal of Federalism*, 20(Winter): 43–54.

Lindbloom, Charles E. 1959. "The Science of 'Muddling Though'," *Public Administration Review*, 19(Spring): 79–88.

MacManus, Susan A. 1991. "Mad About Mandates: The Issue of Who Should Pay for What Resurfaces in the 1990s," *Publius: The Journal of Federalism*, 21(Summer): 59–75.

Maher, Craig S., and Steven C. Deller. 2013. "Measuring the Impacts of TELs on Municipal Finance Conditions." In Helisse Levine, Jonathan Justice and Eric Scorsone (eds.), *Fiscal Health*. New York: Jones and Bartlett: 405–26.

Martell, Christine R., and Paul Teste. 2007. "Fiscal Management Implications of the TABOR Bind," *Public Administration Review*, 67(July/August): 673–87.

McBride, James, and Andrew Chatzky. 2019. "U.S. Trade Deficit: How Much Does It Matter?" U. S. Council on Foreign Affairs, March 8. Accessed at: https://www.cfr.org/backgrounder/us-trade-deficit-how-much-does-it-matter

Monroe, Alan D. 1977. "Operationalizing Political Culture: The Illinois Case," *Publius: The Journal of Federalism*, 7(Winter): 107–20.

Morgan, David R., and John P. Peliserro. 1980. "Urban Policy: Does Political Structure Matter?" *American Political Science Review*, 74: 999–1006.

Mullins, Daniel R., and Philip Joyce. 1996. "Tax and Expenditure Limitations and State and Local Fiscal Structure: An Empirical Assessment," *Public Budgeting & Finance*, 16(Spring): 75–101.

Nickels, Ashley E. 2016. "Approaches to Municipal Takeover: Home Rule Erosion and State Intervention in New Jersey and Michigan," *State and Local Government Review*, 48: 194–207.

O'Sullivan, Arthur. 2001. "Limits on Local Property Taxation: The United States Experience," *Property Taxation and Local Government Review*, 30(3): 177–8.

Pagano, Michael A. 1988. "Effects of Federal Tax Reform on Local Finances," *Publius: The Journal of Federalism*, 18(Summer): 37–50.

Park, Kee Ok. 1996. "Determinants of County Government Growth." In Donald C. Menzel (ed.), *The American County: Frontiers of Knowledge*. University, AL: University of Alabama Press: 34–52.

Park, Ji-Hyung, Sungho Park, and Craig S. Maher. 2018. "The Effects of Tax and Expenditure Limitations (TELs) and Municipal Fiscal Outcomes during a Period of Fiscal Stress," *Public Finance and Management*, 18(1): 84–110.

Petronicolos, Loucas, and William New. 1999. "Anti-Immigrant Legislation, Social Justice, and the Right to Equal Educational Opportunity," *American Educational Research Journal*, 36: 373–408.

Peters, John D., and Susan Welsh. 1977. "Politics, Corruption, and Political Culture: A View from the State Legislature," *American Politics Quarterly*, 6: 345–56.

Savage, Robert L., and Richard J. Gallagher. 1977. "Politico-Cultural Regions in a Southern State: An Empirical Typology of Arkansas Counties," *Publius: The Journal of Federalism*, 7(Winter): 91–105.

Segal, Troy, Robert C. Kelly, and Michael Logan. 2021. "Currency Fluctuations: How They Affect the Economy," *Global Trade Guide*, June 4. Accessed at: https://www.investopedia.com/articles/forex/080613/effects-currency-fluctuations-economy.asp

Simon, Herbert A. 1955. "A Behavioral Model of Rational Choice," *Quarterly Journal of Economics*, 69: 99–118.

Stallman, Judith L., Craig S. Maher, Steven C. Deller, and Sungho Park. 2017. "Surveying the Effects of Limitations on Taxes and Expenditures: What We Do/don't Know," *Journal of Public and Nonprofit Affairs*, 3(2): 197–222.

Sumberger, Jason, and Aakheil Singla. 2022. "Are Tax and Expenditure Limitations Constraining Institutions or Institutionally Irrelevant? Evidence from Minnesota," *Public Budgeting & Finance*, 42(Winter): 3–33.

Sun, Rul. 2014. "Re-Evaluating the Effect of Tax and Expenditure Limitations: An Instrumental and Variable Approach," *Public Finance Review*, 42(1): 92–116.

Wallace, Sally. 2012. "The Evolving Financial Architecture of State and Local Governments." In Robert E. Ebel and John E. Petersen (eds.), *The Oxford Handbook of State and Local Government Finance*. New York: Oxford University Press: 156–75.

Wildavsky, Aaron. 1964. "*The Politics of the Budgetary Process*." Boston: Little, Brown and Company.

Yalmaz, Serdar, Franancois Vaillancourt, and Bernard Dafflon. 2012. "State and Local Government Finances: Why It Matters." In Robert E. Ebel and John E Petersen (eds.), *The Oxford Handbook of State and Local Government Finance*. New York: Oxford University Press: 105–36.

Zhang, Pengju, and Phueng Nguyen-Hoang. 2023. "Home Rule and Municipal Revenue Stability: New Evidence from Texas," *Public Budgeting & Finance*, 43(Spring): 38–60.

# 3 Overview of the Revenue Structure of Local Governments

## The Big Picture

As noted in Chapter 2, local governments in the United States were not created by (or even mentioned in) the U.S. Constitution but instead were established by the states to assist them in the execution of state policies and the provision of myriad (some state- and some local-type) services. Since states created local governments, local governments, in a legal sense, are *inferior* levels of government that have no right of existence and thereby possess only those powers and responsibilities specifically or expressly granted to them by either state constitutions or statutes. Moreover, subsequent judicial interpretations of the relationship between states and their local governments (e.g., Dillon's Rule) have served to reinforce the perspective that local governments are legally inferior and subservient to their states, meaning that local government powers should be construed narrowly or with caution. This hierarchical relationship also implies that states may retract or redefine any of the powers and duties originally granted to local governments, as well as even go so far as to abolish units of local government.

Concomitant with this legal perspective of local governments has been the commonly held belief/perception that local governments should be closely monitored and overseen by their state governments. In fact, it is rather commonplace to hear that state and national government officials as well as people in the media compare the state to a "parent" and local governments to the state's "children." From this viewpoint, the state is seen as being "all-knowing," "wise," "careful," and "more responsible," while local governments are viewed as "immature," "well-meaning ignorant, "careless or even "reckless," and "irresponsible' and often in need of counseling, admonishing, correction, and guidance. Of course, periodic disclosures of local government corruption, slothfulness, gross mismanagement, wastefulness, ineptitude, and unequal treatment of citizens and employees serve to confirm suspicions harbored about these governments. Recent news about local government financial difficulties and bankruptcies (e.g., Detroit, Michigan, Stockton and San Bernardino, California, Hillview, Kentucky, Central Fall, Rhode Island, Orange County, California, Jefferson County Alabama, and several sanitary and improvement districts in Douglas County, Nebraska)

DOI: 10.4324/9781032640389-3

have served to give credence to the belief that local governments must be closely monitored to protect the public interest. Moreover, the news of the disastrous or bumbling mismanagement of the day-to-day operations of local government utilities (e.g., water in Flint, Michigan and sewer in St. Petersburg, Florida), out-of-control police departments (e.g., Ferguson, Missouri, Minneapolis, Minnesota, and Memphis, Tennessee), and countless episodes of corruption has buttressed this perspective.

These characterizations of the legal and real-world relationships between states and their local governments obviously have significant implications for local governments' revenue-raising capabilities and the ability to incur debt. After all, being "creatures of the state" means that local governments can tap only those revenue sources permissible in the state's constitution or state statutes. These types of revenue are commonly referred to as "own source revenues" since they are derived internally from within local governments and from citizens and businesses that live in or are located there. The only other sources of revenue available to local governments are "intergovernmental revenues" that come from a higher level of government (federal or state) in the form of various types of grants-in-aid and statutorily defined shared revenues or from other local governments as payment for the provision of contracted services.

## Total local government revenues

This chapter begins the examination of local government revenues by presenting a global picture of the entire spectrum of monies available to counties, municipalities, townships, special districts, and school districts (i.e., "total revenues") from 1962 to 2017. Scholars who study and analyze public sector budgets, as well as government officials, typically use the expression "total revenues" (TR) as a summative term that captures the inflow of money from the two basic kinds of revenue sources mentioned above—own-source revenues (OSRs) and intergovernmental revenues (IRs). Therefore, for the sake of consistently, this term will also be used throughout this book when referencing "all" or "complete" revenues of a unit of local government.

Local governments must consistently raise lots of money to support constantly escalating service expectations and needs of their respective constituents. Figure 3.1 initially assists in helping us to visualize the growth in the magnitude of these large sums of money from 1962 until 2017 by displaying TR collections of local governments in both actual and constant dollars. As can be seen from this figure, local governments raised over $43 billion in TR in actual dollars in 1962. Over the next 55 years, local governments' TR increased substantially to more than $1.9 trillion in 2017. This means that TR was increasing at a steady pace by about 8.0 percent annually. By comparison, TR of state governments (data not shown in Figure 3.1) was growing by a similar though somewhat higher rate (10.1 percent, on average, per year) over this same period.

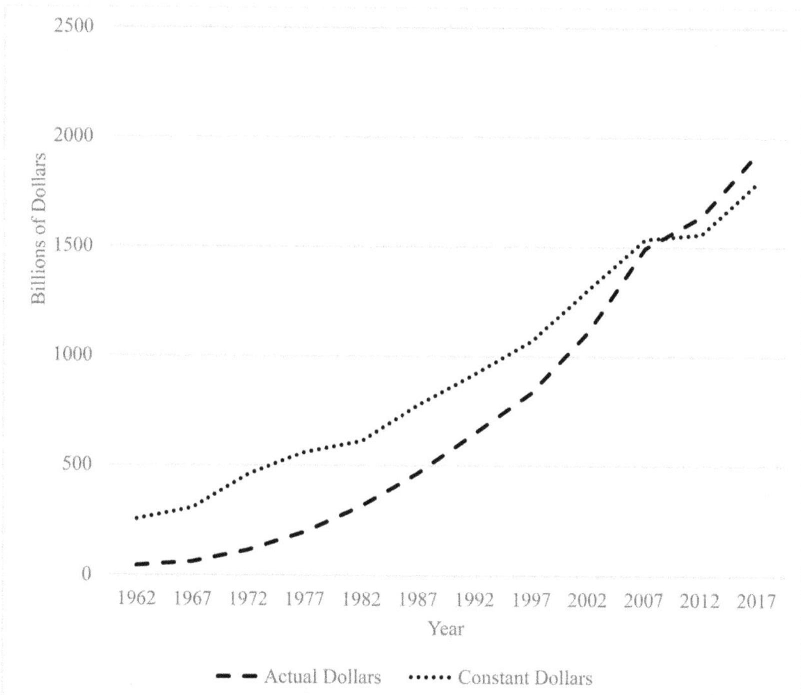


*Figure 3.1* Total Local Government Revenue (TR) in Actual and Constant Dollars, 1962–2017

*Source:* U.S. Bureau of the Census. Census of Governments. Compendium of Government Finances series, 1962–2017.

Figure 3.1 also plots TR collections of local governments in constant dollars over this same period. Here, it appears that, while TR was also increasing over time, the rate of growth was not nearly as impressive as was the case when actual dollars are used. In fact, TR was increasing by around 1.1 percent per year when revenue collections are controlled for inflation. Viewed from a practical perspective, this implies that local government officials were probably not able to do much more than to continue to meet current services demands while also encountering the constant challenge of responding to citizen demands for new or expanded services. In short, local officials had to deal with the fact that actual dollars, although increasing, did not "buy" much more in the way of services than they did during the previous budget year, as inflation reduced the purchasing power of the small amount of additional revenue that was received.

A closer examination of Figure 3.1 provides additional insight into the pattern of TR of local governments in more recent years. Notice the shrinking gap between actual and constant dollars beginning around 1982 and continuing until the present time but becoming especially acute after 2007. Several factors/events explain the decline in the growth rate in both actual and constant dollars. First, the U.S. economy was slowed by several significant recessions during this period (e.g., early 1980s, 1990s, and 2000s), double-digit inflation during the late 1970s, alarming balance of trade deficits becoming more common, outsourcing of private sector jobs overseas, and the continuous and discouraging devaluation of the American dollar against other world currencies. Second, the Congress in 1982, with strong encouragement from the Reagan administration, enacted legislation that substantially curtailed or eliminated a number of federal grant-in-aid programs, thus resulting in an overall net reduction in federal monies to state and local governments by around $5.9 billion. Third, citizen tax revolts—with prime examples being Proposition 13 in California in 1979 and Proposition 2 ½ in Massachusetts in 1982—caused local and even state officials to be more reluctant than usual in proposing tax increases (but particularly property taxes) and incurring additional debt. This was especially so given a political climate best described as one of eroding trust and confidence in government and government officials and a growing belief that there were unacceptable levels of government waste and mismanagement.

In retrospect, much of the period coinciding with the near financial collapse of New York City (around mid-1970s) and continuing through most of the 1980s has been branded by economists as an epoch of fiscal stress and financial hardship for local governments, generally, and for medium and large, declining cities, specifically. A host of underlying problems, including but not limited to large population losses, deteriorating infrastructure, high crime rates, moral and social decay, and out-of-control pension systems coupled with an eroding tax base, resulted in these governments not being able to "make ends meet." Consequently, budget deficits, risky borrowing, and requests for federal and state bailouts became more common. In light of these happenings, Charles Levine (1980) suggested that public officials (state as well as local) accept the possibility that the fiscal stress that they were encountering may not be temporary but instead long-lasting or conceivably permanent. He referred to the daunting task ahead for local governments to be one of "fiscal retrenchment" and "cutback management," which he defined as "managing organizational change toward lower levels of resource consumption and organizational activity" (Levine 1979, 180). Moreover, a number of state and city futures studies in the 1970s and 1980s mentioned severe pressure on government resources, increasing demand for services, and a multitude of infrastructure and environmental problems (Hitchcock and Coates 1985). More recent reports (Warner 2010; Figone et al. 2011) emphasized the persistent problems of escalating service demands, lack of meaningful local government home rule authority in fiscal matters, unfunded federal and state mandates, citizen mistrust, diminishing political capital of local officials, a flawed tax system, and continuing fragmentation of local government.

When attempting to assess the impact that these events singularly or collectively had on local governments, TR figures from 1977–82 help to put things into sharper focus. First, the growth rate in TR in actual dollars declined by 5 percent over the 1977–82 period compared to the previous 15-year average (1962–77)—that is, from 14.5 to 9.5 percent. Moreover, the growth rate in TR in constant dollars shrank from an average of 6.2 percent during 1962–77 to an annual average of 1.9 percent between 1977 and 1982. While the numbers could have been worse, they served as a "wake up" call for local governments

The setbacks associated with retrenchment and cutback management, notwithstanding, local government TR began to show clear signs of sustained, healthy growth shortly thereafter, which was sustained for the next 20 years (1987–2007). During this time, the annual growth rate in TR in actual dollars averaged around 8 percent. The only "fly in the ointment" during this period of optimism (but not noticed immediately) was that the yearly average growth rate in TR in constant dollars dropped to 3.7 percent during the 1987–2007 period compared to what it was from 1962–77 (6.2 percent). This seemingly innocuous matter aside, things were beginning to look so promising that one county budget director optimistically remarked that his government "was beginning to see grand visions of being able to finance projects that had to be moth-balled for many years." However, he and many other local government officials did not suspect that a major downturn in the economy was just around the corner, and it would have a decidedly adverse effect on TR collections and create havoc in balancing their governments' budgets.

With the onset of the Great Recession in 2007, however, the revenue outlook for local governments turned quickly from optimism to gloom and budgeting became a very challenging endeavor for local officials. Further inspection of Figure 3.1 explains why this was so. From the figure, one sees that the growth rate for TR in actual dollars dropped conspicuously (i.e., to 1.9 percent) between 2007 and 2012—remember that TR had been growing by an average annual rate of 7.5 percent from 1962 up until 2007. Furthermore, there was very little growth in TR in constant dollars (a 1.5 percent average annual increase compared to 4.5 percent during the 1962–2007 period).

Described by many economists as the most severe downturn in the economy since the Great Depression of the 1930s, the Great Recession had both direct and indirect negative impacts on the ability of local governments to collect the necessary revenues to sustain even current levels of service delivery. Initially, the sluggish economy leads to a slowdown in the growth rate of TR. Then, the revenue situation worsened as the housing bubble burst and caused massive home forecloses and abandonment of homes when people found that their mortgages were "under water."[1] Not only did this lead to devaluation of real estate but ultimately to reductions in property tax collections. The situation worsened even more so when state governments had to reduce state grant-in-aid money and shared revenues to local government due to their own dwindling revenues caused by the Great Recession. While assistance from the Congress and Obama administration helped offset revenue losses of state and local governments in the form of federal stimulus funds may have succeeded in making a dire situation not quite as bad, these efforts nonetheless were not able to come close to replacing the huge revenue losses experienced by local governments. Unfortunately, the attempt of the federal government to shield local governments somewhat from the sudden and unexpected reduction in traditional, stable revenues stopped when federal stimulus grants ended in late 2013.

While some may have thought it premature to suggest that the slowdown in the growth rate in revenue collections of local governments between 2007 and 2012 had reached a crisis level that could lead to vast cutbacks in services and/or service levels, the continuation of this trend for a prolonged period of time could be a cause for concern. In the aftermath of the Great Recession, some local officials and scholars (Martin, Levey, and Cawley 2012) have argued that the significant downturn in the economy represented a critical breakpoint for local government. Furthermore, they predicted that a "New Normal" would result whereby local governments would have to operate in the future with fewer resources and smaller workforces as well as become more creative and/or innovative in delivering services. Put differently, they envisioned changes precipitated by the "New Normal" as being dramatic, widespread, and permanent, thereby representing a sharp redirection of public policy akin to the disjointed, episodic, and unpredictable change associated with punctuated equilibrium theory (see Jones and Baumgartner 2012). In short, they envision implications that will last long after any economic recovery. Relatedly, other "New Normal" forecasts include the expectation that the condition of restricted and/or precipitously declining resources will persist permanently and that local governments will change fundamentally as a result (Benton 2017, 2018; Hendrick and Degnan 2020).

A different argument made by others (Ammons, Smith, and Stenberg 2012) is that, while a limited number of local governments may respond to the financial pressures and challenges of the "New Normal" with major and lasting changes, most probably will not. Their prediction rests on a reading of the history of how local governments have dealt with similar kinds of fiscal distress in the past and will continue to resist the temptation to make profound changes and opt instead for gradual or few modifications. Their view is consistent with the basic tenets of incrementalism theory (Lindblom 1968), in which gradual change occurs in small increments over an extended period. To buttress their argument, Ammons, Smith, and Stenberg (2012) contend that "relatively few of the major changes in local government across the span of history are associated solely or especially with troubled economic periods, including the Great Depression" (Ammons, Smith, and Stenberg 2012, 66S–67S). They further submit that dramatic change usually has been related to "significant social, political, economic, or technological events or periods like the Progressive Era, urban riots and of the civil

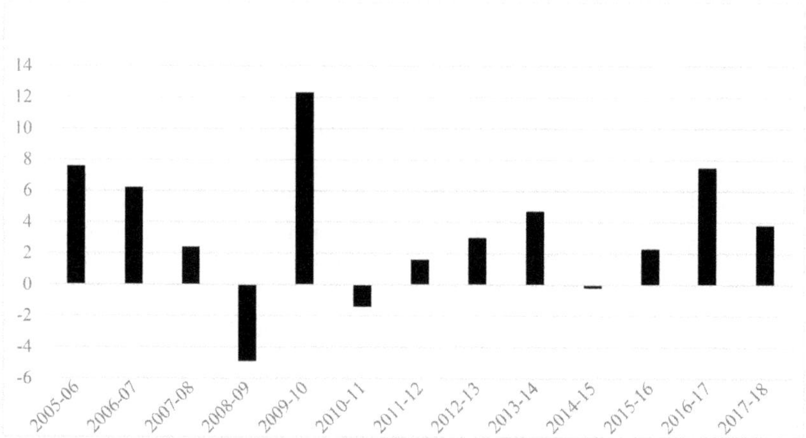


*Figure 3.2* Annual Percent Increase/Decrease in Total Revenue (TR) for All Local Governments, 2005–2018

*Source:* U.S. Bureau of the Census. Census of Governments. Compendium of Government Finances series, 1962–2017 and U.S. Bureau of the Census. 2020 State & Local Government Finance Historical Datasets and Tables. Compendium of Government Finances (Washington, DC: Government Printing Office).

rights movement of the 1960s, and the promises and challenges of the information age" (Ammons, Smith, and Stenberg 2012, 66S).

Given these differing views on the Great Recession's impact on local government's TR, it is important to examine TR figures on a year-by-year basis to determine adequately both short- and long-term effects. These data displayed in Figure 3.2 clearly indicate that the Great Recession produced a longer-lasting negative effect on TR than is the case for the typical recession. One year prior to the start of the Great Recession (2006), TR increased by 7.6 percent from the previous year (2005). This increase was in line with the average yearly growth between 1997 and 2006 (8.0 percent). By 2007, however, the growth rate in TR declined to 6.2. The growth rate declined further to 2.4 percent in 2008, and by 2009, TR fell below the amount received in the previous year and a *negative* growth rate was the result (–4.9). With the receipt of significant amounts of countercyclical federal assistance in 2010, local government TR moved back to the positive side as revenues these governments collected increased by 12.3 percent over what they received in 2009. Nevertheless, this gain appears to have been short-lived and TR receipts remained in a depressed state for most of the remainder of the decade. Again, in 2011 and 2015, *negative* growth rates occurred, and while local governments did see some growth in 2012, 2013, 2014, and 2016, this growth was quite small when compared to the 1997–2006 period. In fact, it was not until 2017 that there was a glimmer of hope that TR collections might return to pre-Great Recession levels, but this small (and perhaps premature) sign was followed in 2018 by yet another decline in the growth rate (around 50 percent). In sum, local government officials were preoccupied with the instability in and uncertainly over their TR in 2020 when the COVID-19 health pandemic delivered another blow to their ability to balance their budgets.

Although financial data on local government TR are not yet available from the Census Bureau for 2019 and 2020, it is reasonable to speculate that the news will not be good and even abysmal. In fact, a number of surveys conducted by the ICMA, NLC, NACo, Pew Institute, and others in the last two years provide ample evidence that the volatility in TR continues to be worrisome for local officials even after economists announced that the Great Recession was officially over in 2010. Even before there was a hint of a coronavirus health pandemic being on the horizon, finance officers from large cities (63 percent) and larger mid-sized cities (49 percent) believed that another recession could occur in the next year or two (McFarland and Pagano 2019, 9). This belief was also shared by a sizable number of finance officers in smaller mid-sized cities (38 percent) and small cities (35 percent) (McFarland and Pagano 2019, 9). As expected, these officials worried as to how a new recession would affect their jurisdiction's various revenue streams. Suffice it to say that similar concerns about the disruption another recession occurring so closely behind the Great Recession could have on the ability to raise sufficient revenues were also common among county, township, special district, and school district officials (e.g., see ICMA 2020; NACo 2020). In short, these expectations as well as other anecdotal information suggest that there was a definite and foreboding sense of uneasiness and caution among local government officials about the prospects for another recession and what it would mean for TR collections.

By the summer of 2020, the worst fears of local government officials were becoming real as revenue collections were beginning to drop for many governments. Although these numbers in local governments' 2020 budgets captured only a few months of the effects of the pandemic-driven recession, they nonetheless provided an early and realistic indication as to what lay ahead. FY 2021 budgets (which started for most local government by either July or October 1) began to capture more fully the bad news about shrinking revenues. In a study conducted in the fall of 2020 that was based on in-depth, focused interviews with 30 city and county officials, most had "serious concerns about the impact that COVID-19 and the [accompanying] recession could have on their governments' revenues" (Benton, Rissler, and Wagner 2020, 32). In addition, these officials provided long lists of cuts to most types of revenue and speculated that this was just the beginning of a long downward spiral with no end in sight. The combined "double-whammy" effect of the Great Recession and the recession caused by COVID-19 is perhaps best articulated by one county government official in this study who summed it up this way: "…after the Great Recession, we had just recovered to prerecession levels when the current recession hit…"

(Benton, Rissler, and Wagner 2020, 33). These views were similar to those reported in the 2020 annual survey conducted by McFarland and Pagano (2020), with an overwhelming majority of respondents in both studies believing that the toll on their finances is likely to be more severe than that experienced during the Great Recession.

While opinion may remain divided on the ultimate and lasting ramifications of the Great Recession and even the COVID-19-driven recession (and if a "New Normal" has resulted), the local government revenue situation (i.e., trends in both OSR and IR) certainly warrants careful and constant monitoring over the next several decades.

## Two sides of the revenue picture: Own-source versus intergovernmental revenues

As stated earlier on, local government revenues can be dissected into two principal parts—OSR and IR. The next two sections of this chapter will examine each of these types of revenue. A closer examination of the various sub-components of these two major revenue streams will be conducted in the next five chapters of this book. That is, Chapters 4–7, respectively, will direct attention to the elements that make up OSR—property taxes, other types of taxes, charges for services, and miscellaneous kinds of revenue. Then, Chapter 8 will focus on a more in-depth inspection of the three basic types of IR—federal, state, and local.

### *Own-source revenue: Stable and normally reliable money over time*

The part that OSR plays in the overall revenue profile of local government budgets is plainly evident from the information shown in Figures 3.3 and 3.4. These two figures, which display the percentage of total local government revenues derived from OSR and IR, leave no doubt that the bulk of the money that local governments require to provide a litany of services is derived from OSR. In fact, according to these figures, approximately two-thirds of the TR of local governments typically has come from this one primary source—internally raised money from their citizens and businesses within each respective jurisdiction or OSR—from 1962 through 2020. Intuitively, this finding makes perfect sense, in that a government and its officials and citizens should not expect any other entities (public or private) to be the principal supplier of funds necessary for the operation of their government or provider of various services.

With that said, it is instructive to take another look at Figures 3.3 and 3.4 to compare the OSR revenue percentages for 1962 and 2020. From this comparison, it is evident that over this 58-year span, local governments have been depending less on OSR. In 1962, local governments received 71 percent of their revenues from OSR; however, by 2020, the proportion had dropped to 65 percent. This is no small change, since a 6-percent decline in the OSR portion

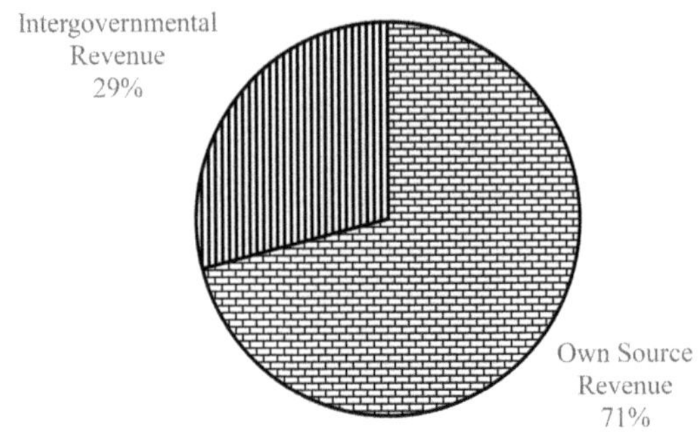


*Figure 3.3* Revenue Sources for Local Governments, 1962

*Source:* U.S. Bureau of the Census. Census of Governments. Compendium of Government Finances series, 1962–2017.

of TR could translate into millions—if not billions of dollars—being spent on the delivery of local government services and therefore coming from another source—IR.

Let us do the math to understand the significance of the fact that OSR constituted a smaller proportion of local governments' TR in 2020. In this year, the five types of local government collectively amassed about $1.917 trillion in TRs. If 71 percent of local government revenues in that year had been OSR (as was the case in 1962), then local governments would have raised somewhere in the neighborhood of an additional $128 billion from within their own jurisdiction than they

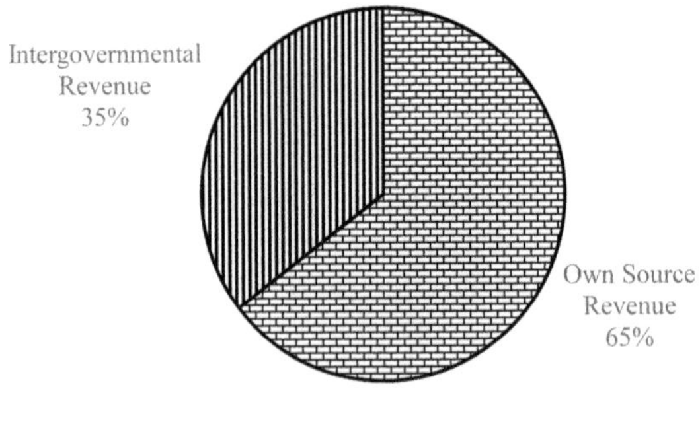


*Figure 3.4* Revenue Sources for Local Governments, 2020

*Source:* U.S. Bureau of the Census. 2020 State & Local Government Finance Historical Datasets and Tables. Compendium of Government Finances (Washington, DC: Government Printing Office).

received from outside sources (i.e., from the federal and state governments and other local governments). That means that citizens and businesses living or located in these local government jurisdictions contributed less money needed to pay the cost of providing countless services they received than they would have otherwise. Put differently, the cost of providing local governments services was, in essence, subsidized by monetary contributions of citizens and business in other states, other parts of their own state, or in other local governments in the same state.

In addition to the trend whereby local governments were deriving a smaller proportion of their TR from OSR, another important trend is noticeable. This trend is analogous to the one described above with regard to TR. That is, the growth rate in local government OSR in both actual and constant dollars began to taper off after 1982 but did begin to rise again noticeably between 2002 and 2007, only to decrease sharply after 2007. In fact, the growth rate all but flattened out over the 2007–17 period (see Figure 3.5). During these last ten years, the average annual growth rate was 1.4 percent and .3 percent, respectively, for actual and constant dollars. The importance of these observations is that local governments might need to reassess current service delivery. Further still, it could mean that they might have to consider a number of things ranging from the diminution of service levels to finding more efficient and economical ways to provide services to delaying the initiation of new services.

To provide some perspective on the relative importance of the contribution that OSRs play in the overall revenue picture of local governments generally, it

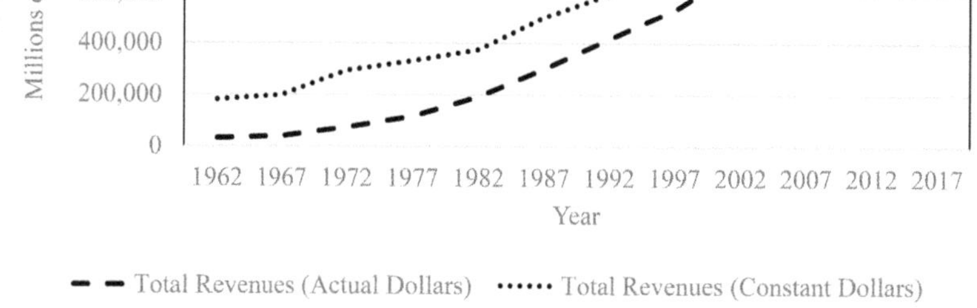


*Figure 3.5* Own-Source Revenues for All Local Governments, 1962–2017

*Source:* U.S. Bureau of the Census. Census of Governments. Compendium of Government Finances series, 1962–2017.

is also valuable to consider the possibility that the contribution that own-source resources make to a local government's TR may vary from one state to another. Simply put, the percentage of local governments' TR accounted for by OSRs may differ considerably from state to state since the percentages reported in Figures 3.3 and 3.4 are a 50-state average. Therefore, OSR percentages for local governments in each state for 2017 were calculated and presented in groupings by their distance from the mean value of 64.4 percent in Table 3.1.

This table highlights the large amount of variability of dependence of local governments across the 50 states. First, there are 27 states where local government OSR collections range from up to 5 percent lower (12 states) or up to

*Table 3.1* Local Government Own-Source Revenue Percentage by State, 2017

| *State* | *Percent* | *State* | *Percent* |
|---|---|---|---|
| 20.1% + Lower than National Average | | Up to 5% Higher than National Average | |
| Vermont | 37.1 | Oklahoma | 65/1 |
| 15.1%–20.0% Lower than National Average | | Iowa | 65.7 |
| Arkansas | 45.6 | Maryland | 66.1 |
| Illinois | 45.9 | New York | 66/2 |
| 10.1%–15.0% Lower than National Average | | Kentucky | 66.3 |
| New Mexico | 50.0 | Connecticut | 68.1 |
| Michigan | 50.3 | Utah | 66.9 |
| Delaware | 53.2 | Maine | 67.0 |
| North Dakota | 53.4 | Washington | 67.2 |
| 5.1%–10.0% Lower than National Average | | Kansas | 68.3 |
| Montana | 55.3 | South Dakota | 68.4 |
| California | 55.9 | Arizona | 68.7 |
| Wisconsin | 56.2 | Missouri | 68.9 |
| Minnesota | 57.4 | New Hampshire | 69.2 |
| Wyoming | 57.9 | Georgia | 69.5 |
| Nevada | 58.3 | 5.1%–15.0% Higher than National Average | |
| Mississippi | 58.5 | Wisconsin | 70.2 |
| Idaho | 58.6 | Rhode Island | 71.0 |
| Up to 5% Lower than National Average | | South Carolina | 71.5 |
| Indiana | 60.0 | Colorado | 71.7 |
| Alaska | 60.1 | Texas | 71.7 |
| West Virginia | 60.1 | Florida | 73.8 |
| Ohio | 61.0 | 10.1%–15.0% Higher than National Average | |
| Oregon | 61.0 | Nebraska | 79.4 |
| Pennsylvania | 61.2 | 15.1% + Higher than National Average | |
| Virginia | 62.9 | Hawaii | 84.4 |
| Louisiana | 63.2 | | |
| Tennessee | 83.6 | | |
| Alabama | 64.3 | | |
| North Carolina | 64.3 | | |
| Massachusetts | 64.5 | | |

*Source:* U.S. Bureau of the Census. Census of Governments. Compendium of Government Finances series, 1962–2017

5 percent higher (15 states) than the mean for all 50 states (65 percent) and thereby constitute the norm. Two other groupings include states with wider variations from the national average. One of these contains eight states whose reliance on OSR extends from over 5 percent up to 10 percent *below* the national mean, while another includes six states whose dependence ranges just over 5 percent to 10 percent *higher* than above the 50-state mean. Of particular note are local governments in the remaining nine states that diverge even more from the national average. On the one end of the spectrum, local governments in two states (Nebraska and Hawaii) receive a considerably larger percentage of their TR from OSR (i.e., almost 15 and 20 percentage points, respectively) than the national mean. On the other end of the spectrum, local governments in four states (New Mexico, Michigan, Delaware, and North Dakota) obtain from over 10 percent to 15 percent less of their TR from OSR than the national average, while local governments in two other states (Arkansas and Illinois) receive from over 15 percent to 20 percent less of their TR from own sources than the national average. Finally, one state (Vermont) collects not much more than one-third of its TR from own-source efforts.

It seems that identifying the unevenness in OSR collections among local governments in the 50 states may be easier than explaining the reasons for this variability. While there appears to be no clear or simple explanation as to why local governments in some states amass a larger/smaller proportion of their TRs from own-source methods than local governments in other states, one possible explanation is worth considering—home rule authority. After all, local governments and local government organizations like the National Association of Counties (NACo), National League of Cities (NLC), and International City/County Management Association (ICCMA), as well as a number of good government groups, have long advocated the granting of greater home rule authority—but especially to municipalities and counties in financial matters (Berman 2019).

To this point, the data analysis indicates that local governments generally have been relying less on OSR over time. But, is this the case for all five types of local government—county governments, municipal governments, townships, special districts, and school districts? This is a reasonable question, given the different kinds of service roles that local governments are expected to play and the rationale used by the states for establishing each type of local governments.

The data in Figure 3.6, showing the degree to which each type of local government has relied on OSR from 1962 to 2012, reveals that the trends do vary. On the one hand, the trend for municipal governments, special districts, and school districts is similar to the trend for all local governments (i.e., decreasing reliance on OSR). The greatest reductions in dependence on OSR were for school districts (dropping from 59 to 45 percent) and special districts (declining from 85 to 75 percent), while a smaller reduction can be seen for municipalities

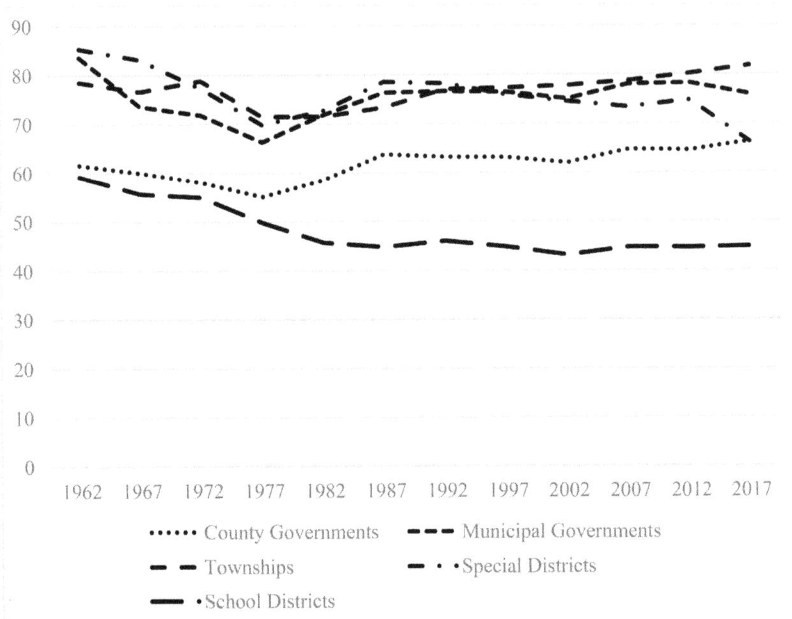


*Figure 3.6* Own-Source Revenue as a Percentage of Total Revenue by Level of Government, 1962–2017

*Source:* U.S. Bureau of the Census. Census of Governments. Compendium of Government Finances series, 1962–2017.

(decreasing from 84 to 78 percent). On the other hand, the trend for county governments and townships diverges from the pattern noted earlier for all local governments. County government reliance on OSR, for instance, increased modestly from 62 to 65 percent, while township dependence increased slightly from 79 to 80 percent.

To understand better the dynamics of what has been happening since the early 1960s and hypothesize reasonably as to what may explain local governments' changes in reliance on OSR, it is important that our analysis turns to an individual, in-depth examination of each type of local government. We begin by taking a closer look at county governments.

### *County governments*

County governments historically have exhibited less reliance on OSR compared to the other types of local governments with the exception of school districts (see Figure 3.6). As of 2017, county governments received around two-thirds of their TR from internally derived sources or OSR. This proportion, while being about 5 percentage points higher than it was in 1962, is still considerably less than the case for municipal governments, townships, and special districts.

The reason for states establishing county governments and the role they envisioned for them helps us understand counties' relatively lower level of dependence on OSR. County governments were created by the states for the primary purpose of having them assist the state in administering state programs and delivering state services at the local (i.e., county) level.[2] From a practical standpoint, it would be difficult for state governments to deliver directly services like welfare, health care, roads, and court system. In fact, it is fair to say that the original 13 states (as well as other states that eventually joined the Union) established county governments as a logical convenience, meaning that they would become administrative arms of the state and therefore serve state and not purely local purposes. From this perspective, counties functioned as "branch" or "satellite" officers of states and thus could serve as a vital connection to state citizens who receive state services at the local level. As such, states could operate from a strategically better position to ensure efficiency, uniformity, equality/fairness, and accountability in the distribution of state benefits and the provision of services.

Therefore, given the design of and purpose for county governments, it became incumbent upon the states to provide a considerable proportion of the money needed to fund these "state" services. As Benton (2002, 8) has succinctly noted, "...generally speaking, the more services a state expects a county to perform, the more revenues will be provided to them to augment county own source revenues." It bears reiterating that services like health care, welfare, courts, roads and highways, and so forth are ones that states want to make available to all of the state's residents. If left to the discretion of various local governments, it is possible that services such as health care and welfare, which often are at the center of bitter ideological and partisan debates, would not exist or, or if provided, would likely be funded at minimal level in states dominated by a traditionalistic or an individualistic culture (see Elazar 1962). Furthermore, state officials, likely cognizant of the unequal distribution of monetary resources across their state as well as the limited revenue-raising abilities of local governments, have often been willing to provide a large part of the money needed to deliver programs in these vital service areas. In sum, county governments, in many respects, are instrumentalities or long arms of their states that provide a number of services to locals with considerable financial assistance from their parent government (Berman 2019). As will become clear shortly, the original purpose and role for county governments continue to be quite different from that of municipalities.

As noted above, there also has been a modest increase in the proportion of OSR collected by county governments in recent years. This is likely attributable to at least two interrelated factors. First, citizen expectations of the modern American county government have changed enormously, but especially in the post-World War II era, due to changing demographics such as ever-increasing urbanization and suburbanization. At one time, county governments were relegated to providing what are often referred to as "traditional" or "mandated" kinds of services (e.g., public health, social services, road construction and maintenance, legal, prosecutorial, and judicial services, tax assessment and collection, other financial administration, recording legal documents collecting vital statistics, disseminating agricultural advice, and supervising elections, among others). Increasingly, however, citizens expect county governments to provide a much longer menu of services commonly called "municipal-type" and "regional" or "urban-type" services. As the term implies, municipal-type services are ones usually associated with cities and include things such as full-time fire protection and emergency medical services, a host of utilities (e.g., water, natural gas, and electric supply), protective inspections (health, safety, building, etc.) modern police services, and libraries. Urban- or regional-type services include things such as natural resource conservation and environmental protection, parks, cultural, and recreational facilities, solid waste and sewer collection and disposal, public mass transit, public parking facilities, low-income public housing, community development/urban renewal, and economic development.

Second, county government officials have been relatively more successful in recent years in convincing state legislatures to grant them greater home rule authority (DeSantis and Renner 1984; Dye and MacManus 2015; Berman 19). To the extent that this has occurred in more states, counties have been able to take advantage of a wider range of revenue-raising opportunities like municipalities, including the ability to levy a large number of taxes and more user fees/charges for services. Yet, these officials acknowledge that they need their states to be more flexible in fiscal matters going forward. What has been accomplished to date is due in no small way to the tireless lobbying efforts of the NACo, state chapters of NACo, ICCMA, the former U.S. Advisory Commission on Intergovernmental Relations (ACIR), good government/reform groups, and the media (see Berman 2019). Collectively, they have been able to make a persuasive argument that, if states expect county governments to function, at least in part, in the capacity as full-service local governments, then states should grant sufficient home rule powers in the area of fiscal decision-making.

### *School districts*

Among the five types of local governments, school districts have always been the least dependent on OSR to fund their operations. Reference back to Figure 3.6 indicates that in 1962, OSR supplied around 59 percent of TR for school districts. By 2017, however, the OSR share had decreased conspicuously to 45 percent—a 14 percent drop. It is interesting to note that the Great Recession had no apparent negative impact on school district OSR.

To explain why school districts depend on OSR much less so than other units of local government requires us to consider the history and rationale behind the establishment of public schools. The decision to create a separate and independent governmental entity to be responsible for the administration and operation of public schools was rooted in Americans' strongly held belief that "free, quality public education is a core societal value" and even considered by some as a "fundamental right" (see Donovan, Mooney, and Smith 2009). In addition to providing students with the knowledge and skills to obtain a job or pursue education at a higher level (i.e., university or technical school), public schools—at all levels—they were also expected to instill in students a sense of civic responsibility. Public education can also produce a number of social side effects that can lead to a better quality of life and economic development for everyone in a community, even beyond the students themselves (Brace 1993; Smith and Rademacker 1999; Hungerford and Wassmer 2014).

Given this historical background and the importance assigned to public education, it is not surprising that Americans were adamant about not wanting education in the United States to become politicalized or for schools to be subject to competing with other interests (e.g., public safety, public works, recreation, health care, libraries, welfare, and courts) for attention and funding. Americans knew all too well about the political give-and-take, stakeholder bargaining, politicians wheeling and dealing, and "smoke filled backroom" political negotiations that normally occur as part and parcel of the city and county budget making process. Thus, there was legitimate and widespread concern that education would never receive adequate funding if it became just one of many services provided by either municipalities or county governments. Simply stated, many believed that the right to a quality education was too much of an integral element of the American ethos and to be tossed about like a "political football" and end up being nothing more than a broken promise (Donovan, Mooney, and Smith 2009).

A logical solution to this dilemma was to create a unique type of government within the family of local governments that would have exclusive authority to provide a public education. Therefore, this creation—school districts—are distinct entities, in that they are "specialized" single-purpose special districts. They are distinct in the sense that they provide only one specific kind of service (education). Nonetheless, states have established other types of single-purpose special districts with the authority to provide a variety of other kinds of services such as fire protection, water or sewer supply, libraries, conservation, and community development. Multi-purpose special service districts have also been created by states, but none of them includes education as one of the services they provide.

Early on, Americans were adamant about the expectation that the provision of public education in the United States would be a partnership between their state government and local school districts. There was also the expectation that the state would operate as the senior partner.[3] Given this arrangement, states could exercise control over curriculum, teacher and administrative hiring and certification, attendance policies, immunization requirements, and other substantive and administrative matters. Furthermore, states would be in a critical position to assist school districts in financing the cost of public education since they created school districts (like county governments) for the explicit purpose of providing a state-level service to citizens at the local level. Therefore, it is reasonable to believe that school districts (like county governments) would rely less on OSR to provide their one service—education.

It was equally important that states would be in a critically strategic position to address funding inequities that may exist between school districts.[4] That is, states would have the opportunity to devise state aid funding formulas so as to allocate more money to those districts with less ability to generate adequate property tax revenues. This would especially be the case where a district may contain a disproportion amount of less valuable real estate to tax. Stated differently, states could provide all districts with a minimum level of fiscal support while also being able to distribute varying amounts of additional aid to poor districts. Unfortunately, most states, however, did not seize the opportunity to correct funding inequities—indeed, gross disparities that developed from the onset of public education until the 1980s.

The unwillingness of most states to take corrective action inevitably led to a number of legal challenges. In the landmark case of *Serrano* v. *Priest* (1971), the California Supreme Court ruled that inequities in school district spending resulting from variations in taxable wealth were unconstitutional. The court stated that local control is a "cruel illusion," in that poor districts simply cannot achieve excellence in education because of a low tax base, even if the state taxed the property at a higher rate. Following *Serrano*, lawsuits in many other states were successful in having states' own property tax-based systems declared unconstitutional because they violated the "equal protection" guarantees (analogous to the U.S. Constitution's 14th Amendment) found in their state constitutions.[5]

These cases resulted in two major changes in the funding of public schools. First, state aid to school districts noticeably increased. Second, and as can be seen in Figure 3.5, OSR as a proportion of TR correspondingly began a precipitous decline, and was detected as early as 1972.

### *Municipal governments*

In contrast to county governments and school districts, municipal governments—along with townships and special districts—have always had a greater dependence on OSR to support their operations and deliver services (see Figure 3.6). In 1962, municipal governments derived 84 percent of their TR from OSR. Only special districts received more of their TR (85 percent) from this source. By 2012, the municipal OSR proportion had declined to 78 percent. Due to the continuing fallout from the Great Recession, the OSR proportion continued to drop by another 2 percent to 76 percent between 2012 and 2017.

Reference to the history surrounding the establishment of municipal governments helps to explain their heavy dependence on OSR. In this regard, it is important to note that municipal governments differ from county governments with respect to the reasoning behind creating them and the process involved in their creation. Repeating what was said earlier, county governments were created by states for the primary purpose of providing state-level services at the local level (e.g., welfare, health care, law enforcement and judicial, and roads). The establishment of municipalities by states was in response to citizens residing in densely populated areas of counties who wanted either a higher level of certain kinds of county services[6] or the provision of a number of services not typically offered by counties.[7] As such, municipal governments were envisioned to serve their local constituents as truly full-service local governments. Moreover, municipalities would provide services only in that area encompassed in the corporate city limits. This is in stark contrast to county governments that were created as appendages and political or administrative subdivisions of their states and were expected (in some instances, mandated) to deliver services to all county residents in both the incorporated and unincorporated parts of the county.

The manner in which states created municipal governments is considerably different from the way in which they established county governments. In the case of counties, the state government simply decides to carve up the state into convenient political subdivisions or administrative units and executes this decision. By contrast, the process to create a municipality begins when a sufficient number of citizens residing in an area smaller than the size of a county formally express the desire to form a municipality by petitioning the state for "incorporation." The area designated for incorporation must satisfy certain criteria like population and density minimums. In most instances, a referendum permitting citizens in the affected area to vote on whether they wish to become an incorporated municipality is required. If the incorporation referendum is successful, then a charter is granted by the state,[8]and the newly created municipality has the legal authority to elect officials, enact regulatory ordinances, and provide services (many of which are not services normally provided by their county government) to its residents. It is significant to note that the charter granted to the new municipality usually contains explicit legal authority to levy taxes and fees and incur debt (typically at levels greater than that for counties) so as to enable the new city to support its operations

Clearly, municipal governments, by virtue of the rationale underpinning their creation and the manner by which states established them, stand out as unique legal entities within the family of local governments in the United States. A noteworthy consequence of this uniqueness is that municipal governments, unlike county governments, usually have greater decision-making authority and discretion and thereby may be able to exercise more independence and practice greater self-governance. According to Krane, Rigos, and Hill (2001), almost all states have included notable home rule provisions in the granting of municipal charters, although in some states, only municipalities that have reached a certain population size can exercise this option.

Given this history and context for the creation of municipal governments, it is plausible to conclude that state governments would expect municipalities—unlike county governments and school districts—to be more self-sufficient financially and therefore assume the responsibility to raise more of their own revenue. In requesting the authority to create their own municipality, citizens knowingly sought the ability to do something that counties were unable to do, as county governments did not possess the legal authority or willingness to provide the kinds of additional services desired by urban dwellers. Concomitantly, with that request was the recognition that they would be expected to raise the revenue necessary to fund more and better services.

In retrospect, then, it becomes obvious that the establishment of municipal governments was a reasonable response of state governments since county governments were ill equipped to provide selected services to pockets of urban dwellers. County governments would have faced a very difficult, if not impossible, task of fairly and strategically providing services to selected residents in a county that may be essentially rural in character. In addition, there would have been the formidable challenge of identifying those who wanted additional services and then administering an equitable tax or fee schedule to pay for the cost of these services.

Yet, in spite of municipalities' greater dependence on OSRs than is the case for most other types of local governments, the own-source proportion of municipal governments has declined somewhat over time. Two factors would appear to account for this phenomenon. One factor has been the conscious decision of many municipalities to identify to the extent possible the users of certain city services (e.g., garbage collection, utilities, sewage collection and disposal, sidewalks, street lighting, parks, storm water management, airports, and sports arenas) and then assess a fee typically called a user charge or special assessment charge. This strategy has been justified in efforts to either reduce or slow the growth rate in property taxes. Another factor has been the greater availability of intergovernmental fiscal assistance, but especially from the federal government beginning in the late 1960s. Chapters 5 and 8 will present a fuller discussion of these two factors.

### *Townships*

Townships have always relied heavily on OSR as a means to finance their operations and provide services to residents and businesses within their jurisdiction (see Figure 3.6). In 1962, OSR accounted for 79 percent of these governments' TR, with only municipal governments and special districts having a slightly less dependence. By 2017, townships relied on this source to supply over $4 out of every $5 or 80 percent of their TR.

To understand better the degree to which townships depend on OSR requires us to understand more about the reasoning for states establishing township governments[9] and the kind of service responsibilities assigned to them by their states. According to Bowman and Kearney (2008, 277), it is commonplace to think of a town or township as "a small community where everyone knows everyone else, where government is informal, and where local leaders gather at the coffee shop to make important decisions." This profile, however, is only partially accurate. While townships usually are smaller, in terms of population, than cities and counties, the extent of their governmental powers is contingent on state government. Furthermore, even where they are relatively weak, township governments increasingly operate in a more formalized manner.

From a legal perspective, township governments are general-purpose units of local governments that are subdivisions of counties. They are distinct from county and city governments but also possess some of the same responsibilities that are typically associated with county and municipal governments. In some instances, they perform many of the functions of county governments at a grassroots level—elections, health care, welfare, road maintenance, land use planning, tax administration, and judicial matters through justices-of-the-peace. In other instances, townships may deliver extensive services similar to those normally associated with municipalities—street lighting, fire and police protection, street cleaning, snow removal, curbs and sidewalks, trash collection, and utilities.

Unlike counties and municipalities, the presence of township governments is limited to 20 states—the northern states from New Jersey to the Midwest; southern and western states have made little use of this unit of local government. Yet, more than 55 million people, or roughly one-fifth of the U.S. population, live under township governments presently. Most townships are unincorporated, meaning that they do not have charters from state government that guarantees their political independence or authorizes them to provide a long list of municipal services. Nevertheless, some states (e.g., Michigan) grant townships a charter under certain conditions. Townships in other states (including Michigan and those in New England,[10] along with those in New Jersey, Pennsylvania, and to some degree, New York and Wisconsin) provide townships with broader powers more suitable to a jurisdiction that is urban in character. As a result, they act, in some ways, like other general-purpose governments (i.e., counties and municipalities). In the remainder of the township states (Illinois, Indiana, Kansas, Minnesota, Missouri, Nebraska, North Dakota, Ohio, and South Dakota), the nature of the township is more rural and hence their autonomy and powers are more circumscribed. It is interesting to note, however, that the closer these rural townships are to large urban areas, the more likely they are to offer an expanded set of services.

This context would suggest two equally plausive but very different scenarios with respect to township governments' reliance on OSR. On the one hand, one would expect that township governments' dependence on OSR would be similar to the dependence that county governments have on this type revenue source, if townships provide a relatively small number of the kinds of services that county governments normally provide. On the other hand, one would assume that township government's reliance on OSR would be comparable to the dependence that municipal governments have on OSR, if township governments are responsible for many of the types of services that municipal government normally provide (usually referred to as "elective services"). Since the proportion of township governments' TR accounted for by OSR is much closer to that for municipal governments, it is reasonable to conclude that townships are providing much more municipal-type services than the traditional kinds of services that states expect or even mandate counties to deliver. Furthermore, it is logical to infer that the cost of providing municipal-type services consumes a large part of the average township government's budget. Therefore, it appears that townships are acting more like municipalities than counties in their role as service providers, given their heavy and increasing reliance on OSR. In fact, by 2012, townships had the greatest dependence on OSR among the five types of local governments.

In spite of these conclusions, it is important to consider the possibility that township government reliance on OSR may vary based on the extent of powers and authority granted to them by their states. Do townships with greater grants of power and authority, like is the case for municipal governments, rely more on OSR, than townships with less latitude in these critical areas? The potential for these different scenarios will be considered in the analyses conducted in Chapters 4–7 when looking at the four major categories of OSR.

### *Special districts*

Much like municipal and township governments, special districts (sometimes referenced as legislative authorities) have also relied on OSR to provide the bulk of the monetary resources necessary to support their service activities (refer back to Figure 3.6). In 1962, OSR supplied 85 percent of special district TR. Over the next 50 years, OSR as a proportion of townships' TR steadily declined. Yet, by 2012, OSR still constituted approximately three-quarters or 75 percent of all revenues of these governments. However, the OSR of special districts took a big hit during the Great Recession, as its proportion of TR dropped noticeably to 66 percent by 2017.

Again, as was the case with the other four units of local government, a familiarity with the rationale for state establishment of special districts will assist in understanding the extent to which these governments depend on OSR collections to function and especially provide services. Over the years, state governments—oftentimes at the strong urging of municipal, county, and township governments, as well as citizens residing in these jurisdictions—have created over 38,000 special districts to provide an array of services to selected populations at the local level (U.S. Bureau of the Census 2012). Simply put, special districts have become convenient mechanisms for states to ensure that vital and highly desirable services are available to the public when other local governments have been either unable legally and financially to provide them or unwilling to do so. Several familiar scenarios illustrate this point.

In the post-World War II era, unincorporated area residents in many states who reside in densely populated parts of the county often have approached their county governments, seeking the provision of services usually delivered by municipalities to their residents. Good examples are fire protection and water and sewer services. However, county officials have often turned down such requests for various reasons, with two of them being the most often cited. First, county governments possess little to no home rule authority and thus do not have the legal authority to provide these and other municipal-type services. In short, counties under these circumstances, even if they wanted to provide these services, are legally unable to do so. Second, county governments inevitably would encounter logistical and financial challenges in acceding to these kinds of requests (e.g., creating service boundaries that would be cost-efficient or satisfy economies of scale). In addition, county officials simply may not want the extra responsibility or hassle of providing services that are not part of the mandated package of services that they have no choice but to provide. In these kinds of situations, the county may request that the state establish a special district.

Another scenario is one in which a municipality (or even a county) has been requested to provide services to the entire city or county that are within its authority to deliver (e.g., airports, storm water management, performing arts facilities, and sports arenas). However, since the city or county is close to or has even reached its property tax limit set by the state or has a history of functioning under fiscal stress conditions, it finds it necessary to decline the appeal to make these kinds of services available. Simply stated, these cities and counties believe that it is not in their best interest or prudent from a financial standpoint to incur extra operating expenses or take on additional debt. Alternatively, the scenario could entail the request for the provision of a service that would benefit primarily residents/businesses located in only a part of the municipality or unincorporated part of the county (e.g., economic development/redevelopment, street lighting and curbs, local parks or recreational facilities, and sidewalks). Regardless of the specific circumstances, the city or county and the requesting parties end up approaching the state government about creating a special district.

Yet, another possible scenario could encompass service issues that transcend city or even county legal boundaries (examples might include water and natural resource conservation, water and pollution, solid and hazardous waste management, strategic planning and zoning, urban mass transit, or even urban development/redevelopment). These kinds of service requests are often prevalent in densely populated areas that know no political or legal boundaries. That is, the need for specialized kinds of government responses stems from acute challenges, problems, and issues that are endemic to the specific area and thereby necessitate a regional or urban-area solution. Sometimes, these type service issues are ones that the state government already has a vested and fundamental interest in, given the regional nature and impact of them. Without question, state officials are inherently concerned about quality of life, economic development, systematic and well-thought-out growth, the quality of the air and water, and the ability of residents to travel easily from Point A to Point B. Therefore, it is logical for the state government to respond to appeals from residents and businesses to assist in these and similar situations in order to provide much-needed guidance and supervision by establishing special districts. Furthermore, the creation of special districts empowers them with the legal and fiscal authority to tackle jointly (and hopefully, successfully) the issues underlying their service needs.

Based on the purposes or rationale for which special districts or legislative authorities (hereafter referred to as special districts) were established, it comes as no surprise that they would receive a considerable percentage of their funds from OSR. Consequently, special districts rely heavily on charges for services and special assessments for most of their OSR and even on additional property taxes levied on residents and businesses to pay for a level of services beyond what city or county residents or businesses usually receive from these governments. While the availability of IR from federal and state governments certainly has increased in recent decades, this source of funding for special districts pales in comparison to OSR. Nevertheless, with the very noticeable decline in receipts from OSR during the aftermath of the Great Recession and possibly an even greater loss of OSR funds due to the COVID-19 pandemic, will special districts become more dependent of federal and state assistance in the short- and possibly the long-term?

### *Intergovernmental revenue: Less stable and sometimes unpredictable money over time*

Whether local government officials like it or not, they would find it virtually impossible to make ends meet if they had to depend solely on OSR; this would be especially so for school districts and to a lesser extent county governments. Nevertheless, the necessity of having to count on the availability of IR—even to a lesser degree than OSR—presents problems for local governments. Compared to OSR, IR is generally less stable and can be unpredictable from one fiscal year to the next or even within any given fiscal year. That being the case, it is important to mention that even OSR is subject to fluctuations over time and therefore can create a sense of uncertainty, anxiety, and frustration for local government officials as they go about the business of preparing a balanced budget. However, history seems to suggest that IR tends to be less certain and more difficult to estimate than is the case with OSR.

A number of factors lend some understanding to the lack of stability and/or reliability of IR, regardless of the source—federal or state government. First, severe downturns in the United States and state and local economies put tremendous pressure on higher levels of governments that provide grants-in-aid or share their revenue with local governments. Facing revenue shortfalls due to declining or stagnant revenues and feeling the need to prioritize the service needs of their direct constituents, the federal and state governments typically look for quick and the least painful ways to reduce expenditures to balance their own budgets. One of the simplest ways to accomplish this task is to reduce fiscal assistance to lower levels of government and usually the political fallout is less than would be the case if they cut programs and services to their respective constituents. This was evident during the most recent Great Recession and the COVID-19 health crisis, when many state governments saw their own revenues decline sharply and found it difficult to meet their service responsibilities. This meant that these states had less money to share with their local government but especially counties, municipalities, and townships. Unfortunately, these kinds of events sometimes trigger a fend-for-yourself scenario, with local governments taking the biggest hit financially and subsequently struggle to make ends meet.

Second, the ideological perspectives of legislative and executive officials at the national and state levels can result in a change in the willingness of granting governments to continue to provide financial assistance to lower levels of government (e.g., state and local governments for the federal government and local governments for state governments). Historically, liberal Democratic members of Congress and Democratic presidents ordinarily have been inclined to be more generous in financially assisting both states and local governments, while conservative Republicans in Congress and Republican presidents have been more miserly and reluctant with regard to sharing their revenue with subnational governments. These contrasting behaviors of Democratic and Republicans are likely rooted in their strongly held convictions about the appropriate size of government and the role in society, in general, and the federal government, in particular. Simply put, Democrats since the New Deal have favored a larger or more active role for organized government, while Republicans have supported a more restrained or limited role. While not usually getting the same level of press attention as is the case for national political figures, it is also accurate to portray many state legislative and gubernatorial officials as mainly sharing the same ideological viewpoint with respect to the appropriate size and role of government as their counterparts at the national level.

A somewhat different but plausible explanation could be that members of Congress and presidents regardless of party affiliation do not like playing the role of the unpopular or vilified tax collector (federal income taxes), while state and local officials reap the political benefits of spending money that they did not raise by imposing higher taxes on their constituents. In fact, members in Congress have frequently argued that there should be more political and financial accountability in federal grant-in-aid and revenue-sharing programs. A very good case in point was the termination of the initially popular general and special revenue-sharing programs begun in 1972 as part of President Richard Nixon's New Federalism initiative. By the mid-1980s, very few influential interest groups supported revenue sharing and there was no clearly identifiable constituency for which to lobby. Another case in point was Congressional enactment of a proposal by the Reagan administration to reduce overall federal grant-in-aid monies by around $5.9 billion in 1982 (see Benton 1986).

Another explanation for sudden increases and decreases in intergovernmental fiscal assistance relates to the specific goals and agendas of presidents and their party members in Congress. As president, Lyndon Johnson missed no opportunity to promote his lofty goal to bring about the "Great Society" in America during his tenure in office. Many of his fellow Democrats in Congress as well as a number of key liberal Republicans shared this goal. Realizing that many state and local governments did not have the fiscal resources—not to mention the political wherewithal—to accomplish this herculean task, President Johnson and Congress significantly increased the number of federal grant-in-aid programs as well as the amount of money available through them. In fact, this was the first time that local governments were the clear target of more federal aid programs and greater amounts of federal money. By the late 1970s, however, many of these programs were mired in controversy amid evaluations that pointed to cost inefficiencies and ineffectiveness. Consequently, a number of them were the focus of heavy bipartisan criticism and ultimately designated for the "chopping block." This setting played into the hands of political opportunists like President Ronald Reagan who made campaign promises to balance the federal budget and spend more money on national defense in the wake of a U.S. military that was perceived to be losing ground to the Soviet Union and People's Republic of China. In order to move forward with his agenda, President Reagan needed to find a way to reduce federal spending, and he found a convenient budgetary tool with which to do it—cut federal grants-in-aid to state and local governments. As stated earlier, President Reagan found an acquiescent Congress that was subsequently able to push through his proposed legislation to reduce substantially grant-in-aid monies flowing to the states and local governments.

In spite of the fact that IR has been somewhat unpredictable and unreliable over the years, the proportion of revenue that local governments derive from this source has increased steadily, generally speaking, over the 1962–2020 time span. As is evident from Figures 3.3 and 3.4 presented earlier in this chapter, the contribution that IR makes to total TR of local governments increased from 29 to 35 percent. As also mentioned earlier, the significance of this increase is huge and has implications for local governments and their citizens. Simply stated, local governments have had to raise a smaller proportion of their TR from own-source monies. This could occur in three ways. First, it could happen when people and businesses in other states (via federal aid transfers) began subsidizing some of the cost of providing local governments services. Second, it could occur when citizens and businesses in more affluent parts of a state began bankrolling less affluent parts of the same state (state government redistribution of wealth through state aid or revenue sharing). A third possibility would be that some local governments are receiving a larger proportion of their revenue from other local governments for the provision of contracted services.

Over this same period of time, another trend—and one that should be of concern going forward—was becoming apparent by the beginning of the Great Recession. After the average annual growth rate in IR in actual dollars increased by a stellar amount from 1997 until 2007 (7.6 percent), it dropped significantly to 1.7 and 2.5 percent, respectively, during the 2007–12 and 2012–17 periods (see Figure 3.7). Perhaps of greater concern was the decline in the growth rate of IR in constant dollars that is also evident from Figure 3.7. During the 2007–12 period, the growth rate in constant dollars all but flattened out (.07 percent annual increase) compared to how it grew on an annual basis from 1997 to 2007 (4.1 percent). While the annual growth rate in constant dollars did improve from 2012 to 2017 to 2.0 percent, this rate of growth was only about one-half of what it was during the ten years preceding the start of the Great Recession. Coupled with the uncertainty of future yields of their OSR, local governments have had to proceed with caution in balancing their budgets in recent years, given the

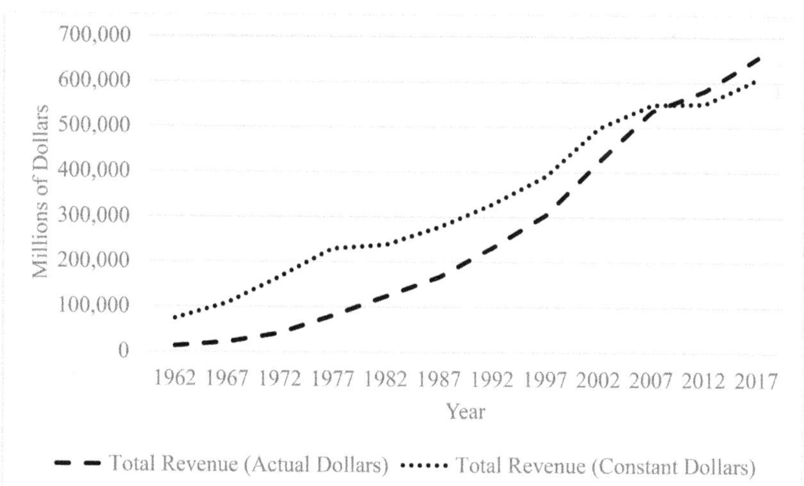


*Figure 3.7* Intergovernmental Revenue for All Local Governments, 1962–2017

*Source:* U.S. Bureau of the Census. Census of Governments. Compendium of Government Finances series, 1962–2017.

slowdown (indeed, uncertainty) about future fiscal assistance from higher levels of government. Cutback management was on full display during the second decade of the 21st century, and the uncertainty of the full impact of the COVID-19 crisis and its after-effects loom large at the present time.

In spite of events of the last decade or so that warrant careful and frequent monitoring in the years ahead, there is nonetheless the unmistaken fact that local governments, in a collective sense, have become more reliant on IR over time,. However, is this the case for all types of local government? Given the different kinds of service roles that local governments must play and the rationale used by the states for establishing different types of local governments, it is therefore reasonable to speculate that variability may exist among types of governments.

The data in Figure 3.8, showing the proportion of TR for each type of local government derived from IR from 1962 to 2017, reveals distinctively different patterns. On the one hand, the patterns detected for municipal governments, special districts, and school districts are analogous to one observed for all local governments (i.e., increasing reliance on IR). The greatest increase in dependence on IR was for school districts (rising from 41 to 55 percent); the next largest increase (i.e., from 15 to 35 percent) was recorded by special districts,

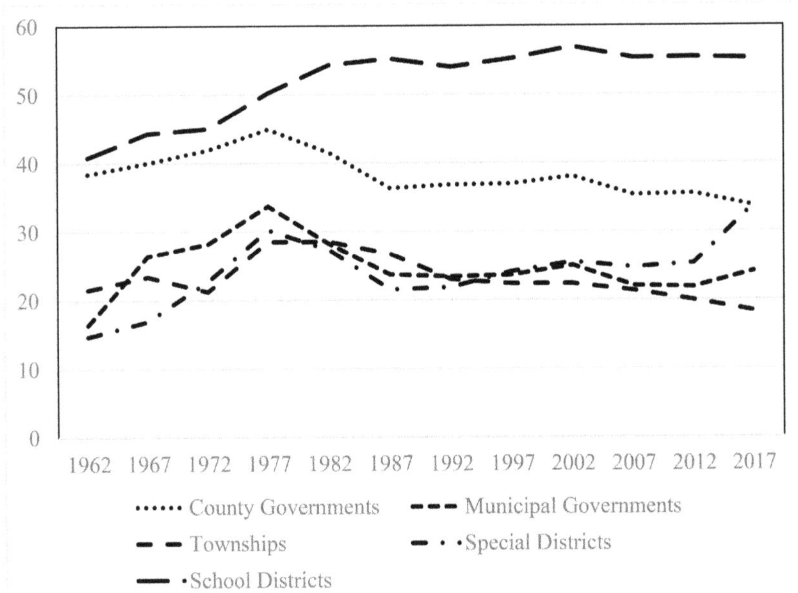


*Figure 3.8* Intergovernmental Revenue as a Percentage of Total Revenues by Level of Government, 1962–2017

*Source:* U.S. Bureau of the Census. Census of Governments. Compendium of Government Finances series, 1962–2017.

while a smaller increase occurred for municipalities (increasing from 16 to 21 percent). On the other hand, the patterns for county governments and townships differ from the one identified for all local governments. That is, county government reliance on IR decreased somewhat from 39 to 36 percent, while township dependence on IR decreased from 22 to 20 percent.

To understand better the dynamics of what has been happening with regard to local government IR since the early 1960s and what may explain changes over time will require separate analyses for each type of local government that breaks down IR into its three basic components—federal and state grant-in-aid monies and revenue sharing and revenue from local governments. Chapter 8 will present these more in-depth analyses.

## Chapter summary

This chapter is the first step in conducting an all-inclusive analysis of local government revenues. In that regard, it provides a broad overview of the revenue systems of and money accessible to counties, municipalities, townships, special districts, and school districts. Referred to in this study as TR, it consists of two basic components—OSR and IR. Based on an examination of these data reported at five-year internals by the U.S. Bureau of the Census in the Census of Governments for the 1962–2017 period, it is evident that local governments derive the largest proportion of their TR from OSR. In 1962, OSR constituted 71 percent of TR, but this proportion had *declined* to 65 by 2017. Over this same period, IR *increased* from 29 to 35 percent of TR.

In the next four chapters of this book, the analysis of trends and patterns of OSR will continue with a close look at the three specific kinds of revenues that make up OSR—taxes, charges for services, and several other types referred to as miscellaneous revenues. The analysis of taxes will be divided into two chapters, with property taxes being the focus of Chapter 4 and other taxes (sales, income, and an assortment of other ones) being covered in Chapter 5. Then, Chapters 6 and 7, respectively, will be devoted to an examination of charges for services and miscellaneous revenues.

## Notes

1 See Benton (2009) for a more in-depth description and examination of the factors that precipitated the Great Recession and the impact that it had on local governments, generally, and on the ability to raise sufficient revenue to pay for services, specifically.

2 See Benton (2002) for a thorough documentation and discussion of the projected role of county governments in the American political system and the unitary relationship that exists between states and their local governments. This is especially so for counties.

3 It is important to remember that the power to provide educational services was a power claimed by the states as one of the reserved powers left to them under the 10th Amendment.

4 The exception, of course, is Hawaii since the state government completely funds and operates public schools.
5 Two years after *Serrano*, plaintiffs in Texas also filed a similar lawsuit in federal court (*San Antonio Independent School District* v. *Rodriguez*, 1973), where they challenged the constitutionality of the state's property tax-based system on the ground that it violated the Equal Protection Clause (EPC) in the U.S. Constitution's 14th Amendment. In its decision, the Court ruled that disparities in financial resources between school districts in a state and resulting inequalities in educational spending per pupil across a state do not violate the EPC. Therefore, states have no duty under the U.S. Constitution to equalize educational resources within a state.
6 Some examples include law enforcement services analogous to a city police department, sidewalks, street curbs, storm water drainage, and traffic signals as an extension of transportation services, specialized municipal courts to handle matters (juvenile, tax, and landlord/tenant issues) within the city, and health and welfare services that exceed what the state or county provides.
7 Some examples include full-time, professionally trained fire protection, utilities (water, electric power, and gas supply), public housing, economic development initiatives, urban renewal programs, regular garbage collection and disposal, transit services, museums and programs in the arts, sports stadiums, and consumer protection services.
8 Not all municipalities, however, have charters, as California municipalities, for example, function under the general state law.
9 Although a distinction is sometimes made between what is a township and what is a town, the term "township" is employed in this book in that both governments function in nearly the same capacity as units of local governments that fit somewhere between county governments and municipal governments. For more explanation, see Bowman, Kearney, and Scavo 2022, 94–95 and Dye and MacManus 2015, 295 and 301–02.
10 In the states of Connecticut, Maine, Massachusetts, New Hampshire, Rhode Island, and Vermont, township government is an especially significant unit of local government, with long traditions and deep roots in the political philosophy of the people of that region. This is particularly the case in Rhode Island and Connecticut since they abolished county governments in 1849 and 1958, respectively. This is also evident in Massachusetts where they had abolished all but one of its 14 original counties as of 1997.

## References

Ammons, David N, Karl W Smith, and Carl W Stenberg. 2012. "The Future of Local Government: Will Current Stresses Bring Major, Permanent Changes?" *State and Local Government Review*, 44(December): 64S–75S.

*Baker v Carr*, 369 U.S.186. 1962.

Benton, J. Edwin. 1986. "Federalism's 'First Principles' and Reagan's New Federalism Policies," *Policy Studies Journal*, 13: 568–75.

———. 2002. "*Counties as Service Delivery Agents: Changing Expectations and Roles.*" Westport, CT: Praeger.

———. 2009. "Coping with Foreclosures." In Miller, Gerald J., and James H. Svara (eds.), *Navigating the Fiscal Crisis: Tested Strategies for Local Leaders*. Washington, DC: ICMA/Alliance for Innovation: 49–51.

———. 2017. "Local Government Service Roles in the U.S.: Constancy and Change." In Kerley, Richard, Joyce Liddle, and Pamela Dunning (eds.), *Handbook of International Local Government*. New York: Routledge: 183–202.

———. 2018. "Intergovernmental Relations in the Early Twentieth-First Century: Lingering Images of Earlier Phases or Emergence of a New Phase?" In Stenberg, Carl, and David Hamilton (eds.), *Intergovernmental Relations in the United States: Reflections and Directions*. New York: Routledge: 15–36.

Benton, J. Edwin, Grant E Rissler, and Spencer Wagner. 2020. "City and County Governments in the Time of COVID-19: The Long and Winding Road," *State and Local Government Review*, 51: 28–52.

Berman, David R. 2019. "*Local Government and the States*." 2nd ed. New York: Routledge.

Bowman, Ann O'M, and Richard C Kearney. 2008. "*State and Local Government*." 7th ed. Boston: Houghton Mifflin Company.

———. and Carmine P.F. Scavo. 2022. "*State and Local Government*." 11th ed. Boston: Cengage.

Brace, Paul. 1993. "*State Government and Economic Performance*." Baltimore: Johns Hopkins University Press.

DeSantis, Victor S, and Tari Renner. 1984. "Governing the County: Authority, Structure, and Elections." In David R. Berman (ed.), *County Governments in an Era of Change*. Westport, CT: Greenwood Press: 15–28.

Donovan, Todd, Christopher Z Mooney, and Daniel A Smith. 2009. "*State and Local Politics: Institutions and Reform*." Belmont, CA: Wadsworth/Cengage Learning.

Dye, Thomas R, and Susan A MacManus. 2015. "*Politics in States and Communities*." 15th ed. Upper Saddle River, NJ: Pearson Education, Inc.

Elazar, Daniel J. 1984. "*American Federalism: A View from the States*." 3rd ed. New York: Harper & Row Publishers.

Figone Debra et al. 2011. What is the Future of Local Government?' *An Alliance White Paper Intended to Provoke a Needed Conversation*." Phoenix, AZ: Alliance for Innovation, Arizona State University.

Hendrick, Rebecca, and Robert P Degnan. 2020. "In the Shadow of State Government: Changes in Municipal Spending After Two Recessions," *American Review of Public Administration*, 50(February): 161–75.

Hitchcock, H. H., and J. F Coates. 1985. "*The Future of State and Local Government as Seen in the Futures Literature*." Washington, DC: Academy for State and Local Government.

Hungerford, Thomas, and Robert Wassmer. 2014. "K-12 Education and the U.S. Economy." National Education Association Research Working Paper. April. Https;//eric.ed.gov/?id=ED490870.

International City Management Association (ICMA). 2020. "*COVID-19 Impacts on Local Governments: Summary of Survey Results*." Washington, DC: International City Management Association. https://icma.org/sites/default/files/COVID-19%20July%202020%20Survey%20Summary%20with%20Key%20Findings%20FINAL%20web.pdf. Accessed May 12, 2020.

Jones, Bryan D, and Frank. R Baumgartner. 2012. "From There to Here: Punctuated Equilibrium to the General Punctuation Thesis to a Theory of Government Information Processing," *Policy Studies Journal*, 40(February): 1–19.

Krane, Dale, Platon N Rigos, and Melvin B Hill Jr. 2001. "*Home Rule in America: A Fifty-State Handbook*." Washington, DC: CQ Press.

Levine, Charles H. 1979. "More on Cutback Management: Hard Questions for Hard Times," *Public Administration Review*, 39: 179–83.

———. 1980. "The New Crisis in the Public Sector." In Levine, Charles H. (ed.), *Managing Fiscal Stress: The Crisis in the Public Sector*. Chatham, NJ: Chatham House: 3–12.

Lindblom, Charles E. 1968. "*The Policymaking Process*." Englewood Cliffs, NJ: Prentice-Hall.

Martin, Lawrence L, Richard Levey, and Jenna Cawley. 2012. "The 'New Normal' for Local Government," *State and Local Government Review*, 44: 17S–28S.

McFarland, Christiana K, and Michael A Pagano. 2019. *City Fiscal Conditions 2019*. Washington, DC: National League of Cities. https://www.nlc.org/resource/city-fiscal-conditions-2019-report/. Accessed May 12, 2020.

McFarland, Christiana K, and Michael A Pagano. 2020. *City Fiscal Conditions 2020*. Washington, DC: National League of Cities.https://gfrc.uic.edu/research/city-fiscal-conditions-2020-by-michael-pagano-and-christiana-mcfarland/. Accessed May 12, 2020.

National Association of Counties (NACo). 2020. *Comprehensive Analysis of COVID-19's Impact on County Finances and Implications for the U.S. Economy*. Washington, DC: National Association of Counties. https://www.naco.org/sites/default/files/documents/Analysis-of-COVID-19s-Impact-on-County-Finances-and-Implications-for-the-US-Economy.pdf. Accessed May 12, 2020.

Reynolds v. Sims, 377 U.S.533. 1964.

*San Antonio Independent School District v. Rodriguez*, 411 U.S. 1. 1973.

*Serrano v. Priest*, 5 Cal.3d 584. 1971.

Smith, Kevin B, and J. Scott Rademacker. 1999. "Expense Lessons: Education and the Political Economy of the American States," *Political Research Quarterly*, 52: 709–27.

U.S. Bureau of the Census. 2012. Census of Governments. Table 9: Special District Governments by Function and State. Accessed at https://www.census.gov/data/tables/2012/econ/gus/2012-governments.html

Warner, Mildred E. 2010. "The Future of Local Government: Twenty-First Century Challenges," *Public Administration Review*, 70(Supplement): S145–7.

Wesberry v. Sanders, 376 U. S. 1. 1964.

# 4 The Property Tax

## The Bountiful but Onerous Tax that Keeps on Giving

While the property tax has always been the foundation of local government financial systems in the United States,[1] it is often viewed in paradoxical terms. Specifically, most assessments of this tax ranging from scholars to practitioners to politicians to the media to the tax-paying public have been both highly critical and laudable. Perhaps, economist C. Lowell Harriss (1973, 16) sums up best this perspective on the property tax in the following statement: "It is the best of taxes. It is the worst of taxes." Anecdotal statements about the property tax would seem to confirm this viewpoint while also suggesting that people have cultivated a "love/hate" opinion with respect to the tax. All of this would suggest that the property tax creates a conundrum of sorts since the tax possesses both good and bad qualities. This inevitably leaves people in the uncomfortable but unavoidable dilemma of having to accept the "good" with the "bad" that the property tax presents. Charlie B. Tyer (1993, 12) seems to capture this sentiment when he notes that the property tax is "the second worst tax consistently in opinions polls of Americans….the tax that people understand the least, hate the most, and yet will continue to pay despite these characteristics because it produces a consistent and stable source of revenue with huge yields."

### Criticisms of and support for the property tax

The property tax is often referred to as the "tax that the public *loves* to hate" (see Cabral and Hoxby 2012), while economist L.L. Ecker-Racz (1970, 77) proffers the view that "the property is not the best tax…or even a good one." Critics of the tax regularly point to several fundamental flaws. First, the property tax is deemed to be an unfair tax based on the way it is calculated and administered. Fairness in these two processes initially hinges greatly on a government assessor making a formal appraisal of the market value of the land and buildings on it. Determining market value may appear to be simple, but ultimately the appraised market value depends on the judgment of the assessor, who may or may not be properly trained for the job or fully cognizant of conditions in the local housing market. This can lead to property being under-appraised or over-appraised; the

DOI: 10.4324/9781032640389-4

same thing can also happen if property is not appraised at reasonably regular intervals (i.e., at least every five years). As a result, property that does not change ownership becomes increasingly undervalued. Then, the fairness of the property tax system is further criticized for exempting government buildings, religious houses of worship, and property owned by charitable organizations from taxation, although they utilize police, fire, EMS, and trash collection services and expect the provision of sidewalks and street lights.

Critics also point to other problems with the property tax. One such problem is that the tax tends to be regressive, meaning that the burden of paying the tax falls more heavily on those with less ability-to-pay. For instance, people trying to buy a house for the first time may find that, while they are able to afford the mortgage payment and insurance premiums, they cannot afford the property tax; therefore, they are prevented from realizing what some have called the "American Dream." In other instances, retires/senior citizens, people living on fixed incomes, or individuals and families experiencing hard financial times may lose their home to foreclosure or are forced to sell it when housing values spiral upward and their annual property tax bills are rising sharply. To make matters worse, the property tax sometimes must be paid in a large lump sum.

The property tax is also criticized because it can lead to a lack of political accountability. This can occur in situations like what sparked a series of property tax revolts across the county in the late 1970s. It started in California where state and local politicians turned a "blind eye" to sharply rising property taxes that doubled or tripled in most areas of the state in only a few years due to rapidly escalating property values. Although elected officials did not explicitly vote to raise property taxes, their inaction nonetheless resulted in out-of-control tax increases. Some senior citizens, people living on fixed incomes, and even employed middle-aged citizens were forced to sell their home to pay their property tax. In the meantime, state and local elected officials stood idly by and basically did nothing to either address the matter or alleviate the economic misery of their citizens. Subsequently, voters had to take matters into their own hands and successfully passed an initiative in 1979 (Proposition 13) that imposed strict limitations on the ability of local governments to raise property and other taxes in the future.

Yet, another criticism of the property tax is that it can result in inequities in burdens and benefits between poorer and more affluent communities. The end result is that the gap between the "haves" and the "have nots" continues to widen while exacerbating the racial and economic divide in countries like the United States that touts itself as the "land of economic opportunity" and a promoter of social equity and justice. The inequity problem becomes quite acute when school districts derive a considerable proportion of the revenue from the local property tax. As explained by Bowman and Kearney (2008, 405), "wealthy districts with much highly valued residential and/or commercial property can afford to finance public schools at generous levels, whereas poor districts (even though they often tax their property at much higher rates than wealthy districts) tend to raise fewer dollars because of their lower property values." The result is that some children receive a more expensive, and probably higher-quality, education than other children do, even though the parents of the advantaged group of children may contribute less money. While the California Supreme Court in 1971 in *Serrano v. Priest* ruled that inequities in school expenditures resulting from variations in taxable wealth were unconstitutional, the U.S. Supreme Court declined to extend the *Serrano* ruling to all states in *San Antonio Independent School District v. Rodriguez* (1973).

Notwithstanding, proponents of the property tax defend its usage on several grounds, not the least of which is that it is the only viable tax alternative left to local governments since the national and state governments have all but monopolized usage of the income and sales taxes, respectively. However, even if local governments were to tax income and sales, these taxes "force individuals and businesses to leave the communities using them" (Dye and MacManus 2015, 571). The strongest and most often mentioned supporting arguments of the property tax are that it is certain (i.e., the tax has been levied year after year for as long as one can remember) and the owners of property must pay it or the government may confiscate and sell their land, buildings, or other taxable possessions. In addition, the subject of the tax (real estate) is less easy to move about and hide from tax assessors unlike income, stocks and bonds, investments, or even a person's purchases. Finally, property taxes are the only kind of taxes that "can be effectively and efficiently collected by relatively untrained local tax officials" (Dye and MacManus 2015, 571).

In spite of the negative appraisals of the property tax, it remains the most widely used tax by all local governments in the United States, if for no other reason than it is convenient and produces an abundant amount of revenue (by far, the largest proportion of local government revenues). While it may seem that criticisms of the property tax overshadow support for it, the tax nonetheless persists. In the end, however, logic, convenience, and, most likely, the necessity to have a dependable and plentiful source of revenue win out over arguments and efforts to do away with the property tax. Like it or not, the property tax is probably here to stay, although reform efforts to minimize the shortcomings of the tax will certainly continue.

## Historical context of the property tax

Contrary to what many Americans may believe, the origins of the property tax predate the founding and colonizing of the United States. The roots of the property tax can be traced back to Europe's feudal system and were instituted in England by William the Conqueror in 1066 (Semuels 2016). The tax system operated in the following way: a monarch would take over all of the land (property) in a given territory and then divide it among his lieutenants and supporters, who would then pay him/her (with money or services) in order to keep the land; in return, the landholders were protected by the monarch and also permitted to rent out the property to others—who would live and work the land—for a fee (Semuels 2016). This system was referred to as "free and common socage," with the person holding the property called a "socman" and his property taxes "socage" (Semuels 2016; Wallis n.d.a). Such an arrangement established a way for people to own property while still remaining loyal to the monarchy, which also had rights to the property.[2]

Once England began to colonize what would eventually become the United States, King James I made sure that this system was transported with the first settlers in Jamestown, so that the Crown could benefit from the profits to be gained from this territorial expansion (Semuels 2016). The charter of the Virginia Company stipulated that—like was the case in feudal times—the king would protect the lands in Jamestown, and in return, the people living on the land would pay the king a share of their profits. Consequently, all property in the Colony would be held in "free and common socage." This meant that all properties could be bought and sold as long as the new holder of the property continued to pay the king. This doctrine eventually spread to all of the original 13 colonies.[3]

After the Revolutionary War ended and property owners no longer had to answer to the king, the new American government had to determine who owned the land in order for the tax system originating under feudalism to continue. With the passage of the Northwest Ordinance, it was decided that the federal government would replace the king as the owner of all land (property) and the state would now become the collector of all fees from the tenants. This is analogous to the feudal system whereby the king owned the land but a knight might have collected the fees (Semuels 2016; Wallis n.d.b). Therefore, when property was sold to an individual, the state had the right to collect payment from that individual in perpetuity (Semuels 2016; Wallis n.d.a and Wallis n.d.b). This was an arrangement comparable to free and common socage, now called "fee simple." That principle and terminology continues today, as individuals buying a home or a commercial establishment will notice the term "fee simple" in their legal documents stating they own the land and property which is still subject to taxes.

It is a rather peculiar note in history that the Founding Fathers, who frequently expressed the desire to abolish the feudal system, retained this remnant of the Old World. But their rationale was quite understandable and simple—governments needed the money. While the federal government, for brief periods, levied a national property tax (1798, 1814, 1815, 1816, and 1861), the property tax became the primary source of revenue for both state and local governments, and this trend continued until the early part of the 20th century (Fisher 1996). Due to a number of factors, including but not limited to adopting new revenue sources (e.g., sales and income taxes) and their inability to make the property tax work as a benefit tax,[4] states began to relinquish much of their claim to it and subsequently this revenue as a proportion of state revenue declined from 45 percent in 1902 to less than 1 percent today. As of 2017, the property tax remains as the chief source of revenue for local governments.

### Analysis of taxes and property tax usage by all local governments

Taxes, including the property tax, have always been the mainstay of the revenue systems of governments for as long as organized governments have existed. Some of the earliest known taxes were those in ancient Egypt (levied on cooking oil), Greece (instituted to pay the costs of war), and the Roman Empire (charged custom duties on imports and exports).[5] Most early taxes were levied on a periodic basis as governments needed revenue to provide services to their citizens. Eventually, most taxes became permanent fixtures of government revenue systems as noted by Benjamin Franklin: "In this world, nothing could be said to be certain, except death and taxes" (Beattie 2010). Moreover, anecdotal references to the enduring nature of taxes described them in this way: "War is hell but taxes last longer" (Beattie 2010).

Having obtained an initial foothold early on in the American colonies, taxes (with the property tax being the most prominent) ultimately became a part of the revenue system of the national, state, and local governments. However, the new American government, for all practical purposes, was understandably cautious and hence took a measured approach to taxation since the U.S. Constitution prohibited the levying of direct taxes. In lieu of direct taxes, government revenues had to be collected through tariffs and duties on certain items (e.g., sugar, tea, tobacco, and legal documents). Likewise, taxation, while also being used judicially, became an increasingly viable and attractive way for local governments to obtain the revenue needed to meet the increasing service needs and expectations of its citizenry. Over time, taxes of one sort or another became the staple and largest source of revenue for these governments.

Tax receipts constitute the largest proportion of local government Total Revenue (TR) and Own-Source Revenue (OSR). No other source of local government revenue (as will become evident in the analyses of chapters to follow) comes close to matching the huge contributions made by taxes. However, as can be seen from Table 4.1, the taxes proportions of TR have been decreasing over time—that is from 49 to 37 percent between 1962 and 2020, while the taxes proportion of OSR remained fairly consistent over time, holding at about 62–64 percent through 2020 (A breakdown by type of local government can be seen in Table A4.1 in the Appendix). Note that, contrary to some predictions about the impact of the COVID-induced recession, the taxes proportion of TR did not decrease any further during the early days of this recession, as there was no change in the percent from 2017 to 2020. Also, it should be noted that the tax proportion of OSR basically stayed the same from 2017 to 2020 (although it did drop slightly from 65 to 64 percent). If this recession had any impact on tax collections and these proportions, it was not apparent from data through 2020.[6] However, it is important that,

*Table 4.1* Total Tax Revenue (TTR) as a Proportion of Total Revenue (TR) and Own-Source Revenue (OSR) for All Local Governments, 1962–2020

| | *1962* | *1967* | *1972* | *1977* | *1982* | *1987* | *1992* | *1997* | *2002* | *2007* | *2012* | *2017* | *2020* |
|---|---|---|---|---|---|---|---|---|---|---|---|---|---|
| TTR as % of Total Revenue | 49 | 48 | 43 | 38 | 33 | 34 | 35 | 34 | 34 | 34 | 36 | 36 | 37 |
| TTR as % of Own-Source Revenue | 68 | 74 | 68 | 64 | 64 | 62 | 64 | 62 | 62 | 62 | 64 | 65 | 64 |

*Source:* U.S. Bureau of the Census. Census of Governments. Compendium of Government Finances series, 1962–2017.

when data for subsequent fiscal years (1921, 2022, and even 2023) become available, they should be examined to determine if there could have been some lagged effect that did not manifest itself until this recession lingered on.

Upon further analysis (see Table 4.2), it is instructive that a pattern is observed for property taxes as a proportion of local governments' TR and OSR that is both similar to and different from the patterns seen in Table 4.1. That is, it appears that property taxes have been accounting for a considerably smaller part of both TR and OSR over time. For example, revenue generated by property tax collections accounted for a much smaller proportion of TR in 2020 than they did in 1962 (i.e., 27 versus 42 percent), while property tax revenues (PTRs) were also responsible for a significantly reduced share of OSR over this same time period (i.e., 46 compared to 69 percent). Again, there is no evidence that the recession caused by the COVID-19 health pandemic negatively impacted the property tax proportions of either TR or OSR. Nevertheless, additional data for 2021, 2022, and 2023 may provide information to the contrary.

Additional analysis, however, does show that while property taxes continue to make up well over one-half of all money collected through taxation, the ad valorem tax has been accounting for a declining portion of total tax-generated

*Table 4.2* Property Tax Revenue as a Proportion of Total Revenue (TR) and Own-Source Revenue (OSR) for All Local Governments, 1962–2020

| | *1962* | *1967* | *1972* | *1977* | *1982* | *1987* | *1992* | *1997* | *2002* | *2007* | *2012* | *2017* | *2020* |
|---|---|---|---|---|---|---|---|---|---|---|---|---|---|
| TTR as % of Total Revenue | 49 | 48 | 43 | 38 | 33 | 34 | 35 | 34 | 34 | 34 | 36 | 36 | 37 |
| TTR as % of Own-Source Revenue | 68 | 74 | 68 | 64 | 64 | 62 | 64 | 62 | 62 | 62 | 64 | 65 | 64 |

*Source:* U.S. Bureau of the Census. Census of Governments. Compendium of Government Finances series, 1962–2017.

*Table 4.3* Property Tax Revenue (PTR) as a Proportion of Total Tax Revenue (TTR) for All Local Governments, 1962–2020

| | *1962* | *1967* | *1972* | *1977* | *1982* | *1987* | *1992* | *1997* | *2002* | *2007* | *2012* | *2017* | *2020* |
|---|---|---|---|---|---|---|---|---|---|---|---|---|---|
| PTR as a % of Total Tax Revenue (TTR) | 86 | 86 | 84 | 81 | 76 | 74 | 76 | 73 | 73 | 72 | 73 | 72 | 72 |

*Source:* U.S. Bureau of the Census. Census of Governments. Compendium of Government Finances series, 1962–2017.

revenues (TTR) of local governments over the last 58 years. In 1962, PTR produced 86 percent of all local government tax revenue, but this proportion had dropped to 72 percent by 2020 (see Table 4.3). Yet, the property tax was still responsible for almost $3 out of every $4 collected from some form of taxation. Moreover, as seen for the Total Tax Revenue (TTR) and PTR proportions of TR and OSR, there appears to be no negative impact of the coronavirus health pandemic as of 2020, but data for years after 2020 may refute these earlier findings.

From the preliminary analysis above, it is obvious that local government reliance on PTR has decreased over time, but especially from 1962 to 2010. It does not matter whether property tax reliance is measured as a proportion of TR or OSR of local government or as a percentage of local government TTR—the trend is the same, although the degree of decline may vary somewhat for these different measures of dependency. But, is the trend the same for all five types of local governments—counties, municipalities, townships, special districts, and school districts? Moreover, what can explain the incidence of lesser or greater dependency on PTRs for each specific type of local government? Furthermore, is the trend for each of type of local government the same in all states or does it vary from state to state, and if so, why? The analyses below should provide answers to these important questions.

### *The property tax: An enduring source of revenue for counties and municipalities*

Counties and municipalities are clearly distinguishable from townships, special districts, and school districts in that they are full-service local governments that provide a much larger menu of staple services. While townships provide a smaller number of services than counties and municipalities, school districts provide only one service—education. Special districts also usually provide only one service but may be responsible for more than a single service—for instance, it is not uncommon for some special districts to provide both water and sewer services rather than just one of them.

*Table 4.4* Total Tax Revenue (TTR) as a Proportion of Own-Source Revenue (OSR) for Counties and Municipalities, 1962–2017

| | *1962* | *1967* | *1972* | *1977* | *1982* | *1987* | *1992* | *1997* | *2002* | *2007* | *2012* | *2017* |
|---|---|---|---|---|---|---|---|---|---|---|---|---|
| TTR as % of Own-Source Revenue (Counties) | 79 | 76 | 73 | 69 | 58 | 57 | 58 | 56 | 55 | 58 | 59 | 60 |
| TTR as % of Own-Source Revenue (Municipalities) | 76 | 74 | 72 | 71 | 62 | 60 | 61 | 59 | 60 | 62 | 63 | 63 |

*Source:* U.S. Bureau of the Census. Census of Governments. Compendium of Government Finances series, 1962–2017.

Like local governments generally, county and municipal governments have always relied very heavily on some form of taxation to produce sufficient revenues to fund basic services (see Table 4.4). In 1962, taxes accounted for 79 percent of county government OSR and 76 percent of municipal OSR. Over the last 40 years, however, this dependency on revenue generated by taxes fell noticeably but more so for counties. By 2002, the proportion of county government OSR made up of tax-generated revenue had declined by 22 percentage points to 57 percent, although it did rebound to 61 percent by 2012 and continued there by 2017. The pattern for municipalities was similar to that for counties (but to a lesser extent) until the 1980s, as the tax proportion of OSR dropped by 16 percentage points to 60 percent. However, the OSR proportion began to rise slightly again and stood at 63 percent in 2017 (the last year for data is available for individual types of local governments). Overall, these data suggest that counties and municipalities have lessened their dependency on taxes and have been tapping other sources of revenue (e.g., charges for services, special assessments, fines and forfeitures, and an assortment of other types of revenues) than they did in the past. The decline in municipal dependency is probably due to the fact that they have relied more on charges for services over the years than have counties. At any rate, we will explore these and other possibilities in later chapters of this book.

Two other important trends are conspicuous in Table 4.4. First, a sharp *decrease* in the proportion of OSR accounted for by taxes (TTR) is evident for both counties and municipalities between 1977 and 1982 (declining by 11 and 9 percentage points for counties and municipalities, respectively). This is likely due to the repercussions of strong anti-tax sentiments prompted by Proposition 13 in California, specifically, and a tax revolt that was spreading across the country, generally, during that time. Second, a modest tick *upward* in county and municipal dependency on TTR is obvious for the 2002–2017 period (rising by 4 and 3 percentage points for counties and municipalities, respectively).

This trend suggests that the impact of the Great Recession probably forced these governments to increase revenue collections from various forms of taxes to make up the loss of revenue typically produced by other non-tax sources (quite likely charges for services, special assessments, interest on earnings, and fees and fines) as the U.S. economy worsened. It will be interesting to see if this pattern continued or even accelerated during the recession resulting from the COVID-19 pandemic. Unfortunately, no data are available for individual local governments beyond 2017 to check for this possibility. A revised version of this book is planned for this explicit purpose.

These overall trends notwithstanding, the amount of money produced by property taxes continues to be the largest component of total tax collections of both counties and municipalities.

The most straightforward way to measure the degree to which counties and municipalities rely on property taxes to finance the provision of public services is to calculate the proportion of OSR that is accounted for by property tax collections.[7] These data, which are displayed in Figure 4.1, indicate what has always been known within state and local government circles and even by the media and informed citizens. That is, while the property tax is a vital source of revenue

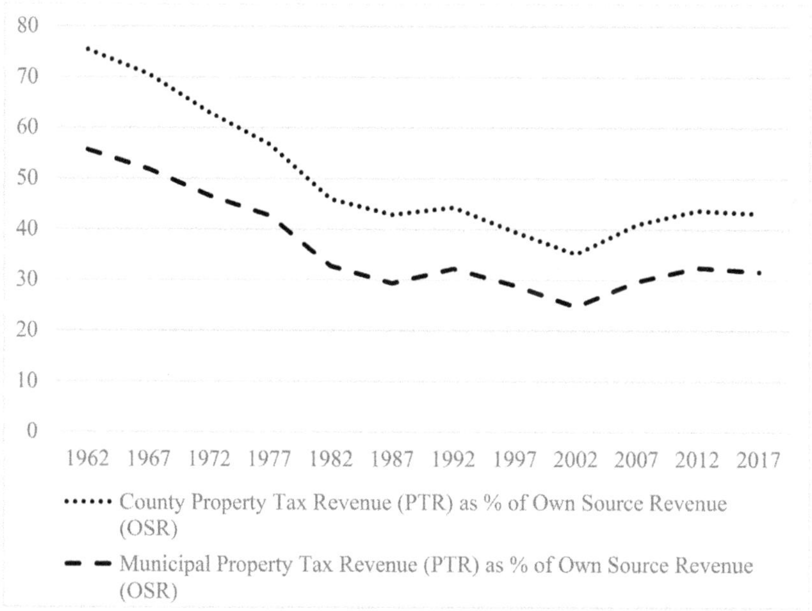


*Figure 4.1* County and Municipal Property Tax Revenue as a Percent of Own-Source Revenue (OSR), 1962–2017

*Source:* U.S. Bureau of the Census. Census of Governments. Compendium of Government Finances series, 1962–2017.

for both of these local governments, it has proven to be more important for county governments. This is clearly evident from Figure 4.1. Yet, it is important to note that the property tax proportion of the OSR gap between counties and municipalities has stayed about the same over the last 58 years.

Several factors are likely to account for the seemingly greater importance of PTR for counties than for municipalities. First, states typically assign county governments a greater number of functions and/or services to deliver than is the case for municipalities. In fact, it is not unusual that many of these services are mandated. These include things such as public welfare, health care, legal and judicial matters, tax assessment and collection, and voter registration and administration, among others. The cost of performing many of these duties and/or providing these kinds of services can be staggering, although states often provide state aid and/or share state revenues with counties as a means to offset some of the costs that they incur. In addition, most states customarily give more latitude to counties to levy property taxes since counties (more likely than municipalities) are called upon to act as administrative or political arms of the state. It is as though states feel that they are obligated to assist counties who are acting as extensions of the state government and thereby assist in providing these services efficiently and evenly across the state.

Second, counties unlike municipalities usually do not perform as many functions or provide services where it is reasonable or feasible to impose a service charge or impose a fee. In those instances where it makes sense for a county to enact a fee charge and if the state permits it, counties are likely to have to share the proceeds from such transactions with the state which may or may not cover the cost of county expenditures. Examples of this include the issuance of marriage licenses, birth and death certificates, occupational certifications and accreditations, and various kinds of permits, recording of deeds, titles, and final judgments in civil court matters, health, safety, and building inspections, and imposition and collection of various fines. Also, many of the services for which the county may be able to charge a fee typically generate little to no revenue or simply inadequate revenue. Seldom are county governments able to collect large sums of money for the provision of various types of utilities (e.g., water, sewer, natural gas, electric power) unless the county has a substantial number of people residing in or businesses located in the unincorporated parts of the county.

Third, counties, in contrast to municipalities, are more likely to provide a larger number of indivisible type services. These kinds of services are ones for which there is no distinctly identifiable recipient or user; yet, these services are important and indispensable to the quality of life and safety of all of the county's residents, as well as to the economic prosperity of the community. Relevant examples include things such as environmental protection/conservation, judicial and court system-related duties, solid waste management, parks and recreational facilities, planning and zoning, county-operated K-12 schools, community colleges, vocational and technical schools, community development/redevelopment programs, mass transit, 911-call centers, libraries, and roads.

In sum, the fact is that counties and municipalities oftentimes provide a different array of services, and this may have important implications for the kinds of revenues each government can realistically utilize. Subsequently, the degree to which they depend on a range of revenue sources may vary widely. This appears to be the case in the utilization of PTR.

A closer examination of the data in Figure 4.1 reveals another significant pattern. In spite of the fact that the property tax historically has been the workhorse of local government tax systems, county and municipal dependency on this source of revenue has noticeably decreased over time. More specifically, property taxes as a proportion of county government OSR declined from 74 to 42 percent between 1962 and 2017, while the property tax proportion for municipal governments also dropped noticeably from 43 to 25 percent over this same period.

This downward trend in dependency on PTR is likely the result of at least three interrelated pressures emanating from the heightened concerns of frustrated and alienated taxpayers. The first of these has been the well-publicized tax revolts of angry homeowners beginning around the mid-1970s who saw their property tax bills increase at unprecedented levels. As noted earlier in this chapter, citizens in California (and shortly thereafter citizens in Massachusetts and Michigan and eventually in many other states) launched massive statewide grassroots campaigns to limit the amount that property taxes could increase from one year to the next.[8] Most of these efforts intentionally bypassed state legislatures and were successful in erecting safeguards against spiraling property tax increases through the constitutional initiative process (e.g., Proposition 13 in California and Proposition 2 ½ in Massachusetts). Given years of inaction and ignoring citizenry pleas of help, frustrated homeowners were in no mood to trust their state legislators to provide them with the much-needed financial relief they sought.

Additional pressure on state and local officials has been brought by taxpayers who often demand greater fairness in both the choice and implementation of various revenue schemes. On the one hand, taxpayers, but especially home and business owners, increasingly complain that they provide a disproportionate part of the revenue needed to pay for local government programs and services. In voicing their complaints, they routinely ask questions like the following: Why should I be forced to contribute to the financing of downtown and airport parking garages, sports stadiums, marinas, civic centers and other entertainment venues, recreational complexes, expressways, or mass transit if I never use these services or facilities? This is a legitimate question in light of the fact that these things historically have been paid for mainly with property tax dollars. Therefore, it is reasonable to expect/demand that service users and not necessarily citizens who pay property taxes should bear these costs. On the other hand, racial minorities and low-income whites complain that the property tax is very regressive and always looms as an obstacle in being able to afford a home when one considers the full cost of home ownership (i.e., mortgage payment, home insurance, and, of course, and the property taxes).

Then, of course, there is the constant influence of citizens who hold conservative fiscal views about the appropriate/acceptable size of government and warn of the potential overreach of what Thomas Hobbes (1996) referred to as the "Leviathan." While Hobbes' portrayal of the Leviathan (term adapted here as a synonym for organized government that was established to ensure "civil peace and social unity"), there are those, while begrudgingly viewing government as a "necessary evil," who would nonetheless argue for restricting the potential for government to become overbearing, at a minimum, and abusive, at its worse. This perspective of government also purports that larger governments and ones that spend lots of money have a greater likelihood for experiencing corruption, inefficiencies, and wastefulness. Therefore, as a means of lessening the opportunity for governments to develop these undesirable attributes (and particularly, to excessively spend the hard-earned money of the very people they serve), fiscal conservatives argue that citizens should limit local governments' access to large sums of money, including their largest source of revenue—the property tax. After all, constantly ballooning property tax bills present the grave threat for citizens to lose their most prized possession and an integral part of the American Dream—their home.

Data displayed in Figure 4.2 provide additional information about the importance that counties and municipalities attach to revenue collected from property taxes. These data are the proportion of TTR that is attributable to property tax collections. As expected, PTR makes up a considerable proportion of the total amount of money that these two full-service governments obtain from some form of taxation. As of 2017, PTR accounted for around 70 percent of all money collected via taxes for counties, while property tax proceeds were responsible for approximately one-half of tax-generated monies of municipalities. Nevertheless, Figure 4.2 also clearly indicates that property taxes as a proportion of TTR for both counties and municipalities have been shrinking over time. While property taxes remain an important component of these governments' total tax receipts, counties and municipalities are nonetheless collecting a larger percentage of their tax revenue from other kinds of taxes. This has been a longtime goal of these governments after many years of pressure from property owners who have complained of having to bear too much of the cost of financing county and municipal operations.

Further examination of Figure 4.2 unveils an important insight as we look to the future. The figure reveals slight (yet noticeable) upward movement in property taxes as a proportion of TTR between 2007 and 2012, which could indicate that counties and municipalities were still likely to be suffering from the ill effects of the Great Recession that had resulted in shortfalls in normal local option

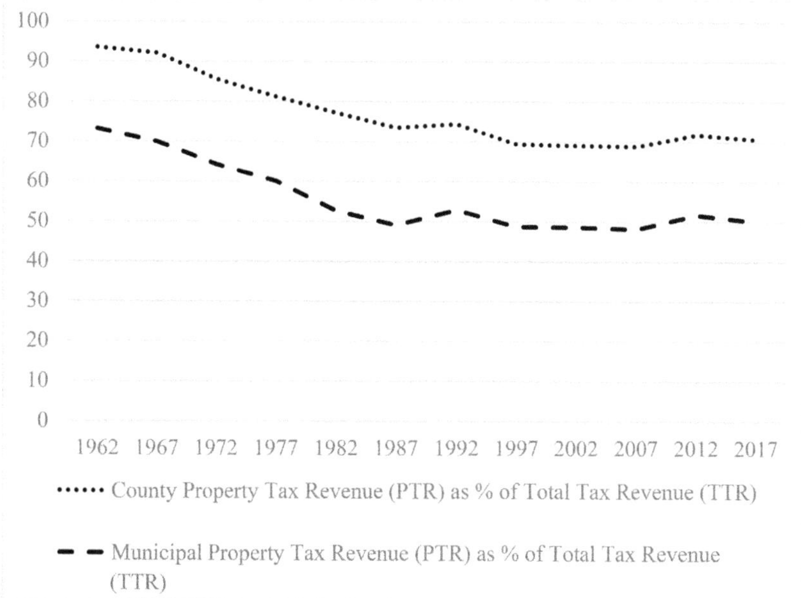


*Figure 4.2* County and Municipal Property Tax Revenue (PTR) as a Percent of Total Tax Revenue (TTR), 1962–2017

*Source:* U.S. Bureau of the Census. Census of Governments. Compendium of Government Finances series, 1962–2017.

sales and income tax collections. Therefore, tracking these data for 2018 and beyond will be essential for us to determine if this trend will continue in both the short- and long term. If the property tax as a proportion of TTR were to continue to increase, this could mean that counties and cities see this as a reasonable option to maintain a steady stream of revenue to support their operations at a time when local option sales and income taxes are dropping. After all, the property tax has had a history of being a bountiful source of revenue that is easy to collect. Furthermore, since many counties and municipalities were still trying to recover from the lingering effects of the Great Recession when the COVID-19-driven recession hit, these governments may find it necessary to increase their reliance—even only in the short-run—on the "old reliable" property tax to get them through these unexpected and unprecedented hard times.

With this said, county and municipal officials, while still committed to shifting reliance away from the property, may view these uncertain times as a temporary detour. As mentioned above, these officials "bought into" the argument made a long time ago by property owners that the property tax is neither the best nor even the fairest way to finance the delivery of local services. Simply stated, there continues to be increasing support for the belief that the expense of providing an increasing number of services should be borne by those who use specific kinds of services. It is also likely that this view continues to be reinforced by financial experts and economists advising county and city officials as well as local government watchdog groups who are vigilantly looking out for the interests of those who tend to pay the greatest proportion of property taxes (i.e., home and business owners). Therefore, the downward trend of dependency on the property tax was clearly visible until 2012 could possibly reappear after the country has been able to shake off the final effects of both the Great Recession and the recession precipitated by the COVID-19 pandemic and even any resultant "New Nomal."[9]

While declining dependency on the property tax by counties and municipalities has been the norm since 1962, this has not always been the case in every state as is evident from Tables 4.5 and 4.6.

From Table 4.5, it is clear that PTR as a proportion of county government TTR experienced a precipitous decline from 1962 to 2017. In fact, that was the case in 40 of 48 states that have counties. In five states (Delaware, Georgia, New Mexico, Maryland, and Kentucky), the decrease was 35 percentage points or greater, while the drop-off surpassed 40 percentage points in three more states

*Table 4.5* County Government Property Tax Revenue (PTR) as a Percentage of Total Tax Revenue (TTR) by State in 1962 and 2017 and Change over Time

| *State* | *1962* | *2017* | *Change* | *State* | *1962* | *2017* | *Change* |
|---|---|---|---|---|---|---|---|
| New Hampshire | 100.0 | 99.6 | −.4 | North Carolina | 98.5 | 75.7 | −33.8 |
| Maine | 100.0 | 99.4 | −.6 | Kansas | 98.2 | 72.2 | −26.0 |
| New Jersey | 99.7 | 99.2 | −.5 | Wyoming | 98.4 | 72.1 | −26.3 |
| Montana | 90.8 | 98.6 | 7.8 | South Carolina | 99.5 | 71.4 | −28.1 |
| Pennsylvania | 97.7 | 95.0 | −2.7 | Florida | 94.8 | 70.7 | −24.1 |
| Minnesota | 99.1 | 94.7 | −4.5 | Colorado | 97.4 | 70.0 | −77.5 |
| Michigan | 99.1 | 94.2 | −4.9 | Tennessee | 95.7 | 65.8 | −29.9 |
| Idaho | 97.8 | 93.9 | −3.9 | Delaware | 100.0 | 64.5 | −35.5 |
| Mississippi | 81.8 | 93.6 | 11.8 | Illinois | 94.0 | 61.3 | −32.7 |
| Texas | 83.9 | 91.2 | 7.3 | Georgia | 96.6 | 60.8 | −35.8 |
| South Dakota | 85.6 | 90.0 | 4.0 | New Mexico | 96.3 | 58.2 | −38.1 |
| Alaska | — | 89.4 | — | Louisiana | 93.7 | 56.8 | −26.9 |
| Vermont | 100.0 | 100.0 | 0.0 | Oklahoma | 100.0 | 55.1 | −44.9 |
| Iowa | 99.1 | 89.1 | −10.1 | Maryland | 92.4 | 53.8 | −38.6 |
| West Virginia | 99.4 | 88.4 | −11.0 | Washington | 76.8 | 52.7 | −24.1 |
| California | 93.6 | 88.1 | −5.5 | Ohio | 97.4 | 52.1 | −45.3 |
| Nebraska | 86.5 | 84.7 | −1.9 | Alabama | 81.9 | 52.1 | −29.8 |
| Hawaii | 57.1 | 83.8 | 26.7 | Utah | 91.2 | 49.0 | −42.2 |
| Wisconsin | 99.1 | 83.7 | −15.4 | Massachusetts | 98.1 | 47.8 | −50.3 |
| North Dakota | 87.1 | 80.9 | −6.2 | Kentucky | 77.2 | 38.2 | −39.0 |
| Virginia | 91.0 | 80.9 | −10.1 | Arkansas | 93.8 | 37.7 | −56.1 |
| Oregon | 98.4 | 77.6 | −20.8 | Nevada | 68.3 | 37.5 | −30.8 |
| Arizona | 96.8 | 77.4 | −19.4 | New York | 87.2 | 36.6 | −50.6 |
| Indiana | 99.6 | 76.7 | −22.9 | Missouri | 98.0 | 26.6 | −71.4 |

*Source:* U.S. Bureau of the Census. Census of Governments. Compendium of Government Finances series, 1962–2017.

*Table 4.6* Municipal Government Property Tax Revenue (PTR) as a Percentage of Total Tax Revenue (TTR) by State in 1962 and 2017 and Change over Time

| *State* | *1962* | *2017* | *Change* | *State* | *1962* | *2017* | *Change* |
|---|---|---|---|---|---|---|---|
| Maine | 98.7 | 98.2 | –.5 | Texas | 89.0 | 52.2 | –36.8 |
| New Hampshire | 98.7 | 97.8 | –.9 | Wyoming | 64.7 | 50.7 | –14.7 |
| Connecticut | 99.3 | 97.4 | –1.9 | Illinois | 61.0 | 50.6 | –10.4 |
| Rhode Island | 98.4 | 96.8 | –1.6 | Kansas | 88.0 | 47.2 | –40.8 |
| New Jersey | 86.5 | 94.5 | 8.0 | New York | 68.3 | 46.8 | –21.5 |
| Massachusetts | 98.5 | 93.6 | –4.9 | Delaware | 89.1 | 46.5 | –42.8 |
| Wisconsin | 96.7 | 91.7 | –5.0 | North Dakota | 87.2 | 44.9 | –42.3 |
| Montana | 93.0 | 87.5 | –5.5 | South Carolina | 76.9 | 43.6 | –33.3 |
| Idaho | 91.1 | 87.2 | –3.9 | California | 59.5 | 42.8 | –16.7 |
| Vermont | 97.4 | 85.2 | –12.2 | South Dakota | 95.4 | 41.3 | –54.1 |
| Indiana | 98.2 | 83.9 | –14.3 | Utah | 60.3 | 40.8 | –22.2 |
| Mississippi | 58.5 | 82.1 | 23.6 | Nebraska | 82.2 | 38.9 | –43.3 |
| Minnesota | 92.0 | 79.8 | –12.2 | Louisiana | 56.3 | 32.7 | –23.6 |
| Iowa | 94.4 | 76.8 | –17.6 | Washington | 61.3 | 31.6 | –29.7 |
| Michigan | 97.2 | 72.5 | –24.7 | West Virginia | 47.7 | 28.8 | –18.9 |
| Alaska | 66.7 | 69.3 | 2.6 | Pennsylvania | 57.3 | 27.8 | –29.5 |
| Hawaii | 69.1 | 67.1 | –2.0 | Kentucky | 50.1 | 24.1 | –26.0 |
| Virginia | 68.6 | 65.4 | –3.2 | New Mexico | 41.1 | 23.1 | –18.0 |
| Oregon | 83.0 | 64.7 | –18.3 | Colorado | 65.5 | 22.4 | –43.1 |
| Tennessee | 76.1 | 64.4 | –11.7 | Arizona | 61.3 | 21.3 | –40.0 |
| Maryland | 89.4 | 62.6 | –26.8 | Arkansas | 58.3 | 19.0 | –39.3 |
| North Carolina | 93.3 | 60.1 | –33.2 | Missouri | 48.9 | 17.6 | –31.3 |
| Nevada | 53.3 | 57.5 | 1.8 | Ohio | 47.6 | 14.9 | –32.7 |
| Georgia | 67.6 | 55.7 | –11.9 | Alabama | 29.5 | 14.7 | –14.8 |
| Florida | 55.8 | 54.9 | –.9 | Oklahoma | 78.1 | 11.0 | –67.1 |

*Source:* U.S. Bureau of the Census. Census of Governments. Compendium of Government Finances series, 1962–2017.

(Oklahoma, Ohio, and Utah). The decline in three additional states (Massachusetts, Arkansas, and New York) exceeded 50 percent. And, in Missouri, it fell by an astounding 71 percent. In addition, Table 4.5 shows that by 2017, the property tax was accounting for less than one-half of all tax revenue for county governments in seven states (Utah, Massachusetts, Kentucky, Arkansas, Nevada, New York, and Missouri) (see the box at bottom of second column of table). It is reasonable to speculate that the property tax revolt that occurred in Massachusetts in the 1980s may be largely responsible for the substantial decline in the property tax component of total taxes among counties in that state.

Table 4.5 also plainly indicates that there are 21 states (New Hampshire, Maine, New Jersey, Montana, Pennsylvania, Minnesota, Michigan, Idaho, Mississippi, Texas, South Dakota, Alaska, Vermont, Iowa, West Virginia, California, Nebraska, Hawaii, Wisconsin, North Dakota, and Virginia) where county governments still derive over 80 percent of their TTR from property tax proceeds. In 2017, as they did in 1962, counties in Vermont collected 100 percent of their tax revenue from the property tax, while counties in New Hampshire, Maine,

New Jersey, Montana, and Pennsylvania were not far behind. Contrary to the national trend, the property tax proportion of TTR increased in counties in five states (Montana, Mississippi, South Dakota, Texas, and Hawaii) between 1962 and 2017. The fact that counties in California continue to collect close to 90 percent of their TTR from the property tax is a bit surprising since the property tax revolt initially gained momentum in that state in the late 1970s.

A significant reduction in the property tax proportion of total tax receipts is also evident for municipal governments between 1962 and 2017 (see Table 4.6). Indeed, this occurred in municipalities in 46 of 50 states. In six states (North Carolina, Texas, South Carolina, Arkansas, Missouri, and Ohio), the drop-off exceeded 30 percentage points or more, while it surpassed 40 percentage points in six additional states (Kansas, Delaware, North Dakota, Nebraska, Colorado, and Arizona). In two other states—South Dakota and Oklahoma—the decline reached as high as 54 and 67 percentage points, respectively. Moreover, Table 4.6 reveals that, as of 2017, property tax collections accounted for less than one-fourth of TTR in nine states (Kentucky, New Mexico, Colorado, Arizona, Arkansas, Missouri, Ohio, Alabama, and Oklahoma).

In spite of the overall trend among most municipal governments whereby the property tax is constituting a smaller proportion of total tax collections, there were a number of states in 2017 that still relied on it to supply the bulk of their TTR. More specifically, there were 14 states (Maine, New Hampshire, Connecticut, Rhode Island, New Jersey, Massachusetts, Wisconsin, Montana, Idaho, Vermont, Indiana, Mississippi, Minnesota, and Iowa) that depended on the property tax to generate at least three-fourths of their TTR. Most of these municipalities are located in Midwest states (Wisconsin, Indiana, Minnesota, and Iowa) and in New England. Municipalities in four of six New England states (Maine, New Hampshire, Connecticut, and Rhode Island) were especially dependent on the property tax, as it makes up at least 95 percent of total tax proceeds. In the other two New England states (Massachusetts and Vermont), the property tax accounted for 94 and 85 percent, respectively, of total tax monies. Municipal governments in one Mid-Atlantic state (New Jersey) and in two Rocky Mountain States (Idaho and Montana) continue to place great emphasis on the property tax. One final state (Mississippi) noticeably increased its reliance on the property tax as a proportion of its total tax collections between 1962 and 2017, as the property tax percentage increased from 59 to 82.

### *The property tax and sub-county local governments: Townships*

In 20 northeastern and Midwestern states, subdivisions of the county governments known as townships usually provide some of the same services that are provided by counties or municipalities. Simply stated, townships are really *subdivisions of counties* since counties are, technically speaking, subdivisions of their state governments. Townships were established by these states for the explicit purpose of making them into "assistants" to county governments. That is, townships were intended to "assist" county governments in the performance of some of their duties (including by not limited to the delivery of a number of services) at the grassroots level in a geographical area smaller than the county itself.

Townships can be placed in one of two categories—those serving basically rural areas and those serving more urbanized places. Townships operating in rural settings typically offer a more limited set of services, while those located in more urbanized areas are more likely to provide a wider menu of services. For instance, in states like Illinois, Indiana, Kansas, Minnesota, Missouri, Nebraska, North Dakota, Ohio, and South Dakota, the character of township government is more rural and their service offerings are often limited to roads and law enforcement (Bowman and Kearney 2008, 278). However, townships in New England and those in New Jersey and Pennsylvania (and to some degree in Michigan, New York, and Wisconsin) usually are found in more urbanized settings and may perform many of the same functions as do county governments (e.g., election administration, road repair, snow removal, tax administration, fire protection, operate libraries, water supply, service collection, and even law enforcement through police departments and local justices of the peace), as well as act in many ways like general-purpose units of local government (Bowman and Kearney 2008, 278).

The decentralized approach to governance and service delivery that characterizes the function and purpose of townships is believed to foster more local control over services and thereby ensure a greater degree of political accountability and encourage greater responsiveness to citizenry service provision needs. While most townships are unincorporated and therefore have not been granted charters from the state governments, a growing number of states do grant townships a charter under certain conditions, thus giving them a degree of independence and the ability to provide many municipal-type services (Dye and MacManus 205, 230—291, 17). Therefore, given the service role of townships—as limited as it might be—it nonetheless means that, like counties and municipalities, township governments are also in need of a plentiful and stable source of revenue to provide a number of vital services to their roughly 55 million constituents or about one-fifth of the U.S. population.

As has always been the case for counties and municipalities, revenue generated by some type of taxation continues to be the primary producer of revenue for townships. According to Table 4.7, townships have a long history of reliance on taxes to pay for the services they provide. In 1962, taxes produced 90 percent of OSR for American township governments. Over the next 55 years, that proportion dropped somewhat to 83 percent. Nevertheless, townships still receive over $8 out of $10 they require to deliver basic services to their citizens from some form of taxation.

If the property tax is an indispensable source of revenue for both county and municipal governments, it is even more so the case for townships. This

*Table 4.7* Total Tax Revenue (TTR) as a Proportion of Own-Source Revenue (OSR) for Townships, 1962–2017

| | *1962* | *1967* | *1972* | *1977* | *1982* | *1987* | *1992* | *1997* | *2002* | *2007* | *2012* | *2017* |
|---|---|---|---|---|---|---|---|---|---|---|---|---|
| Total Tax Revenue (TTR) as % of Own-Source Revenue (OSR) | 90 | 88 | 89 | 88 | 80 | 80 | 79 | 79 | 79 | 79 | 82 | 83 |

*Source:* U.S. Bureau of the Census. Census of Governments. Compendium of Government Finances series, 1962–2017.

can be clearly seen from data found in Figure 4.3. In 1962, PTR accounted for 93 percent of township TR. By 2017, little had changed, as this percentage had declined ever so little to 92 percent. Other data presented in Figure 4.3 tell as a similar story for property tax proceeds as a percentage of township OSR. Specifically, in 1962, revenue received from property taxes comprised over 84 percent of all OSR of township governments. By 2017, the property tax

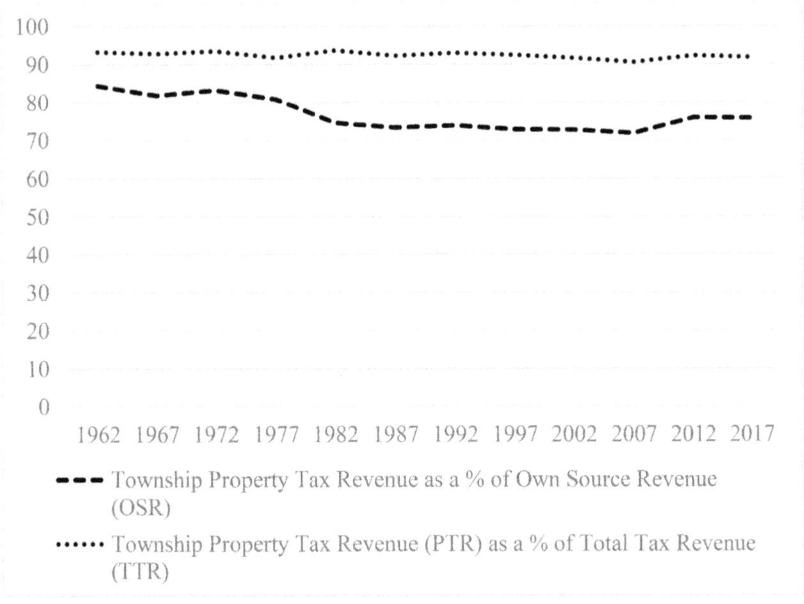


*Figure 4.3* Township Property Tax Revenue (PTR) as a Percent of Own-Source Revenue (OSR) and Total Tax Revenue (TTR), 1962–2017

*Source:* U.S. Bureau of the Census. Census of Governments. Compendium of Government Finances series, 1962–2017.

proportion of OSR had dropped somewhat to 76 percent. Nevertheless, as will be seen later in this chapter, only school districts have a greater dependence on property taxes when measured as a proportion of OSR.

The heavy reliance that township governments place on the property tax can be explained by the same factors that also make the property tax a crucial source of revenue for counties. Like counties, townships are subject to being assigned some of the same functions that are traditional arms-of-the-state ones that county governments are expected to perform (e.g., health-, welfare-, and law enforcement/court-related). It is not unusual for these services to be mandated. In spite of the fact that the state may provide some financial assistance to provide these services, they nonetheless can place a strain on the budgets of townships. As a result, most states with townships provide more latitude to them. It is like states believe that they are obliged to assist township governments that are serving as extensions of the state government and thereby help the state and the county government to provide these services efficiently and evenly across the states' counties.

A second factor that makes it understandable for townships to rely on the property tax has to do with the nature of the services that township governments deliver. Again, similar to county governments, townships provide a number of services that are not amenable to providing on the basis of assessing a charge to the user. While there are some kinds of services for which a fee is charged, they are usually ones that are state-imposed (e.g., issuing fishing, hunting, boating, and marriage licenses, birth and death certificates, occupational certifications, and various permits, conducting building, health, fire, and safety inspections, recording of deeds, titles, and final judgments in judicial matters, and imposing and collecting civil fines). Then, there are other expenditures that townships must make for responsibilities assigned to them by the state or county for which there is very little or no remuneration from either of these two governments (providing jails to temporarily detain arrestees, assessing property for purposes of taxation, providing facilities for courts and court personnel, surveyor, and constable, providing services to senior and disabled citizens, youth, and maintaining cemeteries, and registering voters). It is also not often possible for township governments to collect revenue for the provision of various types of utilities (e.g., water, sewer, natural gas, electric power) unless the township has a sizable number of people residing within their boundaries.

In addition, many of those services that townships provide, like those of counties, are services that are classified as indivisible type services (i.e., ones for which there are no clearly identifiable recipients or users). Nonetheless, these services are staple services that citizens at the local level believe are important to their quality of life and safety, as well as critical to promoting and maintaining the economic prosperity of the community. Some pertinent examples include things such as environmental protection/conservation, law enforcement and court system-related duties, solid waste management, parks and recreational facilities, planning and zoning, K-12 schools, community colleges, and vocational and technical schools, community development/redevelopment programs, mass transit, 911-call centers, libraries, snow removal, street lighting, and construction and repair of roads, streets, and sidewalks.

Although it was mentioned above that the dependency of township governments on the property tax as a major component of OSR had declined over time, it is also significant to note that the decline was not nearly as great as it was for counties and municipalities (8 percentage points for townships versus 32 for counties and 24 percentage points for municipalities). This discrepancy is most likely explained by the simple fact that townships are provided much less leeway in revenue sources, generally, and in taxes, specifically, than are municipalities and even counties. This means that township governments must, of necessity, rely on the property tax to generate a greater proportion of their monetary sources than general-purpose governments, even though they provide many of the same kinds of services that county governments do.

One last glance at Figure 4.3 clearly indicates a clear pattern of constant and consistent reliance on the property tax by township governments over the last 55 years. In 1962, 93 percent of TTR was derived from the property tax (PTR). By 2017, little had changed, as PTR still accounted for 92 percent of TTR.

Since some township governments have been granted authority by their states to provide a longer list of services than is the case in other states, it is important to see if the patterns reported above are different when townships are divided into two groups by degree of service responsibility. These data are be found in Table 4.8. Initially, it can be seen from the figures in the first row of the table that township governments with more service responsibilities are less dependent on tax revenue generally than is true for townships with fewer

*Table 4.8* Total Tax Revenue (TTR) as a Proportion of Own-Source Revenue (OSR) and Property Tax Revenue (PTR) as a Proportion of Own-Source Revenue (OSR) and Total Tax Revenue (TTR) by Scope of Service Responsibility of Township, 1962 and 2017

| | *Less Service Responsibility* | | *More Service Responsibility* | |
|---|---|---|---|---|
| | *1962* | *2017* | *1962* | *2017* |
| Total Tax Revenue (TTR) as % of Own-Source Revenue (OSR) | 93 | 86 | 84 | 74 |
| Property Tax Revenue (PTR) as % of Own-Source Revenue (OSR) | 88 | 82 | 79 | 67 |
| Property Tax Revenue (PTR) as % of Total Tax Revenue (TTR) | 95 | 95 | 93 | 91 |

*Source:* U.S. Bureau of the Census. Census of Governments. Compendium of Government Finances series, 1962–2017.

service responsibilities. This was the case in both 1962 and 2017. It can also be seen from the numbers in the second row of the table that townships which offer more services show less reliance on the property tax specifically to provide a larger proportion of their OSR. Moreover, it is important to note that there is a noticeable pattern among both types of townships whereby there is a declining dependency on the property tax, specifically, and taxes, generally, as a source for OSR. A final observation from the data found in the last row of the table reminds us that one thing has changed very little over time—PTR is still a huge component of all tax collections for both types of townships and the difference between the two types is small.

These data, in addition to demonstrating that township governments with greater service responsibilities depend less on PTR than do townships with fewer service offerings to supply a smaller proportion of OSR, also suggest that this former type of townships may derive a larger proportion of their OSR revenue from the kinds of sources typically utilized by municipalities. That is, townships with greater service responsibilities are more likely to provide a number of municipal- and urban-type services (water, electric power, and gas supply, sewage solid waste collection, parking facilities, and sports arenas) that are amenable to charges for services or user fees. That would be a reasonable scenario since many of the townships that provide a larger array of services tend to be more urban in character and therefore would be expected to deliver more services that are common for a municipality or even a densely populated, highly urban county.

### *School districts and property tax revenue*

School districts, like special districts, are a distinctly different type of local government entities that were established by their states. Unlike counties and municipalities (and even townships) that can provide a long list of local services, school districts provide only one kind of service—education. That is why school districts are sometimes referred to as "special" kinds of special districts. Nevertheless, not all states have created "specialty" units of government to provide for K-12 educational instruction. In fact, four states (Maryland, North Carolina, Tennessee, and Virginia) have opted to entrust the provision of education services to their county governments, while some states have permitted some of their large cities (e.g., New York City, Philadelphia, Detroit, and Chicago) to establish and operate their own schools. In Hawaii, however, neither school districts nor counties nor municipalities are responsible for education services but rather the state government is in charge of a centralized educational system.

Regardless of what governmental entity has been assigned the responsibility for K-12 educational instruction, revenue from some form of taxation has always been a very important source of funding.[10] As can been seen from Table 4.9, school districts have a long history of reliance on tax revenue to fund the operations of their schools. In 1962, taxes of some kind generated 87 percent of OSR

*Table 4.9* Total Tax Revenue (TTR) as a Proportion of Own-Source Revenue (OSR) for School Districts, 1962–2017

| | *1962* | *1967* | *1972* | *1977* | *1982* | *1987* | *1992* | *1997* | *2002* | *2007* | *2012* | *2017* |
|---|---|---|---|---|---|---|---|---|---|---|---|---|
| Total Tax Revenue (TTR) as % of Own-Source Revenue (OSR) | 87 | 86 | 88 | 87 | 81 | 84 | 84 | 83 | 83 | 81 | 85 | 86 |

*Source:* U.S. Bureau of the Census. Census of Governments. Compendium of Government Finances series, 1962–2017.

for America's school districts, and this pattern remained steady through the 1977 time point. By 1982, however, the proportion of OSR made up of taxes (TTR) had dropped conspicuously to 81 percent. Two events quite likely are responsible for this decline—a nationwide tax revolt that was gaining momentum in the mid- to late 1970s and the onset of a recession in the early 1980s. After 1982, the taxes component of OSR rebounded somewhat until it dipped slightly to 81 percent in 2007 and was likely caused by the economic slide known as the Great Recession. With the brunt of the Great Recession becoming more of a memory rather than a reality by 2012, notice that the amount of OSR attributable to TTR had begun the tick upward once again and continued on this path through 2017. The question now becomes one of whether the proportion of OSR attributable to TTR stayed the same or declined again during the COVID-19-driven recession. At this point, we can only speculate until the 2022 Census of Government data becomes available, but some anecdotal information indicates that the TTR proportion may have dropped.

Further analysis of school district revenue sources indicates that money derived from taxes levied on property has always been a significant part of paying for the cost of education. This is a similar pattern that was also observed for county governments and townships (but to a somewhat lesser extent for municipal governments) in efforts to finance the cost of basic services to residents of their jurisdictions. In fact, school districts' dependency on the property tax is much greater than that of all other types of local governments. From Figure 4.4, it can be seen that the proportion of OSR and TR attributable to property tax collections (PT) stood at around 86 and 51 percent, respectively, in 1962 but began to taper off visibly after 1972 and became more pronounced after 1977 but leveled off to 78 percent for OSR and to 36 percent for TR by 2007. This trend is comparable to what was observed above for the proportion of OSR composed of revenue coming from tax proceeds and can be plausibly explained, in part, by growing support nationwide for the tax revolt movement throughout the 1970s as well as the start of a recession in the early 1980s. However, a more compelling explanation

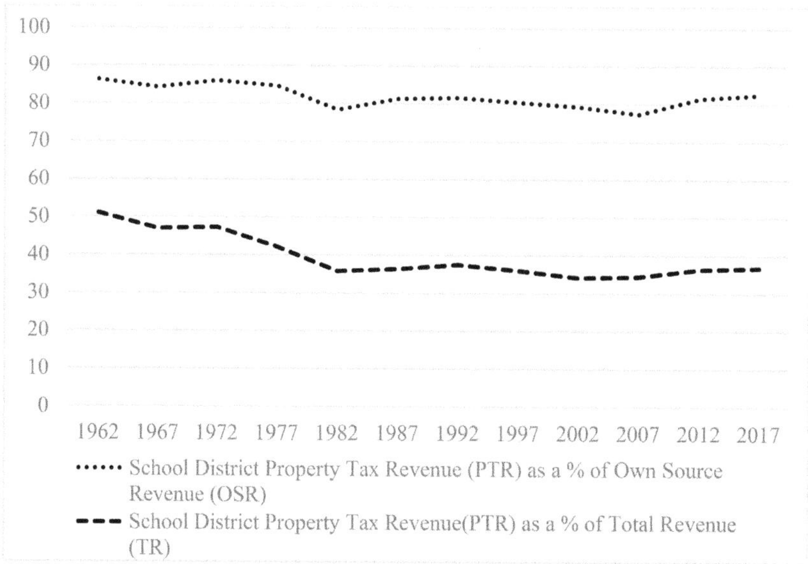


*Figure 4.4* School District Property Tax Revenue (PTR) as a Percent of Total Revenue (TR) and Own-Source Revenue (OSR), 1962–2017

*Source:* U.S. Bureau of the Census. Census of Governments. Compendium of Government Finances series, 1962–2017.

for the reduction in the property tax proportion of school district OSR and TR may be the public's increasing concern about inequity issues that are often found in public education. Simply stated, it can be argued that continued local school district reliance on property taxes as a primary means to fund schools combined with inequalities in property values among communities all but ensures that fiscal disparities among school districts will exist. Consequently, beginning in the early 1970s, a large number of school districts across the country and parents of school-aged children sued their respective state governments, arguing that this practice discriminates unfairly against poorer communities (e.g., see *Serrano* v. *Priest*, 1971). We will explore the plausibility of this latter explanation in more detail in Chapters 5–8.

These trends for PT proportions of OSR and TR between 1977 and 2007 notwithstanding, it is important to re-emphasize that these proportions were trending upward again after 2007 and continued through 2017 (latest data available). At this time, it is not clear whether these trends will continue into the future or if they are a temporary aberration from a roughly 45-year pattern of reduced reliance on PTR to fund local school districts. If the latter, it could be understood in the context of the local governments continuing to grapple with the lingering fiscal uncertainty created by the Great Recession. With this caveat in mind, it is still important that we examine in more detail the 45-year decline (or increase) in the reliance on PTR on a state-by-state basis that occurred between 1962 and 2007.

Since the percentages reported in Figure 4.4 are averages for all U.S. school districts, is it possible that they could hide significant differences existing in individual states? If so, it is important that this analysis be expanded to examine the property tax proportion of OSR and TR in individual states with school districts to determine if they exhibit patterns that differ from the national average. These data are located in Tables 4.10 and 4.11,[11] respectively, for OSR and TR.

Given that the proportion of OSR attributable to property tax receipts had dropped, on average, around 9 percentage points over the 1962–2017 period, it is not surprising to discover that this was the case in 28 out of 45 states that have independent school districts (see Table 4.10). In nine states (California, Indiana, Missouri, Kansas, Arkansas, Louisiana, Iowa, Minnesota, and Montana), the decline was much higher than the mean decrease in other states and ranged from 10 to 32 percentage points, while the decline was drastically higher in Alaska (86), Vermont (87), and Connecticut (91). Moreover, Massachusetts reported

*Table 4.10* School District Property Tax Revenue (PTR) as a Percentage of Own-Source Revenue (OSR) by State in 1962 and 2017 and Change over Time

| *State* | *1962* | *2017* | *Change* | *State* | *1962* | *2017* | *Change* |
|---|---|---|---|---|---|---|---|
| Rhode Island | 100.0 | 92.7 | −7.3 | Pennsylvania | 72.2 | 77.6 | 5.4 |
| New Hampshire | 94.6 | 96.1 | 1.5 | Florida | 72.8 | 76.5 | 3.7 |
| Maine | 87.2 | 95.6 | 8.4 | Montana | 91.6 | 79.8 | −11.8 |
| New Jersey | 93.6 | 95.5 | 1.9 | Missouri | 88/3 | 68.2 | −20/1 |
| New York | 89.7 | 92.4 | 2.7 | Indiana | 89.9 | 74.2 | −15.7 |
| West Virginia | 86.2 | 93.3 | 7.1 | Kansas | 85.6 | 61.5 | −24.1 |
| Wisconsin | 90.7 | 82.5 | −4.3 | New Mexico | 77.9 | 76.0 | −1.9 |
| Illinois | 91.8 | 90.6 | −1.2 | California | 91.1 | 80.2 | −10.9 |
| Texas | 80.2 | 89.7 | 9.5 | Oregon | 89.9 | 78.6 | −11.3 |
| Delaware | 78.6 | 82.4 | 3.8 | Idaho | 86.4 | 81.3 | −5.1 |
| North Dakota | 87.3 | 78.6 | −8.7 | Kentucky | 78.1 | 75.2 | −2.9 |
| Utah | 86.1 | 82.8 | −3.3 | Georgia | 71.7 | 67.5 | −4.2 |
| Nevada | 44.0 | 93.2 | 49.2 | Mississippi | 72.0 | 76.4 | 4.4 |
| Ohio | 90.7 | 81.3 | −9.4 | Iowa | 89.0 | 72.7 | −16.3 |
| South Carolina | 68.8 | 81.1 | 12.3 | Minnesota | 89.4 | 70.4 | −19.0 |
| Wyoming | 89.3 | 80.3 | −9.0 | Alabama | 52.6 | 66.1 | 13.5 |
| South Dakota | 78.8 | 81.8 | 3.0 | Arkansas | 81.6 | 61.5 | −20.1 |
| Colorado | 88.6 | 82.5 | −6.1 | Louisiana | 75.6 | 43.3 | −32.3 |
| Nebraska | 86.0 | 82.2 | −3.8 | Vermont | 91.7 | 4.8 | −86.9 |
| Arizona | 86.7 | 83.9 | −2.8 | Alaska | 85.7 | 0.0 | −85.7 |
| Washington | 79.7 | 85.3 | 5.8 | Connecticut | 91.3 | 0.0 | −91.3 |
| Oklahoma | 79.3 | 85.1 | 5.8 | Massachusetts | 0.0 | 0.0 | 0.0 |
| Michigan | 86.6 | 79.5 | −7.1 | | | | |

*Source:* U.S. Bureau of the Census. Census of Governments. Compendium of Government Finances series, 1962–2017.

*Table 4.11* School District Property Tax Revenue (PTR) as a Percentage of Total Revenue (TR) by State in 1962 and 2017 and Change over Time

| *State* | *1962* | *2017* | *Change* | *State* | *1962* | *2017* | *Change* |
|---|---|---|---|---|---|---|---|
| New Jersey | 75.8 | 65.0 | −10.8 | Iowa | 68.2 | 30.1 | −38.1 |
| Rhode Island | 42.9 | 62.3 | 19.4 | West Virginia | 41.2 | 39.7 | −1.5 |
| New Hampshire | 84.4 | 62.7 | −21.7 | Kansas | 53.4 | 18.6 | −34.8 |
| Illinois | 73.2 | 55.2 | −18.0 | Oregon | 56.9 | 31.8 | −25.1 |
| New York | 46.4 | 50.3 | 3.9 | Wyoming | 47.7 | 22.9 | −24.8 |
| Texas | 41.7 | 50.8 | 9.1 | Oklahoma | 41.6 | 33.8 | −7.8 |
| Nebraska | 78.6 | 48.7 | −29.9 | Kentucky | 35.3 | 30.0 | −5.3 |
| Maine | 47.9 | 52.5 | 4.6 | Delaware | 18.6 | 28.5 | 9.5 |
| Pennsylvania | 43.7 | 42.4 | −1.3 | Washington | 28.3 | 25.8 | −2.5 |
| South Dakota | 61.0 | 44.2 | −16.8 | Montana | 44.8 | 25.7 | −19.1 |
| Wisconsin | 61.8 | 32.7 | −29.1 | California | 53.7 | 27.0 | −26.7 |
| North Dakota | 41.2 | 33.7 | −7.5 | Mississippi | 27.7 | 25.6 | −2.1 |
| Ohio | 88.0 | 42.3 | −45.7 | Idaho | 46.7 | 20.4 | −26.3 |
| Colorado | 54.2 | 41.6 | −12.6 | Alabama | 15.6 | 15.5 | −.1 |
| Florida | 38.6 | 37.1 | −1.5 | Minnesota | 51.8 | 19.5 | −32.3 |
| Missouri | 54.2 | 37.0 | −17.2 | Louisiana | 19.6 | 19.6 | 0.0 |
| South Carolina | 26.4 | 34.0 | 7.6 | New Mexico | 19.0 | 8.2 | −10.8 |
| Arizona | 48.4 | 41.1 | −7.3 | Arkansas | 44.3 | 8.2 | −36.1 |
| Indiana | 61.6 | 22.3 | −39.3 | Vermont | 54.2 | 1.2 | −53.0 |
| Georgia | 25.1 | 29.5 | 4.4 | Alaska | 0.0 | 0.0 | 0.0 |
| Utah | 43.3 | 33.0 | −13.3 | Connecticut | 0.0 | 0.0 | 0.0 |
| Nevada | 26.1 | 25.7 | .4 | Massachusetts | 0.0 | 0.0 | 0.0 |
| Michigan | 55.3 | 28.7 | −26.6 | | | | |

*Note:* State—this is where state where the drop-off in property tax revenue exceeded at least 20 percent, with seven of these states showing a decline of 30 percent or greater.

*Source:* U.S. Bureau of the Census. Census of Governments. Compendium of Government Finances series, 1962–2017.

that school districts received no funds from property taxes for the years 1962 through 2017.

Contrary to the pattern that was observed for a majority of the states in Table 4.10, there were 16 states that experienced an *increase* in the proportion of OSR derived from property tax proceeds between 1962 and 2017. In two of these states (South Carolina and Alabama), the growth was quite evident (12 and 14 percent, respectively), while a much greater increase was obvious for Nevada (49 percent). In the other 13 states (New Hampshire, Maine, New Jersey, New York, West Virginia, Texas, Delaware, South Dakota, Washington, Oklahoma, Pennsylvania, Florida, and Mississippi), the increase was much smaller and well under 10 percent for the most part.

Analogous patterns were also detected when examining individual state data with respect to the proportion of TR that was attributable to PTR (see Table 4.11). As PTR as a proportion of TR had decreased, on average, by 16 percent over the 1962–2007 period, it is predictable that most school districts would exhibit this

*Table 4.12* Property Tax Revenue (PTR) as a Proportion of Total Tax (TTR) for School Districts, 1962–2017

| | *1962* | *1967* | *1972* | *1977* | *1982* | *1987* | *1992* | *1997* | *2002* | *2007* | *2012* | *2017* |
|---|---|---|---|---|---|---|---|---|---|---|---|---|
| Property Tax Revenue as % of Total Tax Revenue | 99 | 98 | 98 | 97 | 97 | 97 | 97 | 97 | 96 | 96 | 96 | 96 |

*Source:* U.S. Bureau of the Census. Census of Governments. Compendium of Government Finances series, 1962–2017.

pattern. In fact, this was the case in 33 of 42 states. In 15 states (New Hampshire, Nebraska, Wisconsin, Ohio, Indiana, Michigan, Iowa, Kansas, Oregon, Wyoming, California, Idaho, Minnesota, Arkansas, and Vermont), the drop-off exceeded 20 percent, with eight of these states showing a decline of 30 percent or greater (Nebraska, Ohio, Indiana, Iowa, Kansas, Minnesota, Arkansas and Vermont). This may indicate that these states were responding to legal challenges to school funding formulas that placed a heavy reliance on property taxes. As discussed above, greater dependence on the property tax has been linked to substantially unequal resources available to school districts and subsequently resulting in a lower-quality education for students residing in districts with lower-valued property. It also may be the case, that in all 33 states experiencing a decline in the PTR proportion of TR (but especially the 23 specific states named above), the state has increased its financial assistance to school districts so that they depend less on PTRs and thus bring about more equity among districts in per student funding (most likely explanation). Another possibility is that school districts have been increasingly raising more money from charges for services or even being permitted by their states to raise money from other types of taxes (e.g., sales and income). All of these possibilities will be explored in Chapters 5–7.

All of this suggests that a lot has changed over the last 55 years with respect to how school districts fund K-12 education in the United States. Nevertheless, there is one thing that has remained constant over this same time period—a persistent and steady reliance of school districts on the property tax as the predominant component of total tax collections (TTR) (see Table 4.12). In 1962, school districts received almost all of their TTR (99 percent) from the property tax. By 2017, not much had changed, as school districts were still depending on the property tax to provide nearly 96 percent of TTR. In fact, school districts' reliance on the property tax for the greatest part of their TTR surpasses that of the other four types of local governments.

### *The property tax and special service districts*

Like school districts, special service districts are clearly different kinds of "political animals" when compared to full-service local governments (i.e., counties and municipalities), and townships (limited-service local governments). First, special districts are limited in the scope of their operations since they typically are established for the purpose of providing only one specific service (a good example is fire protection) and occasionally two closely linked services like water and sewer. Simply put, they fill in the service gaps left by full-service local governments[12] and do not deal with general policy or governance matters. Furthermore, those people who oversee special districts (usually referred to as "board members" or "commissioners") are not necessarily chosen in a way that is reflective of democratic expectations or makes them easily accountable to the public they serve. For instance, while some may be elected by those people they serve (in reality, customers), others may be appointed by city, county, and state officials. In addition, it is not unusual for special districts to operate under greater restrictions than do full-service local governments. For instance, they may not be able to tax at the same level (usually, lower millage rates) or may have less latitude in borrowing money (i.e., lower debt ceilings) for capital improvements.

Another important way in which special districts are distinctively different from full-service local governments is in the approach they take in performing their responsibilities. Since they were created to deliver a service (or a very small number of them), special districts often operate much like private sector entities by adopting business-like practices or entrepreneurial characteristics in providing services to their constituents or customers. That is, they must initially determine the amount of money necessary to construct necessary infrastructure and purchase equipment to get the specific service "up and running" and then calculate reasonable operational costs to deliver the service. In the case of water supply, a special district estimates the cost of installing wells to pump water from the nearest underground aquifer or locating another adequate supply of water (e.g., river or stream) and then construct a filtration plant to treat the water per health code requirements for distribution to residential and business users. Relatedly, reasonable operational and distribution costs for these facilities must be determined and customers billed. Another example would be the provision of fire protection services where the special district must build one or more fire stations and purchase firefighting apparatus and subsequently estimate operating costs of the department (firefighter salaries and fringe benefits, as well as upkeep and maintenance of the stations and fire trucks).

Special service districts like the examples mentioned above oftentimes rely on revenue generated from taxing home owners and business to pay for "up and running" costs and even the expense of expanding or repairing infrastructure facilities in the years after their creation. One possible exception, however, could be fire protection service whereby special districts may elect to levy a property tax on homes and commercial establishments to pay for not only infrastructure costs but also operating costs in lieu of relying on the cumbersome process of billing users of fire services. Nevertheless, money derived from some form of

*Table 4.13* Total Tax Revenue (TTR) as a Proportion of Own-Source Revenue (OSR) and Total Revenue (TR) for Special Districts, 1962–2017

| | *1962* | *1967* | *1972* | *1977* | *1982* | *1987* | *1992* | *1997* | *2002* | *2007* | *2012* | *2017* |
|---|---|---|---|---|---|---|---|---|---|---|---|---|
| Total Tax Revenue as a % of OSR | 32 | 28 | 27 | 25 | 25 | 21 | 23 | 23 | 24 | 25 | 27 | 27 |
| Total Tax Revenue as a % of TR | 17 | 16 | 14 | 12 | 9 | 11 | 12 | 12 | 12 | 13 | 14 | 14 |

*Source:* U.S. Bureau of the Census. Census of Governments. Compendium of Government Finances series, 1962–2017.

taxation, as is evident from Table 4.13, accounts for only a small fraction of the total amount of money needed for special districts to sustain themselves. Since 1962, tax-derived revenue (TTR), at best, has accounted for not more than about a fourth of OSR (and even much less during the 1980s and 1990s) and around 12–14 percent of TR in recent years. A state-by-state analysis (data not shown here) indicates that there is very little variation in this pattern.

A similar picture emerges when examining the proportion of TR and OSR attributable to PTR in Table 4.14. In fact, the percentages, as would be expected, are even lower than they were for TTR as a proportion of TR and OSR. Between 1962 and 2017, the PTR part of OSR dropped from 32 to 27 percent, while PTR as a proportion of TR declined from 17 to 9 percent. Indeed, special districts have by far the lowest dependency on the property of any of the other four types of local governments. Furthermore, the property tax is becoming a steadily shrinking source of funding for special service districts—a trend that is likely to continue into the future. Again, when these data are broken down by individual states (data not shown here), there is no discernible variation in this pattern.

*Table 4.14* Total Tax Revenue (TTR) as a Proportion of Own-Source Revenue (OSR) and Total Revenue (TR) for Special Districts, 1962–2017

| | *1962* | *1967* | *1972* | *1977* | *1982* | *1987* | *1992* | *1997* | *2002* | *2007* | *2012* | *2017* |
|---|---|---|---|---|---|---|---|---|---|---|---|---|
| Total Tax Revenue as a % of OSR | 32 | 28 | 27 | 25 | 25 | 21 | 23 | 23 | 24 | 25 | 27 | 27 |
| Total Tax Revenue as a % of TR | 17 | 16 | 14 | 13 | 8 | 11 | 8 | 9 | 8 | 8 | 9 | 9 |

*Source:* U.S. Bureau of the Census. Census of Governments. Compendium of Government Finances series, 1962–2017.

One final observation about the PTR and special districts is that the tax is also becoming a smaller part of the total amount of funds that these governmental entities derive from some form of taxation. In 1962, the PTR accounted for all of the revenues collected from some form of taxation. By 2017, a little less than two-thirds of total tax collections (63 percent) came from property tax proceeds.

## Summary thoughts and looking ahead

From the founding of the United States until the present time, the property tax has been a major and heavily relied upon source of revenue for four of five types of local government—the exception being special service districts (also sometimes referred to legislative authorities). This is abundantly clear from the analysis conducted in this chapter that covers the 1962–2017 period. Nevertheless, it is also evident from our analysis that the property tax proportion of both TR and OSR has been declining over time. This trend has been especially pronounced for county and municipal governments. Like what was seen for counties and municipalities, PTR as a proportion of TR declined (but not as sharply) over time as well for school districts; yet, the percentage of OSR composed of property tax proceeds dropped only slightly. The least amount of change among these four types of local governments was for townships. While there was a drop-off in the proportion of TR and OSR that was comprised by property tax collections, the decline was modest at best. Then, there was one common trend across all five types of local governments—money derived from the property tax was still the largest part of their TTR, accounting for well of 50 percent of it.

In the chapters ahead, we will identify and describe how other types of revenue sources (i.e., other kinds of taxes, an assortment of miscellaneous funding, charges for services, user fees, and intergovernmental fiscal assistance) have been accounting for a larger share of money that the property tax once provided for local governments.

## Notes

1 It should be noted, however, that until the early 1900s, most states routinely were entitled to a portion of property tax proceeds.
2 For a comprehensive treatment of this subject, see Fisher (1996).
3 For an in-depth historical account of the diffusion of this practice, see Hughes (1991).
4 All governments would like to levy "benefits" taxes—taxes paid by people who benefit directly from the government services the taxes finance. Local governments are consistently able to levy property taxes on the justification that the tax benefits they provide to their citizens. Expenditures by local governments on services like schools, police, fire protection, EMS roads, sidewalks, parks and recreational facilities, street lighting, and so forth raise local property values and generate property revenues.
5 See "The History of Taxation," assessed at http://www.taxworld.org/History/TaxHistory.htm

6 A state-by-state analysis was also conducted and did not reveal any noticeable effect on local government tax revenues as a proportion of total revenue (TR) or own-source revenue (OSR) that could be attributed to the recession accompanying the COVID-19 health pandemic.
7 The interested reader can view analogous data for the proportion of TR attributable to revenue generated by property taxes for the 1962–2017 interval in Table A4.1 located in the Appendix.
8 For an excellent review of the tax revolts in the 1970s and 1980–2003 and citizenry views on property taxes, see the following: Buchanan 1979; Ladd 1979; Lowery and Seligman 1981;Dye and Beck 1982; Hansen 1983; Mullin and Wallin 2004.
9 The best description of the "New Normal" has been given by Martin, Levey, and Cawley (2012). They assert that what a growing number of practitioners and scholars are referring to as a "New Normal" for local governments was precipitated by Great Recession on 2008–09 and represented a critical breakpoint for them with implications that were likely to persist long after any subsequent economy recovery. According to them, the aftermath for local governments was projected to consist of fewer resources, smaller workforces, and new ways of delivering services.
10 This could be due to the long held American belief that education was so highly valued and integral to an ordered and democratic society and that it should be made available to all citizens without charge or regardless of one's income or social class. In fact, it has often been said that the very logic of democracy led inevitably to K-12 public education. Another expectation was that that free public schools were to advance a long list of societal goals as well as serve as a catalyst for economic development. For these and other reasons, Americans have always believed that education should be funded by some mechanism that best taps into the wealth of the nation, state, or community, such as taxes.
11 Since no independent school districts exist in Hawaii, Maryland, North Carolina, Tennessee, and Virginia, the analysis referencing Tables 4.9 and 4.10 and Figure 4.4 does not include any Census of Government data for public schools located in these states.
12 There has been an increasing use of special districts as special purpose taxing districts to assist county governments and even cities to provide new services or a higher level of current services since both of the full-service governments are constrained by state constitutional and statutory limits of property tax rates and bonded indebtedness. A good example is in Illinois where they have been often utilized to assist municipalities in providing parks and business improvement.

## References

Beattie, Andrew. 2010. "A Short History of Taxation."

Bowman, Ann O'M, and Richard C. Kearney. 2008. *State and Local Government*. 7th ed. Boston: Houghton Mifflin Company.

Buchanan, James M. 1979. "The Potential for Taxpayers Revolt in American Democracy," *Social Science Quarterly*, 59(March): 691–696.

Cabral, Marika, and Caroline Hoxby. 2012. *The Hated Property Tax: Salience, Rates, and Tax Revolts (No. w18514)*. National Bureau of Economic Research. Assessed at: https://papers.ssrn.com/sol3/papers.cfm?abstract_id=2170637

Dye, Thomas R., and Susan A. MacManus. 2015. *Politics in States and Communities*. 15th ed. Upper Saddle River, NJ: Pearson Education, Inc.

Dye, Thomas R., and Paul Allen Beck. 1982. "Sources of Public Opinion on Taxes," *Journal of Politics*, 44(February): 172–82.
Ecker-Racz, L.L. 1970. *The Politics and Economics of State-Local Finance*. Englewood Cliffs, NJ: Prentice-Hall, Inc.
Fisher, Glenn W. 1996. *The Worst Tax? A History of the Property Tax in America*. Lawrence, KS: University of Kansas Press.
Hansen, Susan. 1983. *The Politics of Taxation*. New York: Praeger.
Harriss, C. Lowell. 1973. "Property Taxation: What's Good and What's Bad," *Challenge: The Magazine of Economic Affairs*, 16(September–October); 16–21.
Hobbes, Thomas. 1996. *Leviathan*. In Richard Tuck (ed.), New York: Cambridge University Press.
Hughes, Jonathan R.T. 1991. *The Governmental Habit Redux: Economic Controls from Colonial Times to the Present*. Princeton, NJ: Princeton University Press.
Ladd, Carl. 1979. "The Polls: Taxing and Spending," *Public Opinion Quarterly*, 43(Spring): 126–35.
Lowery, David, and Lee Seligman. 1981. "Understanding the Tax Revolt: Eight Explanations," *American Political Science Review*, 75(December): 963–74.
Martin, Lawrence L., Richard Levey, and Jenna Cawley. 2012. "The 'New Normal' for Local Government," *State and Local Government Review*, 44(December): 17S–28S.
Mullin, Daniel R., and Bruce A. Wallin. 2004. "Tax and Expenditure Limitations: Introduction and Overview," *Public Budgeting and Finance*, 34(Winter): 2–15.
Semuels, Alana. 2016. "The Feudal Origins of American's Most-Hated Tax," *The Atlantic*, August 24.
*San Antonio Independent School District v. Rodriguez*, 41 U.S. 1. 1973.
*Serrano v. Priest*, 5 Cal.3d 584. 1971.
Tyer, Charlie B. 1993. "The Property Tax. Why It Persists," *The South Carolina Policy Forum Magazine*, 4(Spring): 12–21.
Wallis, John Joseph. n.d.a. "Property Rights in Land."
———. n.d.b. "A History of the Property Tax in America."

## Appendix

*Table A4.1* Total Tax Revenue (TTR) as a Proportion of Own-Source Revenue (OSR), by Type of Local Government, 1962–2017

| | *1962* | *1967* | *1972* | *1977* | *1982* | *1987* | *1992* | *1997* | *2002* | *2007* | *2012* | *2017* |
|---|---|---|---|---|---|---|---|---|---|---|---|---|
| County Governments | 80 | 77 | 74 | 70 | 58 | 58 | 59 | 57 | 62 | 59 | 61 | 61 |
| Municipal Governments | 76 | 74 | 72 | 71 | 62 | 60 | 61 | 59 | 60 | 62 | 63 | 63 |
| Townships | 90 | 88 | 89 | 88 | 80 | 80 | 79 | 79 | 79 | 79 | 82 | 83 |
| Special Districts | 32 | 28 | 27 | 25 | 18 | 21 | 23 | 23 | 24 | 25 | 27 | 27 |
| School Districts | 87 | 86 | 88 | 87 | 81 | 84 | 84 | 83 | 83 | 81 | 85 | 86 |

*Source:* U.S. Bureau of the Census. Census of Governments. Compendium of Government Finances series, 1962–2017.

# 5 Other Types of Taxes

## Sales, Income, and Other/ Miscellaneous

While it is likely that the property tax will remain as the tax of choice and necessity for counties, municipalities, townships, and school districts (and even to a lesser extent for special service districts) in the foreseeable future, it is also expected that these governments increasingly will turn to other types of taxes and/or other revenue sources to augment their funding needs. This prediction is based on a number of factors and events, not the least of which was the data presented in Chapter 4 that shows that these four local governments (but particularly counties and municipalities) have been exhibiting a conspicuous reduction in their dependency on the property tax since 1962. Simply put, money derived from the payment of property taxes has been accounting for less and less of both total and own-source revenue (i.e., TR and OSR) and total tax revenue (i.e., TTR) of all local governments with the exception of special service districts. Since local governments are continuing to spend more and not less money, this realistically must mean that they are now relying on other sources of revenue to make up the difference which used to come from property taxes.

As noted in the previous chapter, the estimated value of real estate and structures located on it historically has been considered a reasonable yardstick—although not necessarily the most preferred—to gauge local government service needs and expectations as well as the ability of homeowners and owners of businesses and industries to pay for these services. This rationale along with the fact the property tax was a "convenient" tax greatly influenced local officials to make it the most widely used form of taxation. The term "convenient" means that the property tax was fairly straightforward and easy to implement (compared to the sales or income tax), with local tax officials performing the following simple tasks: identify all taxable property located within the local government's boundaries while granting some exemptions (e.g., religious and charitable organizations and government property); assess the value of the taxable property; determine the tax (millage) rate to be applied to certain categories of property (e.g., agricultural, residential, business, and industrial); calculate the tax due and send out tax notices; and, of course, collect the revenue. Furthermore, the fact that the object to be taxed (property) is difficult to

DOI: 10.4324/9781032640389-5

hide from tax officials (unlike the case for one's income, investments in stocks and bonds, or purchases) has made the property tax an even more appealing tax for local governments. Then, there is also the argument that local governments have the exclusive opportunity to collect revenue from the property tax and therefore not have to compete with the federal government or their states for a share of the proceeds of a sales or income tax. Why should local governments make it more difficult for themselves to raise revenue when there is an easy-to-follow process and little or no competition from the bigger federal and state governments to generate a plentiful and steady source of revenue like the property tax?

But, with that said, it is important to consider whether the property tax is really the best and fairest or even the most convenient way for local governments to fund the cost of providing a long list of services—but especially for indivisible services[1]—to their citizens. Indeed, critics of the property tax have long argued that the tax has a number of significant shortcomings that would make it a much less desirable means for local governments' revenue-raising needs, while also pointing out that the sales, individual and corporate income, vehicle licenses, and several other miscellaneous types of taxes would be better alternatives. To understand better the merits of this perspective and utility of the property tax, it is important to examine the tax in light of five commonly cited tax policy principles (i.e., equity, adequacy, simplicity, exportability, and progressivity) to get some sense of how the property tax stacks up against other types of taxes. Furthermore, such an examination should provide considerable insight as to the motives behind local governments increasingly opting to depend more on revenue generated by other types of taxes as a superior, or at least a better, alternative to revenue usually produced by the property tax.

## A case for greater reliance on other types of taxes

### *Equity*

Equity is just another way of referring to tax fairness. While there are two ways to look at tax equity (vertical and horizontal), the second term is directly relevant to evaluating the property tax. Horizontal equity is a measure of whether taxpayers in similar circumstances pay similar amounts of tax. For example, if a homeowner pays a higher property tax than a homeowner for a home with the same true market value, then that violates horizontal fairness. This happens more times than not in the real world when the value of property is not reassessed at reasonably short intervals, but especially in times of rampant inflation. Moreover, this situation is exacerbated when one of the homes is sold at true market value and the selling price then becomes the new assessed value for taxing purposes. The result is that the property taxes on the recently sold home will be higher than the other homes in the same vicinity because its value for taxing purposes is outdated and therefore less than what the owner could get in the open market if it were to be sold.

### *Adequacy*

Adequacy refers to whether a tax raises enough money to support the level of public services demanded by citizens. Stated differently, adequacy is what separates successful taxes and tax systems from unsuccessful ones. While the primary concern for local officials is typically about short-term adequacy (making sure that there is enough revenue to fund public services in the upcoming fiscal year), it is equally important for them to pay sufficient attention to the development of long-term adequacy strategies (balancing budgets not just this year or the next, but for five to ten years down the road).

Two factors that are vital to the adequacy of a tax are its stability and elasticity. A stable tax is one that grows at a predictable rate. Predictable growth makes it easier for local government officials to put together budgets that match projected revenues to projected spending. However, stability itself is not sufficient to guarantee adequacy in the long-run. For instance, property taxes, while they grow predictably, also usually grow more slowly than the cost of services that local governments provide. Elasticity is a measure of whether the growth in a specific kind of tax keeps up with the economy. This is an important consideration since the cost of providing public services typically grows at least as fast as the economy. Therefore, an elastic tax is one for which the tax revenue grows faster than the economy over the long-run.

There is however some fundamental tension between the goals of elasticity and stability. Elastic taxes, like a personal income tax (and to a lesser degree the sales tax), are more likely to ensure sufficient revenues in the long-run, but may vacillate from year to year. In fact, history indicates that the long-term growth of the personal income tax is substantially greater than that of the sales or property tax, although the income tax is more volatile in the short-run. All of this points to the necessity—indeed, wisdom—of creating and maintaining a diverse local government revenue base to help in smoothing out the ups and downs associated with periodic fluctuations in the economy, as history has shown that too great of a reliance on one or just a few revenue sources usually results in diminished revenue collections. In contrast, prudently managed income (and to a lesser extent, sales) taxes in combination with the property tax will likely ensure a more sustainable funding source over the long-run than is probable with a continued heavy reliance on property tax. In short, it should be reiterated that stable taxes, like the property tax, will grow typically predictably, but the slower growth rate in the tax will probably mean that tax increases will be necessary in the long-run so as to fund adequately services at the same level compared to previous years.

### *Simplicity*

Simplicity is another often-mentioned goal associated with prudent tax policy principles. Complicated tax rules make a tax system difficult for citizens to understand. Complexity also makes it difficult for local governments to oversee and enforce tax collections and makes for easier adoption of targeted tax breaks benefitting certain groups. This happens quite often when either state legislatures or citizens via referenda adopt numerous exemptions for the property tax, thus costing local governments millions of dollars in potential revenue. For years, home rule proponents have argued that local governments should be granted complete authority to create property tax exemptions rather than state legislators who have their own political agendas and citizens and interest groups who are looking for special treatment and either do not care or consider the fiscal consequences of shrinking local government revenues that are needed to provide vital services to their citizens.

### *Exportability*

A fourth tax policy principle relevant to an examination of local governments' heavy reliance on the property tax is exportability. Going largely unnoticed by the average citizen is the fact that public services provided by their local government revenues are enjoyed by individuals and businesses in other states—including businesses that hire a state's high school graduates and tourists who use a local government's transportation infrastructure, parks and recreational faculties, or requires/utilizes police, fire, EMS, water, and sewer services. This is why local government tax systems should be designed to make outer-state businesses and residents pay their fair share of the cost involved in providing various services which they take advantage of (state government tax systems have always been devised in this way). For a local government, there are three ways that taxes can be exported: by having non-residents pay the tax directly (e.g., sales taxes on items purchased by tourists), by levying taxes on businesses which are passed on to non-residents, and through interaction with a state income tax (e.g., local governments being permitting to piggyback on the state income tax for out-of-state people working temporarily within their jurisdiction).

### *Progressivity*

The last principle is progressivity. This refers to the degree to which the incidence of paying a tax is reflective of and sensitive to the notion or goal of "ability to pay." Simply stated, a progressive tax is one that taxes people (or businesses) to a greater extent if they have a greater ability to pay, with the personal income tax being the best example. The logic and defense of the income tax are that, as a person's income increases, so does his/her means to pay a tax. The property tax does not satisfy this principle and instead the burden of paying it typically falls more heavily on the poor and ends up being a regressive tax.

In sum, this evaluation of the property tax in terms of its consistency/compatibility with the goals implicit in important tax policy principles helps in understanding and explaining the decline in local governments' dependency on the property tax as the primary source of both OSR and TR since 1962. In all likelihood, acute awareness of the shortcomings of the property tax along with concerns expressed by local government citizens and tax reform groups prompted local officials to seek greater authority from their state governments to tap other taxing options. This explanation certainly is consistent with the trends that were identified in Chapter 4. Nevertheless, as will be discussed later in this chapter, there are likely to be other factors that can assist in explaining the decrease in local government's reliance on the property tax.

## Examination of sales, income, and other-type tax usage by all local governments

One of the major reforms advanced by home rule proponents over the years has been for states to grant their local governments greater latitude in revenue-raising alternatives, including the ability to levy sales, income, and a variety of other types of taxes. Their reasoning is that the restrictions states historically have placed on local governments' revenue-raising capabilities have forced especially counties, municipalities, townships, and school districts to utilize revenue systems that are contrary to the old principle of "don't place all of your eggs in one basket." But, in granting greater fiscal authority, states, in theory, could make it possible for local governments to diversify both their tax and revenue base and may be able to raise revenue in a more citizen-friendly manner. Since many states have been increasingly responsive to calls for greater home in recent decades, it is therefore likely that the decline in local governments' dependency on the property tax since 1962—as suggested above—has been due, at least in part, to them taking advantage of expanded home authority in the area of finances that allows them to levy a number of other kinds of taxes besides the tax on property.

The first indication that revenue generated by non-property tax sources has been filling the void left by a decline in the growth rate in property tax revenue is its significant increase over the last 55 years. In 1962, non-property tax revenue amounted to a little over $2.5 billion. By 2020, this figure had climbed to nearly $223 billion, or by about 79 times. By comparison, property tax revenue grew from $18.4 billion to $581 billion, or by about 28 times. In short, while both property and non-property taxes were growing over the 1962–2020 period, the growth rate for non-property taxes was increasing by a much higher rate. This pattern persists when examining constant dollar figures (not shown here).

Other evidence to support the likelihood that non-property tax monies were helping to make up for a slowdown in the growth rate of property tax collections can be seen from the data in Figure 5.1. This figure shows the proportion of OSR for all local governments accounted for by total non-property tax proceeds from 1962 and 2020. Notice that the non-property tax total almost doubles over this period, with much of this increase attributive to the increase in sales tax revenue. Over time, revenue from the general sales tax has been growing at a somewhat

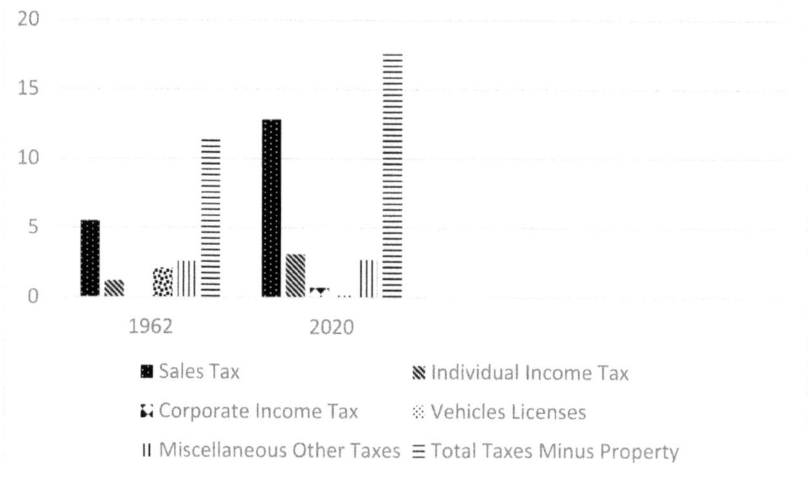


*Figure 5.1* Sales, Individual Income, Corporate Income, Vehicle Licenses, Miscellaneous Other Taxes, and Total Taxes Minus Property as a Percentage of Own-Source Revenue for All Local Governments, 1962 and 2020

*Source:* U.S. Bureau of the Census. Census of Governments. Compendium of Government Finances series, 1962–2017 and U.S. Bureau of the Census. 2020 State & Local Government Finance Historical Datasets and Tables. Compendium of Government Finances (Washington, DC: Government Printing Office).

higher rate compared to taxes on selective sales (data not shown in the figure). Although the individual income tax accounts for a smaller proportion of total non-tax revenue than does the sales tax, the revenue from it has more than doubled during this time. Also, worthy of mention is the fact that while there was no revenue recorded for a corporate income tax in 1962, this new source of revenue for local governments surfaced in 1982 and proceeds from it are likely to grow in the coming years.

Other data confirm this pattern whereby non-property tax revenue has been becoming a more important source of revenue for local governments since 1962. In addition to accounting for a much larger proportion of local governments' OSR from 1962 to 2020, non-property tax revenue is also accounting for an increasing proportion of TTR. This is clearly evident from the data found in Figure 5.2. Here, it can be seen that the total non-property proportion of TTR for all local governments increased substantially from 1962 to 2020 and accounted for nearly a third of TTR (32 percent) in 2020. Closer examination of Figure 5.2 reveals that the sales tax proceeds made up the largest share of specific types of total non-property tax revenue other than the assortment of "miscellaneous" revenue in both 1962 and 2020, and this percentage was increasing over time. By 2020, sales tax monies accounted for close to two-thirds of total non-property

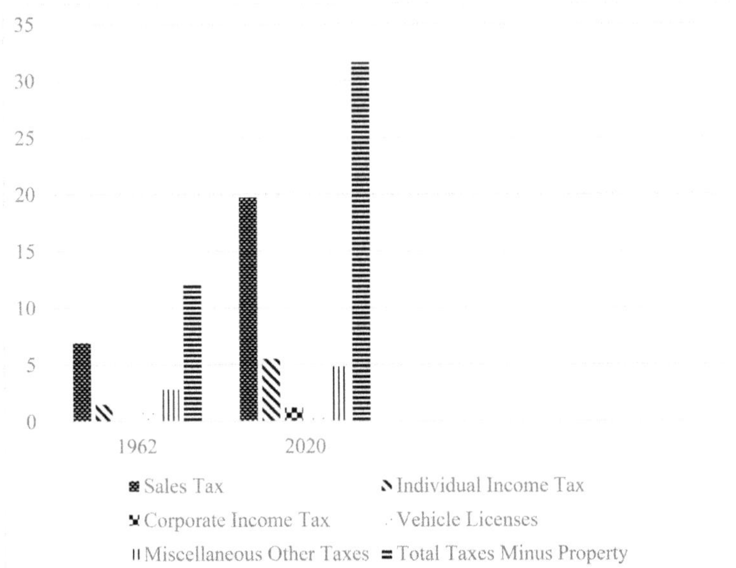


*Figure 5.2* Sales, Individual Income, Corporate Income, Vehicle Licenses, Miscellaneous Other Taxes, and Total Taxes Minus Property as a Percentage of Total Tax Revenue (TTR) for All Local Governments, 1962 and 2020

*Source:* U.S. Bureau of the Census. Census of Governments. Compendium of Government Finances series, 1962–2017 and U.S. Bureau of the Census. 2020 State & Local Government Finance Historical Datasets and Tables. Compendium of Government Finances (Washington, DC: Government Printing Office).

tax funds. When breaking down sales tax revenue into general sales and selective sales, it is apparent that general sales account for the larger portion of it and this share has been increasing slightly over time (74 percent in 2020 versus 66 percent in 1962). Sizably smaller proportions of TTR were accounted for by the other non-property taxes, with the individual income tax, corporate income tax, and other/miscellaneous tax constituting 6, 1, and 5 percent, respectively, of the total in 2020. Nonetheless, it is important to mention that these percentages were increasing noticeably between 1962 and 2020.

From this point, it will be interesting to find out if the patterns and trends observed here for each type of non-property tax (sales, individual income, corporate income, vehicle licenses, and miscellaneous/other) are the same or different when the analysis shifts to an examination of counties, municipalities, townships, special districts, and school districts separately. The rest of this chapter is devoted to learning about the direction of these patterns generally and on a state-by-state basis between 1962 and 2017 (the last year for which these financial data are reported for each of the five types of local governments).

**Varying usage of the sales tax by the type of local government**

As has been theorized and documented in the preceding chapters of this book, revenue patterns of specific local governments are expected to vary and can be explained by a number of factors, not the least of which is the purpose or rationale for their creation by their states and the functions they were expected to perform. Yet, one common theme prevails—local governments receive most of the revenue (presently, about two-thirds of it) from OSR. Additionally, it was learned from Chapter 4 that the largest proportion of OSR continues to be derived from some form of taxation for four of five local governments (the exception being special districts), with the primary source of tax revenue coming from the property tax. In two of these governments (school districts and townships), heavy dependence on the property tax is still the case, although township reliance on the property tax has dropped a little over time. For two other local governments (counties and municipalities), reliance on the property (always being greater for the former government than the latter) declined noticeably from 1962 to 2017. The consequences of these changes for counties and municipalities and to a lesser extent for townships are obvious. That is, these governments must be collecting a larger proportion of their OSR and TTR from some other types of taxes other than the property tax.

From the previous section, it was seen that there were increases in all local governments' dependency on non-property tax proceeds from 1962 to 2020, but especially for the sales tax. But what does that mean for each of the five types of local governments? The data presented in Figure 5.3 assists in making this determination. Clearly, counties and municipalities are making greater use of the sales tax to augment their revenue collections. More specifically, these two governments are relying on the sales tax to produce a greater proportion of their OSR. A closer look at the trend lines in Figure 5.3 for these two governments reveals several other pieces of important information. While both governments presently derive about the same proportion of their OSR from the sales tax (around 18 percent for municipalities and about 13 percent for counties), counties have greatly increased their use of the sales tax over time. In point of fact, county revenue collected from the sales tax when calculated as a percentage of OSR increased by more than six-fold between 1962 and 2017; by comparison, the sales tax proportion of municipal OSR, while also increasing, did so at a slower pace—just under 150 percent. Another point worth noting is that the sales tax proportion of OSR for both governments has increased very little since 1997. This could be due to the effects of two recessions during the first few years of the 21st century and the Great Recession of the late 2000s and the early 2010s.

By contrast, special districts, townships, and school districts typically have not depended on the sales tax to supply much of their OSR (see Figure 5.3). As of 2017, sales tax revenue produces only 1 and 2 percent of OSR, respectively,

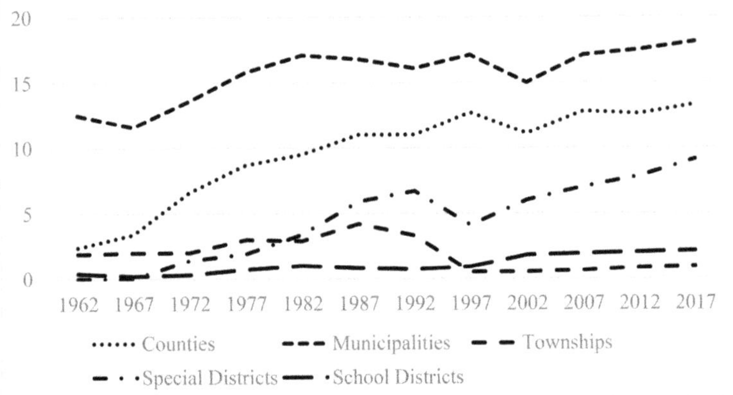


*Figure 5.3* Sales Tax Revenue as a Percentage of OSR for Counties, Municipalities, Townships, Special Districts, and School Districts, 1962–2017

*Source:* U.S. Bureau of the Census. Census of Governments. Compendium of Government Finances series, 1962–2017 and U.S. Bureau of the Census.

for townships and school districts. However, the sales tax proportion of OSR for school districts generally has been trending upward in recent years and bears watching, as this may be an indication that school districts are attempting to assuage the funding inequity problems that can result from too-heavy of a reliance on the property tax. In addition, the data in Figure 5.3 pertaining to special districts also suggest that it will be important to monitor their sales tax receipts in the future since the sales tax proportion of OSR has been trending upward noticeably as well since 1997 and now constitutes a little over 9 percent of their OSR.

In spite of the desire of local governments to levy a sales tax, the degree to which they are able to do so is controlled by their states. There are two kinds of sales taxes that are permissible. One is the tax on general sales and is levied on top of (usually expressed as "piggybacking") on the state sales tax. The other is a sales tax levied on selective purchases for things like motor fuel, alcohol beverages, tobacco purchases, public utilities (e.g., electric power, natural gas, and water service), admission to entertainment (movie theaters, amusement parks, plays, concerts, etc.) and sporting events, among others. As can be seen from Table 5.1, most states (N = 35) permit their local governments to levy both kinds of sales taxes, although it is not unusual for states to restrict usage to certain types of local governments. County and municipal governments are the most likely to be granted the authority to levy both types of sales taxes, while the power to do so is less likely to be given to townships and special and school districts. Table 5.1 also indicates that 14 states permit certain local governments to levy a selective sales

*Table 5.1* State Authorization for Local Government Usage of the General and Selective Sales Tax, 2017

| *Permitted Usage of Both Tax (N = 35)* | *Permitted Usage of Only Selective Tax (N = 14)* | *No Permitted Usage of Either Tax (N = 1)* |
|---|---|---|
| Alabama | Delaware | Connecticut |
| Alaska | Idaho | |
| Arkansas | Indiana | |
| Arizona | Kentucky | |
| California | Maine | |
| Colorado | Maryland | |
| Florida | Massachusetts | |
| Georgia | Michigan | |
| Hawaii | Montana | |
| Illinois | New Hampshire | |
| Iowa | New Jersey | |
| Kansas | Oregon | |
| Louisiana | Rhode Island | |
| Minnesota | West Virginia | |
| Mississippi | | |
| Missouri | | |
| Nebraska | | |
| Nevada | | |
| New Mexico | | |
| New York | | |
| North Carolina | | |
| North Dakota | | |
| Ohio | | |
| Oklahoma | | |
| Pennsylvania | | |
| South Carolina | | |
| South Dakota | | |
| Tennessee | | |
| Texas | | |
| Utah | | |
| Vermont | | |
| Virginia | | |
| Washington | | |
| Wisconsin | | |
| Wyoming | | |

*Source:* Adapted from Jared Walczak and Scott Drenkard 2017. State and Local Sales Tax Rates in 2017. Washington, DC: Tax Foundation.

tax but not a tax on general sales, and one other state (Connecticut) does not allow any of their local governments to levy either kind of sales tax.

However, being given the authority to charge either or both kinds of sales taxes does not mean that local governments are given unfettered power in the usage of them. With regard to both types of sales taxes, state constitutions and statues place limits on the maximum amount (percentage) that can be charged. Presently, the maximum total local government rate for the both kinds of sales taxes ranges from .50 percent in Hawaii to 8.30 in Colorado (Walczak and Drenkard 2017). The average total rate is 3.4855 percent (Walczak and Drenkard 2017). Other restrictions are not uncommon for both types of sales taxes and can include the following: voter approval in addition to adoption by the local government governing body; approval/adoption may be valid for only a specific period of time and then "sunsets"; only certain local governments may approve/adopt and collect monies (e.g., only county governments in Florida can levy the tax although they may share the proceeds with other local governments), whereas only municipalities in California are allowed to use the tax); and states may mandate that local governments grant exemptions for certain items (e.g., food) or prohibit local governments from charging a sales tax at certain times of the year designated as "tax holidays" where citizens can purchase items such as back-to-school supplies (many states) or hurricane supplies (Florida). Many states also mandate that a portion of the revenue collected must be earmarked for certain kinds of services or purposes (e.g., recent tax monies collected by Florida counties had to be spent for services and programs such as indigent health care, roads, mass transit, environmental protection, public safety, schools, sports facilities, among other things).

But, in spite of a state's willingness to permit its local governments to utilize a sales tax, there must also be a concomitant willingness on the part of local governments to take advantage of the opportunity to tax either or both general and selective sales. The extent to which local governments do this is referred to as "tax effort." The data arrayed in Table 5.2 provides some indication of local government "tax effort" on a state-by-state basis for the 35 states that levy a general sales tax. The heading at the top of the table titled "Percent Usage" provides a fairly reasonable measure or indicator of "tax effort." The average "tax effort" for local governments in all states is 57 percent, but as can be seen from Table 5.2, "tax effort" varies widely from state to state. The least effort is recorded for Mississippi local governments, while the greatest effort is found in Texas. The ranking for other states is also reported in the table.

One additional way to gauge usage of the sales tax by local governments is to take into account the amount of revenue that is generated by each of the two types of the tax. It comes as no surprise that the general sales tax is both the more popular of the two and the larger producer of revenue. That was true in 1962 and remains so today. In 1962, 66 percent of all revenue collected from taxes on "sales and gross receipts" was produced by the general sales tax. By 2017, the general sales tax was accounting for an even larger proportion—75 percent.

While the identification of these general practices and trends for sales tax usage for all local governments is certainly enlightening, it will also be beneficial to examine the different patterns that exist within and among the 50 states for each type of local government in their use of the sales tax.

*Table 5.2* State Authorization for and Local Government Usage of the General Sales Tax, 2017

| *State* | *Maximum Allowable Tax Rate* | *Average Local Tax Rate* | *Percent Usage* | *Rank* | *State* | *Maximum Allowable Tax Rate* | *Average Local Tax Rate* | *Percent Usage* | *Rank* |
|---|---|---|---|---|---|---|---|---|---|
| Alabama | 7.00 | 5.01 | 72 | 9 | New Mexico | 3.5625 | 2.43 | 68 | 15 |
| Alaska | 7.50 | 1.76 | 23 | 32 | New York | 4.875 | 4.49 | 92 | 2 |
| Arkansas | 5.125 | 2.80 | 55 | 19 | North Carolina | 2.75 | 2.15 | 78 | 6 |
| Arizona | 5.30 | 2.65 | 50 | 23 | North Dakota | 3.50 | 1.78 | 51 | 21 |
| California | 2.50 | 1.00 | 40 | 27 | Ohio | 2.25 | 1.39 | 62 | 17 |
| Colorado | 8.30 | 4.60 | 55 | 18 | Oklahoma | 6.50 | 4.36 | 67 | 16 |
| Florida | 2.00 | 0.80 | 40 | 28 | Pennsylvania | 2.00 | 0.34 | 17 | 34 |
| Georgia | 4.00 | 3.00 | 75 | 7 | South Carolina | 2.50 | 1.22 | 49 | 24 |
| Hawaii | 0.50 | 0.35 | 70 | 12 | South Dakota | 4.50 | 1.89 | 42 | 26 |
| Illinois | 4.75 | 2.39 | 50 | 22 | Tennessee | 2.75 | 2.46 | 89 | 3 |
| Iowa | 1.00 | 0.80 | 80 | 5 | Texas | 2.00 | 1.94 | 97 | 1 |
| Kansas | 4.00 | 2.12 | 53 | 20 | Utah | 2.15 | 0.81 | 38 | 29 |
| Louisiana | 7.00 | 4.98 | 71 | 11 | Vermont | 1.00 | 0.18 | 18 | 33 |
| Minnesota | 1.50 | 0.42 | 28 | 30 | Virginia | 0.70 | 0.33 | 47 | 25 |
| Mississippi | 1.00 | 0.07 | 7 | 35 | Washington | 3.40 | 2.42 | 71 | 10 |
| Missouri | 5.00 | 3.66 | 73 | 8 | Wisconsin | 1.75 | 0.42 | 24 | 31 |
| Nebraska | 2.00 | 1.39 | 70 | 14 | Wyoming | 2.00 | 1.40 | 70 | 13 |
| Nevada | 1.30 | 1.13 | 87 | 4 | | | | | |

*Source:* Adapted from Jared Walczak and Scott Drenkard 2017. State and Local Sales Tax Rates in 2017. Washington, DC: Tax Foundation.

But, in spite of a state's willingness to permit its local governments to utilize a sales tax, there must also be a concomitant willingness on the part of local governments to take advantage of the opportunity to tax either or both general and selective sales. The extent to which local governments do this is referred to as "tax effort." The data arrayed in Table 5.2 provides some indication of local government "tax effort" on a state-by-state basis for the 35 states that levy a general sales tax. The heading at the top of the table titled "Percent Usage" provides a fairly reasonable measure or indicator of "tax effort." The average "tax effort" for local governments in all states is 57 percent, but as can be seen from Table 5.2, "tax effort" varies widely from state to state. The least effort is recorded for Mississippi local governments, while the greatest effort is found in Texas. The ranking for other states is also reported in the table.

One additional way to gauge usage of the sales tax by local governments is to take into account the amount of revenue that is generated by each of the two types of the tax. It comes as no surprise that the general sales tax is both the more popular of the two and the larger producer of revenue. That was true in 1962 and remains so today. In 1962, 66 percent of all revenue collected from taxes on "sales and gross receipts" was produced by the general sales tax. By 2017, the general sales tax was accounting for an even larger proportion—75 percent.

While the identification of these general practices and trends for sales tax usage for all local governments is certainly enlightening, it will also be beneficial to examine the different patterns that exist within and among the 50 states for each type of local government in their use of the sales tax.

### *Counties*

Over the last 55 years, the number of states permitting county governments to levy a sales tax has grown considerably. In 1962, only about a third of the states authorized their counties to charge a tax on either general sales or gross receipts transactions as a means to raise additional revenue and thereby potentially enable them to reduce their dependency on the property tax (Bowman and Kearney 2008; Dye and MacManus 2015). States, if they granted counties to levy a sales tax, were more likely to authorize the usage of a general sales tax rather than a selective sales tax. By 2017, however, all but four states that had organized county governments (the exceptions being Maine, Montana, New Hampshire, and Vermont) had the authority to levy either a general or a selective sales tax; there is no type of county sales tax in two additional states (Connecticut and Rhode Island) since county governments were abolished in 1842 and 1958, respectively. Most states (29) permit their counties to levy both a general and selective sales tax, while 13 states allow counties to charge only a selective sales tax; two other states limit counties to only a general sales tax (Bowman and Kearney 2008; Dye and MacManus 2015; Walczak and Drenkard 2017; Afonso 2017).

Regardless of the type of authority states grant to counties to impose a sales tax, these governments' reliance on it to supply necessary resources to fund services and programs varies substantially as measured by the proportion of OSR that is accounted for by total sales tax collections. This is clearly visible from the data contained in Table 5.3. In 2017, county governments in 15 states (Alabama, Arkansas, Georgia, Illinois, Louisiana, Massachusetts, Missouri, Nevada, New Mexico, New York, Ohio, Oklahoma, Tennessee, Utah, and Washington) relied on the total receipts from both types of sales taxes to supply at least one-fifth of their OSR; in two of these states (Arkansas, New York, and Missouri), total

*Table 5.3* Sales Tax Revenue of County Governments as a Proportion of OSR, 2017

| *State* | *(Percent)* | | | *State* | *(Percent)* | | |
|---|---|---|---|---|---|---|---|
| | *General Sales* | *Selective Sales* | *Total* | | *General Sales* | *Selective Sales* | *Total* |
| Alabama | 24 | 4 | 28 | Montana | 0 | 0 | 0 |
| Alaska | 4 | 2 | 6 | Nebraska | 0 | 1 | 1 |
| Arizona | 11 | 1 | 12 | Nevada | 14 | 15 | 29 |
| Arkansas | 43 | 1 | 44 | New Hampshire | * | * | * |
| California | 1 | 1 | 4 | New Jersey | 0 | 0 | 0 |
| Colorado | 17 | 2 | 19 | New Mexico | 31 | * | 31 |
| Connecticut | — | — | — | New York | 41 | 1 | 42 |
| Delaware | 0 | 1 | 1 | North Carolina | 13 | 2 | 15 |
| Florida | 5 | 8 | 13 | North Dakota | 10 | 1 | 11 |
| Georgia | 20 | 6 | 26 | Ohio | 23 | 1 | 24 |
| Hawaii | 0 | 7 | 7 | Oklahoma | 20 | 1 | 21 |
| Idaho | 0 | 1 | 1 | Oregon | 0 | 5 | 5 |
| Illinois | 18 | 8 | 26 | Pennsylvania | 1 | 2 | 3 |
| Indiana | 0 | 2 | 2 | Rhode Island | — | — | — |
| Iowa | 3 | 1 | 4 | South Carolina | 10 | 3 | 13 |
| Kansas | 15 | 1 | 16 | South Dakota | 0 | 1 | 1 |
| Kentucky | 0 | 6 | 6 | Tennessee | 13 | 2 | 20 |
| Louisiana | 19 | 2 | 21 | Texas | 3 | 1 | 4 |
| Maine | 0 | 0 | 0 | Utah | 25 | 7 | 32 |
| Maryland | 0 | 5 | 5 | Vermont | 0 | 0 | 0 |
| Massachusetts | 0 | 22 | 22 | Virginia | 6 | 4 | 10 |
| Michigan | 0 | 1 | 1 | Washington | 22 | 4 | 26 |
| Minnesota | 2 | 0 | 2 | West Virginia | 0 | 4 | 4 |
| Mississippi | 0 | 1 | 1 | Wisconsin | 9 | 0 | 9 |
| Missouri | 39 | 2 | 41 | Wyoming | 7 | 1 | 8 |

— Connecticut and Rhode Island have no county governments.

* Less than 1 percent.

*Source:* U.S. Bureau of the Census. Census of Governments. Compendium of Government Finances series, 1962–2017.

sales tax revenue provided 44, 42, and 41 percent, respectively, of their OSR. In another eight states (Arizona, Colorado, Florida, Kansas, North Carolina, North Dakota, South Carolina, and Virginia), total receipts from the sales tax supplied from 10 to 19 percent of OSR. In stark contrast, revenue from total taxes on sales and gross receipts contributed a small (ten states) to a negligible (eight states) proportion of OSR, while OSR in three states (Maine, Montana, and Vermont) contained no sales tax monies.

It is also worth mentioning that the bulk of total sales and gross receipts tax revenue was made up of money received from the general sales tax. In fact, the general sales tax proportion increased from 73 to 79 percent between 1962 and 2017. Revenue that counties collected from the selective sales tax, while continuing to grow, pales in comparison to general sales tax proceeds. As is seen from Table 5.3, there were only two states where the selective sales tax proportion reached double digits (Massachusetts at 22 percent and Nevada at 15 percent). Nevertheless, there was a modest increase in the proportion of OSR accounted for by proceeds from selective services in recent years, as the general sales tax proportion of total gross sales and receipts revenue peaked in 1987 at 83 percent and continued to decline slightly to 79 percent by 2017.

A breakdown of selective sales revenue for 2017 is provided in Figure 5.4. The largest proportion of this money (47 percent) comes from sales taxes imposed on a large variety of non-specified items that are labeled as "Other" in the figure. The next largest proportion (33 percent) derives from a tax on public utilities, while a much smaller percentage (14) is obtained from a tax on motor fuel. The smallest proportions are attributable to alcoholic beverage and tobacco product sales (3 percent for each).

### *Municipalities*

Early on, states were more likely to grant their municipal governments the authority to levy taxes on sales and gross receipts than they were for other types of local governments. In 1962, there were 40 states that permitted municipal governments to levy some type of sales tax (Walczak and Drenkard 2017). Unlike what was the case with county governments, states in 1962 were much more inclined to allow municipalities to levy a selective rather than a general sales tax—39 states had only a selective tax, while no state had just a general tax on sales (Walczak and Drenkard 2017). An additional 13 states were granted authority to levy both kinds of sales taxes. By 2017, the number of states having the authority to charge some type of a sales tax had increased to 49 (Connecticut being the lone exception), with the largest number of them (32) being able to levy both a general and a selective sales tax (Walczak and Drenkard 2017). Sixteen other states have granted municipalities the authority to levy only a selective tax, and one state is permitted to charge just a general sales tax (Walczak and Drenkard 2017).

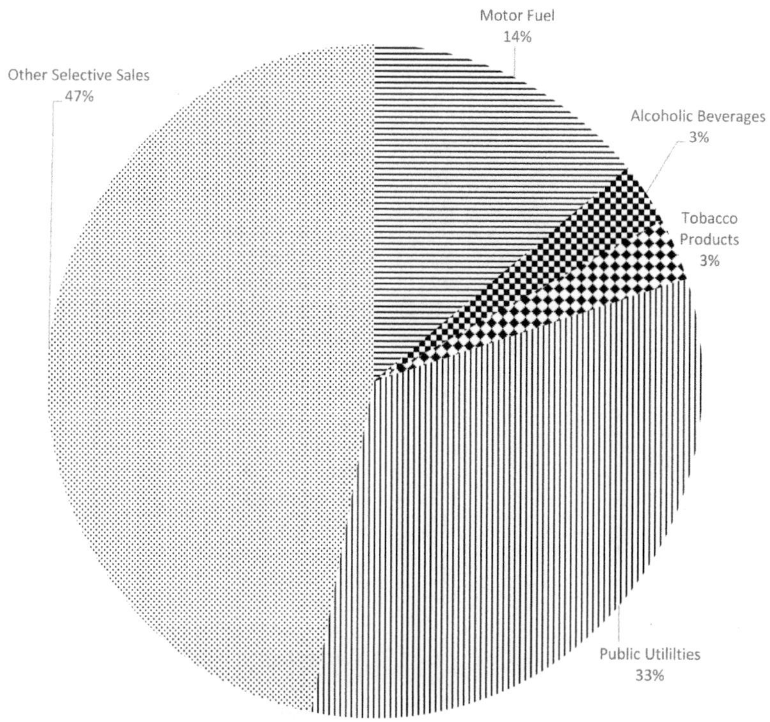


*Figure 5.4* Breakdown of Selective Sales Taxes for County Governments, 2017

*Source:* U.S. Bureau of the Census. Census of Governments. Compendium of Government Finances series, 1962–2017.

Like what was observed for county governments, there is also a considerable amount of variability among the states as to municipal government dependency on a sales tax to pay for the cost of service provision. This can be seen in Table 5.4 where municipal sales tax revenue as a proportion of municipal government OSR has been calculated. In 2017, total sales tax revenue supplied slightly more than one-half of municipal OSR in one state (Alabama). In five other states (Arizona, Arkansas, Colorado, New Mexico, and Oklahoma), municipal sales tax proceeds made up at least 40 percent of these governments' OSR, while municipal governments in three additional states (Louisiana, Missouri, and South Dakota) depended on sales tax revenue to provide a minimum of 30 percent of their OSR. Furthermore, municipalities in nine more states (California, Illinois, Kansas, Nebraska, North Dakota, Tennessee, Texas, Utah, and Washington)

*Table 5.4* Sales Tax Revenue of Municipal Governments as a Proportion of OSR, 2017

| *State* | *(Percent)* | | | *State* | *(Percent)* | | |
|---|---|---|---|---|---|---|---|
| | *General Sales* | *Selective Sales* | *Total* | | *General Sales* | *Selective Sales* | *Total* |
| Alabama | 44 | 7 | 51 | Montana | 0 | 1 | 1 |
| Alaska | 11 | 5 | 16 | Nebraska | 20 | 2 | 22 |
| Arizona | 39 | 4 | 43 | Nevada | 2 | 13 | 15 |
| Arkansas | 30 | 10 | 40 | New Hampshire | 0 | * | * |
| California | 13 | 10 | 23 | New Jersey | 0 | 2 | 2 |
| Colorado | 37 | 7 | 42 | New Mexico | 38 | 6 | 44 |
| Connecticut | 0 | 0 | 0 | New York | 10 | 3 | 13 |
| Delaware | 0 | 3 | 3 | North Carolina | 15 | 3 | 18 |
| Florida | 2 | 12 | 14 | North Dakota | 22 | 2 | 24 |
| Georgia | 0 | 15 | 15 | Ohio | * | 1 | 1 |
| Hawaii | 9 | 5 | 14 | Oklahoma | 41 | 3 | 44 |
| Idaho | 1 | 3 | 4 | Oregon | 0 | 11 | 11 |
| Illinois | 7 | 17 | 24 | Pennsylvania | 5 | 4 | 9 |
| Indiana | 0 | 2 | 2 | Rhode Island | 0 | 1 | 1 |
| Iowa | 6 | 4 | 10 | South Carolina | 5 | 8 | 13 |
| Kansas | 19 | 8 | 27 | South Dakota | 32 | 3 | 35 |
| Kentucky | 0 | 12 | 12 | Tennessee | 13 | 7 | 20 |
| Louisiana | 31 | 6 | 37 | Texas | 19 | 7 | 26 |
| Maine | 0 | * | * | Utah | 17 | 8 | 25 |
| Maryland | 0 | 6 | 6 | Vermont | 2 | 3 | 5 |
| Massachusetts | 0 | 3 | 3 | Virginia | 7 | 12 | 19 |
| Michigan | 0 | 3 | 3 | Washington | 15 | 13 | 28 |
| Minnesota | 2 | 4 | 6 | West Virginia | 5 | 5 | 10 |
| Mississippi | 0 | 4 | 4 | Wisconsin | * | 2 | 2 |
| Missouri | 26 | 9 | 35 | Wyoming | 0 | 7 | 7 |

* Less than 1 percent.

*Source:* U.S. Bureau of the Census. Census of Governments. Compendium of Government Finances series, 1962–2017.

counted on the total receipts from both types of sales taxes to provide, at a minimum, one-fifth (20 percent) of their OSR. It is important to call attention to the fact that ten of these states (Alabama, Arkansas, Illinois, Louisiana, Missouri, New Mexico, Oklahoma, Tennessee, Utah, and Washington) are ones in which county governments also place a heavy dependence on proceeds from the sales tax. Could this present a potential situation where citizens in these states believe that the sales tax is overused and might urge their state and their local governments to be more cognizant of the need to practice greater tax diversity? In fact, critics of greater home rule authority in fiscal matters might point to the situation above as a reminder of the need for the state government to be more circumspect in their responsibility to protect the tax-paying public from being overly burdened by a duplicative tax. Beyond these observations and cautionary note, further examination of Table 5.4 reveals that there are municipalities in 12 states (Delaware, Idaho, Indiana, Massachusetts, Michigan, Mississippi, Montana, New Jersey, Ohio, Rhode Island, Vermont, and Wisconsin) where total sales tax revenue accounts only for between 1 and 5 percent of municipal government OSR. Then, municipalities in one state (Connecticut) collect no money from either type of sales tax.

As is the case of counties, municipal government revenue derived from the general sales tax also accounts for the larger share of all sales tax collections. Nevertheless, the general sales tax proportion has always been noticeably lower for municipalities than it has been for counties; it was 15 percentage points lower in 2017 (i.e., 44 percent for municipal governments versus 79 percent for counties). This means that proceeds from selective taxes have been accounting for a larger part of the money produced by taxes on total sales and gross receipts. Municipalities in seven states (Georgia, Illinois, Kentucky, Nevada, Oregon, Virginia, and Washington) reported selective tax collections that amounted to at least 10 percent of total sales tax proceeds.

A summary of selective sales revenue for 2017 is found in Figure 5.5. Tax collections originating from a sales tax imposed on public utilities constitutes the largest proportion of this type of revenue (54 percent). The second largest proportion (41 percent) originates from a sales tax from a group of non-specific items that are identified as "Other" in the figure. Much smaller proportions come from taxes on motor fuel and alcoholic beverages sales (2 percent each) and tobacco products (1 percent).

### *Townships*

Township governments, like county and municipal governments, are considered to be full-service local government, although they usually provide a shorter menu of services than do counties and municipalities. Nevertheless, the number of services that townships deliver is much larger than the few services provided by any particular special district or the one service provided by school districts. In addition, townships, much like their county and municipal counterparts, must always be conscious of the expectation to carefully weigh the pros and cons and cost efficiency and cost effectiveness of an array of services that often compete against one another for scarce resources. Moreover, the task of allocating scarce resources is made more difficult for townships, as well as for municipal and county governments, because of the activity of highly charged and well-organized vested interests in the community. Yet, when it comes to deciding what kinds of revenue to rely on the most to pay for the costs of service provision, townships can be clearly distinguished from counties and municipalities. That is, townships, unlike counties and municipalities, make limited usage of taxes on sales and gross receipts and also derive a much smaller proportion of their OSR from them.

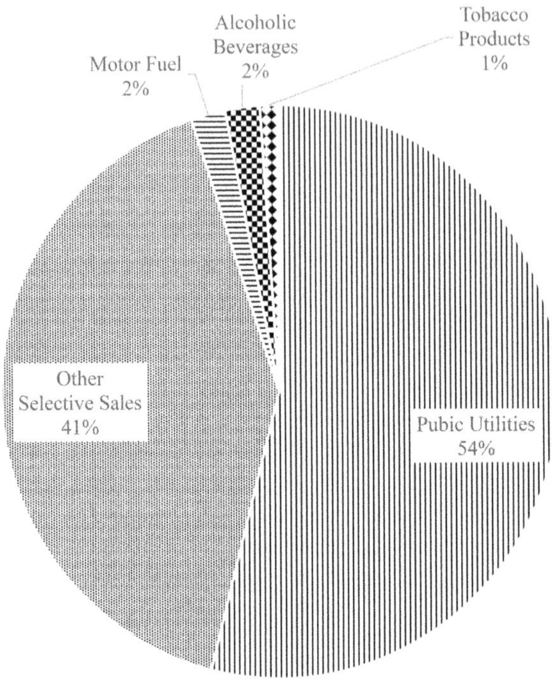


*Figure 5.5* Breakdown of Selective Sales Taxes for Municipal Governments, 2017

*Source:* U.S. Bureau of the Census. Census of Governments. Compendium of Government Finances series, 1962–2017.

One of the primary reasons that townships historically have not been very dependent on revenue derived from a tax on sales and gross receipts is that the 20 states in which they are found have not granted them the authority to do so. In 1962, townships in only five of these 20 states were permitted to charge a sales tax—four had the power to use both a general and selective sales tax and one could tax selective items only (Walczak and Drenkard 2017). By 2017, the number of states allowing their townships to levy a sales tax had increased to 14 states, with six states (Minnesota, Missouri, New York, Ohio, Vermont, and Wisconsin) permitting townships to use both a general and selective sales tax and eight states (Illinois, Maine, Massachusetts, Michigan, New Hampshire, New Jersey, Pennsylvania, and Rhode Island) allowing the utilization of only a selective sales tax (Walczak and Drenkard

2017). While states with townships appear to be somewhat more willing to let these governments levy a sales tax in recent years, it is possible that their reluctance to grant wider taxing authority is due to concerns about having multiple layers of government (i.e., the state, county, municipality, and township) dipping into the pockets of the same citizens, thus potentially creating a financial hardship for them.

If the ability of township governments to charge a sales tax is quite restricted, it is also the case for the amount of revenue that they collect from this tax. It should be remembered from the analysis above where all local governments were compared with respect to the proportion OSR composed of sales tax collections (see Figure 5.3) that townships ranked last behind municipal governments, county governments, special districts, and school districts. The data presented in Table 5.5 confirm that revenue collected from a tax on general or selective sales accounts for only a very small proportion of all township governments' OSR. The largest proportion is only 2.2 percent (Vermont), while townships in four states receive no money from a sales tax and townships in four other states (Missouri, New Hampshire, North Dakota, and South Dakota) collect a negligible amount from this source.

It should also be noted that an overwhelming amount of the revenue produced by a sales tax (97 percent in 2017) comes from a tax on selective items. In fact, until 1982, the tax on selective items accounted all sales tax revenue for townships. Presently, townships in only four states (North Dakota, Ohio, South Dakota, and Vermont) collect money via a general sales tax, which constitutes just 4 percent of total sales tax revenue.

*Table 5.5* Sales Tax Revenue of Township Governments as a Proportion of OSR, 2017

| *State* | *(Percent)* | | | *State* | *(Percent)* | | |
|---|---|---|---|---|---|---|---|
| | *General Sales* | *Selective Sales* | *Total* | | *General Sales* | *Selective Sales* | *Total* |
| Connecticut | 0 | 0 | 0 | New Hampshire | 0 | * | * |
| Illinois | 0 | 0.2 | 0.2 | New Jersey | 0 | 0.9 | 0.9 |
| Indiana | 0 | 0 | 0 | New York | 0 | 1.9 | 1.9 |
| Kansas | 0 | 0 | 0 | North Dakota | * | * | * |
| Maine | 0 | 0.3 | 0.3 | Ohio | 0.2 | 0.7 | 0.9 |
| Massachusetts | 0 | 1.3 | 1.3 | Pennsylvania | 0 | 0.6 | 0.6 |
| Michigan | 0 | 0.5 | 0 5 | Rhode Island | 0 | 0.6 | 0.6 |
| Minnesota | 0 | 0.4 | 0.4 | South Dakota | * | * | * |
| Missouri | 0 | * | * | Vermont | 1.8 | .4 | 2.2 |
| Nebraska | 0 | 0 | 0 | Wisconsin | 0 | 1.7 | 1.7 |

* Less than .5 percent.

*Source:* U.S. Bureau of the Census. Census of Governments. Compendium of Government Finances series, 1962–2017.

Although it is only of incidental concern, given the small proportion of township OSR attributable to taxes on sales and gross receipts, the majority of selective sales tax revenue (54 percent) comes from taxes on an assortment of things referred to as "Other." The remaining part (46 percent) derives from taxes on public utilities.

### *Special districts*

Special districts can be classified in a number of ways, depending on the service roles they are intended to play and the functions they are tasked with performing. The most common type of special district is one that provides a single service and sustains itself financially on the basis of collecting fees/charges from users of a service. One good example is a district that provides potable water to residents and businesses in a specifically defined area and charges a user fee for the service. Similarly, districts may collect and dispose of sewage or provide fire prevention and suppression services with users paying a fee or being assessed a set charge. Other type of districts, however, may be created that have no clearly defined users that can be assessed a fee or charge. Instead, these type of districts (often called "authorities") provide services for part of a county or city, an entire county or city, or even region of a state where everyone to some extent benefits (i.e., the service can be thought of as a general or collective, or better still, an indivisible good). Examples include water or natural resource conservation districts, transit authorities, children's welfare authorities, housing authorities, and library districts. Here, since everyone in the district potentially benefits, then everyone should pay and a tax would be a reasonable way to pay for the service. An alternative means of financing could be a combination of a fee and a tax. For instance, a local option sales tax could be used to ensure that residents and business within the boundaries of an entire county, city, or region would help pay for the availability of mass transit services, while a fee could also be charged for actual users of transit services.

The fact that most special districts resemble the first type described above would seem to explain why most of them rely heavily on charges for services as a primary source of revenue (this will be explored in more detail in Chapter 6). Therefore, it is not surprising to find out that states traditionally have not granted special districts wide authority to levy a sales tax. In 1962, only six states permitted special districts to charge a tax on sales and gross receipts (Walczak and Drenkard 2017). In short, most special districts being like water, sewer, or sanitation districts were thought to have a ready-made and logical means of financing their operations—that is, charge their customers a user fee. This made a lot of sense since it could be impossible or cumbersome at best to levy a tax on selected people and businesses within a larger political unit such as a county or city. By 2017, the number of states permitting special districts to place a tax on sales had increased to 28 (Walczak and Drenkard 2017).

*Table 5.6* Sales Tax Revenue of Special Districts as a Proportion of OSR, 2017

| *State* | *(Percent)* | | | *State* | *(Percent)* | | |
|---|---|---|---|---|---|---|---|
| | *General Sales* | *Selective Sales* | *Total* | | *General Sales* | *Selective Sales* | *Total* |
| Alabama | 0.0 | * | * | Nebraska | 0.0 | 0.0 | 0.0 |
| Arizona | 13.0 | 0.0 | 13.0 | Nevada | 0.0 | .9 | .9 |
| Arkansas | 1.7 | 0.0 | 1.7 | New Mexico | 12.1 | 0.0 | 12.1 |
| California | * | * | * | Ohio | 18.1 | .2 | 18.3 |
| Colorado | 14.0 | * | 14.0 | Pennsylvania | 0.0 | .6 | .6 |
| Florida | * | 0.0 | * | Rhode Island | 0.0 | 1.9 | 1.9 |
| Idaho | * | .7 | .7 | Tennessee | 0.0 | 0.0 | 0.0 |
| Illinois | 16.2 | 0.0 | 0.0 | Texas | 21.3 | 1.0 | 22.3 |
| Indiana | 0.0 | 0.0 | 0.0 | Utah | 0.0 | 0.0 | 0.0 |
| Iowa | 0.0 | .1 | .1 | Virginia | 0.0 | 0.0 | 0.0 |
| Kentucky | 0.0 | * | * | Washington | 14.1 | 2.0 | 16.1 |
| Louisiana | 10.1 | 1.9 | 12.1 | Wisconsin | 5.1 | 5.5 | 10.6 |
| Missouri | 2.4 | .7 | 3.1 | Wyoming | 0.0 | .4 | .4 |
| Montana | 0.0 | 2.1 | 2.1 | | | | |

* Less than .5 percent.

*Source:* U.S. Bureau of the Census. Census of Governments. Compendium of Government Finances series, 1962–2017.

It is speculated that the granting of authority to use a sales tax in additional states in more recent years could be due to an increase in the number of special districts in the second type of classification described above where a user fee may not be either the appropriate or fairest way to pay for the cost of providing a particular kind of service.

This increase in the number of states granting special districts the authority to levy a tax on sales and gross receipts has inevitably enabled these governments to raise additional money to support their operations. In most instances, this has meant that sales tax revenue has been accounting for a larger proportion of these governments' OSR. However, as the data found in Table 5.6 indicates, revenue derived from a sales tax still amounts to only a small fraction of the OSR for special districts in many of the states that permit the usage of a tax on sales and gross receipts, while there are only eight states where sales tax proceeds are greater than 10 percent of OSR. Yet, there are six states, in which, special districts receive no revenue from a sales tax or, at best, a negligible amount.

It is noteworthy that almost all of the revenue that special districts receive from a tax on sales and gross receipts (95 percent in 2017) comes from a general sales tax that is piggybacked on a state sales tax. Furthermore, it is not unusual for the proceeds to be earmarked for a specific kind of countywide or citywide program or service.

Although only a very small fraction of total sales tax revenue originates from a charge on selective products or items, a huge proportion of it (94 percent in 2017) come from a sales tax on things designated as "Other." The remaining portion (6 percent in 2017) derives from a tax on public utilities.

### *School districts*

Fewer states permit school districts to levy a sales tax than is the case for any other type of local government. At present, only 13 states have given school districts the authority to use a sales tax to supplement their revenues which primarily have come from property taxes and state financial assistance (districts in only 12 states took advantage of this option in 2017). However, this is a sizable increase since there were only four states in 1962 that were permitted to levy a tax on sales. Many of the additional states that now grant school districts the power to charge a tax on sales have done so in the last two decades. Therefore, it is important to see if this upward trend continues, given the uncertainty that surrounds fiscal assistance from state governments in the wake of the Great Recession's impact (and now the effect of the COVID-19-induced recession) and the desire of local governments to reduce their reliance on the property tax (see Sheiner and Campbell 2020; U..S. Government Accounting Office 2021). In short, state governments may revert a posture of "fend for yourself" federalism during downturns in the economy and to school reform advocates may stress the need to tap other revenue sources that are less regressive (see Shannon 1987; Benton 2018).

Variability in school district dependency on sales tax revenue is apparent when looking at the figures in Table 5.7. Among the 12 states that derived money for a tax on sales and gross receipts in 2017, the proportion of OSR that is attributable to sales tax revenue ranges from a low of 1 percent or less in five states to a high 21 percent in Georgia and 50 percent in Louisiana. As mentioned above, it will be interesting to see if other states in the next few years are willing to let

*Table 5.7* Sales Tax Revenue of School Districts as a Proportion of OSR, 2017

| *State* | *(Percent)* | | | *State* | *(Percent)* | | |
|---|---|---|---|---|---|---|---|
| | *General Sales* | *Sales* | *Total* | | *General Sales* | *Sales* | *Total* |
| Colorado | * | 0.0 | * | Nebraska | 0 | .1 | .1 |
| Florida | 4.8 | 0.0 | 4.8 | Nevada | 0 | .3 | .3 |
| Georgia | 20.7 | 0.0 | 20.7 | New York | 0 | .2 | .2 |
| Iowa | 0.0 | 2.3 | 2.3 | Pennsylvania | 2.6 | .1 | 2.7 |
| Kentucky | 0.0 | 9.0 | 9.0 | South Dakota | 2.9 | 0.0 | 2.9 |
| Louisiana | 50.2 | 0 | 50.2 | Washington | 0.0 | * | * |

* Less than .5 percent.

*Source:* U.S. Bureau of the Census. Census of Governments. Compendium of Government Finances series, 1962–2017.

school districts assess a tax on sales as a buffer against recurring recessions, dwindling state financial assistance, and unwise/unpopular heavy dependence on property tax revenue.

To date, most of the revenue that school districts receive from a tax on sales and gross receipts comes from the general sales tax. In 1962, around two-thirds of the revenue was derived from the general sales tax but that proportion had increased to 93 percent by 2017.

## The income tax and local governments

If states have been somewhat reluctant to grant their local governments the authority to charge a tax on sales and gross receipts, they have been even more restrained and deliberative about allowing their local governments to levy a tax on income. This is undoubtedly due in large measure to the fact that the proceeds from the individual and corporate income tax constitute the second largest source of revenue for all but a handful of states.[2] Understandably, states have been much less willing to allow their local governments to compete with them for a part of the revenue that could be generated from an income tax, as states already must play "second fiddle" to the national government for this coveted type of revenue. In fact, it is often said that the federal government has first claimed on the use of an income tax and validation of this claim can be found in the fact that the federal government collects the lion's share of all income tax monies (usually around two-thirds). Moreover, by the early 1900s, most states had ceded all claim to property tax revenue to their local governments. But, since states do not have to compete with the federal government for sales tax revenue,[3] they then have been somewhat more willing to share this revenue source with their local governments as was seen in the earlier part of this chapter. Therefore, the bottom line is that states continue to be much less agreeable to allowing their local governments to siphon off a considerable portion of their second most important source of revenue—the sales tax.

This point is quite evident from a quick comparison of sales and income tax revenue over the last 55 years. While sales tax revenue has been the most significant component of the non-property tax component of local government revenues since 1962, the income tax accounts for far less of it. However, the income tax proportion of non-property tax revenue did increase from 12 to 21 percent from 1962 to 2017. This meant that, by 2017, proceeds from the income tax made up about one-third as much of non-property tax revenue of local governments as did the sales tax (i.e., 21 percent versus 63 percent). This is an improvement in comparison to 1962, when the income tax accounted for only about one-fifth of the amount of what the sales tax did. Going forward, it appears that the income tax could become a larger contributor to local government budgets. But will that be the case for each type of local government?

**Different levels of usage of the income tax by four types of local government**

The limited use of an income tax by local governments can be seen from another vantage point. In 1962, just five states granted their municipalities the authority to use an income tax. By 2017, still only 13 states (Alabama, Delaware, Indiana, Iowa, Kansas, Kentucky, Maryland, Michigan, Missouri, New York, Ohio, Oregon, and Pennsylvania) permitted at least one of five types of local governments (the exception being special districts) to levy an income tax (Urban Institute & Brookings Institution 2022). This compares to 49 states that currently allow at least some of their local governments to adopt a sales tax.

Although greater usage of the income tax in recent years is confirmed by financial data reported to the U.S. Bureau of the Census by local governments, this usage and its impact on OSR and TR varies significantly from one type of local government to another. This can be seen from Figure 5.6.

From the figure, it is clear that municipal governments have been the most conspicuous beneficiaries of revenue produced by an income tax. In 1962, income tax proceeds constituted about 2 percent of municipal governments' OSR. Within ten years, this percentage had more than tripled, with income tax proceeds staying fairly stable around 8 percent until a slowdown in the economy that occurred in the early part of the 21st century led to a noticeable decline

*Figure 5.6* Income Tax Revenue as a Percentage of OSR for Counties, Municipalities, Townships, and School Districts, 1962–2017

*Source:* U.S. Bureau of the Census. Census of Governments. Compendium of Government Finances series, 1962–2017.

by 2002. Yet, the income tax proportion of municipal government OSR had rebounded by 2007 but only to decline somewhat once again by 2012 as a result of wide sweeping effects of the Great Recession. Since the end of the Great Recession, the OSR proportion has remained steady.

Further examination of Figure 5.6 indicates that county governments, townships, and school districts have a history of considerably less reliance on an income tax. County and township government dependence on an income tax as a proportion of their OSR has followed a very similar path. Until around 1972, the income tax proportion of county government OSR amounted to less than 1 percent. From that point, the OSR proportion steadily climbed to 2 percent and has remained at that close to that level, although it declined slightly from 2012 to 2017. A parallel pattern can be seen for townships except that the rise to 2 percent began somewhere between 1972 and 1977 but became clearly evident by 1977. In 2017, it remained at that level, in spite of the Great Recession.

School districts are the least reliant on revenue generated from an income tax. In 1962, revenue from an income tax as a proportion of school district OSR amounted to about .5 percent. Over the years, this proportion increased only so slightly and had barely risen to 1 percent by 2012 and continued at that level throughout the Great Recession and its aftermath. As seen in earlier chapters, the overwhelming proportion of school district OSR comes from property tax collections.

Conspicuously absent from Figure 5.6 is data for special districts since no state permits these governments to levy an income tax.

Given this preliminary assessment of local governments' usage of an income tax, it will be instructive to examine in more detail this usage by municipalities, counties, townships, and school districts.

### *Municipalities*

By far, there are more states that permit their municipalities as opposed to their counties, townships, or school districts to levy an income tax. In 2017, municipalities in ten states had such authority (see Table 5.8). While proceeds from an income tax made up a small proportion of municipal OSR in six of these states, this was not the case in four other states. In New York, money derived from income tax collections accounted for about one-fourth of municipalities' OSR, while it amounted to over a third of municipal OSR in Pennsylvania. In the other two states (Ohio and Kentucky), income tax revenue constituted over one-half of municipal OSR there. It would seem likely that cities like Louisville, New York City, Buffalo, Rochester, Philadelphia, Pittsburg, Cleveland, and Cincinnati were major users of the income tax, as well as other cities in these states.

It is also important to point out that most of the revenue derived from a municipal tax on income was produced by the individual income tax. Not surprisingly, municipalities in New York and Pennsylvania collected a much larger

*Table 5.8* Income Tax Revenue of Municipal Governments as a Proportion of OSR, 2017

| *State* | *(Percent)* | | | *State* | *(Percent)* | | |
|---|---|---|---|---|---|---|---|
| | *Individual Income* | *Corporate Income* | *Total* | | *Individual Income* | *Corporate Income* | *Total* |
| Alabama | 2.8 | 0.0 | 2.8 | Michigan | 8.0 | 0.0 | 8.0 |
| Indiana | 3.9 | 0.0 | 3.9 | Missouri | 6.4 | 1.2 | 7.6 |
| Kansas | * | 0.0 | * | New York | 15.8 | 8.8 | 24.6 |
| Kentucky | 29.6 | 5.6 | 55.2 | Ohio | 48.3 | 2.0 | 50.3 |
| Maryland | 14.7 | 0.0 | 14.7 | Pennsylvania | 29.0 | 6.0 | 35.0 |

* Less than .5 percent.

*Source:* U.S. Bureau of the Census. Census of Governments. Compendium of Government Finances series, 1962–2012.

proportion of its total income tax revenue from a corporate income tax (around 9 and 6 percent, respectively) than did cities in the other eight states.

***Counties***

County governments are even less likely to have the authority to use an income tax. No state permitted county governments to levy a tax on income in 1962. Not much had changed by 2017, as only five states (Indiana, Kansas, Kentucky, Maryland, and Oregon) had given into pleas from home rule proponents to give counties greater latitude in raising revenue (see Table 5.9). It is noteworthy that all five of these states also give this same permission to their municipalities. In three of these five states, the proportion of county OSR attributable to income tax proceeds was fairly small or negligible. However, this is not true in Kentucky and Maryland. In Kentucky, income tax revenue amounts to nearly 16 percent of OSR, while in Maryland, money coming from income tax revenue makes up over one-quarter of the county OSR (26 percent). One final glance at Table 5.9 indicates that most of the money collected through an income tax is derived from a tax on individuals' income.

*Table 5.9* Income Tax Revenue of County Governments as a Proportion of OSR, 2012

| *State* | *(Percent)* | | | *State* | *(Percent)* | | |
|---|---|---|---|---|---|---|---|
| | *Individual Income* | *Corporate Income* | *Total* | | *Individual Income* | *Corporate Income* | *Total* |
| Indiana | 9.4 | 0.0 | 9.4 | Maryland | 28.2 | 0.0 | 28.2 |
| Kansas | * | 0.0 | * | Oregon | * | 3.4 | 3.4 |
| Kentucky | 15.5 | 5.6 | 15.5 | | | | |

* Less than .1 percent.

*Source:* U.S. Bureau of the Census. Census of Governments. Compendium of Government Finances series, 1962–2017.

In spite of the historical unwillingness of state governments to grant county governments expanded revenue-raising authority, will states with highly urbanized and/or rapidly growing counties be more receptive to persistent calls to convey greater fiscal latitude to counties and even the ability to levy an income tax? Speculation along these lines gains added credence in the wake of what seems to be a parade of downturns in the economy in recent years that create great revenue uncertainty for all local governments, including counties (see Benton 2012; Perlman and Benton 2012). But this is especially so for an increasing number of counties that are densely populated and experiencing rapid growth and are therefore under considerable pressure to provide more municipal- and urban-type services (see Benton 2002a, 2002b, 2003a, 2003b, 2010, 2019) as well as comply with an increasing number of unfunded federal and state mandates.

### *School districts*

In 1962, no state allowed their school districts to collect revenue from an income tax, but by 2017, school districts in four states (Iowa, Kentucky, Ohio, and Pennsylvania) had been granted the authority to do so. All of these states also permit other local governments to levy an income tax: Iowa (municipalities, counties, and townships); Ohio and Pennsylvania (municipalities, special districts); Kentucky (counties and municipalities). Therefore, there is evidence of a growing pattern of granting greater leeway in revenue-raising capabilities in these states. School districts in all four states can levy only a tax on an individual's income.

From Table 5.10, it can be seen that revenue coming from an income tax provides only a small part of OSR in two of these states (Iowa and Ohio), although the percent is somewhat higher in Kentucky and Pennsylvania. Nevertheless, greater ability of school districts to levy an income tax could become a reality down the road. Several factors or conditions could be a harbinger of things to come.

For many years, financial experts have warned that the way in which public schools are typically funded is a classic example of "placing too many eggs in

*Table 5.10* Income Tax Revenue of School Districts as a Proportion of OSR, 2017

| *State* | *(Percent)* | | | *State* | *(Percent)* | | |
|---|---|---|---|---|---|---|---|
| | *Individual Income* | *Corporate Income* | *Total* | | *Individual Income* | *Corporate Income* | *Total* |
| Iowa | 3.2 | 0.0 | 3.2 | Ohio | 3.5 | 0.0 | 3.5 |
| Kentucky | 8.4 | 0.0 | 8.4 | Pennsylvania | 9.0 | 0.0 | 9.0 |

* Less than .5 percent.

*Source:* U.S. Bureau of the Census. Census of Governments. Compendium of Government Finances series, 1962–2017.

one basket," given the usual very heavy reliance on property tax revenue. As seen in Chapter 4, school districts' dependence on the property tax supersedes that of all other local governments. In 2017, property tax collections accounted for around 83 percent of OSR and 95 percent of all tax revenue (TTR). But, beyond the concern about too great of a reliance on the property tax, there are more serious issues to consider. While the property tax is a stable tax (i.e., it grows at a predictable rate), predictability and stability are not sufficient to guarantee fiscal adequacy in the long-run. Property taxes, for example, while they grow predictably, usually grow more slowly than the cost of operating public school systems. Therefore, it is important that a tax also be characterized as having elasticity, which is the ability of a tax to produce the kind of growth that keeps up with the growth in the economy. This is an important consideration since the cost of providing public services such as education typically grows at least as fast as, if not greater than, the economy. As this book goes to press in 2023, local governments officials at all levels are very troubled by the challenge posed to them to balance their budgets due to the high rate of inflation. Simply put, they are discovering that the elasticity of their primary sources of revenue (but especially the property tax) is insufficient to keep pace with the sharply rising costs of providing staple services. As an example, Dr. Sandra Yudice, the City Administrator in the Georgetown, South Carolina with a population of around 10,000, recently informed the Mayor and City Council at a budget workshop that she did not know if it would be possible for the city to bridge the gap between projected expenditures and the grossly devalued anticipated revenue for FY 2024. Even with a slight uptick in revenue over last year, many local officials like Dr. Yudice are finding out that their revenue will not buy what the same amount of money bought last year.

The increasing volatility in the economy and uncertainly of intergovernmental financial assistance poses another challenge to amassing the revenue necessary to operate a viable public school system. What seems to be the greater frequency and intensity of upheavals in the economy has been a cause of concern for school district officials and the parents of school-aged children alike. The most recent Great Recession, which was marked by the "bust" in the housing market and a record number of mortgages "being under water" (but especially in California and Florida), was a wakeup call for school districts that experienced significant reductions in what was supposed to be a stable and predictable source of revenue (the property tax). The large number of home foreclosures, along with the subsequent sharp drop in many states of the market and assessed value of real estate, has led to well-founded fears concerning the adequacy and reliability of the property tax in both the short- and long-run. A parallel concern for school districts is whether their state governments (and to a lesser extent the federal government) who are also still experiencing the aftershock of the Great Recession can be counted on during economic slowdowns to continue to provide financial assistance at expected or promised levels. Certainly, experience over the last several decades indicates that the federal and state governments are also having to deal with the loss of their revenue due to recessions have not been reticent about exhibiting an attitude of "fend-for-yourself" federalism when it comes to intergovernmental fiscal assistance (see Shannon 1987; Benton 2018).

Then, who could have predicted or even imagined the economic dislocation that has been caused by the COVID-19 health crisis (see Seager and Campbell 2020; U..S. Government Accounting Office 2021). School districts have been sent reeling in every way conceivable—having to shift to remote instruction, attending to unimaginable health and safety protocols, adjusting to the disruption of family life, and, of course, worrying about the increased cost of providing educational services in unprecedented and uncertain times. Our ability to determine the extent to which school systems have fared financially will take years and perhaps decades. At this point, we do know that American Rescue Plan Act (ARPA) will provide some much-needed financial assistance. However, mixed messages are being received from state government leaders as to prospects for a quick economic recovery in their states which could permit them to render some additional monetary assistance to local school districts.

But, even during times of a steady and predictable flow of intergovernmental aid and a strong economy, there are other drawbacks to placing a great deal of dependency on financial assistance from state governments. The most obvious drawback is the fact that most state governments receive the largest proportion of their OSR revenue from some type of a sales tax. As mentioned earlier in this chapter, the sales tax is a prime example of a regressive tax, even if there are exemptions for things like food, medicine, and other necessities. In short, school districts find themselves in the untenable position of financing education with a less than desirable type of tax (i.e., one which is paid disproportionately by lower-income individuals and families). However, permitting school districts to levy an income tax would constitute a better and fairer option than depending on state fiscal assistance because an individual income tax is generally regarded as a progressive type of tax, meaning that it is paid by people with a greater ability to pay.

Another situation that could result in greater pressure being brought to bear on states to allow their school districts to levy an income tax is the ever-present concern to close the gap between rich and poor school districts with respect to how education is financed. Since the California Supreme Court in 1971 in the case of *Serrano v. Priest* ruled that inequities in school expenditures resulting from variations in taxable wealth were unconstitutional, courts of last resort in over one-half of the states have handed down similar decisions. In spite of the fact that all states have made efforts to equalize funding by using distribution formulas that target districts with lower property values, significant variations and other problems still remain. These efforts cannot take away the regressive nature of how the state raises the revenue that they share with their

*Table 5.11* Income Tax Revenue of Townships as a Proportion of OSR, 2017

| *State* | *(Percent)* | | | *State* | *(Percent)* | | |
|---|---|---|---|---|---|---|---|
| | *Individual Income* | *Corporate Income* | *Total* | | *Individual Income* | *Corporate Income* | *Total* |
| Indiana | 3.9 | 0.0 | 3.9 | Ohio | .3 | * | .3 |
| Kansas | * | 0 | * | Pennsylvania | 26.4 | 0.0 | 26.4 |

* Less than .5 percent.

*Source:* U.S. Bureau of the Census. Census of Governments. Compendium of Government Finances series, 1962–2017.

school districts. In addition, the increase in the number of charter schools and growing number of states that permit the use of vouchers often can siphon off vital funds that could be used to equalize funding across the state and from one school district to another.

In sum, these conditions and factors could eventually convince naysayers and opponents of a local government income tax to support a school district income tax or could even result in more states' willingness to grant their school district this authority.

#### *Townships*

Of the 20 states that have organized township governments, only four of them (Indiana, Kansas, Ohio, and Pennsylvania) have conferred authority on these type local governments to levy a tax on income (see Table 5.11). All such revenue is derived from an individual income tax. In Kansas and Ohio, income tax revenue constitutes an insignificant amount of township governments' OSR. Even in Indiana, income tax revenue makes up a very meager proportion of township OSR. In stark contrast, money coming from an income tax is a major source of revenue for townships in Pennsylvania. In fact, income tax revenue accounts for over one-fourth of these governments' OSR (26 percent), which is close to the same proportion that is reported for municipalities in the Keystone State.

### Miscellaneous taxes: Augmenting local government resources

In addition, to granting their local governments the authority to levy a tax on sales and income, states also permit these governments to place a tax on a long list of other activities and items (e.g., vehicles, businesses, stadium, entertainment admission, occupational licenses, utilities, document stamp fees, recording of titles and deeds, and updating the title on one's property) that are referred to here as miscellaneous taxes. The most recognizable miscellaneous tax and the

*Table 5.12* Miscellaneous Tax Revenue for All Governments as a Proportion of Own-Source Revenue (OSR), Total Revenue (TR), and Total Tax Revenue (TTR), 1962 and 2017

| | *(Percent)* | |
|---|---|---|
| | *1962* | *2017* |
| Own-Source Revenue (OSR) | 2.6 | 2.8 |
| Total Revenue (TR) | 1.6 | 1.6 |
| Total Tax Revenue (TTR) | 3.3 | 4.4 |

*Source:* U.S. Bureau of the Census. Census of Governments. Compendium of Government Finances series, 1962–2017.

one that accounts for the largest proportion of this category of taxes is the vehicle license tax; in 2017, 7 percent of funds collected via miscellaneous taxes came from this source.

Over the years, not much has changed with regard to the role played by miscellaneous taxes in the revenue system for local governments. Simply put, miscellaneous taxes historically have accounted for a very small proportion of local government revenues no matter how one measures it—that is as a percent of OSR, TR, or TTR (see Table 5.12). Regardless of this fact, local governments would be hard pressed to have to replace money derived from this source of revenue if it were suddenly not there any longer.

What has changed over time, however, is the proportion of non-property tax revenue that is attributable to miscellaneous taxes when a comparison is made with the sales and income tax (see Table 5.13). Not surprisingly, miscellaneous tax revenue has always made up a smaller percentage of non-property tax revenue collections than has sales tax proceeds. As of 2017, the miscellaneous revenue percentage is now smaller than the income tax proportion as well. Other data contained in the table also indicate that the

*Table 5.13* Non-Property Tax Revenue Proportions, 1962 and 2017

| | *(Percent)* | |
|---|---|---|
| | *1962* | *2017* |
| Sales Tax | 58 | 63 |
| Income Tax | 12 | 21 |
| Miscellaneous (Other) Taxes | 30 | 16 |
| TOTAL | 100 | 100 |

*Source:* U.S. Bureau of the Census. Census of Governments. Compendium of Government Finances series, 1962–2017.

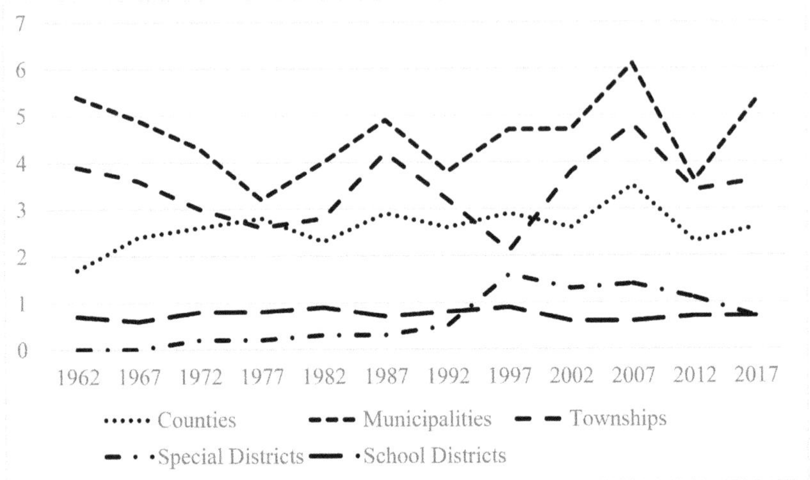


*Figure 5.7* Other Tax Revenue as a Percentage of OSR for Counties, Municipalities, Townships, Special Districts, and School Districts, 1962–2017

*Source:* U.S. Bureau of the Census. Census of Governments. Compendium of Government Finances series, 1962–2017.

miscellaneous tax proportion of all non-property tax revenue in 2017 is only about one-half of what it was in 1962 (i.e., 16 versus 30 percent). Also, worthy of mention is the fact that the proportion of non-property tax revenue accounted for by the sales and income tax is noticeably higher (somewhat more so for the latter than the former). Given the analysis of changing trends and patterns for the sales and income taxes earlier in this chapter, these findings should have been expected.

Examination of the importance of miscellaneous tax revenue for each of the five types of local governments provides a final perspective. From the data presented in Figure 5.7, it is easy to see that there is not a lot of variation among various local governments as to the part that revenue produced by a number of miscellaneous taxes plays in these governments' overall budgetary picture. From 1962 to 2012, miscellaneous tax revenue constituted a slightly greater proportion of OSR for municipal, township, and county governments, although somewhat higher for the first two of these governments. However, there is a very conspicuous decline in the respective proportion for each of these three governments evident in 2012 and likely due, at least in part, to the economic dislocation associated with the Great Recession. However, note a slight uptick in the ORS proportion after 2012. Furthermore, it is clear that special and school districts depend even less so on this type of tax revenue and perhaps is explained by the limited or specialized nature of these type of governments.

## Summary and conclusions

The analysis in this chapter clearly indicates that local governments are increasingly relying on revenue produced by non-property kinds of taxes to fill the vacuum left by a decline in the growth rate in property tax yields. While there are differing explanations as to why local governments have reduced their dependency on the property tax, it is quite possible that it has something to do with the growing belief in many circles that the property tax is not viewed as either the best or fairest way to finance the provision of local government services. For a number of years, there have been persistent complaints about property owners having to bear too much of the burden of financing local government programs and services. The fact that there was a very noticeable pattern whereby the property tax revenue proportion of TR, OSR, and TTR has been declining in the wake of the national tax revolt movement (became clearly evident with 1982 data) gives considerable credence to this explanation.

But, as will be seen in the next two chapters, other sources of OSR revenue (charges for services and miscellaneous proceeds) are also accounting for a larger proportion of the monetary resources required to finance the provision of local government services.

## Notes

1 An indivisible local government service is one that cannot be broken down into smaller parts and is always provided to all citizens in a jurisdiction. In addition, indivisible services are ones for which no clear-cut individual users can be identified and thereby assessed a charge or fee for its usage. Good examples are fire and police protection, roads and traffic control devices, environmental protection and resource conservation, criminal, civil, and specialty courts, general health care (e.g., immunization for school-aged children, animal control, food and restaurant inspections, tests for commutable diseases, mosquito abatement), economic development, libraries, and planning and zoning. By contrast, divisible services are ones in which users of a service can be readily pinpointed and required to pay for it through some kind of fee, charge, or special assessment.

2 There are only seven states (Alaska, Florida, Nevada, South Dakota, Texas, Washington, and Wyoming) that do not have an individual income tax, while residents of New Hampshire and Tennessee tax only dividends and income from investments. South Dakota and Wyoming also do not have a corporate income tax, while four other states (Nevada, Ohio, Texas, and Washington) charge a gross receipts tax in lieu of having a corporate income tax.

3 There are a few minor exceptions like federal excise taxes.

## References

Afonso, Whitney B. 2017. *Local Sales Tax Laws: State by State Details*. Chapel Hill, NC: Institute of Government.

Benton, J. Edwin. 2002a. *Counties as Service Delivery Agents: Changing Expectations and Roles*. Westport, CT: Praeger.

———. 2002b. "County Service Delivery: Does Structure Matter?" *Public Administration Review*, 62(July/August): 423–31.

———. 2003a. "County Government Structure and County Revenue Policy: What the Connection?" *State and Local Government Review*, 35(Spring): 78–89.

———. 2003b. "The Impact of Structural Reform on County Government Service Provision," *Social Science Quarterly*, 84(December): 858–74.

———. 2010. "Trends in Local Government Revenues: The Old, the New, and the Future." In Ingram, Gregory K., and Yu-Hung Hong (eds.), *Municipal Revenues and Land Policies*. Cambridge, MA: Lincoln Institute of Land Policy: 81–112.

———. 2012. "State-City and County Fiscal Relations: A Look at Past and Present Relations and a Glimpse at Relations in the Future." In Thurmaier, Kurt, and Jack Meek (eds.), *Networked Governance: The Future of Intergovernmental Management*. Washington, DC: Congressional Quarterly Press: 39–69.

———. 2018. "Intergovernmental Relations in the Early Twentieth-First Century: Lingering Images of Earlier Phases or Emergence of a New Phase?" In Stenberg, Carl, and David Hamilton (eds.), *Intergovernmental Relations in the United States: Reflections and Directions*. New York: Routledge: 15–36.

———. 2019. "Local Government Service Roles in the U.S.: Constancy and Change." In Kerley, Richard, Joyce Liddle, and Pamela Dunning (eds.), *Handbook of International Local Government*. New York: Routledge: 183–202.

Bowman, Ann O'M, and Richard C. Kearney. 2008. *State and Local Government*. 7th ed. Boston: Houghton Mifflin Company.

Dye, Thomas R., and Susan MacManus. 2015. *Politics in States and Communities*. 15th ed. Upper Saddle River, NJ: Pearson.

Perlman, Bruce J, and J. Edwin Benton. 2012. "Going It Alone: New Survey Data on Economic Recovery Strategies in Local Government," *State and Local Government Review*, 44(Special Issue): 5S–16S.

U.S. Government Accounting Office. 2021. *State and Local Governments: Fiscal Conditions during the COVID-19 Pandemic in Selected States*. Washington, DC: U.S. Government Accounting Office. https://www.gao.gov/products/gao-21-562. Accessed on March 23, 2023.

Shannon, John. 1987. "The Return to Fend-For-Yourself Federalism: The Reagan Mark," *Intergovernmental Perspective*, 13 (Summer–Fall): 34–37.

Sheiner, Louise, and Sophia Campbell. 2020. *How Much Is COVID-19 Hurting State and Local Revenues*. Washington, DC: Brookings Institution. https://www.brookings.edu/blog/up-front/2020/09/24/how-much-is-covid-19-hurting-state-and-local-revenues/. Accessed on March 23, 2023.

Urban Institute & Brookings Institution. 2022. *The State of State (and Local) Tax Policy*. Washington, DC: Tax Policy Center, Urban Institute and Brookings Institution. https://www.taxpolicycenter.org/briefing-book/how-do-state-and-local-individual-income-taxes-work. Accessed on March 19, 2023.

Walczak, Jared, and Scott Drenkard. 2017. *State and Local Sales Tax Rates in 2017*. Washington, DC: Tax Foundation. https://www.google.com/search?client=firefox-b-1-d&q=county+government+use+of+local+option+sales+taxes&dlnr=1&sei=Z2QWZO77KJ2XwbkPjfCk0A8. Accessed on March 18, 2023.

## Appendix

*Table A5.1* County, City, Township, Special District, and School District Usage of the General and Selective Sales Tax, 2017

| *Permit General and Selective Sales Taxes for:* | | | |
|---|---|---|---|
| *Counties, Cities, Special Districts, and School Districts* | *Counties, Cities Townships, and Special Districts* | *Counties, Cities, and Special Districts* | *Counties, Cities Townships* |
| Colorado | Missouri | Arizona | Massachusetts |
| Kentucky | Wisconsin | California | Michigan |
| Louisiana | | Florida | Minnesota |
| Washington | | Idaho | New Jersey |
| | | New Mexico | Ohio |
| | | Oregon | Texas |

*Source:* U.S. Bureau of the Census. Census of Governments. Compendium of Government Finances series, 1962–2017.

# 6 Charges for Services

## Paying Directly for What One Gets in Services

While four of five types of local governments (counties, municipalities, townships, and school districts) have traditionally relied heavily on revenue produced by some form of taxation to supply the necessary money to fund a long list of programs and services, these governments increasingly have been looking for ways to reduce this dependency. In Fiscal Year (FY) 1962, counties, municipalities, townships, and school districts collected slightly more than $20 billion in revenue from taxes which translates into 68 percent of OSR and 64 percent of TR. By FY 2020, the combined amount of revenue produced by some type of tax for these four local governments had grown exponentially to nearly $804 billion, but the tax revenue proportion of OSR and TR had dropped appreciably to 64 and 37 percent, respectively. As seen from the data analysis in Chapter 4, municipal and county governments have led the way in reducing their reliance on tax revenue, while school and special districts have not been as successful in this regard. And, in spite of the fact that special districts have never depended very much on tax proceeds to fund the cost of providing their services, the proportion of special district OSR and TR accounted for by tax-generated funds also declined from 32 to 27 percent (OSR) and from 17 to 14 percent (TR) between 1962 and 2017.

Before proceeding to a discussion and detailed analysis of the principal way that local governments have been able to reduce (or at least minimize) their dependency on tax revenue (i.e., utilizing "charges for services" or "user fees" where practical), it is important to explain or understand the reasoning behind the desire to find an alternative to levying various kinds of taxes as a viable and acceptable means to fund the provision of as many local government services as possible. Since taxes historically have produced an ample amount of revenue for governments at all levels to satisfy the service needs and expectations of their citizens, why would local governments, in particular, and governments, in general, want to switch to a different kind of funding scheme?

DOI: 10.4324/9781032640389-6

## Rationale for charges for services and user fees

The subtitle to this chapter should provide us with a good starting point for understanding the reasoning behind local governments wanting to fund part or all of the cost of providing as many services as possible by requiring charges for services rendered or a user fee. The subtitle "paying directly for what one gets" speaks directly to the logical way in which people think about purchases in general, and it sounds something like the following: "If I want something, then I purchase it, assuming I have the money to do so; but if I do not want something, then I do not buy it, whether I have the money or not." In the marketplace of life, people as consumers often are presented with the opportunity to make choices from among products that are for sale and can decide either to buy or not buy the product or even decide to buy a similar product or service. Likewise, as citizens of a local government, citizen "consumers" also have the right to the same kind of options when it comes to publicly provided services. Proponents of charges for services and user charges/fees do so because it is easy to understand and accept by the public since they directly link the benefits and cost of public goods in the fashion of the marketplace (Dye and MacManus 2015, 415). Moreover, proponents of these means to fund the cost of local government services do so because charges and services and users clearly satisfy the benefits principle (Bowman and Kearney 2008).

Several examples illustrate how citizens exercise these options. In one example, citizens can choose to drive on a toll road and pay a user fee to do so or elect to take regular streets and roads to travel to the same destination without being charged for it. Other examples involve citizens leaving their vehicle in a publicly owned airport parking garage, being transported by EMS personal via ambulance to a hospital, or seeking medical treatment at a government-owned hospital. In all three cases, citizens pay a user fee for the use of the parking garage or are assessed a charge for EMS transport and services rendered by the hospital. Take note that citizens in these scenarios who choose not to use the toll road or the parking garage, opt for EMS initial medical treatment and transportation, or obtain advanced medical treatment pay nothing to the respective governments to fund these services, and, of course, why should they? The point is that local government citizens can elect to use some government services with the understanding that they will incur a charge or fee, while citizens who choose not to utilize various services offered by their local governments are under no obligation to help pay for the construction of facilities or operating expenses associated with these services. More and more, local governments and their citizens are seemingly in agreement as to the reasonableness and fairness of the kind of citizen consumer model described above.

In the examples mentioned above, charges for services and user fees are often calculated so as to generate close to the 100 percent of the money required to provide the service. However, that is not necessarily the case with a number of other kinds of local government services for which a fee is charged. For instance, the money local governments receive in the form of charges and fees for using library services, going to a park, visiting or attending a function at a cultural facility (museum, art gallery, performing arts center, etc.), using a recreational facility (gym, playing field, pool, etc.), living in public housing, having sewage and solid/toxic waste properly disposed of, and attending a K-12 school or community college usually does not cover the full cost of providing library, parks and recreational/cultural, airport, housing and community development, sewage, solid waste management, and educational services. In reality, revenue from several sources (taxes, intergovernmental grants-in-aid, miscellaneous funds, and proceeds from the sale of bonds), in addition to money derived from charges and user fees, is required to finance the cost of these and many other services.

## Importance of different kinds of user fees/charges

What kinds of non-utility-type charges for services and user fees do local governments regularly utilize and which ones produce the most revenue? The U.S. Bureau of the Census in its Census of Governments identifies 12 types of non-utility kinds of charges for services/user fees which are associated with the following service areas: education, hospitals, highways, airports, parking, port facilities, parks and recreation, natural resources, housing and community development, sewage, solid waste management, and other. Figures 6.1 and 6.2 display the percentage of total charges for services/user fees revenue derived from each type in 1962 and 2020 for counties, municipalities, townships, and special districts (school districts were excluded from this analysis since they obtain money only from education-related charges for service).

To understand fully the implications for the data displayed in these two figures, it is instructive to keep three important things in mind. First, there was a significant increase in the total amount of money that local governments were collecting for all types of non-utility charges for services and user fees in 2020 compared to 1962. Over this period, the amount of money that was generated by charges for services increased from $3.2 billion to approximately $300 billion or by an average of $5.4 billion per year. Second, as mentioned in the previous section, the proportion of OSR accounted for by all non-utility charges for services and user fees almost doubled from 13 to 24 percent over this 58-year period. Third, the ratio of charges for services revenue to property tax revenue increased significantly from 22 percent in 1962 to 59 percent in 2020, meaning that local governments were relying less on property tax revenue and more on money derived from charges for services.

Looking first at Figure 6.1, one can see that hospital charges for services and charges for a variety of "other" miscellaneous services produced the largest proportion of this type of revenue for local governments (i.e., 24 and

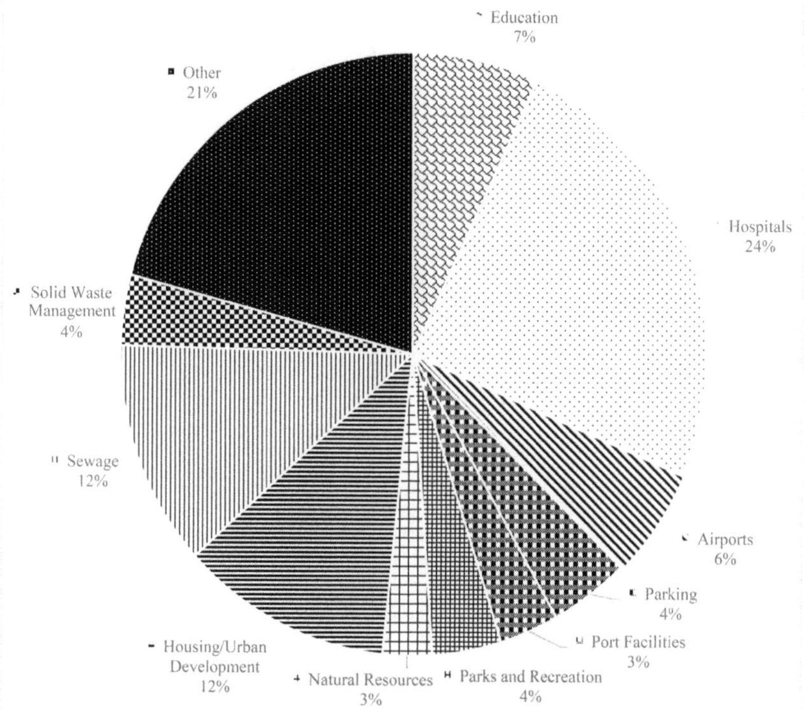


*Figure 6.1* Distribution of Charges for Services for All Local Governments, 1962

*Source*: U.S. Bureau of the Census. Census of Governments. Compendium of Government Finances series, 1962–2017 and U.S. Bureau of the Census and 2020 State & Local Government Finance Historical Datasets and Tables. Compendium of Government Finances (Washington, DC: Government Printing Office).

21 percent, respectively) in 1962. Two other service areas (sewage and housing/urban renewal) accounted for the next highest proportions of charges for services revenue (12 percent for both areas). Another 7 and 6 percent of local governments' charges for services money was obtained from charges assessed for education- and airport-related services, respectively. The remaining 18 percent was generated by charges for services on parking (4 percent), solid waste management (4 percent), parks and recreation (4 percent), natural resources (3 percent), and port facilities services (3 percent). Less than 1 percent was received from highway charges for services.

Turning to Figure 6.2, it is evident that some things had remained about the same, while other things had changed over the past 58 years. As to things that remained about the same, it appears that the proportion of non-utility-type charges for services accounted for by several types of services (e.g., natural resources, parks and

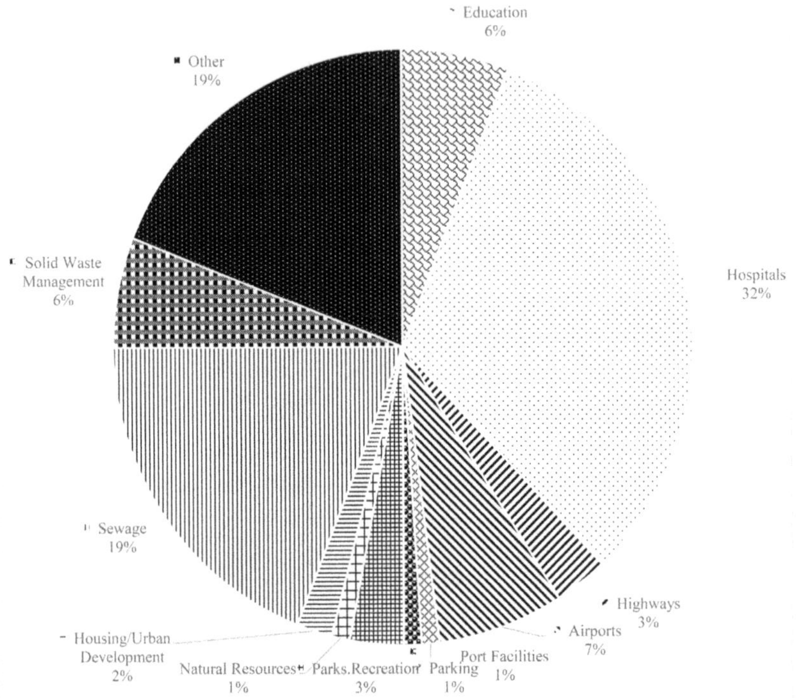


*Figure 6.2* Distribution of Charges for Services for All Local Governments, 2020

*Source:* U.S. Bureau of the Census. Census of Governments. Compendium of Government Finances series, 1962–2017 and U.S. Bureau of the Census and 2020 State & Local Government Finance Historical Datasets and Tables. Compendium of Government Finances (Washington, DC: Government Printing Office).

recreation, parking, and port facilities) remained quite low and even declined slightly since 1962. The education proportion, while somewhat smaller, virtually remained the same by 2020. Also note the conspicuous drop in the proportion for housing/urban renewal from 12 to 2 percent over the last 58 years. Although responsible for only a tiny proportion of charges for services income in 1962, charges for the use of highways had increased by 2020 (i.e., from less than .5 to 3 percent). Moreover, it can be seen that the proportion of charges for services revenue attributable to "other" miscellaneous services in 1962 (21 percent) had declined to 19 percent by 2020.

Very noticeable changes, however, are noted for charges for services in other service areas. Most conspicuous was the sharp rise in the charges for services proportion recorded for hospitals. It increased by 8 percentage points from 24 percent in 1962 to 32 percent in 2020. Nevertheless, one has to wonder how much of the increase in hospital charges for services is related to the rapidly escalating cost of health care in the United States and not to calculated efforts to wean themselves from property tax revenue. Another noteworthy increase is seen for sewage charges for services, as the proportion for this service area jumped from 12 to 19 percent between 1962 and 2020.

Somewhat less conspicuous but still notable are changes that occurred in some other service areas. For instance, between 1962 and 2020, the charges for services proportion rose for solid waste management (from 4 to 6 percent), while the proportion for airports climbed from 6 to 7 percent.

In addition to the services mentioned above, counties, municipalities, townships, and special districts often provide their residents with utilities like water, electric power, natural gas, and mass transit for which they charge a consumption or user fee.[1] Utilities are typically viewed differently than are other kinds of services for which local governments levy a charge. More specifically, each type of utility is considered to be an expressly designated enterprise operation and funds collected by them are usually segregated from the operating budget and general fund of the parent local government. In fact, utilities are legally viewed as and should be run like an independent or private sector businesses and therefore are self-sufficient entities in the sense that they are self-sustaining (i.e., they generate enough revenue from the sale of water, electricity, or natural gas to support their operations). In short, utility services are established with the expectation that they operate on the basis that they will at least break even financially.[2]

However, utilities are different from other types of local government charges for services in that they many times are expected to make a modest "profit," as a result of charge proceeds exceeding capital costs and operational expenses. This can occur in two ways. One is where the utility, much like a private sector company, sets the rates it charges its citizens at a level higher than what it is expected to cost to operate. To make this scenario viable and also be able to offer rates comparable to private sector providers, the Cities of Lakeland and Tallahassee, Florida have long operated their own electric generating plants; in another example, the City of Georgetown, South Carolina purchases electric power at a wholesale rate from a state-owned utility (Santee Cooper) and then resells it to its citizens at a cheaper rate than what citizens could buy electricity directly from Santee Cooper. It also helps that these cities have been granted authority to operate what can be best described as a local government "friendly monopoly." Another way this happens is where the local government sells a service (e.g., water) at a higher rate than it charges its own citizens to residents of neighboring communities (for instance, the City of Tallahassee, Florida has been selling water to residents of unincorporated Leon County for several decades at a cost of 150 percent of what it charges city residents and businesses). As such, local governments like the ones mentioned above are in a better position to augment their revenue base and perhaps avoid or at least minimize financial hardships during times of a slowed economy, as they can have the luxury of transferring some of their "profit" to their general or even "rainy day" fund (this is what the Cities of Georgetown and Tallahassee do).

Like local governments, state governments and even the federal government also take advantage of charges for services and user fees to pay for the cost of services they provide to their respective citizens and businesses. In fact, state governments often use charges for services and user fees for many of the same services (e.g., electric power, toll highways and bridges, health care in state-owned hospitals and clinics, occupational licenses and certifications, admissions to state parks and fairgrounds, hunting and fishing licenses, business licenses, and a host of court-related fees). The federal government also charges a number of fees that are similar to those imposed by state and local governments, but its most well-known charge for service, of course, is paid every time someone sends a letter or package through the United States Postal Service or visits a national park or landmark.

In spite of a local government's desire to raise additional revenue from charges for services as a means to lessen their dependence on property taxes, these governments have to consider the practicality of this type of revenue. This initially requires determining the nature of the service: Is it a divisible or an indivisible service? A divisive service is one that must satisfy two important criteria. First, it is one in which a clearly identifiable user can be established. Examples would include users of recreational facilities, water, electricity, natural gas, public housing, ambulance services, mass transit, cable TV services, marinas, port facilities, parking garages, drivers on toll roads and bridges, individuals seeking marriage licenses, building and burning permits and construction fees, divorce decrees, businesses needing health and safety inspections, building contractors who are required to obtain plumbing, electrical, and frame inspections, patients at publicly owned hospitals, school-aged children receiving free or reduced cost lunches or inoculations against diseases, homeowners and rental property owners needing sewage and solid waste collection, among others. Second, local officials must be able to establish and then easily collect a reasonably priced fee or user charge for a divisible service.

Unlike with the case for divisible-type services, consumption of indivisible-type services is not easy to measure and cannot be easily apportioned to users. Examples of indivisible-type services include fire, police, consumer and environmental protection, water conservation, planning and zoning, traffic control, libraries, mosquito abatement, courts, jails, animal control, coroner functions, tax assessment and collection, flood/drainage control, conducting elections, and collecting vital statistics. Needless to say, local governments cannot determine the amount of police or fire services or mosquito control that citizens use and what would be a fair price to charge them. Therefore, indivisible services are not amenable to being paid for with user fees or charges for services.

Since local governments cannot fund indivisible services through a user fee or charge, they are then inevitably left with paying for them primarily by a less desirable means—usually some kind of tax.[3] As such, local governments become the only realistic service provider out of default since the private sector is driven by the profit motive. With no other provision options available, local governments are resigned to providing indivisible services that their citizens expect and demand unless they are willing to contract out to private, for-profit vendors or non-profit entities. Therefore, local governments, when presented with the opportunity to fund in part or in whole a service with a user fee or charge, are increasingly doing so since taxpayers—but particularly, property owners—are demanding that more of the burden of paying for the cost of government services be shifted to clearly identifiable users than has heretofore been the case. For property owners who feel as though that they have shouldered too much of the burden of financing local government services, the matter simply boils down to a matter of fairness and a way to minimize the obvious service "freeloader" problem.

As will be seen in the analysis below, there has been mounting and conspicuous evidence over the last several decades of a concerted effort on the part of local governments to shift—to the extent possible—the financing of divisible-type services away from all kinds of taxes (but especially property taxes) to charges for services and user fees.[4] In fact, this trend is one of the most important ones identified and discussed in this book.

## Growing use of charges for services and user fees

If there was one common pattern that seemed to characterize the structure of the typical local government revenue system in early America, it was the obvious heavy reliance on taxes (but especially, property taxes) to supply the resources needed to perform the many day-to-day functions of these governments and provide a growing menu of basic services. This pattern was still obvious by the middle of the 20th century. However, with the growth in the size and scope of local government and changes in public opinions and attitudes about public financing by the post-World War II era, local government officials sensed the urgency and rationality to rethink how their governments should fund the provision of services. Specifically, a clear-cut consensus began to form that taxpayers were being unfairly burdened with providing a disproportionate share of the resources needed to pay for local government services. Consequently, local government officials—where feasible—began the process of shifting the financing of their services away from tax-based revenue sources (but particularly, the property tax) to ones that required clearly identifiable users of specific services to pay a user fee or charge. As will be seen in the analysis below, that practice and pattern is still ongoing as we have now entered the third decade of the 21st century.

Table 6.1 provides a first glimpse of the growth of charges for services, generally, and by comparison to tax revenue for all local governments from 1962 to 2020. Here, one sees that the amount of total local government revenue generated from charges for services, while smaller than that for taxes, is still impressive. This is especially so when comparing the growth rate in each of these two sources of local government revenue over time. It is obvious that charges for services collections

*Table 6.1* Comparison of Dollar Amount of Revenue from Local Government Charges for Services and Percent Change from Year to Year to Amount of Local Government Total Tax Revenue (TTR) and Change from Year to Year, 1962 and 2020

| | *Total Tax Revenue (TTR) Amount (in billions of dollars)* | *Percent Change* | *Charges for Services Amount (in millions of dollars)* | *Percent Change* |
|---|---|---|---|---|
| 1962 | $ 4,063 | — | $ 20,940 | — |
| 1967 | 6,285 | 54.7 | 29,074 | 38.8 |
| 1972 | 17,069 | 71.6 | 49,741 | 71.1 |
| 1977 | 19,097 | 11.9 | 74,852 | 50.5 |
| 1982 | 35,817 | 87.7 | 103,783 | 38.7 |
| 1987 | 55,546 | 103.0 | 153,973 | 48.4 |
| 1992 | 85,364 | 53.7 | 228,679 | 48.5 |
| 1997 | 118,474 | 99.9 | 284,399 | 24.4 |
| 2002 | 152,291 | 29.1 | 425,149 | 49.5 |
| 2007 | 210,353 | 37.5 | 526,932 | 23.7 |
| 2012 | 252,976 | 20.0 | 589,885 | 12.1 |
| 2017 | 299,992 | 19.0 | 706,752 | 19.8 |
| 2020 | 336,221 | 12.1 | 804,294 | 13.8 |

*Source:* U.S. Bureau of the Census. Census of Governments. Compendium of Government Finances series, 1962–2017 and 2020 State & Local Government Finance Historical Datasets and Tables. Compendium of Government Finances (Washington, DC: Government Printing Office).

were, generally speaking, growing at a much faster clip than tax proceeds for several of the five-year intervals than was the case for tax revenue (but particularly for the 1972–77, 1997–2002, 2002–07, 2012–17, and 2017–20 periods), although the growth rate in both types of revenue slowed down considerably after 2007 and likely was due to the faltering economy during the Great Recession.

Other evidence of the strong and vibrant growth rate in charges for services revenue from an examination of the data in Table 6.2 where charges for service collections are calculated as the proportion of total revenue (TR) and own-source revenue (OSR) and then can be compared to comparable figures for Total Tax Revenue (TTR). Specifically, these figures clearly indicate that revenue derived from charges for services over the 1962–2020 period has been making up a larger part of local governments' TR and OSR, while TTR is constituting an increasingly smaller and smaller proportion of these governments' TR and OSR over the same time period. Success in this regard has been the result of the sustained lobbying efforts of home rule advocates, states being amenable to giving their local governments greater latitude in fiscal matters, and local governments' willingness to take advantage of the opportunity to becoming more creative and bold in adopting new charges for services for the sake of fairness and equity, and, when necessary, "selling" these ideas to their citizens. Certainly, this information should be encouraging for local governments who had steadfastly sought to become less reliant on revenue produced by some form of taxation but especially property taxes.

*Table 6.2* Charges for Services as a Proportion of Own-Source Revenue (SR) and Total Revenue (TTR) for All Local Governments, 1962–2020

| | *1962* | *1967* | *1972* | *1977* | *1982* | *1987* | *1992* | *1997* | *2002* | *2007* | *2012* | *2017* | *2020* |
|---|---|---|---|---|---|---|---|---|---|---|---|---|---|
| Charges for Services as a % of OSR | 15 | 17 | 17 | 19 | 22 | 22 | 23 | 25 | 26 | 25 | 27 | 27 | 27 |
| Charges for Services as % TR | 9 | 10 | 10 | 9 | 11 | 12 | 13 | 14 | 15 | 15 | 16 | 16 | 16 |
| TTR as % of Total Revenue | 49 | 48 | 43 | 38 | 33 | 34 | 35 | 34 | 34 | 34 | 36 | 36 | 37 |
| TTR as % of Own-Source Revenue | 68 | 74 | 68 | 64 | 64 | 62 | 64 | 62 | 62 | 62 | 64 | 65 | 64 |

*Source:* U.S. Bureau of the Census. Census of Governments. Compendium of Government Finances series, 1962–2017 and 2020 State & Local Government Finance Historical Datasets and Tables. Compendium of Government Finances (Washington, DC: Government Printing Office).

In spite of this good news for local governments, challenges still lie ahead. While local governments in a number of states seem to have made the most of the opportunities afforded to them by their states to increase their revenue base and yields, much additional work remains for them and citizenry-led home rule advocacy groups to press for greater authority in their fiscal affairs. Other formidable challenges but none more daunting is having to cushion themselves from sharp downturns in the economy like that experienced during the Great Recession and its aftermath and the recession resulting from the COVID-19 health pandemic and the extraordinary high rate of inflation that followed. The data in Tables 6.1 and 6.2 would seem to suggest that these two recessions were the likely cause for a conspicuous slowdown in the growth rate in charges for services revenue (as was also the case for the tax proceeds) and the proportion of OSR and TR accounted for by charges for services after 2002. More precise information on the full of extent of these effects on both charges for services and tax revenue is speculative at the present time, and as mentioned elsewhere in this book, will not be known until data for 2021 and beyond becomes available from the Census of Governments.

As previously discussed, local government utility operations and their use of user fees are quite different than the typical local government department and its use of charges for services. On the one hand, local government utilities function as enterprise operations, meaning that they bill water, electricity, sewer, solid waste customers for the consumption of a divisible service or product (i.e., water, electricity, sewer and solid waste collection) to cover the cost of providing the service. Related kinds of one-time user fees could include things such as water and sewer tap-on fees or electric hook-on fees. On the other hand, local government departments and agencies often levy or impose a charge for services to help fund the cost of public goods and services they provide in the exercise of their mandatory (i.e., required by their state) regulatory and service delivery functions. Some examples include a city, county, or township building department levying a charge for services fee for issuing contractors' licenses, building permits, subdivision or plat approvals, or preforming various safety building inspections (plumbing, electrical, framing, mechanical, etc.) or a county clerk of court imposing a charge for services for issuing marriage licenses, copies of a birth or death certificates, final decrees in divorces, or recording deeds or titles for homes, vehicles, or boats.

Consistent with long-established and accepted business practices, local governments typically do not comingle revenue collected from utility user fees with their OSR fund. More specially, user fee proceeds must be segregated to ensure that they are utilized only for those enterprise operations that provide specific kinds of utility services in a manner consistent with the private sector model of being self-sufficient and operating on the basis of minimally breaking even financially. With this in mind, let's take a look at the amount of local government utility revenue collected from user fees from 1962 to 2020 (see Figure 6.3). Utility user fee revenue has grown steadily over the years. The same is true if these figures are cast in constant dollars (data not shown here). It is assumed that this

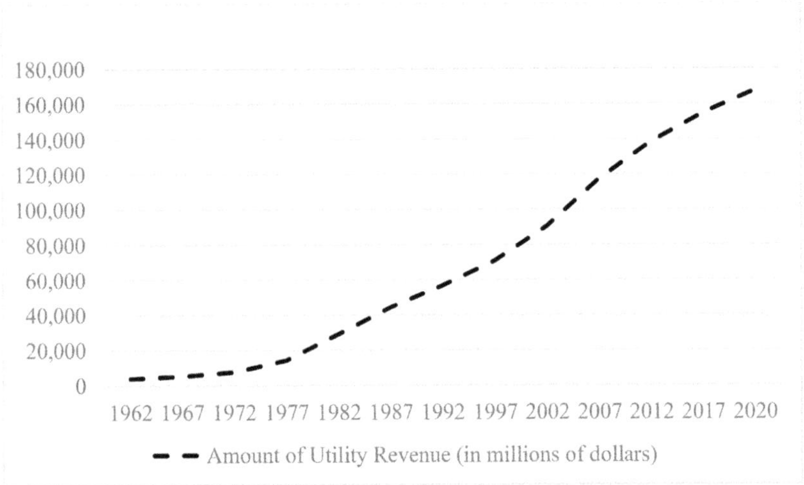


*Figure 6.3* Total Local Government Utility Revenue, 1962–2020

*Source:* U.S. Bureau of the Census. Census of Governments. Compendium of Government Finances series, 1962–2017 and U.S. Bureau of the Census and 2020 State & Local Government Finance Historical Datasets and Tables. Compendium of Government Finances (Washington, DC: Government Printing Office).

revenue was sufficient to cover the cost of providing the various utility services that were available to the public (and may even reflect a small "profit"[5]). There are no other kinds of local government revenue that utility revenue can be compared to or can be used as a meaningful "yardstick." These yearly figures stand on their own and can be compared only to figures for other years and how they may have changed. To make sure that user fees are always adequate to cover the cost of their utility operations, local government officials should always be mindful that they must regularly adjust user fee rates to make sure that revenue collections keep up with inflation, as well as the need for regularly scheduled maintenance or unanticipated breakdowns or emergencies. If not, they have to take money from their general fund to keep the utility financially solvent.

## Different patterns of usage of charges by the level of local government

As to be expected, there are notable differences in the degree to which each type of local government depends on charges for services and income from utility sales to supply revenue for their respective jurisdictions (see Figure 6.4). Not

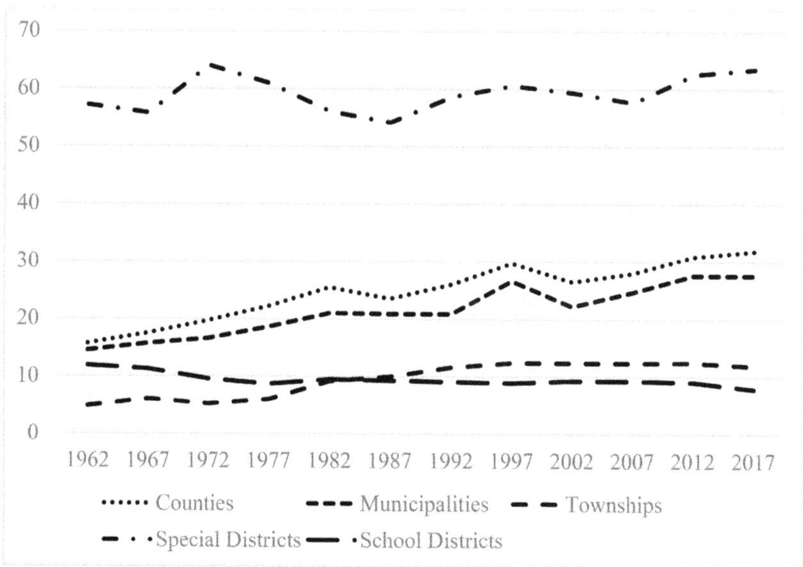


*Figure 6.4* Charges for Services Revenue as a Percentage of OSR for Counties, Municipalities, Townships, Special Districts, and School Districts, 1962–2020

*Source*: U.S. Bureau of the Census. Census of Governments. Compendium of Government Finances series, 1962–2017 and U.S. Bureau of the Census. 2020 State & Local Government Finance Historical Datasets and Tables. Compendium of Government Finances (Washington, DC: Government Printing Office).

surprisingly, data presented in this figure indicates that special districts have always relied more heavily on these kinds of revenue than the other types of local governments to finance the various services that they make available to citizens and business within their service area. After all, the primary reason for the creation of special districts was for them to be, first and foremost, vehicles to provide services that counties and municipalities could or would not provide due to constitutional and statutory restrictions placed on them. Furthermore, it is important to remember that special districts were never intended or envisioned to function as instruments of governance or serve as deliberative general policymaking bodies like county and municipal government but instead were expected/intended to serve as appendages to or "helpers" for county and municipal governments. Therefore, given the distinct role that special districts were supposed to play, it would be logical that they would amass the largest part of their revenue from charges for services. This is confirmed in Figure 6.4, where it can be seen that special districts obtained nearly two-thirds of their OSR from charges for services in both 1962 and 2017.

Another important piece of information can be gleaned from the data for special districts in Figure 6.4. Note the sizable growth in the proportion of OSR accounted for by charges for services from 1962 to 2017. In all likelihood, this is due to deliberate efforts of special district officials to pass on more of the costs associated with service provision to the users of specific non-utility-type services (examples include medical treatment at a hospital, use of a toll road/bridge, parking garage, marina, facilities at an airport, or attendance at an event held in a sports stadium/arena or civic auditorium).

County governments are the next largest user of charges for services, although not to the extent that special districts are. From Figure 6.4, it can be seen that counties relied on this kind of revenue to produce a little more than 30 percent of their OSR in 2017. Further inspection of the figure indicates the proportion of OSR accounted for by charges for services doubled over the 1962–2017 time period from 16 to 32 percent. The fact that counties derive a sizable percentage of their OSR from charges for services is not surprising because county governments serve as administrative arms of the state and therefore must perform a lot of state-mandated regulatory functions for which they exact a charge for things like a multitude of court recording charges, civil fines, as well as many kinds of traditional local government services and duties (see Benton 2002). Most of the charges for services revenue are derived from counties in the form of providing myriad services related to the operation of county health departments and hospitals, schools, libraries, and airports, the treatment and disposal of sewage, and solid waste management and disposal. It is also significant to mention that the TTR and PTR proportion of county government OSR drastically dropped from 79 to 61 and 75 to 43 percent, respectively, between 1962 and 2017 (see Chapter 4), while these governments were beginning to receive a larger percentage of their OSR from charges for services.

While municipal government revenue obtained from charges for services has usually accounted for a smaller proportion of these governments' OSR than has been the case of counties, this source of revenue has grown at a similar pace over the same 55-year time frame—doubling from 14 to 28 percent (see Figure 6.4). The growth rate in the municipal charges for services proportion of OSR also does not come as a surprise like what was seen for counties, but there is an additional reason for municipal governments. In regard to municipalities, the public historically has requested their states' permission to incorporate so as to satisfy rising service expectations brought on by greater population density and diversity. It goes without saying that municipalities are also required by their states to perform a host of regulatory functions like conducting inspections and enforcing traffic laws (like county governments) which means that they collect a lot of additional revenue that they would not otherwise receive. Most importantly, however, municipalities in recent years have been under increasing pressure to reduce their reliance on taxes, in general, and property taxes, in particular, and subsequently shift most of the cost of providing as many services as possible to other types of OSR. Clear evidence of this shift in municipal budgeting was seen in Chapter 4 where it was reported that TTR and PTR as a proportion of OSR had declined noticeably from 76 to 63 percent and from 56 to 32 percent, respectively, between 1962 and 2017. And, of course, a series of highly celebrated tax revolt movements that emerged in the 1970s, along with the mounting fiscal stress experienced by cities of all sizes, accelerated the move away from heavy reliance on tax revenue, generally, and property taxes, specifically, to other forms of OSR like charges for services.

Further examination of the data shown in Figure 6.4 suggests that townships historically have had a fairly limited reliance on changes for services. Still, proceeds from this form of revenue accounted for around 12 percent of township OSR in 2017. In comparison to the other types of local governments, the proportion of township government OSR accounted for by charges for services was the smallest in both 1962 and 2017, although the OSR percentage did more than double over this 55-year period (i.e., from 5 to 12 percent). Of important note, however, is that townships appear to be following the same pattern that was detected for special districts, municipalities, and counties whereby they were relying appreciably more on revenue produced by charges for services while simultaneously depending much less on taxes, generally, and property taxes, specifically, from 1962 to 2017 (data from Chapter 4 indicates that the TTR and PTR proportion of township OSR had decreased from 90 to 83 and 84 to 75 percent, respectively). Although the increase in the proportion of OSR was rather modest (12 percent in 2017 compared to 4 percent in 1962), it is nonetheless consistent with what appears to be obvious local governments' intentions to identify discrete users of services and charge them accordingly. Evidence of this inclination comes from the fact that township reliance on property taxes decreased over the same time frame (i.e., the property tax proportion of township OSR decreased from 80 percent in 1962 to 72 percent by 2017).

School districts stand alone among the five types of local governments since they collect revenue only from charges for education services. They neither operate utilities nor do they provide any type of utility service. From Figure 6.4, it can be seen that charges for services and user fees accounted for about 8 percent of school districts' OSR in 2017. The percentage had remained virtually static at 10 percent for several decades before dropping to 9 percent in 1992 and eventually to 8 percent more recently. Not surprisingly and as discussed in Chapter 4, school districts remain strongly dependent on some kind of taxes (primarily property). In 1962, school districts received 86 percent of their OSR from property tax proceeds, and by 2017 this proportion had decreased to 83 percent. Thus, school districts were mimicking a trend similar (although to a smaller degree) to what the other four types of local governments were doing. Since property tax collections still make up a very large part of school district TTR (96 percent in 2017), school districts were still heavily dependent on property tax money to fund their schools in 2017. By 2017, school districts still depended on this tax to produce 83 percent of its OSR. Further inspection of school district data also reveals that the small reduction in dependence on the property tax over the 1962–2017 period might actually be due to additional money coming from sales and income taxes and state aid and not necessarily from more money being received from charges from services collections. This pattern of very heavy reliance on property taxes proceeds remains a major concern for educators who worry about the financial sustainability of public schools, given what seems to be an increasing number of downturns in the economy in recent decades. Such recessions (with the most recent example being the Great Recession and the recession caused by the COVID-19 health pandemic) typically result in steep reductions in property tax yields, thus creating greater uncertainty in school district budgets. And, as mentioned throughout this book, the concern over the unending heavy reliance on the property tax is due to the lack of elasticity of the tax—that is, the slow growth in the revenue produced by the tax does not grow as fast as the cost of providing educational services. Furthermore, this problem only gets worse over the years if not corrected, and reminds us of the old adage of "continuing to kick the old can down the road."

As discussed at the outset of the chapter, utility user fees are crucial to local governments that provide things such as water, electric power, natural gas, and transit services. Set up as self-sufficient enterprise operations and intended to collect enough money in consumption or user fees to at least cover the cost of service provision, the money that these charges and fees produce is enormous and should be noted as was done in an earlier section of the chapter where the focus was on all local governments. In 2017, local governments collected over $167 billion in such revenue. But how much money in utility revenues did each of the four types of local governments (counties, municipalities, townships, and special districts) collect from 1962 to 2017 and did each government experience a steady and healthy increase in these type of proceeds to sustain their

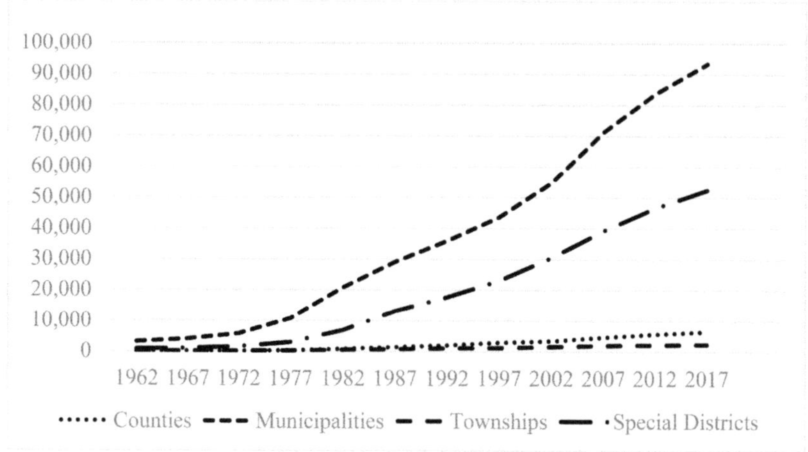


*Figure 6.5* Utility Revenue for Counties, Municipalities, Townships and Special Districts, 1962–2017

*Source:* U.S. Bureau of the Census. Census of Governments. Compendium of Government Finances series, 1962 and 2017.

utility operations? The data arrayed in Figure 6.5 should shed some light on these questions.

The data displayed in this figure indicates that, as anticipated, municipalities accounted for the largest amount of revenue collected from user or consumption fees. In 1962, they received a little more than \$3 billion, with this amount increasing significantly to over \$93 billion by 2017. Special districts amassed the second largest amount of money from these kinds of fees—around \$800 million in 1962 and rising to nearly \$53 billion by 2017. Historically, counties and townships have received smaller amounts of money from consumption or user fees. That is, county government receipts were at \$46 million in 1962 and increased to almost \$7 billion by 2017, while townships proceeds amounted to \$75 million in 1962 and then climbed to nearly \$2.5 billion by 2017. Given the huge role that municipal governments have always played in the United States in providing a variety of utility services, it is not surprising to find out that they have collected huge amount of money from these types of fees over the 1962–2017 period. Similarly, given the increasing role that special districts have been asked to play in making a number of important utility services (but especially water) available to residents and businesses in unincorporated areas of counties that are highly urbanized, it is reasonable to learn that they have also received large sums of revenue from user or consumption fees. However, county governments would have never been expected to collect a lot of money from utility user or consumption fees since they were created by their states to serve primarily as administrative arms or political subdivisions of the state and basically required to provide state level services at the local level (many of them mandated) and were never envisioned to perform like municipal governments that would provide a long list of services (many of which are utilities) typically referred to as "municipal-type services" (see Benton 2002). Townships also would not be expected to collect large amounts of money from user or consumption fees due to the fact they are sparsely populated, meaning that any utility operations they had would probably be small in scope. Looking at these data in Figure 6.5, one would think and hope that the revenue received from user and consumption fees for these four types of local governments would have been adequate to cover the cost of providing various kinds of utility services, but the only way to know for sure would be to examine the finances of each utility operation separately.

## State-by-state analysis of non-utility-type charges for services and linkage to tax dependency

Given the growing importance of non-utility-type charges for services and user fees as a source of revenue for local governments, additional analysis is warranted for counties, municipalities, townships, and school districts. More specifically, is the use of non-utility kinds of charges for services/user fees widespread across all states and is it more common in certain regions of the country and what may account for different patterns? Also, to what extent has increased utilization of non-utility-type charges for services and user fees led to a decreased reliance on property tax revenue? A more in-depth analysis begins with the oldest unit of local governments—counties.

### *County governments*

While county governments are often lauded as the cornerstone of local government, they continue to be caught in a proverbial quagmire because they often must serve two masters—their state government and their local constituents. On the one hand, they are creatures of their states and expected and oftentimes required to perform many unwanted and costly functions as legal extensions, administrative subdivisions, or satellite entities of their state governments. For instance, they are frequently mandated to provide myriad health and welfare services, operate a far-reaching and complicated civil and criminal court system, register voters and hold periodic elections, maintain a huge record keeping system to document everything from ownership of real property and vehicles to births, deaths, marriages, and dissolution of the same to conducting health and safety inspections to granting legal status to profit and non-profit corporations to certifying and licensing people to engage in most vocations and then regulating their work and conduct to dispensing horticultural information to organizing and holding the annual county fair.

On the other hand, county governments are expected to make available an increasing array of services that once were considered to be ones that were provided traditionally to residents of municipal governments. That has changed, however, with the increasing urbanization and suburbanization of the land within the boundaries of the American county or its counterparts in Louisiana (parishes) and Alaska (boroughs). Who would have thought a hundred years ago that county governments would be providing an assortment of utilities (water, natural gas, and electric power), 24/7 fire protection with full-time professionally trained personnel as well as fire prevention services, specialized police services usually found only in cities, sidewalks and curbing, street lights, traffic signalization, mosquito abatement, animal control and emergency medical services; constructing and operating huge sports facilities, marinas, museums, and civic arenas; determining the future economic direction and landscape of the community through prudent land use plans, planning and zoning decisions, and urban renewal projects, solid and hazardous waste management, sustainability initiatives, natural resource conservation, homeland security responsibilities, and so forth.

Keeping up with these massive responsibilities is a daunting challenge in and of itself. Even more formidable is the challenge to find the necessary financial resources to adequately and fairly fund the provision of these services. But this challenge entails much more than simply finding enough money to cover program and service costs. It also involves the necessity to be creative and even innovative in identifying sources of funding and then fairly apportioning the burden of extracting money from the citizens they serve. Although it is beyond the scope of this book, it additionally involves the efficient and cost-effective use of both monetary and personnel resources while being ever-vigilant about conserving resources and protecting the fragile community and global environment.

In order to utilize more fully monetary resources that meet the tests of adequacy (with both stability and elasticity qualities) and fairness and equity, local governments have been relying more and more often on charges for services and user fees since 1962. But has this practice been universal across the spectrum of counties in all of the states, and if not, where has it gained traction? Moreover, has greater usage of charges for services resulted in county governments reducing their historically huge dependency on revenue coming from property taxes? Data on the non-utility charges for services proportion of county government OSR in 2017 by state is contained in Table 6.3 and provides a useful starting point to address these important questions.

These most recent data indicate that there is wide diversity among the states with respect to their county governments' usage of and amount of revenue derived from charges for services. The proportion of county government OSR originating from charges for services ranged from a low of 5 percent in Virginia to a high of 58 percent in Indiana in 2017. Besides Indiana, there were eight other states (Mississippi, Wyoming, Vermont, Kentucky, Michigan, Iowa, California, and

*Table 6.3* Rank Ordering of Charges for Services Proportion of OSR for County Governments by State, 2017

| *Rank*[1] | *State*[2] | *Percent* | *Rank*[1] | *State*[2] | *Percent* | *Rank*[1] | *State*[2] | *Percent* |
|---|---|---|---|---|---|---|---|---|
| 1 | Indiana | 58 | 17 | Nevada | 33 | 33 | Illinois | 23 |
| 2 | Mississippi | 57 | 18 | Texas | 33 | 34 | Montana | 23 |
| 3 | Wyoming | 56 | 19 | Idaho | 32 | 35 | New York | 23 |
| 4 | Vermont | 54 | 20 | Florida | 32 | 36 | Oregon | 23 |
| 5 | Kentucky | 52 | 21 | Minnesota | 32 | 37 | Utah | 22 |
| 6 | Michigan | 46 | 22 | North Carolina | 32 | 38 | Colorado | 20 |
| 7 | Iowa | 46 | 23 | Oklahoma | 31 | 39 | Georgia | 19 |
| 8 | California | 44 | 24 | New Hampshire | 30 | 40 | Arkansas | 17 |
| 9 | Nebraska | 42 | 25 | West Virginia | 30 | 41 | Arizona | 16 |
| 10 | Tennessee | 39 | 26 | Kansas | 28 | 42 | Maine | 16 |
| 11 | Delaware | 38 | 27 | Pennsylvania | 28 | 43 | Maryland | 15 |
| 12 | Louisiana | 37 | 28 | South Carolina | 24 | 44 | North Dakota | 14 |
| 13 | Massachusetts | 37 | 29 | Washington | 27 | 45 | New Mexico | 13 |
| 14 | Ohio | 36 | 30 | Alabama | 26 | 46 | South Dakota | 13 |
| 15 | Missouri | 36 | 31 | Alaska | 24 | 47 | Hawaii | 11 |
| 16 | Wisconsin | 35 | 32 | New Jersey | 24 | 48 | Virginia | 5 |

1 The change percentage for each state was rounded off to the nearest tenth so that there would be no ties in the rankings.

2 Connecticut and Rhode Island were omitted because they do not have county governments.

*Source:* U.S. Bureau of the Census. 2017 Census of Governments. Compendium of Government Finances (Washington, DC: Government Printing Office), Table 4.3.8.

Nebraska) where counties depended on charges for services to produce at least 40 percent of their OSR. By comparison, counties in only one state in 1962 collected as much as 40 percent of their OSR from charges for services. Also, counties in another 16 states relied on charges for services to provide 30–39 percent of their OSR. This contrasts with counties in only four states in 1962.

Not only is the OSR proportion much higher in counties in more states by 2017, but there are many instances where the county proportion has increased significantly over the last 55 years (see Table 6.4). The OSR proportion for counties in one state (Vermont) shot up by an amazing 54 percent, while the OSR proportion in other three states (California, Michigan, and Iowa) rose by an impressive 30 percent or greater. Counties in an additional nine states posted OSR gains of at least 20 percent, and the county OSR proportion in four more states reached to 15–19 percent. Yet, there were still nine states where their counties posted small gains of less than 10 percent in the proportion of OSR collected from charges for services. Counties in seven states (Hew Hampshire, Nevada, Virginia, South Carolina, Hawaii, New Mexico, and Arkansas) actually experienced an overall reduction in the OSR proportion attributable to charges for services.

What has this 55-year documented history of substantial increases in the non-utility-type charges for service proportion of county OSR had on county governments' traditional heavy dependency on revenue generated by property taxes? The "Charges for Services/Property Tax" ratios reported in Table 6.5 assist in

*Table 6.4* Rank Ordering of Changes in Charges for Services Proportion of OSR for County Governments between 1962 and 2017 by State

| *Rank*[1] | *State*[2] | *1962* | *2017* | *Change* | *Rank*[1] | *State*[2] | *1962* | *2017* | *Change* |
|---|---|---|---|---|---|---|---|---|---|
| 1 | Vermont | 0 | 54 | 54 | 25 | Washington | 14 | 27 | 13 |
| 2 | California | 10 | 44 | 34 | 26 | North Dakota | 2 | 14 | 12 |
| 3 | Michigan | 16 | 46 | 30 | 27 | Idaho | 20 | 32 | 12 |
| 4 | Iowa | 16 | 46 | 30 | 28 | Pennsylvania | 16 | 28 | 12 |
| 5 | Mississippi | 29 | 57 | 28 | 29 | Florida | 21 | 32 | 11 |
| 6 | Indiana | 30 | 58 | 28 | 30 | Alabama | 16 | 26 | 10 |
| 7 | Nebraska | 15 | 42 | 27 | 31 | Illinois | 13 | 23 | 10 |
| 8 | Kentucky | 26 | 52 | 26 | 32 | Georgia | 9 | 19 | 10 |
| 9 | Massachusetts | 14 | 37 | 23 | 33 | South Dakota | 4 | 13 | 9 |
| 10 | Minnesota | 9 | 32 | 23 | 34 | Arizona | 7 | 16 | 9 |
| 11 | Wyoming | 35 | 56 | 21 | 35 | Delaware | 29 | 38 | 9 |
| 12 | Louisiana | 17 | 37 | 20 | 36 | Colorado | 12 | 20 | 8 |
| 13 | Wisconsin | 15 | 35 | 20 | 37 | Maine | 10 | 16 | 6 |
| 14 | Tennessee | 21 | 39 | 18 | 38 | Oregon | 17 | 23 | 6 |
| 15 | Montana | 7 | 23 | 16 | 39 | Utah | 18 | 22 | 4 |
| 16 | Kansas | 8 | 23 | 15 | 40 | North Carolina | 29 | 32 | 3 |
| 17 | Missouri | 21 | 36 | 15 | 41 | Maryland | 14 | 15 | 1 |
| 18 | Alaska | 10 | 24 | 14 | 42 | New Hampshire | 31 | 30 | −1 |
| 19 | Texas | 19 | 33 | 14 | 43 | Nevada | 37 | 33 | −1 |
| 20 | New Jersey | 11 | 24 | 13 | 44 | Virginia | 14 | 5 | −9 |
| 21 | Oklahoma | 18 | 31 | 13 | 45 | South Carolina | 42 | 28 | −14 |
| 22 | Ohio | 23 | 36 | 13 | 46 | Hawaii | 26 | 11 | −15 |
| 23 | New York | 10 | 23 | 13 | 47 | New Mexico | 34 | 13 | −21 |
| 24 | West Virginia | 17 | 30 | 13 | 48 | Arkansas | 38 | 17 | −21 |

1 The change percentage for each state was rounded off to the nearest tenth so that there would be no ties in the rankings.

2 Connecticut and Rhode Island were omitted because they do not have county governments.

*Source:* U.S. Bureau of the Census. Census of Governments. Compendium of Government Finances series, 1962 and 2017.

addressing this question. Interpreting the meaning of the ratios is rather straightforward. A ratio of 1.0 indicates that a county government receives practically the same proportion of their OSR from both property taxes and charges for services. Therefore, a ratio greater than 1.0 means that a county receives a larger proportion of its OSR from charges for services than it does from property taxes. For example, counties in Kentucky in 2017 collected a little over three times the amount of OSR from charges for services than what they received from property taxes. Table 6.5 also shows that there were 14 other states that received more revenue from charges for services than for property taxes. Then, a ratio of less than 1.0 indicates that counties receive less of their OSR from charges for services than they do for property taxes. According to Table 6.5, county governments in most states fall into this latter category.

A comparison of these ratios for 1962 and 2017 and especially changes in them provide credible evidence that increases in the proportion of county OSR

*Table 6.5* County Government Charges for Services/Property Taxes Ratios by State in 1962 and 2017 and Change over Time

| *Rank*[1] | *State*[2] | *1962* | *2017* | *Change* | *Rank*[1] | *State*[2] | *1962* | *2017* | *Change* |
|---|---|---|---|---|---|---|---|---|---|
| 1 | Kentucky | .467 | 3.039 | 3.572 | 25 | West Virginia | .218 | .599 | .381 |
| 2 | Missouri | .286 | 1.603 | 2.068 | 26 | Arkansas | .256 | .631 | .376 |
| 3 | Mississippi | .586 | 1.696 | 1.660 | 27 | Utah | .263 | .633 | .370 |
| 4 | Indiana | .448 | 2.031 | 1.583 | 28 | Illinois | .176 | .538 | .363 |
| 5 | Michigan | .207 | 1.724 | 1.517 | 29 | Georgia | .113 | .495 | .342 |
| 6 | Vermont | .000 | 1.429 | 1.429 | 30 | Idaho | .261 | .593 | .332 |
| 7 | Wyoming | .574 | 1.924 | 1.350 | 31 | Alaska | .135 | .421 | .286 |
| 8 | Massachusetts | .171 | 2.409 | 1.238 | 32 | Texas | .321 | .607 | .286 |
| 9 | Louisiana | .173 | 1.248 | 1.075 | 33 | Montana | .092 | .398 | .256 |
| 10 | Ohio | .355 | 1.297 | .942 | 34 | Colorado | .139 | .391 | .252 |
| 11 | Iowa | .194 | 1.134 | .940 | 35 | Oregon | .232 | .472 | .240 |
| 12 | California | .121 | 1.023 | .902 | 36 | New Jersey | .123 | .361 | .238 |
| 13 | Nevada | .938 | 1.772 | .824 | 37 | Pennsylvania | .204 | .430 | .226 |
| 14 | New York | .130 | .936 | .797 | 38 | Arizona | .090 | .292 | .202 |
| 15 | Tennessee | .297 | 1.092 | .795 | 39 | Maryland | .183 | .373 | .190 |
| 16 | Nebraska | .210 | .942 | .732 | 40 | North Dakota | .025 | .185 | .160 |
| 17 | Oklahoma | .223 | .916 | .693 | 41 | South Dakota | .045 | .180 | .135 |
| 18 | Delaware | .429 | 1.109 | .680 | 42 | North Carolina | .451 | .566 | .115 |
| 19 | Washington | .224 | .836 | .612 | 43 | Maine | .147 | .175 | .028 |
| 20 | Florida | .316 | .919 | .603 | 44 | New Hampshire | .457 | .465 | .008 |
| 21 | Wisconsin | .183 | .687 | .504 | 45 | Virginia | .196 | .176 | −.020 |
| 22 | Kansas | .094 | .563 | .469 | 46 | New Mexico | .551 | .312 | −.239 |
| 23 | Minnesota | .108 | .575 | .467 | 47 | South Carolina | .866 | .685 | −.281 |
| 24 | Alabama | .308 | .771 | .463 | 48 | Hawaii | .818 | .185 | −.633 |

1 The change percentage for each state was rounded off to the nearest hundredth so that there would be no ties in the rankings.

2 Connecticut and Rhode Island were omitted because they do not have county governments.

*Source:* U.S. Bureau of the Census. Census of Governments. Compendium of Government Finances series, 1962–2017.

derived from charges for services are responsible, at least in part, for a noticeable reduction in county governments' long-time extremely heavy reliance on property tax proceeds. Two specific observations are particularly noteworthy. First, the highest ratio in any state in 1962 was 93.8 (Nevada). But, by 2017, counties in 16 states had ratios that were greater than this high-water mark 55 years earlier, with 15 of them (Kentucky, Missouri, Mississippi, Indiana, Michigan, Vermont, Wyoming, Massachusetts, Louisiana, Ohio, Iowa, California, Nevada, Tennessee, Nebraska, and Delaware) having ratios that exceeded 1.0 in 2017. Second, impressive ratio gains had been made by counties in many states by 2017. The ratio increased to over 100 percentage points for counties in nine states (Kentucky, Missouri, Mississippi, Indiana, Michigan, Vermont, Wyoming, Massachusetts, and Louisiana), while the ratio increased to over 90 percentage points in another three states (Ohio, Iowa, and California). The ratio increased to over 80 percentage points in one state (Nevada), to over 70 in three additional states (New York, Tennessee, and Nebraska), and from 50–69 percent in five other states. In spite of these and other gains, the ratio decreased for counties in four states (Virginia, New Mexico, South Carolina, and Hawaii).

***Municipal governments***

Unlike county governments, municipalities, for the most part, have not been caught in a tug-a-war between their state government and their local constituents. Nonetheless, they have always been expected to provide a long list of local or municipal-type services. For instance, municipalities routinely have provided things such as garbage, yard waste, hazardous materials, and sewage collection, a number of building, health, and safety inspections, storm water management, cable TV, paved driveways, public housing, cemeteries, libraries, hospitals, airports, animal control, mosquito abatement, museums, animal control, and parking. Moreover, this list of service offerings greatly has expanded through the years. Many of these services were usually funded primarily or even entirely by tax-generated (typically, property) proceeds. As a result, municipalities came under increasing pressure from their citizens (but especially property owners) to depend less on property tax collections to pay for services and instead increase their usage of revenue sources that pinpointed and billed specific users of services (i.e., charges for services) so as to better and more fairly apportion government costs.

As discussed earlier, municipal governments, like counties, have also been collecting a larger proportion of their OSR from non-utility-type charges for service over the last 55 years. Which states have municipalities that receive some of the largest and smallest proportions? Table 6.6 indicates that municipalities in Mississippi and West Virginia collected nearly one-half (48 percent) of their OSR from charges for services in 2017. Municipalities in another state (Indiana) also received at least 40 percent of their OSR from non-utility-type charges for services

*Table 6.6* Rank Ordering of Charges for Services Proportion of OSR for Municipal Governments by State, 2017

| *Rank*[1] | *State* | *Percent* | *Rank*[1] | *State* | *Percent* | *Rank*[1] | *State* | *Percent* |
|---|---|---|---|---|---|---|---|---|
| 1 | West Virginia | 48 | 18 | Washington | 27 | 35 | North Dakota | 21 |
| 2 | Mississippi | 48 | 19 | Vermont | 27 | 36 | Kansas | 23 |
| 3 | Indiana | 40 | 20 | Maine | 26 | 37 | Georgia | 20 |
| 4 | Arizona | 37 | 21 | Arkansas | 26 | 38 | Ohio | 20 |
| 5 | Idaho | 35 | 22 | South Dakota | 25 | 39 | Maryland | 20 |
| 6 | Iowa | 34 | 23 | Florida | 25 | 40 | New Hampshire | 18 |
| 7 | Utah | 33 | 24 | New Mexico | 25 | 41 | Alaska | 17 |
| 8 | Oklahoma | 32 | 25 | Missouri | 24 | 42 | Virginia | 17 |
| 9 | Nevada | 32 | 26 | Hawaii | 24 | 43 | South Carolina | 17 |
| 10 | Montana | 32 | 27 | Colorado | 23 | 44 | Delaware | 15 |
| 11 | Wyoming | 32 | 28 | Kentucky | 23 | 45 | Massachusetts | 14 |
| 12 | Michigan | 30 | 29 | Texas | 23 | 46 | Tennessee | 13 |
| 13 | Minnesota | 28 | 30 | Illinois | 22 | 47 | New York | 13 |
| 14 | California | 28 | 31 | Wisconsin | 22 | 48 | New Jersey | 11 |
| 15 | Louisiana | 28 | 32 | North Carolina | 22 | 49 | Alabama | 11 |
| 16 | Oregon | 27 | 33 | Pennsylvania | 22 | 50 | Connecticut | 5 |
| 17 | Nebraska | 27 | 34 | Rhode Island | 22 | | | |

1 The change percentage for each state was rounded off to the nearest tenth so that there would be no ties in the rankings.
*Source*: U.S. Bureau of the Census. 2017 Census of Governments. *Compendium of Government Finances* (Washington, DC: Government Printing Office), Table 4.3.8.

in that year, while another nine states (Arizona, Idaho, Iowa, Utah, Oklahoma, Nevada, Montana, Wyoming, and Michigan) derived at least 30 percent of their OSR from this type revenue. At the other end of the spectrum, municipalities in 11 states (New Hampshire, Alaska, Virginia, South Carolina, Delaware, Massachusetts, Tennessee, New York, New Jersey, Alabama, and Connecticut) counted on non-utility-type charges for services for less than 20 percent of their OSR. As a comparison, county governments more so than municipal governments in 2017 received much more of their OSR from charges for services. For instance, counties in nine states obtained 40 percent or more of their OSR from charges for services compared to municipal governments in only three states.

In addition to municipalities in more states obtaining a higher proportion of their OSR from non-utility-type charges for services in 2017 compared to 1962, there were several instances where the municipal proportion increased noticeably from 1962 to 2017 (see Table 6.7). In particular, the OSR proportion climbed by 37 percentage points in Mississippi, while the proportion increased by at least 20 percentage points in other eight states (Indiana, Arizona, Utah, Idaho, Iowa, Maine, Vermont, and Nevada). Municipalities in most states (20) registered gains greater than 10 but less than 19 percentage points. There were three states (Alabama,

*Table 6.7* Rank Ordering of Changes in Charges for Services Proportion of OSR for Municipal Governments between 1962 and 2017 by State

| *Rank*[1] | *State* | *1962* | *2017* | *Change* | *Rank*[1] | *State* | *1962* | *2017* | *Change* |
|---|---|---|---|---|---|---|---|---|---|
| 1 | Mississippi | 11 | 48 | 37 | 26 | North Carolina | 10 | 22 | 12 |
| 2 | Indiana | 11 | 40 | 29 | 27 | Pennsylvania | 11 | 22 | 11 |
| 3 | Arizona | 11 | 37 | 26 | 28 | West Virginia | 37 | 48 | 11 |
| 4 | Utah | 8 | 33 | 25 | 29 | Colorado | 12 | 23 | 11 |
| 5 | Idaho | 11 | 35 | 24 | 30 | North Dakota | 11 | 21 | 10 |
| 6 | Iowa | 12 | 34 | 22 | 31 | New Hampshire | 8 | 18 | 10 |
| 7 | Maine | 5 | 26 | 21 | 32 | Oklahoma | 23 | 33 | 10 |
| 8 | Vermont | 7 | 27 | 20 | 33 | Texas | 13 | 23 | 10 |
| 9 | Nevada | 12 | 32 | 20 | 34 | Louisiana | 19 | 28 | 9 |
| 10 | South Dakota | 9 | 25 | 19 | 35 | Maryland | 11 | 20 | 9 |
| 11 | Hawaii | 5 | 24 | 19 | 36 | Georgia | 11 | 20 | 9 |
| 12 | Minnesota | 12 | 30 | 18 | 37 | Kansas | 13 | 21 | 8 |
| 13 | California | 10 | 28 | 18 | 38 | New Mexico | 18 | 25 | 7 |
| 14 | Rhode Island | 4 | 22 | 18 | 39 | New Jersey | 5 | 11 | 6 |
| 15 | Nebraska | 9 | 27 | 18 | 40 | Massachusetts | 8 | 14 | 6 |
| 16 | Wyoming | 14 | 32 | 18 | 41 | Alaska | 23 | 17 | 6 |
| 17 | Montana | 15 | 32 | 17 | 42 | Virginia | 13 | 17 | 4 |
| 18 | Illinois | 5 | 22 | 17 | 43 | Kentucky | 19 | 23 | 4 |
| 19 | Michigan | 16 | 32 | 16 | 44 | New York | 10 | 13 | 3 |
| 20 | Washington | 12 | 27 | 16 | 45 | Tennessee | 10 | 13 | 3 |
| 21 | Oregon | 14 | 28 | 14 | 46 | Delaware | 14 | 15 | 1 |
| 22 | Wisconsin | 8 | 22 | 14 | 47 | Connecticut | 5 | 5 | 0 |
| 23 | Missouri | 11 | 24 | 13 | 48 | Alabama | 13 | 11 | –2 |
| 24 | South Carolina | 4 | 17 | 13 | 49 | Arkansas | 26 | 21 | |
| 25 | Florida | 12 | 25 | 13 | 50 | Ohio | 38 | 20 | –18 |

[1] The change percentage for each state was rounded off to the nearest tenth so that there would be no ties in the rankings.

*Source:* U.S. Bureau of the Census. Census of Governments. Compendium of Government Finances series, 1962–2017.

Arkansas, and Ohio) where the non-utility-type charges for services proportion of OSR for municipalities showed a declined during the 1962–2017 period.

Given the information found in Tables 6.6 and 6.7, to what extent has greater municipal usage of non-utility-type charges for services impacted dependency on property tax revenue? The data in Table 6.8 suggests that municipalities in many states have been able to reduce their reliance on property tax proceeds over time as they collected a larger proportion of their OSR from non-utility-type charges for services. More specifically, the charges for services/property tax ratios in 30 states in 2017 exceeded 1.0, meaning that municipalities collected more revenue from charges for services than they were receiving from property taxes. This compares to only six states (Oklahoma, Arkansas, West Virginia, New Mexico, Ohio, and Alabama) in 1962; however, it should be noted that municipalities in these six states in 1962 were far ahead of municipalities in other states in reducing their dependency on property tax revenue. Looking again at Table 6.8, it can be seen that there were a half-dozen states where

*Table 6.8* Municipal Government Charges for Services/Property Taxes Ratios by State in 1962 and 2017 and Change over Time

| *Rank*[1] | *State* | *1962* | *2017* | *Change* | *Rank*[1] | *State* | *1962* | *2017* | *Change* |
|---|---|---|---|---|---|---|---|---|---|
| 1 | Oklahoma | 1.233 | 7.000 | 5.767 | 26 | Minnesota | .253 | 1.115 | .862 |
| 2 | West Virginia | 1.946 | 4.727 | 2.051 | 27 | Florida | .496 | 1.106 | .670 |
| 3 | Wyoming | .576 | 4.149 | 4.073 | 28 | Kansas | .383 | 1.097 | .714 |
| 4 | Arkansas | 1.295 | 3.719 | 2.424 | 29 | Texas | .339 | 1.016 | .677 |
| 5 | Missouri | .385 | 3.429 | 3.044 | 30 | Idaho | .323 | 1.011 | .688 |
| 6 | Mississippi | .417 | 2.783 | 2.366 | 31 | Montana | .342 | .999 | .657 |
| 7 | Ohio | 1.212 | 2.613 | 1.401 | 32 | Delaware | .337 | .972 | .635 |
| 8 | Arizona | .421 | 2.498 | 2.077 | 33 | South Carolina | .129 | .971 | .842 |
| 9 | Colorado | .423 | 2.474 | 2.051 | 34 | Oregon | .378 | .956 | .578 |
| 10 | New Mexico | 1.059 | 2.409 | 1.350 | 35 | Vermont | .116 | ,913 | .797 |
| 11 | Utah | .270 | 2.227 | 1.957 | 36 | Illinois | .269 | .889 | .620 |
| 12 | Kentucky | .931 | 2.030 | 1.099 | 37 | North Carolina | .273 | .821 | .548 |
| 13 | Washington | .693 | 1.942 | 1.249 | 38 | Alaska | 1.000 | .783 | −.217 |
| 14 | Nebraska | .263 | 1.925 | 1.662 | 39 | Tennessee | .524 | .728 | .204 |
| 15 | Georgia | .402 | 1.876 | 1.414 | 40 | Hawaii | .112 | .603 | .491 |
| 16 | Louisiana | .491 | 1.728 | 1,237 | 41 | Wisconsin | .133 | .558 | .425 |
| 17 | Indiana | .200 | 1.639 | 1.439 | 42 | Maryland | .169 | .506 | .337 |
| 18 | California | .358 | 1.434 | 1.076 | 43 | Virginia | .314 | .406 | .092 |
| 19 | Nevada | .386 | 1.405 | 1.109 | 44 | New York | .213 | .285 | .172 |
| 20 | Pennsylvania | .293 | 1.287 | .994 | 45 | Maine | .052 | .383 | .331 |
| 21 | Alabama | 1.222 | 1.223 | .001 | 46 | New Hampshire | .102 | . 264 | .162 |
| 22 | South Dakota | .223 | 1.201 | .977 | 47 | Rhode Island | .050 | .233 | .183 |
| 23 | Michigan | .326 | 1.147 | .821 | 48 | Massachusetts | .093 | .211 | .118 |
| 24 | North Dakota | .337 | 1.141 | .804 | 49 | New Jersey | .068 | .170 | .102 |
| 25 | Iowa | .261 | 1.136 | .875 | 50 | Connecticut | .063 | . 113 | .050 |

[1] The change percentage for each state was rounded off to the nearest hundredth so that there would be no ties in the rankings.

*Source:* U.S. Bureau of the Census. Census of Governments. Compendium of Government Finances series, 1962–2017.

municipalities were approaching the 1.0 level by 2017. These numbers take on added significance when considering the huge increases in these ratios over time as indicated in the last column of the table that reports changes in these ratios. That is, the ratio had increased substantially from 1962 to 2017 in 19 states, with municipalities in Oklahoma and Wyoming experiencing a five-fold and four-fold gain, respectively.

### *Townships*

In some respects, township governments resemble municipal and county governments since they provide some of the same kinds of services, although usually smaller in number and scope. For instance, it is not unusual for them to be responsible for things such as fire and police protection, welfare, health care, hospitals, highways, parks and recreational services, sewage and solid waste disposal, and libraries. Thus, it would be logical to conclude that townships would have a revenue structure like counties and municipalities. In one way, they are similar since all three governments historically have depended on tax (but especially, property tax) revenue to fund their operations. However, townships differ from both counties and municipalities in two ways. One, they obtain a much smaller proportion of their OSR from non-utility-type charges for services. In 2017, township governments, on average, depended on charges for services to supply just under 12 percent of their OSR compared to 32 and 28 percent, respectively, for counties and municipalities. Second, townships continue to be heavily dependent on property tax collections to supply a large part of their OSR (76 percent in 2017).

The data presented in Table 6.9 clearly show that 20 township governments, for the most part, rely on non-utility-type charges for services to supply only a small part of their OSR. With the exception of townships in Pennsylvania and Michigan, these governments received 14 percent or less of their OSR from

*Table 6.9* Rank Ordering of Charges for Services Proportion of OSR for Townships by State, 2017

| *Rank*[1] | *State* | *Percent* | *Rank*[1] | *State* | *Percent* | *Rank*[1] | *State* | *Percent* |
|---|---|---|---|---|---|---|---|---|
| 1 | Michigan | 27 | 8 | Massachusetts | 9 | 15 | Illinois | 4 |
| 2 | Pennsylvania | 24 | 9 | Rhode Island | 8 | 16 | Minnesota | 3 |
| 3 | Wisconsin | 14 | 10 | Connecticut | 7 | 17 | Nebraska | 3 |
| 4 | New Jersey | 13 | 11 | Indiana | 7 | 18 | South Dakota | 2 |
| 5 | New York | 12 | 12 | New Hampshire | 7 | 19 | Kansas | 1 |
| 6 | Vermont | 11 | 13 | Ohio | 7 | 20 | North Dakota | * |
| 7 | Maine | 10 | 14 | Missouri | 5 | | | |

1 The change percentage for each state was rounded off to the nearest tenth so that there would be no ties in the rankings.

* Less than .5 percent.

*Source*: U.S. Bureau of the Census. 2017 Census of Governments. Compendium of Government Finances (Washington, DC: Government Printing Office), Table 4.3.8.

*Table 6.10* Rank Ordering of Changes in Charges for Services Proportion of OSR for Townships between 1962 and 2017 by State

| *Rank*[1] | *State* | *1962* | *2017* | *Change* | *Rank*[1] | *State* | *1962* | *2017* | *Change* |
|---|---|---|---|---|---|---|---|---|---|
| 1 | Michigan | 5 | 27 | 22 | 11 | Missouri | 0 | 5 | 5 |
| 2 | Wisconsin | 4 | 14 | 18 | 12 | Massachusetts | 4 | 9 | 5 |
| 3 | Pennsylvania | 11 | 24 | 13 | 13 | Rhode Island | 4 | 8 | 4 |
| 4 | Vermont | 2 | 11 | 9 | 14 | Nebraska | 0 | 3 | 3 |
| 5 | New Jersey | 4 | 13 | 9 | 15 | Illinois | 1 | 4 | 3 |
| 6 | Indiana | 0 | 7 | 7 | 16 | Connecticut | 5 | 7 | 2 |
| 7 | Maine | 3 | 10 | 7 | 17 | South Dakota | 0 | 2 | 2 |
| 8 | Ohio | 0 | 7 | 7 | 18 | Minnesota | 4 | 1 | 3 |
| 9 | New Hampshire | 1 | 7 | 6 | 19 | North Dakota | 0 | * | 0 |
| 10 | New York | 6 | 12 | 6 | 20 | Kansas | 8 | 1 | −7 |

* Less than .5 percent.

1 The change percentage for each state was rounded off to the nearest tenth so that there would be no ties in the rankings.

*Source:* U.S. Bureau of the Census. Census of Governments. Compendium of Government Finances series, 1962–2017.

charges for services in 2017. This pales in comparison to the typical county or municipality. One possible explanation of the greater usage of charges for services in townships in these two states is that they are typically located in highly urbanized areas and thus likely to have more service responsibilities.

If township governments were receiving only a small proportion of their OSR from non-utility-type charges for services in 2017, then it is highly likely that this type of revenue has not been growing very much over time. This reasonable assumption is confirmed by the data in Table 6.10. Increases in the OSR proportion attributable to charges for services are moderate at best (see the 22, 18, and 13 percent increases for townships in Michigan, Wisconsin, and Pennsylvania, respectively) and are quite low OSR percentages for townships in the other states.

Consequently and as expected, the limited usage of non-utility charges for services has not reduced township governments' reliance on property tax revenue by very much. This supposition is supported by the data in Table 6.11. While the ratio of charges for services to property taxes rose noticeably for townships in Pennsylvania and even moderately in Michigan from 1962 to 2017, it barely changed in other 18 states that have townships, meaning that property tax revenue remains the overwhelmingly dominant source of revenue for these governments.

### School districts

School districts, like township governments, have a history of minimal use of non-utility-type charges for services. This, of course, would be expected of a governmental entity that provides only one service and has limited opportunities

*Table 6.11* Township Charges for Services/Property Taxes Ratios by State in 1962 and 2017 and Change over Time

| *Rank*[1] | *State* | *1962* | *2017* | *Change* | *Rank*[1] | *State* | *1962* | *2017* | *Change* |
|---|---|---|---|---|---|---|---|---|---|
| 1 | Pennsylvania | .183 | .884 | .701 | 11 | Minnesota | .000 | .059 | .059 |
| 2 | Michigan | .101 | .625 | .524 | 12 | Rhode Island | .043 | .098 | .055 |
| 3 | Wisconsin | .014 | .198 | .184 | 13 | Illinois | .000 | .041 | .041 |
| 4 | New Jersey | .068 | .170 | .102 | 14 | Missouri | .000 | .035 | .035 |
| 5 | New York | .088 | .183 | .095 | 15 | South Dakota | .000 | .035 | .035 |
| 6 | Indiana | .000 | .090 | .090 | 16 | Nebraska | .000 | .033 | .033 |
| 7 | Ohio | .000 | .085 | .085 | 17 | Vermont | .026 | .146 | .020 |
| 8 | Maine | .035 | .113 | .078 | 18 | Connecticut | .062 | .071 | .009 |
| 9 | New Hampshire | .015 | .081 | .069 | 19 | North Dakota | .000 | * | * |
| 10 | Massachusetts | .051 | .118 | .064 | 20 | Kansas | .085 | .013 | –.072 |

[1] The change percentage for each state was rounded off to the nearest tenth so that there would be no ties in the rankings.

* Less than .5 percent.

*Source:* U.S. Bureau of the Census. Census of Governments. Compendium of Government Finances series, 1962–2017.

for levying charges for education-related services. Looking at Table 6.12, it is clear that school districts in 40 of 45 states that had them in 2017 received a much smaller proportion of their OSR from charges for services when compared to county and municipal governments. In these 40 states, school districts collected 18 percent or less of their OSR from charges for services. By comparison, counties and municipalities in only 9 and 11 states, respectively (see Tables 6.3

*Table 6.12* Rank Ordering of Charges for Services Proportion of OSR for School Districts by State, 2017

| *Rank*[1] | *State* | *Percent* | *Rank*[1] | *State* | *Percent* | *Rank*[1] | *State* | *Percent* |
|---|---|---|---|---|---|---|---|---|
| 1 | Connecticut | 82 | 16 | Missouri | 12 | 31 | Washington | 7 |
| 2 | Massachusetts | 55 | 17 | Montana | 12 | 32 | Texas | 6 |
| 3 | Vermont | 47 | 18 | Wyoming | 12 | 33 | South Carolina | 6 |
| 4 | Arkansas | 22 | 19 | South Dakota | 11 | 34 | Georgia | 5 |
| 5 | Kansas | 21 | 20 | New Mexico | 11 | 35 | Pennsylvania | 5 |
| 6 | Mississippi | 18 | 21 | Arizona | 11 | 36 | Kentucky | 4 |
| 7 | Alabama | 18 | 22 | Colorado | 11 | 37 | Maine | 3 |
| 8 | Iowa | 17 | 23 | Wisconsin | 11 | 38 | New Jersey | 3 |
| 9 | Oregon | 17 | 24 | Indiana | 10 | 39 | New Hampshire | 3 |
| 10 | Minnesota | 16 | 25 | Ohio | 10 | 40 | West Virginia | 3 |
| 11 | Michigan | 15 | 26 | Nebraska | 9 | 41 | Delaware | 2 |
| 12 | North Dakota | 14 | 27 | Utah | 9 | 42 | New York | 2 |
| 13 | Florida | 13 | 28 | California | 8 | 43 | Nevada | 2 |
| 14 | Oklahoma | 13 | 29 | Illinois | 7 | 44 | Louisiana | 1 |
| 15 | Idaho | 12 | 30 | Rhode Island | 7 | 45 | Alaska | 0 |

[1] The change percentage for each state was rounded off to the nearest tenth so that there would be no ties in the rankings

*Source:* U.S. Bureau of the Census. Census of Governments. Compendium of Government Finances series, 1962–2017.

and 6.6), received 18 percent or less of their OSR from this source. In this respect, school districts are very much like township governments which also have a minimal reliance on non-utility-type charges for services. At the other end of the continuum, school districts in two states (Arkansas and Kansas) obtained 22 and 21 percent, respectively, of their OSR from charges for services, while school districts in another state (Vermont) received 47 percent of its OSR from this source. School districts in other two states (Connecticut and Massachusetts) reported the highest OSR proportion of 82 and 55 percent, respectively.

Given school districts' minimal usage of non-utility-type charges for services in most states as seen above, it is not surprising that little change is detected in reliance on this source of revenue between 1962 and 2017 (see Table 6.13). In all but 2 of the 45 states with school districts, there was an increase of 9 percentage points or less in the charges for services proportion of OSR in 18 states and a decrease in the charges for services proportion in another 25 states over this interval. While the decline in the OSR proportion attributable to charges for services was huge for school districts in Massachusetts, school districts there still obtained 55 percent of their OSR from this source.

*Table 6.13* Rank Ordering of Changes in Charges for Services Proportion of OSR for School Districts between 1962 and 2017 by State

| *Rank*[1] | *State*[2] | *1962* | *2017* | *Change* | *Rank*[1] | *State*[2] | *1962* | *2017* | *Change* |
|---|---|---|---|---|---|---|---|---|---|
| 1 | Connecticut | 9 | 82 | 73 | 24 | Nebraska | 11 | 9 | −2 |
| 2 | Vermont | 6 | 47 | 41 | 25 | Nevada | 4 | 2 | −2 |
| 3 | Oregon | 8 | 17 | 9 | 26 | New Jersey | 5 | 3 | −2 |
| 4 | Kansas | 12 | 21 | 9 | 27 | Utah | 11 | 9 | −2 |
| 5 | Iowa | 9 | 17 | 8 | 28 | Oklahoma | 18 | 13 | −5 |
| 6 | Minnesota | 8 | 16 | 8 | 29 | Pennsylvania | 10 | 5 | −5 |
| 7 | Arkansas | 15 | 22 | 7 | 30 | New York | 7 | 2 | −5 |
| 8 | Rhode Island | 0 | 7 | 7 | 31 | Mississippi | 24 | 18 | −6 |
| 9 | Michigan | 9 | 15 | 6 | 32 | Maine | 9 | 3 | −6 |
| 10 | Montana | 7 | 12 | 5 | 33 | New Mexico | 19 | 11 | −8 |
| 11 | North Dakota | 9 | 14 | 5 | 34 | Washington | 16 | 7 | −9 |
| 12 | Wisconsin | 6 | 11 | 5 | 35 | West Virginia | 12 | 3 | −9 |
| 13 | Wyoming | 8 | 12 | 4 | 36 | Alaska | 9 | 0 | −9 |
| 14 | South Dakota | 8 | 11 | 3 | 37 | Texas | 17 | 6 | −11 |
| 15 | Ohio | 8 | 10 | 2 | 38 | Florida | 25 | 13 | −12 |
| 16 | Colorado | 9 | 11 | 2 | 39 | Kentucky | 19 | 4 | −15 |
| 17 | California | 7 | 8 | 2 | 40 | Louisiana | 17 | 1 | −16 |
| 18 | Indiana | 9 | 10 | 1 | 41 | Delaware | 21 | 2 | −19 |
| 19 | Idaho | 12 | 12 | 0 | 42 | Georgia | 26 | 5 | −21 |
| 20 | Illinois | 7 | 7 | 0 | 43 | South Carolina | 30 | 6 | −24 |
| 21 | Missouri | 13 | 12 | −1 | 44 | Alabama | 44 | 18 | −26 |
| 22 | New Hampshire | 4 | 3 | −1 | 45 | Massachusetts | 91 | 55 | −36 |
| 23 | Arizona | 12 | 11 | −1 | | | | | |

1 The change percentage for each state was rounded off to the nearest tenth so that there would be no ties in the rankings.

2 Manyland, North Carolina, Tennessee, and Virginia were omitted because schools are operated by county governments in those states, while Hawaii was omitted since schools in that state are run by the state government.

*Source:* U.S. Bureau of the Census. Census of Governments. Compendium of Government Finances series, 1962–2017.

Not unexpected, data contained in the two preceding tables which reveal very limited usage and growth in charges for services by school districts over the last 55 years leads to the inevitable conclusion that districts in most states have made little or no progress in reducing their heavy dependency on property taxes. In fact, school districts in 25 states have actually regressed, meaning that they were relying more on property tax revenue in 2017 than they were in 1962. In spite of the fact that school districts in a handful of states have increased their usage of charges for services since 1962, this has had, at best, a modest impact on reliance on property tax proceeds. As the ratios presented in Table 6.14 suggest, there is scant evidence to indicate that school districts collected significantly large enough revenue from charges for services to reduce their reliance on property tax revenue. At this writing, it would appear that school districts in most states are content or have resigned themselves to accept the fact that they must depend on money collected from property taxes to supply the overwhelming majority of their OSR.

*Table 6.14* School District Charges for Services/Property Taxes Ratios by State in 1962 and 2017 and Change over Time

| *Rank*[1] | *State*[2] | *1962* | *2017* | *Change* | *Rank*[1] | *State*[2] | *1962* | *2017* | *Change* |
|---|---|---|---|---|---|---|---|---|---|
| 1 | Arkansas | .157 | .360 | .203 | 24 | Utah | .127 | .111 | −.016 |
| 2 | Kansas | .143 | .332 | .189 | 25 | New Jersey | .057 | .034 | −.023 |
| 3 | Oregon | .084 | .220 | .136 | 26 | Arizona | .141 | .117 | −.024 |
| 4 | Montana | .076 | .156 | .133 | 27 | Oklahoma | .223 | .156 | −.026 |
| 5 | Michigan | .101 | .213 | .112 | 28 | Nevada | .092 | .035 | −.067 |
| 6 | Minnesota | .225 | .248 | .092 | 29 | New York | .084 | .021 | −.067 |
| 7 | Wisconsin | .071 | .147 | .076 | 30 | Pennsylvania | .139 | .064 | −.075 |
| 8 | Rhode Island | .000 | .070 | .070 | 31 | Maine | .106 | .030 | −.076 |
| 9 | North Dakota | .106 | .166 | .060 | 32 | Mississippi | .337 | .328 | −.088 |
| 10 | South Dakota | .093 | .135 | .042 | 33 | Connecticut | .095 | .000 | −.095 |
| 11 | Ohio | .083 | .122 | .039 | 34 | New Mexico | .249 | .142 | −.107 |
| 12 | Indiana | .100 | .138 | .038 | 35 | West Virginia | .136 | .027 | −.109 |
| 13 | Wyoming | .086 | .124 | .038 | 36 | Texas | .217 | .073 | −.109 |
| 14 | Iowa | .102 | .235 | .037 | 37 | Alaska | .114 | .000 | −.114 |
| 15 | Vermont | .070 | .100 | .030 | 38 | Washington | .201 | .084 | −.117 |
| 16 | Colorado | .106 | .129 | .014 | 39 | Florida | .345 | .165 | −.180 |
| 17 | Missouri | .159 | .146 | .013 | 40 | Kentucky | .249 | .051 | −.198 |
| 18 | Idaho | .139 | .145 | .006 | 41 | Louisiana | .232 | .029 | −.203 |
| 19 | California | .081 | .087 | .006 | 42 | Delaware | .273 | .021 | −.252 |
| 20 | Massachusetts | .000 | .000 | .000 | 43 | Georgia | .367 | .087 | −.280 |
| 21 | Illinois | .074 | .073 | −.001 | 44 | South Carolina | .433 | .076 | −.357 |
| 22 | New Hampshire | .043 | .026 | −.006 | 45 | Alabama | .833 | .271 | −.565 |
| 23 | Nebraska | .123 | .106 | −.011 | | | | | |

1 The change percentage for each state was rounded off to the nearest hundredth so that there would be no ties in the rankings.

2 Manyland, North Carolina, Tennessee, and Virginia were omitted because schools are operated by county governments in those states, while Hawaii was omitted since schools in that state are run by the state government. In addition, Vermont was omitted due to inaccurate data.

*Source:* U.S. Bureau of the Census. Census of Governments. Compendium of Government Finances series, 1962–2017.

## Differing usages of types of charges for services by the type of local government

At this point in the analysis, it will be instructive to ascertain the degree to which counties, municipalities, townships, and special districts depend on 11 specific kinds of non-utility-type charges for services to supply part of their OSR. In so doing, the analysis will not direct any attention to the "other" category because it includes a smattering of a large number of less recognizable services and no clearly identifiable or tangible service. Given the differing rationale for the creation of these four types of local government and the service roles they are expected to play, there is bound to be some variability in the usage of charges for services by these governments.

### *County governments*

While county governments received revenue from all 11 kinds of charges for services (as well as from less notable services in the "Other" category) in both 1962 and 2017, they obtained the largest proportion from charges for services related to treatment at county hospitals (see Table 6.15). It is also interesting to note that counties derived essentially the same percentage from these sources in both years (43 percent in 1962 and 42 percent in 2017).[6] The large proportion received for hospital charges for services is no surprise because county governments in many states have a well-known and long history of providing hospital/heath care services to their residents. In fact, state governments and county residents alike have typically viewed hospital/heath care services as staple, core, or "must" services that county governments should either provide through

*Table 6.15* Rank Ordering of Non-Utility Charges for Services for Counties in 2017 and 1962

| *Service* | *2017* | | *Service* | *1962* | |
|---|---|---|---|---|---|
| | *Rank* | *Percent* | | *Rank* | *Percent* |
| Hospitals | 1 | 42 | Hospitals | 1 | 43 |
| Other | 2 | 30 | Other | 2 | 37 |
| Sewage | 3 | 8 | Education | 3 | 11 |
| Solid Waste | 4 | 7 | Airports | 4 | 3 |
| Education | 5 | 5 | Sewage | 6 | 1 |
| Highways | 8 | 2 | Natural Resources | 8 | 1 |
| Housing & CD[1] | 9 | 1 | Port Facilities | 9 | * |
| Port Facilities | 10 | * | Parking | 10 | * |
| Natural Resources | 11 | * | Highways | 11 | * |
| Parking | 12 | * | Housing & CD[1] | 12 | * |

[1] Housing & Community Development (once referred to as Housing & Urban Renewal).

* Less than 1 percent.

*Source:* U.S. Bureau of the Census. Census of Governments. Compendium of Government Finances series, 1962–2017.

county-owned and -operated facilities or assure their availability through alternative means (e.g., establishment of local government hospital authorities).[7]

Table 6.15 also indicates that changes have occurred over the last 55 years as to where charges for services revenue have been originating. Conspicuous declines in the proportion of charges for services revenue have taken place in two areas ("other" and education) between 1962 and 2017. The result has been that county governments are now getting a larger proportion of their charges for services revenue from charges and/or fees that have been levied on users of sewage and solid waste collection and disposal services. Two factors seem to explain the increase in revenue from these two sources. One has been actions taken by the federal government to encourage (making grants-in-aid and low interest loans available) and/or require (issuing mandates) counties and other local governments to be more cognizant of the environmental hazards related to the careless way in which garbage and sewage had been collected and disposed of in the past. A second factor has been the conscious effort of county government officials to transition away from funding sewage and solid water operations from taxes (primary property) to a more business-like and fairer model whereby residents and businesses pay for these services through a service charge or user fee.

In viewing the proportion of charges for services that counties (and also municipalities, townships, and special districts) collect from the 11 types of charges (see Tables 6.15–6.18), it is very important to keep in mind that the figures are average percentages for all counties (or as the case may be, for all municipalities or for all townships or for all special districts). As such,

*Table 6.16* Rank Ordering of Non-Utility Charges for Services for Municipalities in 2017 and 1962

| *Service* | *2017* | | *Service* | *1962* | |
|---|---|---|---|---|---|
| | *Rank* | *Percent* | | *Service* | *Rank* |
| Sewage | 1 | 36 | Sewage | 1 | 19 |
| Other | 2 | 16 | Other | 2 | 16 |
| Hospitals | 3 | 12 | Hospitals | 3 | 16 |
| Solid Waste | 4 | 11 | Housing & CD[1] | 4 | 10 |
| Airports | 5 | 10 | Parking | 5 | 8 |
| Parks and Recreation | 6 | 5 | Education | 6 | 7 |
| Highways | 7 | 3 | Solid Waste | 7 | 7 |
| Housing & CD[1] | 8 | 3 | Airports | 8 | 7 |
| Parking | 9 | 2 | Parks and Recreation | 9 | 6 |
| Port Facilities | 10 | 2 | Port Facilities | 10 | 3 |
| Education | 11 | 1 | Highways | 11 | * |
| Natural Resources | 12 | * | Natural Resources | 12 | 0.0 |

[1] Housing & Community Development (once referred to as Housing & Urban Renewal).

* Less than 1 percent.

*Source:* U.S. Bureau of the Census. Census of Governments. Compendium of Government Finances series, 1962–2017.

*Table 6.17* Rank Ordering of Non-Utility Charges for Services for Townships in 2017 and 1962

| *Service* | *2017* | | *Service* | *1962* | |
|---|---|---|---|---|---|
| | *Rank* | *Percent* | | *Service* | *Rank* |
| Sewage | 1 | 46 | Education | 1 | 34 |
| Other | 2 | 21 | Sewage | 2 | 25 |
| Solid Waste | 3 | 13 | Other | 3 | 16 |
| Parks and Recreation | 4 | 9 | Hospitals | 4 | 7 |
| Education | 5 | 6 | Solid Waste | 5 | 7 |
| Hospitals | 6 | 2 | Parks and Recreation | 6 | 5 |
| Parking | 7 | 1 | Parking | 7 | 3 |
| Airports | 8 | 1 | Highways | 8 | 2 |
| Highways | 9 | 1 | Airports | 9 | * |
| Housing & CD[1] | 10 | 1 | Housing & CD[1] | 10 | * |
| Port Facilities | 11 | * | Port Facilities | 11 | * |
| Natural Resources | 12 | * | Natural Resources | 12 | 0.0 |

[1] Housing & Community Development (once referred to as Housing & Urban Renewal).

* Less than 1 percent.

*Source:* U.S. Bureau of the Census. Census of Governments. Compendium of Government Finances series, 1962–2017.

*Table 6.18* Rank Ordering of Non-Utility Charges for Services for Special Districts in 2017 and 1962

| | *2017* | | | *1962* | |
|---|---|---|---|---|---|
| *Service* | *Rank* | *Percent* | *Service* | *Service* | *Rank* |
| Hospitals | 1 | 48 | Housing & CD[1] | 1 | 28 |
| Other | 2 | 13 | Hospitals | 2 | 23 |
| Sewage | 3 | 12 | Other | 3 | 12 |
| Airports | 4 | 10 | Natural Resources | 4 | 10 |
| Housing & CD[1] | 5 | 4 | Sewage | 5 | 8 |
| Highways | 6 | 4 | Port Facilities | 6 | 8 |
| Parks and Recreation | 7 | 2 | Airport | 7 | 8 |
| Port Facilities | 8 | 2 | Parks and Recreation | 8 | 1 |
| Natural Resources | 9 | 2 | Parking | 9 | 1 |
| Solid Waste | 10 | 2 | Solid Waste | 10 | * |
| Parking | 11 | * | Highways | 11 | * |
| Education | 12 | 0.0 | Education | 12 | * |

[1] Housing & Community Development (once referred to as Housing & Urban Renewal).

* Less than 1 percent.

*Source:* U.S. Bureau of the Census. Census of Governments. Compendium of Government Finances series, 1962–2017.

there is the real possibility for considerable variability from one state to another. Let's take the case of county government hospital charges for services. As reported above, counties in 2017 received, on average, 43 percent of all charges for services revenue from hospital/health care charges. However, this does not mean that county governments in each state necessarily received this same percentage (43) from this particular source. In examining 2017 data on a state-by-state basis, one would find the following: county governments in 16 states collected no hospital charges for services revenue since there were no county hospitals[8]; county governments in five states (Indiana, Iowa, Mississippi, Oklahoma, and Wyoming) obtained 80–90 percent of their charges for services revenue from hospitals, while county governments in another two (Louisiana and Tennessee) and four (Missouri, Nebraska, South Carolina, and Texas) states received 70–79 percent and 60–69 percent, respectively, from this source; and counties in another four states got less than 10 percent of their charges for services revenue from hospital fees.

The important point here is that there is usually not just one pattern that describes charges for services revenue collections for county governments (or for municipal governments or for township governments or for special districts) but a number of different patterns that result from the unique history, culture, politics, and social and economic characters found in each state.

### *Municipal governments*

When looking at Table 6.16, it is clear that money obtained from charges for services has always been more spread out for municipal governments than for county governments. By far, the most important source of this money in both 1962 and 2017 are charges levied for sewage services. This is hardly a surprising finding since sewage services—like fire and police, garbage collection, sidewalks, street lighting, and utilities—have long been viewed as indispensable services for densely populated areas like cities. It is also important to draw attention to the fact that the sewage proportion of total charges for services increased significantly between 1962 and 2017 (i.e., from 19 to 36 percent), thus confirming earlier speculation that municipal and (even county) officials have been addressing documented inequities in service funding schemes by progressively shifting from a heavy dependency on property tax revenue to greater reliance on charges for services.

Besides deriving 16 percent of charges for services revenue from a wide variety of "other" service areas in both 1962 and 2017, municipalities, by 2017, were obtaining sizable proportions of this type of revenue from charges and fees related to the usage of hospitals (12 percent), solid waste collection and disposal (11 percent), and airports (10 percent). Subsequently, this meant that municipalities in 2017, when compared to 1962, were deriving smaller proportions of their charges for service revenue from services such as housing and community development, parking and education. It is also the case that the proportion of charges for services generated by hospital charges declined from 16 percent in 1962 to 12 percent in 2017, in spite of the fact that this source was still one of the top producing types of charges in 2017; this reduction in the hospital charges for services proportion is likely explained by the nationwide trend whereby municipalities have been attempting to lessen their city's legal liability to malpractice suits by establishing hospital authorities and to more fairly distribute the burden of funding hospitals.

### *Township governments*

In some ways, there are some similarities between townships and municipalities in recent years when it comes to the proportional distribution of revenues derived from various charges for services (see Tables 6.17 and 6.16). For example, both type of governments received the largest part of this type of revenue from charges for sewage services in 2017. In fact, townships had the higher proportion (i.e., 46 percent for townships versus 36 percent for municipalities). In addition, both governments collected nearly the same proportion from solid waste charges (13 percent for townships and 11 percent for municipalities). In both service areas, it is apparent that townships like municipal governments are funding their operations more with charges for services revenue and less with property tax revenue than was the case in 1962. By 2017, township governments were also collecting a larger proportion of their charges for services revenue (9 percent) from the provision of another common municipal-type service—parks and recreation.

From Table 6.17, it is clear that charges for the services proportion for some areas had dropped noticeably over the last 55 years, but especially for education. In comparing the actual amount of money received by townships in 1962 for education and sewage charges versus what was received in 2017, it can be seen (data not shown here) that the amount of money received for the former grew at a very modest pace, while the latter increased at an astronomical rate. In short, revenue derived from education charges did not shrink over the 1962–2017 period but instead the massive growth in charges for sewer services greatly overshadowed the much smaller rate of growth in education charges. Then, the conspicuous decline in hospital charges for services can be attributed to townships "getting out of the hospital business" because of the financial risk involved. The best guess is that former township hospitals were either sold to private sector companies or converted to hospital authorities.

### *Special districts*

While special districts are perhaps best known for providing some essential utilities (i.e., water and gas supply and electric power) to residents and businesses which are located beyond the city limits of municipalities and charging a user fee for them, special districts also deliver some of the same non-utility services as do counties, municipalities, and townships and levy a charge for services. In fact, it is often asserted that special districts fill the service void left by counties and municipalities and even townships and are the providers of last resort. As the case may be, these other local governments may not have the legal authority to provide non-utility-type services, may not be financially able to fund these services due to tax or bonded indebtedness limitations, or cannot realize economies of scale in the provision of certain services.

At any rate, service districts collect a lot of money from the provision of several non-utility kinds of services (see Table 6.18). In 1962, special districts collected over one-half of their non-utility-type revenue from the provision of housing/community development and hospital services. Special districts also receive a smaller portion of non-utility revenue from charges related to the conservation of natural resources. By 2017, however, the receipt of non-utility revenue became more focused, as close to one-half of it (48 percent) was derived from hospital charges for services. Much smaller portions came from sewage and airport charges. The much greater proportion received from hospital charges for services is most likely the result of the ownership and control of a large number of city and some county and township hospitals being transferred to newly established state legislative authorities or special districts. The financial and risk management reasons for this change have been discussed earlier.

## Trends in usage of utility user fees by the level of local government

As was seen earlier in this chapter (refer back to Tables 6.1 and 6.2), there has been a substantial increase in revenue collected by local governments from charges for services that subsequently resulted in a noticeable amount of growth in the proportion of local governments' OSR accounted for by this source of revenue (increasing from 15 to 27 percent between 1962 and 2017). Likewise, there has been significant growth in the amount of revenue (in the form or user fees or charges) received by local government to fund the cost of their utilities (i.e., enterprise operations). While local governments collected a little over $4 billion in 1962, the amount of this revenue increased to over $167 billion by 2020. However, this growth rate has not been uniform across the two basic types of charges for services—non-utility- and utility-type charges. The greatest amount of growth—indeed, all of it—has occurred in non-utility-type charges, where it rose from 13 percent in 1962 to 24 percent in 2017. In point of fact, there was no change in the proportion of total local government OSR attributable to utility-type charges for services/user fees, as it was the same in 2017 as it was in 1962—13 percent.

Nonetheless, revenue derived from utility-type charges for services or user fees is still an important source of money since it supposedly covers the cost (and in some instances, it may include the making of a small "profit") incurred by local governments in providing vital services such as water supply, electric power, natural gas supply, and mass transit to people and businesses within their jurisdictions. These are services that are immediately recognizable as ones which should be funded by charges assessed to "users" or clear "beneficiaries" of them. To fund them entirely or even mostly with property and other kinds of tax proceeds would seem to be an unfair and unjustified burden imposed on what could turn out to be angry and resentful taxpayers and likely to invite severe criticism. It would also likely engender sharp rebukes from civic groups and the media, as well as the exodus of business and middle- to upper-income residents in accordance with Tiebout's (1956) allusion to "voting with [one's] feet." In addition, it would have the logical potential for creating an unwanted and unpopular "freeloader" stigma. Simply put, local government officials are always mindful of doing whatever is necessary to avoid this kind of public relations nightmare that can have serious political repercussions at election time.

With this said, which governments received the largest part of total local government revenue generated by various kinds of utility charges for services/ user fees from the most recent data in 2017? These data are shown in Figure 6.6. Total local government utility user fees/charges collections amounted to just under $155 million. According to the figure, municipalities collected the bulk of these funds (60 percent) and supposedly at least enough money to permit them to cover their costs of service provision). The second largest proportion of utility revenue was received by special districts (34 percent). Smaller proportions of

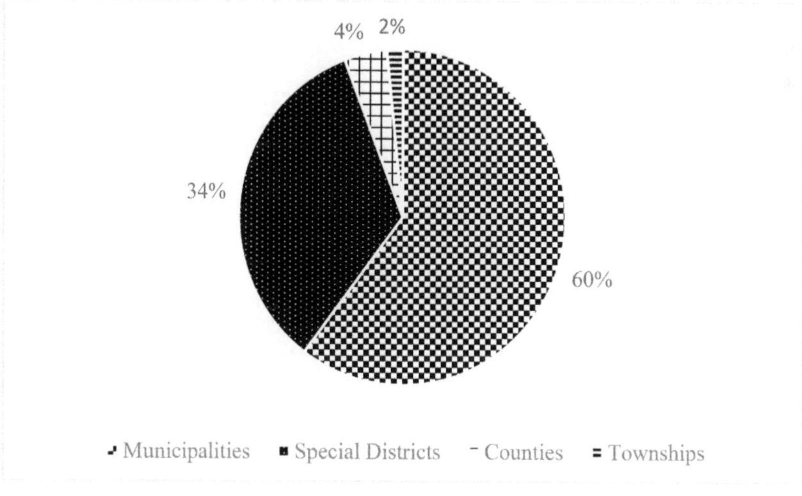


*Figure 6.6* Distribution of Utility Revenue, 2017

*Source:* U.S. Bureau of the Census. Census of Governments. Compendium of Government Finances series, 1962–2017.

the total amount were paid by utility customers to county governments (4 percent) and townships (2 percent). These findings are consistent with expectations, as municipalities have always been the leader in local governments in providing a number of utility services (but especially water, sewer, and solid waste collection) to their residents and businesses. And, of course, special districts in recent decades have been accounting for a fairly large part of these revenues in their role of providing utility services when municipalities and counties cannot or will not provide them to residents and business in the unincorporated areas of highly urbanized and densely populated counties (see Benton 2002).

Given this information, how did the distribution of utility receipts break down among the four kinds of utility services (water, electric power, natural gas, and transit)? The answer is found in Figure 6.7, where it appears that municipalities benefitted the most (actually collecting at least enough money to permit them to cover their costs of service provision) than other types of local governments in all four kinds of service charges (i.e., water, electric power, natural gas supply, and mass transit in 2017, although special districts did take in a sizable share of the proceeds from these same service areas. Figure 6.7 also indicates that special districts collected the largest proportion of money collected by all government for transit charges for services/user fees. Unfortunately, no meaningful long-term comparisons can be made over time since the Census Bureau did not begin reporting of revenue amounts for specific utility services until 2002.

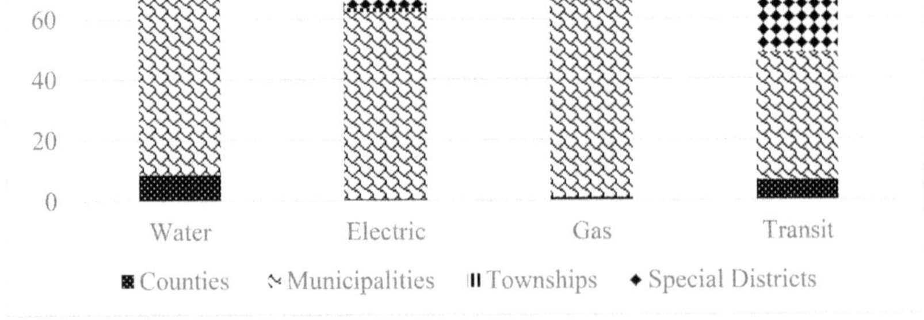


*Figure 6.7* Local Government Proportions of Revenue Proceeds from Water, Electric, Gas, and Transit Charges for Services/User Fees, 2017

*Source:* U.S. Bureau of the Census. Census of Governments. Compendium of Government Finances series, 1962–2017.

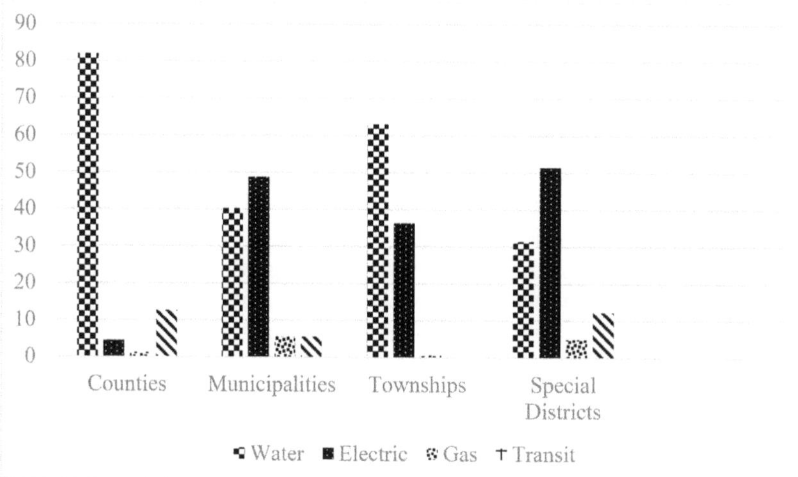


*Figure 6.8* Revenue from Various Utility Charges for Services, 2017

*Source:* U.S. Bureau of the Census. Census of Governments. Compendium of Government Finances series, 1962–2017.

Another way to estimate the importance of each type of utility-type revenue for each of the four local governments is to examine the proportion of total utility receipts derived from water, electric, gas, and transit charges. This information for counties, municipalities, townships, and special districts in 2017 is contained in Figure 6.8.

For county governments, it is obvious that the overwhelming majority of utility revenue (over 80 percent) is received from water charges. It is reasonable to speculate that counties (but especially ones with large and densely populated unincorporated areas) have chosen to provide water services to citizens and businesses that expect the provision of this vital municipal-type service. It can be seen from additional data not shown here that there are counties in two states that collect an unusually large amount of money and proportion of their total utility revenue from these kinds of charges. This is the case for county governments in Washington and Wisconsin. Counties in Washington received approximately $245 million in their utility revenue or 98 percent of it from transit charges, while county governments in Wisconsin collect 100 percent of their utility revenue (over $54 billion) from this source.

In looking at the data for municipal governments in the figure, it is apparent that they derive similar proportions from water supply and electric power charges, with much smaller portions coming from natural gas supply and transit charges. While it is common knowledge that cities have been major suppliers of water services, it was somewhat surprising that they are also major suppliers of electricity. It would be interesting to know if municipalities entered into the electric power business in an effort to provide electricity to their residents or viewed it as an opportunity to supply a vital service while also taking advantage of the opportunity to earn a "profit" and thereby be able to supplement their city's general revenue sources.

Township governments, while they receive a much smaller proportion of their OSR from utility charges for services compared to counties, municipalities, and special districts, seem to have a distributional pattern similar to that of municipalities. More specifically, their largest proportions of charges for services revenue come from water supply and electric power (about 99 percent of it). Again, one also has to wonder about the motivation for township governments for entering into the field of electric power provision.

Finally, the pattern detected for special districts bears close resemblance to the pattern seen for municipalities. Over 80 percent of special district utility-type revenues are collected from the same two services—water supply and electric power. The largest proportion (51 percent) comes from the sale of electricity, while a substantial amount (31 percent) is derived from the provision of water. Although special districts in most states receive a much smaller proportion of their utility revenue from transit charges or user fees, there are some notable exceptions. For example, special districts in New York collected 78 percent of their utility revenue from transit charges, while special districts in Illinois received 62 percent of their utility revenue from this one source. Relevant data indicates that charges for services in special districts in two other states (Ohio and Pennsylvania) accounted for 55 and 41 percent, respectively, of their utility-type revenue. As such, special districts (rather than counties and cities) in these states appear to be leaders in the provision of transit services. This information about special districts in all four of these states, along with similar data for counties in Washington and Wisconsin, would suggest that they are more active in funding mass transit services and thus would be more likely to receive a substantial proportion of their utility revenue from transit charges/user fees.

## Summary observations and conclusions

With local governments' commitment to reduce their historically heavy dependency on property tax proceeds in early 1960s, they have been successful in part in doing so because of their willingness to substantially increase their usage of non-utility charges for services and user fees. However, it is important to point out that the actual growth in this type of OSR has been realized only by counties, municipalities, townships, and special districts; this has not been the case for school districts. Furthermore, there is strong evidence to suggest that there is a significant link between increases in the proportion of revenue coming from non-utility charges/fees and the simultaneous decreases in the percentage of revenue derived from property tax collections. The largest amounts of non-utility charges/users revenues have been in the following service areas: hospitals, sewage, solid waste, airports, and parks and recreation. It is also significant to note that, while these four types of local governments were receiving a much larger proportion of their OSR from charges for services since 1962, the proportion of their OSR derived from utility-type sources basically remained the same over this same 55-year period. Most of their utility-type revenue originated from charges for water.

In the next chapter, attention will shift to a number of lesser known yet important "other" or miscellaneous types of local government revenue that supplement what these governments receive from a variety of taxes and charges for services/ user fees. The "other" revenues include but are not limited to things such as special assessments, fines and forfeitures, sale of property, and proceeds from the operation of liquor stores, rents, royalties, donations, and interest earnings.

## Notes

1 Local governments have long operated public utilities, as well as public facilities such as ports, parking lots, and airports. Many are now entering fields traditionally dominated by private companies. This is motivated partially by political resistance to tax increases and new user fees as local governments (but especially, cash-strapped municipalities) seeking to raise revenues, as well as public pressure to create jobs as the economy has faltered. Examples from across the country include the development of city-owned hotels to promote economic development through tourism (such as a convention center hotel owned by the City of Dallas), the provision of cable and broadband services by public power companies, and the increasingly sophisticated use of real estate development to generate lease revenues, especially to help finance public transit development. See Mikesell (2018) for a history of local governments, but especially municipalities, providing these kinds of services and paying for them with user fees and charges for services.

2 One exception, however, is mass transit services. Local government-owned mass transit systems have rarely been able to operate even on a break-even basis. Subsequently, they are typically subsidized with tax money or other types of revenue.

3 Of course, local governments can also use funds derived from several types of miscellaneous or "other" revenues (subject of Chapter 7) or intergovernmental revenue (subject of Chapter 8) to pay for the provision of indivisible services.

4 Although it is beyond the scope of this book, local governments since the 1970s have also been engaging in stepped-up efforts to shed services in order to relieve the ever-increasing pressure emanating from both rising citizen service expectations and more frequent episodes of fiscal stress. Efforts have included but not limited to the following: contracting out service delivery (or even part of a service) to private for-profit or non-profit entities and other local governments; transferring service responsibility to another level(s) of government (federal or state) or to another local government (e.g., from a municipal to a county government); providing a service through volunteers; and even eliminating services (see Hatry 1983; Honadle 1984; ICMA 2021).

5 A good example is the City of Georgetown, South Carolina which has provided electric power to residents and business in the City for over 70 years. Over the years, the Electric Department enterprise operation has consistently made a tidy profit, thus allowing the City to transfer some of this extra revenue to the general fund to cover

occasional shortfalls. In fact, it has been said that the City uses this extra money as a de facto "rainy day" or "reserve" fund. Also, see Mikesell 2018.

6 Although the data are not shown here, this proportion has remained amazingly constant during the entire 55-year span covered in this book and has not increased or decreased by more than 1 percentage point at any time.

7 Of course, hospital and health care services can and are offered by private sector companies, and thereby, fill any unmet need and provide healthy competition.

8 These states were Alaska, Connecticut, Delaware, Georgia, Hawaii, Maine, Maryland, Massachusetts, New Hampshire, North Dakota, Oregon, Pennsylvania, Rhode Island, Vermont, Virginia, and Washington.

## References

Benton, J. Edwin. 2002. *Counties as Service Delivery Agents: Changing Expectations and Roles*. Westport, CT: Praeger.

Bowman, Ann O'M, and Richard C. Kearney. 2008. *State and Local Government*. 7th ed. Boston, MA: Houghton Mifflin Company.

Dye, Thomas R., and Susan MacManus. 2015. *Politics in States and Communities*. 15th ed. Upper Saddle River, NJ: Pearson.

Hatry, Harry. 1983. *Review of Private Approaches for Delivery of Public Services*. Washington, DC: The Urban Institute.

Honadle, Beth Walter. 1984. "Alternative Service Delivery Strategies and Improvement of Local Government Productivity," *Public Productivity Review*, 8(4): 301–13.

International City/County Management Association. 2021. *Service Delivery Alternatives in the Age of COVID-19 – Summary of Survey Results*. Washington, DC: ICMA. https://icma.org.

Mikesell, John L. 2018. *Fiscal Administration: Analysis and Application for the Public Sector*. 8th ed. Boston: Cengage.

Tiebout, Charles. 1956. "A Pure Theory of Local Expenditures," *Journal of Political Economy*, 64(October): 416–24.

# 7 Miscellaneous Revenues

## Relatively Small but Still Vital Money for Local Governments

As seen in earlier chapters of this book, local governments, like their federal and state government counterparts, obtain a substantial portion of their revenue needed to sustain their operations and provide a litany of services from two major internally derived sources (i.e., OSR)—taxes and charges for services. In 2017, local governments collected over $1.25 trillion or about 93 percent of their OSR (or 61 percent of their Total Revenue—TR) from a variety of taxes and charges. The remaining amount or roughly 7 percent of local governments' OSR (or about 4.4 percent of TR) was collected from an assortment of what is usually referred to as "Miscellaneous" revenue sources. According to the U.S. Census of Governments' five-year reports on Local Government Finances, miscellaneous revenues consist of special assessments, sale of property, interest earnings, proceeds from the operation of liquor stores, and "other general revenue" (fines and forfeits, rent, royalties, and donations).

### Small money to help balance the budget

While it might be easy for some causal observers to downplay the importance of the approximately 7 percent of local governments' OSR (or a little more than 4 percent of their TR) that comes from miscellaneous sources, the loss of this revenue certainly would have created a conspicuous hole in these governments' budgets and probably would have led to significant—and perhaps long-term—repercussions for them and their citizens. More to the point, we are not talking about the loss of perhaps a few thousand dollars or even a hundred thousand dollars or so but rather these governments having to experience the loss of millions or perhaps billions of dollars that could significantly alter a local government's budget and its ability to satisfy citizen service needs and expectations. Given the enormity and complexity of the local government financial picture, this is no small matter and should never be dismissed as these governments have to make minor adjustments to their budgets. For a municipality, it could result in the inability to employ three fewer firefighters, meaning that it would have one less engine or aerial ladder apparatus in service for one of the fire department's

DOI: 10.4324/9781032640389-7

*Table 7.1* Miscellaneous Revenue for Local Government, 2017

| *Government Type* | *Amount (in billions)* | *% of Own-Source Revenue (OSR)* | *Total Revenue (TR)* |
|---|---|---|---|
| County Government | $20.7 | 7.4 | 4.8 |
| Municipal Governments | $34.9 | 9.1 | 5.8 |
| Townships | $ 2.5 | 5.5 | 4.3 |
| Special Districts | $11.5 | 9.0 | 4.7 |
| School Districts | $15.2 | 5.9 | 2.6 |
| TOTAL | $84.7 | 8.3 | 4.8 |

*Source:* U.S. Bureau of the Census. 2017 Census of Governments. Compendium of Government Finances (Washington, DC: Government Printing Office).

three shifts. For a county government, less money derived from miscellaneous sources could result in laying off five patrol deputies from the sheriff's department which could mean fewer officers protecting the communities and inadequate back-up for other on-duty deputies. Fewer miscellaneous dollars could also cause a diminution in the educational experience for K-12 children when the number of students per classroom must be increased because the school district can no longer retain its current number of teachers while enrollments are increasing. Similar financial hardships and service consequences would be expected for townships and special service districts and their residents/customers.

Table 7.1 shows the huge monetary loses that counties, municipalities, townships, special districts, and school districts would have been experienced in 2017 if they had not collected money from a number of miscellaneous types of revenue. Collectively, these local governments would have had $84.7 billion less money to spend in fiscal year 2017. Municipalities would have been hit the hardest ($34.9 billion), while counties would not have been far behind ($20.7 billion). School and special districts also would have had much less money at their disposal, although their projected loses would have been only about one-third of what it would have been for municipalities ($15.2 billion and $11.5 billion, respectively). In spite of the fact that townships stood to lose the smallest amount of money ($2.5 billion), this would have been no insignificant amount of money and likely would have imposed a hardship on these governments.

Perhaps more important than the actual amount of money that would have been lost by various local governments was the level of dependency that each had on miscellaneous revenue. Notice that, while special districts stood to lose only about one-third as much money as would have municipalities, miscellaneous revenue constituted a similar proportion of special districts' OSR (9.0 percent versus 9.1 percent). This means that the budgets of special districts would have been impacted negatively to almost the same degree as municipal government budgets in spite of losing much less total dollars. Further, note that, while school districts lost more money than special districts ($15.2 million compared to $11.5 billion), the burden on school districts would have been somewhat less than special districts, given the former's lesser dependency on miscellaneous revenue (5.9 versus 9.0 percent of OSR). In short, the greater dependency that a local government has on miscellaneous revenue could lead to greater difficulty in balancing one's budgets if it were to lose a substantial amount of this source of money. Similar conclusions can be reached by considering the importance (dependency) of miscellaneous revenue as a percentage of TR.

Needless to say, the loss of miscellaneous revenue would be no inconsequential matter, as each of these governments and their citizens potentially could be presented with some tough and painful choices. On the one hand, local governments hypothetically might have to face the prospect of having to slash their budgets by the exact amount of money that they would have obtained from various types of miscellaneous revenue. On the other hand, local governments theoretically could be forced to raise the same amount of money normally derived from miscellaneous revenues by tapping other revenue sources to maintain current service levels. That is, they could have to institute new taxes and/or increased rates of existing taxes; in addition, they could impose new charges of services and/or raise the rate for current charges. Another possibility could be for local governments to confront their dilemma by cutting funding for some services while also raising more money from other OSR sources. Other possible ways of addressing the loss or unavailability of miscellaneous revenue would be to outsource service provision, find ways to cut the cost of the delivery of in-house provided services, or obtain additional funding from the federal or their state governments. In sum, revenue derived from miscellaneous sources, while it may be small in the eyes of some observers, is critical to the fiscal sustainability of local governments.

The closest comparison that can be made to local governments' loss of miscellaneous types of revenue would be to consider the consequences of a reduction in one's personal or family income or the loss of income derived from one's business. Without doubt, one's personal or family lifestyle would inevitably be different if he/she/they did not have the current level of income. Likewise, one's personal or family lifestyle of necessity would have to change if there were a sudden and permanent change in income. In a similar way, the loss of business income would also produce economic hardships and consequences. The ability to keep a desirable level of inventory in stock, advertise in various venues as deemed necessary, employ a requisite and skilled workforce, and make an acceptable profit could be negatively impacted, and, of course, having to declare bankruptcy could become a harsh reality. In short, the dreadful realities of economic dislocation of any sort by individuals, families, one's business, and even governments like counties, municipalities, townships, special districts, and school districts can necessitate unwanted changes.

The important point here is that miscellaneous local government revenues, while small in comparison to revenue derived from some form of taxation and charges for services, are clearly vital to local governments' ability to balance their budgets and thereby satisfy the service needs and expectations of their citizens and businesses at the grassroots level of the federal system of government.

Before beginning a comprehensive analysis of the part that miscellaneous revenues play in the finances of local governments, it is instructive for us to have a better understanding of the specific kinds of revenue sources that make up what is typically referred to as "Miscellaneous Revenue."

## What is miscellaneous revenue?

While local government financial management experts may sometimes differ as to what kinds of monetary receipts should be included in the category referred to as "Miscellaneous Revenues," they usually agree on the ones singled out for analysis here. They normally include the following: special assessments, sale of surplus property, interest earnings, proceeds from the operation of liquor stores, and "other general revenue" (i.e., fines and forfeits, rents and royalties, and donations).

Special assessments consist of compulsory contributions collected from property owners who benefit from special public improvements (street pavement, sewer and water services, street lighting, sidewalks, storm water management, solid and yard waste and hazardous material collection, neighborhood parks, fire protection, etc.) to defray the cost of such improvements (either directly or through the payment of debt service or indebtedness incurred to finance the improvements) and apportioned according to the assumed benefits to the property affected by the improvements.

Local governments, like citizens and private companies and businesses own property in the form of real estate and structures or buildings that may be situated on them. From time to time, local governments may designate some of the property they own to be "surplus property" because they deem it to be something that they will not need in either the immediate or long-term future. Therefore, they decide to sell the property and then add the proceeds from the sale to their available revenues for future budgets. The sale of securities and commodities, equipment, and other personal property are usually not included in this fund classification.

Interest earnings represent interest earned on deposits, securities, including amounts for accrued interest on investment securities sold. However, receipts for accrued interest on bonds issued are classified as offsets to interest expenditure. It is also important to note that the interest earnings normally listed under general revenue do not include earnings on assets of employee-retirement systems.

Liquor store revenue refers to monies received from the sale of liquor by state and/or local-owned liquor stores and other revenue from state and/or liquor store operations. Excluded from such revenues are any state taxes collected by state liquor monopoly systems. The type of revenue is available to local governments in just five states (Arkansas, Maryland, Minnesota, North Carolina, and South Dakota) and limited to counties in Maryland and North Carolina and municipalities in (Arkansas, Minnesota, North Carolina, and South Dakota). It should also be mentioned that any state taxes collected by state liquor store monopoly systems are not included.

The "other general revenue" part of miscellaneous revenue consists of three basic and unrelated sources. First, fines and forfeits (usually based on a state-imposed formula whereby the state and local governments split these funds) are penalties imposed for violation of law and forfeits of amounts on deposit as performance guarantees but does not include penalties on delinquent taxes. Second, rents and royalties consist of rents from leased properties, mineral leases, royalties, and miscellaneous rentals not related to the performance of a particular function; rental revenue from such facilities is classified as revenue from current charges for the activity of the function concerned. Lastly, donations include money gifted to local governments by private persons or businesses with nothing in the way of services rendered expected in return.

## Examination of local governments' dependency on miscellaneous revenue

As noted in Chapters 4–6, local governments have historically relied much more heavily on a variety of taxes (but primarily property) and charges for services to supply the financial resources necessary to fund a long list of well-known services. Miscellaneous revenue, while by no means a trivial source of additional money, tends to augment local government coffers and thereby helps these governments to close the gap between desired expenditures and the revenue needed to cover the cost of anticipated spending. As would be expected, elected and appointive local officials (but especially, budget personal) usually pay much more attention to designing and tweaking the two major revenue "workhorses" (taxes and charges for services) because of the obvious political and economic ramifications. As a result, less scrutiny is normally given to the amount that will come from a somewhat "given" source of revenue (i.e., miscellaneous funds) about which they have much less discretion or control. Hopefully, the following analysis will shed more light on what sometimes has been an overlooked or unexplored small yet critical part of the local government budget.

Figure 7.1 reinforces the reality that revenue obtained from miscellaneous sources has always been much smaller than the money derived from taxes and charges for services. In 1962, funds originating from miscellaneous sources accounted for almost 6 percent of local governments' OSR. By the late 1970s and early 1980s, there was a noticeable surge in local governments' miscellaneous revenue collections, with this revenue source amounting to as much as 16 percent of OSR in the 1987 reporting period. After 1987, miscellaneous revenue declined somewhat and leveled off to around 12–13 percent for the next 20 years.

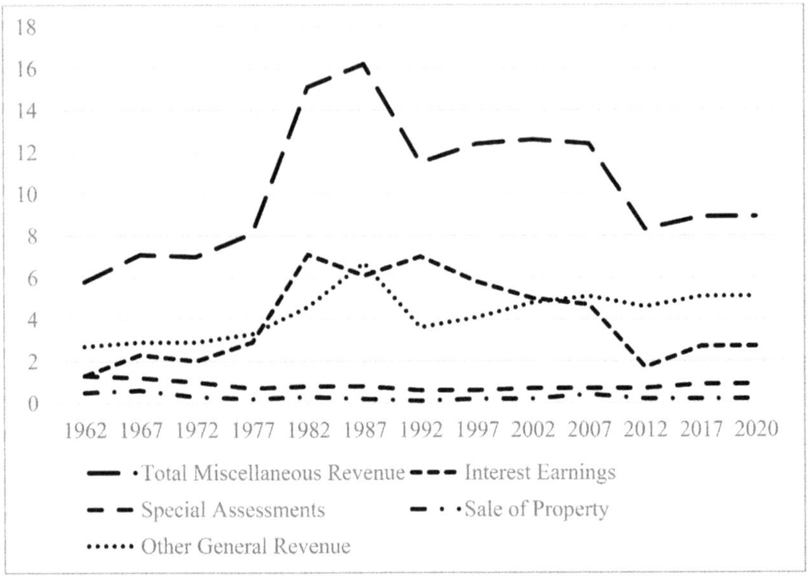


*Figure 7.1* Total Miscellaneous Revenue and Types of Miscellaneous Revenue as a Proportion of Own-Source Revenue for All Local Governments, 1962–2017

*Source:* U.S. Bureau of the Census. Census of Governments. Compendium of Government Finances series, 1962–2017.

With the onset of the Great Recession in 2007, miscellaneous revenues dropped again to around 8 percent of OSR but had increased to nearly 9 percent by 2017. These latter findings would suggest that the strong negative effects produced by the Great Recession have persisted for a much longer period of time than was the case in previous economic downturns and thereby giving credence to the assertion that local government officials may have to adapt to the reality of a "New Normal" in government finances.

Further inspection of Figure 7.1 aids in understanding the primary reason behind the conspicuous increase in miscellaneous revenue as a percentage of local governments' OSR from the 1970s until the 1990s. This increase was likely associated with the simultaneous growth in revenue obtained from interest earnings during that period. Astute local government financial officers took advantage of unusually high interest rates being paid to investors by banking and lending institutions and investment companies. In fact, it was fairly common knowledge that local government budget officials and certified public accountant firms retained to advise on fiscal matters strongly urged local government elected officials about the wisdom of investing as much of their contingency funds and surplus money in high interest-bearing (but particularly, short-term) savings plans. In short, local governments took advantage of letting their idle cash grow their money that was not needed for either operating or capital expenditures.

Other data presented in Figure 7.1 provide more perspective on the size and content of local governments' miscellaneous revenue. Over time, a modest increase in the amount of money collected from a variety of "other general revenue" sources have also contributed to the overall increase in the total amount of miscellaneous funds that are at the disposal of local governments. Interestingly, the increase in these funds followed a very similar pattern to what was seen for interest earnings and could be due to local government reformers' efforts to convince state legislators to share larger portions of proceeds from fines and forfeitures with their local governments, but especially counties and municipalities. Specifically, local officials and civic reformers have been successful in a number of states in lobbying their legislatures to give them a larger cut of the money that the state receives from fines and forfeitures in lieu of expanded authority to enact new taxes, increase the rates of existing taxes, or tap other kinds of revenue sources. Finally, other data presented in Figure 7.1 reveals that money generated from a number of special assessments as well as from the sale of surplus property has consistently made up only a negligible proportion of miscellaneous revenue.

At this point, it is important to determine if the patterns identified here are uniform across all types of local governments or if different patterns are the norm.

## Trends in reliance on miscellaneous revenues by the type of local government

The proportion of OSR that is accounted for by miscellaneous revenue varies among the five types of local government (see Figure 7.2). Early on, county governments relied less on miscellaneous revenue than all other local governments with the exception of school districts. These governments' dependence on miscellaneous revenue was similar to that of townships (i.e., this revenue source provided about 4–6 percent of township OSR). This pattern of dependency on miscellaneous revenue contrasted sharply with the patterns for municipalities and special districts, as these two types of local governments relied on miscellaneous kinds of revenue to supply 10–19 percent and 11–25 percent of their OSR, respectively. However, by 1982, county government revenue derived from miscellaneous sources started to increase significantly. As a result, miscellaneous revenue began to constitute a larger proportion of county governments' OSR, with the county OSR proportions becoming similar to municipal government proportions. The miscellaneous revenue proportion of OSR of county governments peaked at 18 percent in 1987, while the municipal government OSR figure also reached its highest point (19 percent) in 1987. It should not go unnoticed that miscellaneous revenue as a proportion of school district OSR increased

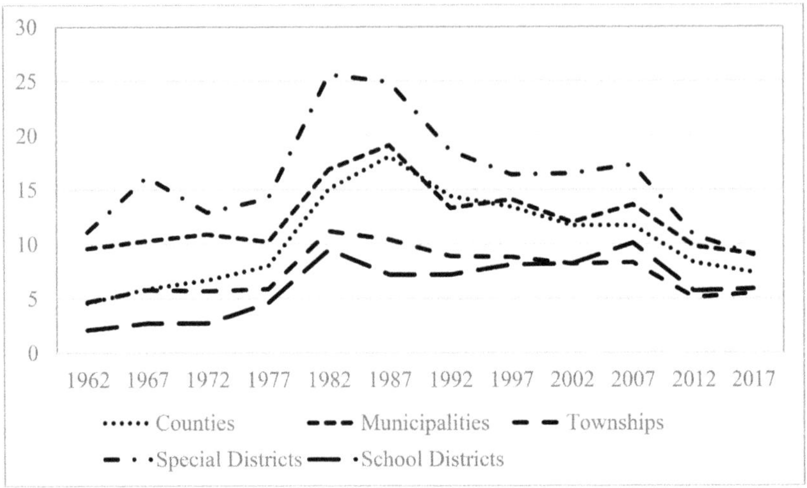


*Figure 7.2* Miscellaneous Revenue as a Percent of Own-Source Revenue (OSR) by Type of Local Government, 1962–2017

*Source:* U.S. Bureau of the Census. Census of Governments. Compendium of Government Finances series, 1962–2017.

considerably after 1977 and climbed to a high water mark of 10.1 percent in 2007. Finally, it is quite clear that miscellaneous revenue as a proportion of OSR began to noticeably decrease for all five types of local governments after 2007. This was likely due to the impact of the Great Recession and its lingering impact beyond the supposed end in 2009, and no local government was spared from the financial fallout that this most significant slowdown in the economy since the Great Depression of the 1930s had on these governments. This is analogous to the rippling effect observed for local governments' tax and charges for service receipts that was reported in Chapters 4–6. That is, there is every indication that the chilling effect that the Great Recession had on miscellaneous revenues starting in 2007 (beginning of the Recession) continued long after the economic recovery had supposedly begun in late 2009 for four of five types of local governments (the exception being school districts), as the miscellaneous revenue proportion of OSR was continuing to drop by 2017. This finding is contrary to the rather short-term negative repercussions that previous recessions of the 20th century had on revenues of all governments (federal and state, as well as local). Moreover, there is more recent data from annual Census of Governments and surveys conducted by the ICMA and the League of Cities that indicate that there is still a strong negative lingering effect of the Great Recession.[1] In fact, a *Wall Street Journal* article (see Harrison 2020), citing statistics and analyses of leading economists, reports that local government revenue levels did not fully recover from the 2007–09 recession until the fall of 2019, a decade after the downturn supposedly had ended and only a few months before COVID-19 resulted in significant reductions in local government revenue. These predictions do not bode well for the larger or even the smaller types of local government revenue, including those from miscellaneous sources.

As a matter of curiosity, an examination of the data for individual states was conducted to see if there were any appreciable variations for each of the five types of local governments. This check revealed a handful of cases where the miscellaneous revenue proportion of OSR for some local governments was at least two times greater than the mean proportion for comparable governmental units in other states from 1962 to 2017. As can be seen in Table 7.2, municipalities

*Table 7.2* Governments with Greater and Lesser Reliance on Miscellaneous Revenue, 2017

*Greater Reliance*

| *Counties* | *%* | *Municipalities* | *%* | *Townships* | *%* | *Special Districts* | *%* | *School Districts* | *%* |
|---|---|---|---|---|---|---|---|---|---|
| *Mean %* | *7.4* | | *9.1* | | *5.5* | | *9.0* | | *5.9* |
| | | ND | 19.4 | ND | 40.6 | RI | 53.7 | VT | 47.2 |
| | | WY | 19.2 | MI | 14.7 | UT | 20.9 | MA | 44.1 |
| | | | | | | MD | 19.3 | CT | 18.9 |
| | | | | | | PA | 16.7 | KS | −17.3 |
| | | | | | | | | DE | 16.0 |
| | | | | | | | | IN | 15.5 |
| | | | | | | | | AR | 15.4 |
| | | | | | | | | AL | 15.1 |
| | | | | | | | | MN | 13.7 |
| | | | | | | | | NM | 13.2 |

*Lesser Reliance*

| *Counties* | *%* | *Municipalities* | *%* | *Townships* | *%* | *Special Districts* | *%* | *School Districts* | *%* |
|---|---|---|---|---|---|---|---|---|---|
| *Mean %* | *7.4* | | *9.1* | *5* | *5.5* | | *9.0* | | *5.9* |
| HI | 3.2 | AZ | 4.1 | KS | 2.5 | ID | 4.5 | IL | 3.8 |
| SD | 3.2 | SD | 4.1 | MO | 2.0 | MI | 4.5 | NE | 2.5 |
| | | PA | 3.6 | CT | 1.9 | WI | 4.5 | ME | 1.6 |
| | | NC | 3.2 | NE | 1.1 | MS | 4.4 | CA | 1.5 |
| | | KY | 2.9 | | | WY | 4.4 | NJ | 1.3 |
| | | | | | | WA | 4.3 | RI | .8 |
| | | | | | | KS | 4.2 | AK | 0.0 |
| | | | | | | ME | 4.1 | | |
| | | | | | | DE | 3.3 | | |
| | | | | | | SC | 3.2 | | |
| | | | | | | NE | 3.0 | | |
| | | | | | | LA | 2.3 | | |

*Source:* U.S. Bureau of the Census. 2017 Census of Governments. Compendium of Government Finances (Washington, DC: Government Printing Office).

in two states (North Dakota and Wyoming) and townships in two states (North Dakota and Michigan) have a consistent pattern of obtaining a larger percentage of their OSR from miscellaneous sources. Additionally, special districts in four states (Rhode Island, Utah, Maryland, and Pennsylvania) and school districts in ten states (Vermont, Massachusetts, Connecticut, Kansas, Delaware, Indiana, Arkansas, Alabama, Minnesota, and New Mexico) have typically received a larger proportion of their OSR from miscellaneous sources compared to similar governments in other states. There were no aberrant cases among county governments.

It also can be seen from Table 7.2 that there are local governments in some states where they exhibit a reliance on miscellaneous revenue that is 50 percent or lower than the national average for similar type governments. This is the case for the following: counties in two states (Hawaii and South Dakota); municipalities in five states (Arizona, South Dakota, Pennsylvania, North Carolina, and Kentucky); townships in four states (Kansas, Missouri, Connecticut, and Nebraska); special districts in 12 states (Idaho, Michigan, Wisconsin, Mississippi, Wyoming, Washington, Kansas, Maine, Delaware, South Carolina, Nebraska, and Louisiana), and school districts in seven states (Illinois, Nebraska, Maine, California, New Jersey, Rhode Island, and Alaska).

The tendency for some jurisdictions to obtain a much larger or smaller proportion of their OSR from miscellaneous sources could be due to a number of particular factors or combination of factors. On speculation, this pattern could have been an artifact of not being able to depend on more traditional sources of OSR that over time developed into a tradition of being more self-reliant to buffer the jurisdiction in the event of unanticipated revenue shortfalls. Another plausible explanation could be that these patterns could be an artifact of the unique political culture of a state and thereby embedded in specific local governments' normal fiscal practices. Otherwise, these patterns may be nothing more than simple happenstance. At any rate, it does seem like there could be something unique, not understood, or clearly identified about local governments in several specific states where several types of local governments are more likely to be below the mean (Nebraska for townships, special districts, and school districts, South Dakota for counties and municipalities, Kansas for townships and special districts, and Maine for special districts and school districts). It can also be observed that counties and municipalities are more likely to be above the national mean in another state (North Dakota). Somewhat contradictory and worthy of mention is that school districts in Kansas are considerably above the mean.

## Patterns of miscellaneous revenue receipts by funding source

It is obvious that the four funding sources that are included in the miscellaneous revenue category (other general revenue, interest earnings, special assessments, and sale of property) are distinctively different in their substance and origin, although they are conveniently lumped together for financial accounting purposes. Furthermore, each type of miscellaneous revenue accounts for a conspicuously different proportion of the OSR for counties, municipalities, townships, special districts, and school districts. Therefore, it is reasonable that in the analysis below, each is examined separately.

***Other general revenue***

As seen in Figure 7.1, there is variability among the four sources of money that collectively are referred to as miscellaneous revenue. Over the 1962–2017 time frame, "Other General Revenue" was clearly the most stable of the four funding sources that make up the miscellaneous revenue category. Moreover, with only a few exceptions, this funding source accounted for the largest proportion of OSR since 1962. (The most notable exception was when "Interest Income" accounted for a larger percentage.) It should also be mentioned that, unlike "Interest Income," the OSR proportion produced by "Other General Revenue" decreased only so slightly during the Great Recession (2007–09) and the Recession's lingering aftermath (from 2010 to the present). In other words, "Other General Revenue" has proven over the last 55 years to be a resilient and dependable source of revenue, even though it constitutes only a small part of the OSR of all local governments (around 4.6 percent in 2017).

With these important initial observations in mind, let's see if there are any differences in reliance on this particular kind of miscellaneous revenue by the five types of local governments. Figure 7.3 provides the necessary data to make

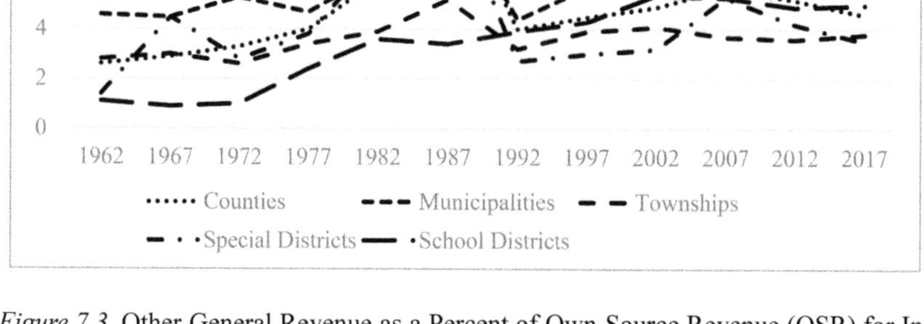


*Figure 7.3* Other General Revenue as a Percent of Own-Source Revenue (OSR) for Individual Local Governments, 1962–2017

*Source:* U.S. Bureau of the Census. Census of Governments. Compendium of Government Finances series, 1962–2017.

this determination. Generally speaking, "Other General Revenue" has made up a somewhat larger proportion of the OSR for counties and municipalities than has been the case for townships and special districts. Based on the most recent figures (2017), "Other General Revenue" accounts for between 4 and 5 percent of both county and municipal government OSR. Until 1987, the county and municipal "Other General Revenue" OSR proportions were also higher than that for school districts. However, since 1992, the proportion of school districts' OSR accounted for by "Other General Revenue" has been slightly more than 5 percent. The latest figures available indicate that the OSR proportions of townships and special districts stood at 3.6 and 2.5 percent, respectively.

A closer look at Figure 7.3 reveals that there was an obvious spike in the OSR proportion for counties, municipalities, and special districts between 1982 and 1987. There seems to be no substantive explanation for this short-term phenomenon (e.g., substantial increase in the amount of additional money collected by these governments compared to previous years) whereby the "Other General Revenue" proportion increased sharply after 1982 and then dropped back close to the 1982 level in ten years or less. In fact, a data check indicates that there was no appreciable increase in the amount of money listed as "Other General Revenue" that was collected during this period, but there was a noticeable decline in the amount of money that was received from taxes (especially property) and charges for services that was likely due to two recessions that occurred during the early and latter parts of the 1980s. Therefore, it is logical to conclude that the uncharacteristic sudden rise and fall of the "Other General Revenue" proportion of OSR was the result of a reduction in the OSR proportion normally attributable to taxes and charges for services collections.

The OSR figures mentioned above are averages (i.e., the mean) for all 50 states. Are there local governments in some states that are more (or even less) dependent on "Other General Revenue" to help close the gap in their budgets not covered by some type of tax, charges for services/user fees, and other types of miscellaneous revenue? Table 7.3 provides a list of those local governments by state where "Other General Revenue" makes up either a larger and smaller proportion of a government's OSR than is normally the case in the typical state.

From the top panel of the table, it can be seen that, as of 2017, special districts in 11 states rely more on "Other General Revenue" than do special districts in other states. Likewise, a greater reliance is also found for school districts in ten different states. Among traditional general-purpose local governments, greater reliance on "Other General Revenue" is the norm for counties in three states (North Dakota, Arizona, and West Virginia) and in municipalities in another three states (Wyoming, New Jersey, and Florida). In addition, limited general-purpose local governments (i.e., townships) in three states (North Dakota, South Dakota, and Michigan) show more of a tendency to rely on this type of miscellaneous revenue than other townships.

Looking at the bottom panel of the table, one sees about as many instances of lesser reliance on "Other General Revenue" (i.e., being appreciably below the

*Table 7.3* Governments with Greater and Lesser Reliance on "Other General Revenue," 2017

*Greater Reliance*

| *Mean %* | *4.5* | | *4.7* | | *3.6* | | *2.5* | | *5.1* |
|---|---|---|---|---|---|---|---|---|---|
| *Counties* | *%* | *Municipalities* | *%* | *Townships* | *%* | *Special Districts* | *%* | *School Districts* | *%* |
| ND | 18.9 | WY | 13.7 | ND | 38.1 | HI | 71.9 | MA | 43.4 |
| AZ | 10.0 | NJ | 11.1 | SD | 7.7 | RI | 43.5 | VT | 42.5 |
| WV | 9.5 | FL | 10.0 | MI | 7.3 | MD | 14.3 | KS | 16.7 |
| | | | | | | AZ | 8.4 | CT | 16.5 |
| | | | | | | UT | 7.8 | DE | 15.2 |
| | | | | | | NV | 6.7 | IN | 14.3 |
| | | | | | | AR | 6.5 | AR | 13.1 |
| | | | | | | NC | 6.5 | AL | 12.5 |
| | | | | | | ND | 6.4 | NM | 12.0 |
| | | | | | | VA | 5.5 | MN | 11.9 |
| | | | | | | OH | 5.1 | | |

*Lesser Reliance*

| Mean % | *4.5* | | *4.7* | | *3.6* | | *2.5* | | *5.1* |
|---|---|---|---|---|---|---|---|---|---|
| *Counties* | *%* | *Municipalities* | *%* | *Townships* | *%* | *Special Districts* | *%* | *School Districts* | *%* |
| OH | 2.1 | TN | 2.3 | MN | 1.8 | TX | 1.1 | IL | 2.3 |
| CA | 2.0 | SD | 2.1 | KS | 1.7 | KY | 1.0 | NE | 2.1 |
| KS | 1.5 | KY | 1.1 | MO | 1.6 | AR | .9 | OK | 1.6 |
| KY | 1.3 | | | NE | 0.0 | ID | .9 | ME | 1.5 |
| SD | .7 | | | | | NE | .8 | CA | 1.3 |
| PA | .6 | | | | | NY | .8 | NH | 1.3 |
| NM | .2 | | | | | WI | .7 | NJ | 1.2 |
| | | | | | | LA | .1 | RI | .6 |
| | | | | | | NM | .1 | | |

*Source:* U.S. Bureau of the Census. 2017 Census of Governments. Compendium of Government Finances (Washington, DC: Government Printing Office).

mean) for both kinds of general-purpose local governments—county governments in seven states (Ohio, California, Kansas, Kentucky, South Dakota, Pennsylvania, and New Mexico), municipal governments in three states (Tennessee, South Dakota, and Kentucky), and townships in four states (Minnesota, Kansas, Missouri, and Nebraska). However, this is not the case for special and school districts. Special districts in nine states (Texas, Kentucky, Arkansas, Idaho, Nebraska, New York, Wisconsin, Louisiana, and New Mexico) report that "Other General Revenue" makes up a much smaller part of their OSR than is true for the typical special district across the country. A similar situation exists for school districts in eight states (Illinois, Nebraska, Oklahoma, Maine, California, New Hampshire, New Jersey, and Rhode Island), as their reliance on "Other General Revenue" is appreciably below the national mean.

While there is nothing that immediately stands out as clear reasons as to why some local governments in some states would be more likely to depend more or less on "Other General Revenue" than would other type of local governments in the same state, several explanations seem plausible. A simple but intuitive explanation for special districts is related to the rationale and purpose for their creation. The typical special district was established to provide a specific municipal- or urban-type service (e.g., water, sewer, and fire protection) to the residents and businesses of a densely populated unincorporated area of a county, with the expectation that users of the service are expected to pay the full cost of its availability. However, there are other types of special districts that encompass an entire county, municipality, or township and provide a certain service or program. All residents and businesses of the jurisdiction of this second kind of special district are expected to pay for its cost of operation whether they benefit directly from it or not. Examples include housing authorities, urban renewal/redevelopment or economic development districts, conservation districts, library districts, children's welfare and health care boards, among others. Since these special districts function to provide for the "total good" of the entire jurisdiction, one would expect that states would be more apt to share more of what is called "Other General Revenue" with them. Therefore, it is possible that special districts in states having more of this second kind of special districts would exhibit a greater dependency on "Other General Revenue" to supply a larger proportion of their OSR. Conversely, special districts in states with more traditional kinds of special districts would be predicted to depend less on this additional kind of "shared revenue."

As for school districts, it is reasonable to speculate that states would be more inclined to share "Other General Revenue" monies with school districts (and subsequently districts would be more reliant on this type of funding) in states that meet one or more of several criteria—being less affluent, fewer own-source revenue-raising options, states provide small amounts of state aid and traditional kinds of shared revenue, and significant inequities in per pupil spending between the state's school districts. Lesser dependency on "Other General Revenue" would be anticipated for school districts in states that displayed just the opposite characteristics (i.e., being more affluent, greater own-source revenue-raising alternatives, receipt of larger amounts of money from mainline shared revenues and state grants-in-aid, and little, if any, inequities in per pupil spending between the state's school districts.

Lastly, it is reasonable to speculate that greater or lesser dependence on "Other General Revenue" by county governments, municipalities, and townships may be a straightforward function of what one's state intended for them to do—reduce the direct service provision role of the state in matters that are more local in nature and more appropriate for smaller governments. For example, states, while wanting to make sure that the important law enforcement, judicial/court, welfare, health care, revenue collection, and record keeping functions of the state are carried out uniformly across the state, are cognizant of the utility and value of decentralization as a means of legitimizing the role of government in society. Moreover, decentralization generally tends to lead to greater policy implementation efficiencies, effectiveness, and even cost savings. Simply put, these governments serve as "branch" or "satellite" offices for various state agencies and function to implement state policy decisions and provide a myriad of services in a seamless fashion (see Benton 2002).

The latter point would seem to be reinforced by the fact that approximately 80 percent of the money referred to as "Other General Revenue" originates from funds that states derive from "fines and forfeits." In almost all cases, states split or share part of these revenues with their local governments. These type of funds, although they are sometimes referred to as "state shared revenue," should not be confused with other kinds of shared revenue (e.g., motor fuel, gross receipts, intangible, tobacco, alcohol beverage, cigarette insurance premium, public utilities, personal and corporate income, and severance taxes vehicle and drivers licenses) that are normally provided to local governments and more likely to be thought of as traditional kinds of intergovernmental revenue (see Chapter 8 for a comprehensive analysis). Fines and forfeiture-shared revenue is usually distributed based on a state-imposed formula whereby the state agrees to divide or "share" with some or all five types of local governments. As such, these funds should be viewed as a quasi-type of state aid, separate from the more obvious kinds of state aid. The manner in which these funds are distributed may also provide a rough approximation of the priority that states place on the intended service provision roles played by different type of local governments in different states.

### *Interest earnings*

As seen earlier in Figure 7.1, revenue derived from interest earnings accounted for a significant proportion of miscellaneous revenue collected by local governments, but especially during the 40-year period stretching from about 1977 until 2007. The recent drop-off in importance of this type of miscellaneous, as noted earlier in the chapter, is most likely due to an underperforming economy attributable to the Great Recession and its enduring effect throughout most of the second decade of the 21st century. Prior to the Great Recession, interest earnings made up a little less than half of all miscellaneous revenue and represented around 5 percent of local government OSR (see Figure 7.4). Does dependency on interest earnings vary among different types of local governments?

While this is a legitimate and interesting question, any analysis of recent data probably would not yield any insightful or reliable findings, given the sharp decline in these funds as a percentage of OSR in the last decade or so. If the importance of this source of revenue were to increase in the future, such an analysis would be warranted and would probably provide useful information. However, it is probably safe to say that much of the variability between different

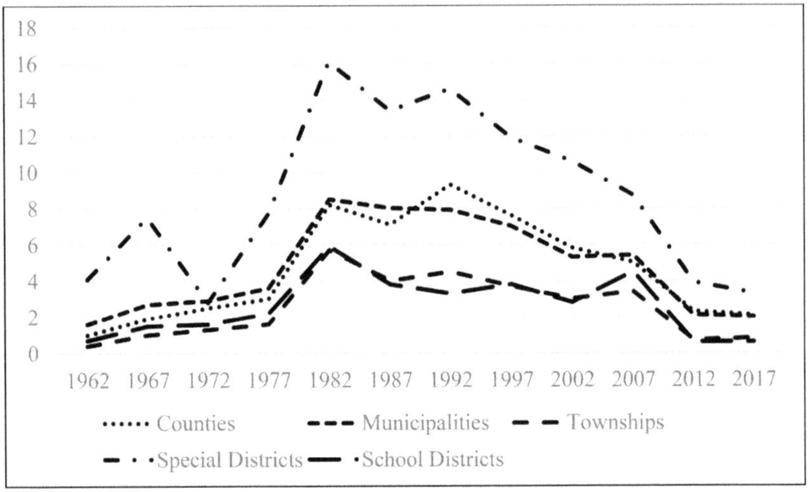


*Figure 7.4* Interest Earnings as a Percentage of Own-Source Revenue (OSR) for Individual Local Governments k 1962–2017

*Source:* U.S. Bureau of the Census. Census of Governments. Compendium of Government Finances series, 1962–2017.

types of local governments could be explained by the unique financial situation of a particular local government, whether it is a county, municipality, townships, special district, or school district. Simply stated, the ability of a local governments to invest money to earn interest income is a direct function of having surplus money in a contingency or "rainy-day" fund that is not encumbered in the operating budget, prudent to keep on hand to cover unforeseen emergencies, or required to satisfy the government's creditors. Therefore, governments that are more fiscally stable and healthy are more likely to be able to derive more revenue from interest earnings.

#### *Special assessments*

Money collected by local governments from special assessments represents only a small proportion of the funds that are referred to as miscellaneous revenue and consequently account for a very tiny part of these governments OSR (see Figure 7.1). Suffice it to say that there is no appreciable variation between different types of local governments or within these governments in the degree to which they rely on this source of revenue to fund their operations or pay for the cost of providing certain kinds of services (data not shown here). In short, one type of local government is no more likely to rely more on special assessment revenue than other governments and there is no variation within a state for any of the five types of local governments.

With that said, it is rather surprising that local governments (but particularly, counties, municipalities, and townships) do not make greater use of special assessments as a valuable revenue-raising alternative. This observation is made in light of the documented trend reported in earlier chapters whereby local governments have been reducing their historically heavy reliance on property tax revenue while increasingly depending on user fees/charges for services and even selective taxes to make up the difference. This trend is very clear from the data that shows a conspicuous decline in property tax revenue accounting for a smaller proportion of OSR and a concomitant increase in the percentage of local governments' OSR coming from user fees and even selective taxes on fuel and other petroleum products, motor vehicles, hotel occupancy, airport landing fees, etc. Again, it seems odd that counties, municipalities, and townships have not expanded their use of special assessments as a means to provide amenities to residents and businesses for things such as storm water/drainage projects, street lightings, curbs and sidewalks, parks and recreational facilities, among other things. In fact, special assessments would seem to be a cross between a charge for services and a selective tax and can be readily employed as a revenue enhancer. Moreover, special assessments would seem like a no-brainer since they are capable of helping these local governments realize their goal by achieving greater fairness in the provision of certain services by linking better the actual users of services with those who should pay for them. Special assessments can also be quicker to set up and implement than a special district, and if desired, abolished (i.e., local government would only need to repeal the enabling ordinance and not have to get involved in what could be a cumbersome legal and contentious political process or abolishing a special service district).

In addition to the customary kinds of special assessments mentioned above, there is a "special type" of special assessment (impact fee/charge) that has unique relevance for local governments although its importance varies. Impact fees have the potential to provide substantial amounts of revenue but usually only for jurisdictions that are experiencing rapid growth in their population and are highly urbanized, while ensuring that "new growth" pays for itself. Simply put, impact fees are charges levied on new residential and business construction and help local governments pay for the additional costs associated with providing a variety of services such as fire protection, water and sewer, transportation, education, parks and recreation. However, it is important to note that the use of funds collected from impact fees is normally restricted to paying for costs associated with capital improvements (e.g., new or expanded roads and bridges, additional traffic signals, fire and police stations, firefighting apparatus, water and sewer treatment plants, storm water drainage systems, new schools or additions to existing ones, new or enlarged parks and recreational facilities, jails, new or expanded solid waste collection facilities, equipment, and disposal sites, and additional library facilities or expansions of existing ones). Impact fees, however, typically cannot be used to pay for the operating costs associated with service expansion or entirely new services necessitated with new growth (e.g., salaries and fringe benefits of new firefighters, police officers, emergency medical responders, sanitation and public works employees, health care professional workers, librarians, teachers, detention officers, and employees in human resource, finance, IT, planning, and other administrative departments).

As just mentioned, the adoption of impact fees is more likely to occur in jurisdictions that are experiencing rapid and sustained growth in their population and find it challenging to keep up with increasingly rising service expectations and demands from the public. The State of Florida is a good case in point since its population has boomed since the end of World War II (see Benton and Feiock 2008; MacManus 2008; Benton 2023, Benton, Foreman, and Lee 2023; Deslatte and Hawkins 2023). Although the State's population growth rate slowed somewhat during the first decade of the 21st century, the growth rate has begun to climb again and presently the state is growing by around 800 persons per day. Currently, the state remains the third fastest growing state, outpaced only by California and Texas. Therefore, it is not an overstatement to conclude that Florida's population growth rate is nothing short of mind-boggling. As one Florida newspaper reporter has noted: "It is not your imagination. People really are flocking to Florida" (Perry, Rogers, and Wilder 2022).

What makes Florida especially best suited for utilizing impact fees compared to California and Texas is the fact that most of Florida's growth has occurred in the unincorporated areas of its rapid-growth counties (e.g., Dade, Broward, Hillsborough, Pinellas, Orange, Palm Beach, Sarasota, Manatee, Polk, Pasco, and Seminole). This is significant because this is where most of the demand for new and expanded services is coming. Residents there (many of them who are transplants from highly urbanized Northeastern and Midwest states or immigrants from nearly 30 Central and South America and Caribbean counties) bring with them expectations that their county governments provide a litany of municipal-type services (24/7 fire protection and emergency medical response, water and sewer, street lights and sidewalks, curbside solid waste collection, adequate roadways and traffic control devices, professionalized and modern police departments, to name just a few).[2] Needless to say, the state has also experienced significant growth in the number of special service districts in many of these same counties as county governments have been unable to keep up with unprecedented service demands, while existing districts experienced a significant surge in the number of clients they must serve.

It is also important to note that record-setting growth in the K-12 student population has also occurred within school districts in these same Florida counties (school district boundaries in the State are coterminous with county lines) and consequently has resulted in the need to either enlarge existing schools or build new ones. A case in point is the Hillsborough County School District (Tampa) where it has had to build 31 new elementary schools, 12 new middle schools, and 11 new high schools and add classroom space at over 100 existing schools from 1980 to 2020. It has also been the case that a number of rapidly growing large- as well as medium-sized cities in Florida have witnessed an appreciable increase in the demand for more new services and expansion of the level of services that they presently provide.

Given this tremendous growth in Florida's population over the last 40–50 years, it comes as no surprise that revenue generated from impact fees in those counties, cities, school districts, and special districts experiencing the greatest amount of growth far exceeded collections in those jurisdictions with smaller growth rates or experiencing no growth or even losing population.[2] In 2020, local governments in Florida amassed over $1.8 billion from impact fees, an increase of about three-fold since 2003.[3] In fact, it was not unusual for these faster growing governments to collect 10 to 20 times more revenue from impact fee assessments than slower growing or no-growth comparable jurisdictions. Therefore, it is reasonable to speculate that similar kinds of differences would be found in Texas and California as well as in some other states (Arizona, South Carolina, North Carolina, Georgia, and Colorado) that have also experienced population growth albeit at a more modest pace.

## Review and reflections

Revenue obtained from miscellaneous sources, while constituting only a small fraction of local governments' OSR, is nonetheless indispensable for them in balancing their budgets on an annual basis. In looking at the contribution that miscellaneous revenues make to the typical local government over time, it appears that it is in the range of 6–7 percent in a normal economy. Exceptions occur when banks and other lending institutions are paying unusually high interest rates as was the case during most of the 1980s and 1990s and the early part of the first decade of the 21st century. But, in spite of accounting for the smallest percentage of both OSR and TR, these governments would be hard pressured to make ends meet if they did not have this type of revenue available to them.

To recap some of the particulars about miscellaneous revenue, a few points are worth noting. First, an assortment of several monetary sources that include things such as fines and forfeits, rents and royalties, and donations (but primarily fines and forfeits) usually referred to collectively as "other miscellaneous revenue" have consistently made up the majority of miscellaneous revenue. Second, "interest income" has occasionally accounted for nearly the same proportion as "other miscellaneous revenue" from time to time, but normally "interest income" has been the second most important component of miscellaneous revenue. Then, proceeds from the sale of surplus government property and the levying of special assessments have accounted for much smaller percentages of miscellaneous revenue.

The analysis conducted in this chapter also indicates that there is not a lot of variability among local governments as to the proportion of OSR they obtain from miscellaneous revenue, although counties, municipalities, and special districts historically have received a somewhat larger percentage than have townships and school districts. Additional analysis reveals no major variations in revenue collections within states for each type of local government. Of special note, however, is that rapid population growth in states like Florida (or in specific fast-growth counties and municipalities in other states with more moderate growth rates) is associated with larger collections of funds from specific kinds of special assessments—impact fees or charges.

With the analysis of this last important type of OSR now complete, it is time to turn attention to the quest of local governments to secure outside funds to help cover the cost of the service needs and expectations of the public they serve. This typically entails efforts to obtain funds from the federal government, their state, or other local governments. As will be seen, "outside" or intergovernmental funding is a significant source of revenue for local governments, especially since they are often limited by their states when it comes to raising their own revenue.

## Notes

1 See an annual publication of the Center for City Solutions and Applied Research at the National League of Cities that is titled *City Fiscal Conditions [Year] Report*. Also, see Warner, Aldag, and Kim 2021.

2 For a more detailed description and discussion of the case of Florida, see Benton 2002, 2023, Benton, Foreman, and Lee 2023, and Deslatte and Hawkins 2023.

3 In FY 2020, county governments in Florida collected about half of all impact fee revenue (50 percent), with school districts and municipalities receiving 27 and 21 percent, respectively, and special districts getting the remainder (2 percent). The largest percentage of impact fee revenue, by government, was spent for the following programmatic purposes: transportation (counties), physical environment (municipalities), public safety (special districts), and education (school districts). (See State of Florida 2021.)

## References

Benton, J. Edwin. 2002. "*Counties as Service Delivery Agents: Changing Expectations and Roles*." Westport, CT: Praeger.

———. 2023. "Introduction to Government and Politics in the Sunshine State." In Benton, J. Edwin (ed.), *Government and Politics in Florida*, 4th ed. Gainesville, FL: University Press of Florida: forthcoming.

———. and Richard Feiock. 2008. "Local Governments: Institutions of Governance and Agents of Service Delivery." In J. Edwin Benton (ed.), *Government and Politics in Florida*, 3rd ed. Gainsville, FL: University Press of Florida: 240–64

———. Sean Foreman, and Robert E. Lee. 2023. "Local Governments in Florida: Counties, Municipalities, and Special Districts." In J. Edwin Benton (ed.), *Government and Politics in Florida*, 4th ed. Gainesville, FL: University Press of Florida: forthcoming.

Deslatte, Aaron, and Christopher Hawkins. 2023. "Florida's Shifting Agenda in Growth Management and Environmental Protection." In J. Edwin Benton (ed.), *Government and Politics in Florida*, 4th ed. Gainesville, FL: University Press of Florida: forthcoming.

Harrison, David. 2020. "State and Local Government Budget Woes Create Drag for Economic Recovery Prospects: Cuts to Employment, Spending, and Revenue Likely to Weigh on Growth for Years, Economists Say." May 24. https://www.wsj.com/articles/state-and-local-budget-woes-create-drag-for-economic-recovery-prospects-11590312600. Accessed on May 28, 2020.

Perry, Mark, Luke Rogers, and Kristie Wilder. 2022. "New Florida Estimates Show Nation's Third Largest State Reaching Historic Milestone." Washington, D.C.: U.S. Bureau of the Census. December. https://www.census.gov/library/stories/2022/12/florida-fastest-growing-state.html. Accessed on October 27, 2023.

MacManus, Susan A. 2008. "The Economics and Politics of Financing Florida's Many Governments." In J. Edwin Benton (ed.), *Government and Politics in Florida*, 3rd ed. Gainsville, FL: University Press of Florida: 294–327.

National League of Cities. 2020. *City Fiscal Conditions [Year] Report*. Washington, DC.

State of Florida. 2021. Florida House of Representatives and Florida Department of Revenue. Report of Revenue Estimating Conference. http://edr.state.fl.us/Content/conferences/revenueimpact/archives/2021/_pdf/page173-195.pdf. Accessed on September 7, 2021.

Warner, Mildred E, Austin M Aldag, and Yunji Kim. 2021. "Pragmatic Municipalism: U.S. Local Government Responses to Fiscal Stress," *Public Administration Review*, 81: 389–98.

# 8 Intergovernmental Revenue

## "Outside" Money to Stretch the Budget

Providing for the welfare of the general public has always been a primary and basic goal of government in the United States and refers to the concern of government for essentials like the health, morality, safety, piece of mind, and prosperity of its citizens. In fact, the preamble to the U.S. Constitution mentions promotion of the "general welfare" as a primary reason for creation of the Constitution. Promotion of the general welfare is also stated as an explicit purpose or goal in state constitutions and general legislation and is integral to the establishment of state and local governments.

The impetus for local governments to spend for the general welfare can originate from a number of sources, including but not limited to the people within these jurisdictions. Obviously, residents of counties, cities, and townships and people who live within the boundaries of special and school districts periodically make their service needs and desires known to their respective local governments as do owners of businesses and industries. Additionally, their views may be shared with local governments via citizens, civic, good government, or advocacy groups that have been created to perform a function labeled by David Easton (1965) as "interest articulation." Then, of course, the media, serving as the "conscience of the community," may voice concerns about the general welfare, in general, and about service needs, in particular.

This chapter will examine the role of two high-profile other entities (state governments and the federal or national government) that historically have had a valid, if not, overriding interest in the existence and service provision role of local governments. As will be seen in the analysis that follows, states and the federal government provide substantial amounts of additional money to local governments which can be used to stretch their service delivery capabilities. In addition, this chapter examines how funding received by local governments from other local governments serves to augment the pool of money that is available for enlarging the service provision capabilities of these governments in current times of greater expectations from the consuming public.

DOI: 10.4324/9781032640389-8

## History and logic behind intergovernmental revenue

Since state governments have the constitutional authority to establish local governments, they naturally have a legitimate stake in the success of these governments with respect to them being able and willing to carry out a number of functions and provide a wide-ranging menu of well-known services and justify the *raison d'être* for local governments. Simply stated, states established local governments to assist them in the delivery of state-level services and programs (e.g., welfare, roads, health care, police protection, criminal and civil courts, conservation of natural resources, registering voters and holding elections, tax assessment and collection, among others) as well as in providing a long list of services to meet the needs and wishes of the local constituents (e.g., fire prevention and suppression, libraries, potable water, electric power, sewage and solid waste collection and disposal, parks and recreation, cultural amenities, sidewalks, streets and traffic signalization, street lighting, and so forth). Concomitant with the state's stake in local governments is also the real, if not, tacit expectation and responsibility for states to be significantly involved in the financial affairs of their local county and municipal governments, townships, and special and school districts. But, what form does this involvement take?

One obvious type of involvement has been in the area of revenue-raising authority. States through their constitutions and statutes provide explicit guidance in both the establishment and operation of local government revenue systems. With respect to what types of revenue that local governments may collect, all state constitutions and statutes permit the levying of a property tax but a much smaller number of states allow the adoption of a sales or income tax, as was seen in Chapters 4 and 5. Then, Chapter 6 details the extent to which that states permit their local governments to generate additional revenue by charging residents, businesses, and industries a fee for the provision of a host of services, while Chapter 7 provides information on the importance of states permitting their local government to obtain additional and much needed money from a variety of miscellaneous sources, although this type of funding usually does not produce nearly as much revenue as do taxes and charges for services. Chapter 9 closes out the discussion of the traditional ways in which local governments raise a sufficient amount of money to pay for the provision of services from their general fund with a thorough analysis of state supervision of local governments' efforts to borrow money in both the short- and long-terms to finance most capital improvements.

In addition to identifying the kinds of revenue sources that local governments may take advantage of (or as the case may be, enumerating the ones that are expressly prohibited), state constitutions and statutes often specify certain conditions that apply to the usage of various revenue sources, including but not limited to taxes and user fees/charges for services and other miscellaneous types of revenue options. The property tax is a good example. As a matter of fact, states routinely delineate a number of restrictions on the property tax such as the maximum rate (usually expressed in mills) that can be charged, exemptions that must be granted to offset tax liability (e.g., homestead recognition, agricultural usage of property, charitable, religious, and non-profit organizations, military veterans, disabled persons, and senior citizens), and prohibitions against exorbitant increases from one year to the next. States also regularly oversee local governments' determination of the "market" or "true" value of real estate and structures located on it that is subject to the property tax.

Other examples of state oversight of local governments' administration of their revenue system are evident in the types of restrictions that are commonly placed on the usage of sales and income taxes and charges for services. For instance, states determine whether or not their local governments may levy a general sales tax (usually piggy-backed on a state general sales tax) or levy a tax on selective items (e.g., tobacco products, alcoholic beverages, utilities such as electric power, water, gas, phones, hotel/motel room rates, and cable TV), as well as maximum rates. Additionally, states normally require that user fee rates be set at a reasonable level to prevent local governments from engaging in price gouging or taking advantage of a monopoly they may have over the provision of certain services.

In short, the long arm of the state is often evident in local governments' ability to raise the revenue necessary to provide an extensive list of services expected of their citizens.

Another form of involvement is for states to require (i.e., mandate) that their local governments bear primary responsibility for the provision of a list of highly visible types of services (e.g., health care, road construction and maintenance, voter registration and elections, protective inspections, agricultural information, adjudicating criminal and civil matters, among others), as well as be responsible for providing some, if not all, of the funding for these services. Responsibility for these duties is congruent with the legal configuration of government at the subnational level and presumptive notion that local governments were expected or intended to serve as administrative arms and/or political subdivisions of their states. Upon being granted statehood, states recognized that it was neither prudent nor desirable for them to be directly involved in the delivery of several important, staple services, as a decentralized administrative arrangement seemed to be more conducive to ensuring greater organizational efficiency, effectiveness, and economy. In sum, the kinds of services mentioned above seemed to call for a more localized, personal, and "closer to home" delivery approach, while the state could still provide the necessary administrative oversight and ensure uniformity.

Over time, the national or federal government also has developed a growing stake in the service provision capabilities of local governments. This has resulted from the significant rise in the federal government's interest in and concern for domestic policy matters and its concomitant willingness to provide large sums of more money to promote the "general welfare" since the early part of the 20th century. This was especially evident from the New Deal legislation designed to relieve the misery of the Great Depression of the 1930s and America's quest to achieve the goals of the Great Society during the 1960s. Both of these epic periods were marked by the enactment of numerous and significant pieces of congressional legislation and resulted in massive amounts of money flowing to state and local governments in the form of grants-in-aid and revenue sharing. While most of this money was earmarked for state governments, an undetermined amount of it eventually reaches local governments as states either willingly shared this new-found revenue with their local governments or did so because of the "pass-through" language imbedded in legislation enacted by Congress. At any rate, it is clear that the federal government vitally needs the assistance of local governments to carry out the purpose of congressional legislation which logically entailed the provision of services at the local level (e.g., decent and affordable housing, urban renewal, safe drinking water, treatment of sewage, disposal of solid and hazardous waste, accessibility for the disabled, environmental protection and conservation, health care, welfare, police and fire protection, and so forth).

Although revenue received by local governments from other local governments is strictly not the same as revenue obtained from federal and state grants-in-aids or revenue-sharing programs, it is nonetheless a type of additional revenue that could be used by these governments and potentially allows them to stretch their spending capacity. Generally speaking, there are two kinds of revenue that can be received from other local governments: one, it can be payment from one local government to another for the provision of services as part of a contractual arrangement. For instance, it is not uncommon for local governments (but especially, municipalities) to provide water and sewer service, police or fire protection, solid waste collection and disposal, parks and recreation services, maintenance of vehicles, buildings, and other facilities, planning and zoning expertise, payroll and other administrative functions, libraries, etc., to county governments, townships, or other municipalities. Funds received from another local government could also be the cost share of one or more governments to another government as part of a service co-production agreement/arrangement. The extent to which revenue obtained from other local governments represents additional money that can be used to enlarge one's expenditure capabilities, however, depends on whether the government providing a service via a contract is able to make a reasonable "profit."

## Types of federal and state financial assistance

Make no mistake about it and as Mikesell (2018, 654) brings to our attention, "grants transfer spending power from one government to another." While it can be argued that federal and state monetary grants-in-aid can lead to the intrusion of these higher levels of government into the internal affairs of lower levels of government like counties municipalities, townships, and special and school district, grants also can be seen in a positive light because they permit local governments to take advantage of a supposedly stronger revenue administration capacity of the higher level government to raise money for them. In this kind of arrangement, federal and state grants "can compensate local governments for benefit spillovers to nonresidents, reduce the problems created by fiscal disparity, encourage programs of special national or state merit, reduce special problems associated with regional economic decline, and encourage local governments to implement management reforms by making it a condition for receiving aid" (Mikesell 2018, 854). In also speaking to the potential positive fiscal impact of federal and state grants-in-aid, Thomas R. Dye (1966) refers to this kind of revenue as "outside money" that allows lower levels of government to provide services to their citizens that otherwise would not be possible given their own limited resources. If the truth be told, local government officials, for the most part, have been willing to endure the negative side effects of federal and state grants-in-aid in order to receive what has often been referred to as "a vital financial shot in the arm" of much-needed additional money to provide more and higher quality services to their constituents. Or, to paraphrase Dye, grant money permits local government officials to stretch their budgets.

Both federal and state governments operate intergovernmental financial assistance programs. The federal grant system has included three types of assistance: categorical grants, block grants, and from 1972 through 1986, general revenue sharing. The last is a type of general fiscal assistance that bears a close resemblance to state-to-local grant programs. Since there are a number of grants that have elements of all three basic types, it is sometimes difficult to classify them. However, most federal grant programs—measured in terms of both numbers and outlay totals—are categorical grant programs. A federal government website provides the *Catalog of Domestic Federal Assistance* (https://www.investopedia.com/terms/c/catalog-of-federal-domestic-assistance-cfda.asp) to assist anyone through about 2,300 federal assistance programs (the count as of 2023).

### *Categorical grants*

Categorical grants pay for specific and narrowly defined programs, normally restricted to spending for certain kinds of activities such as building a fire station, water or sewer treatment facility, or parking garage, or paying salaries of social or victims' advocate workers and remedial education school teachers. This kind of fiscal assistance is usually on a matching-funds basis (i.e., the federal government puts up only part of the funding with the state or locality putting up the rest) and "in accordance with prescribed standards or requirements." No state or local government is *required* to accept grants-in-aid. Participation in the program is voluntary. If state and local governments find the conditions attached to the grant money to be unacceptable, they can just decline to participate. As is well-known, such aid is intended to induce the recipient government to act in a manner other than the way it would act without the aid. Stated differently, these types of grants try to persuade recipient governments to redirect expenditures to different or new specific purposes to ensure provision of specific recipient government services in a manner consistent with national interest. In these areas, narrow local interests typically are not the same. As articulated by Mikesell (2018, 659), "the [federal] grant changes the returns as seen by the recipient government to make certain activities more attractive—the federal share makes the aided activity cheaper for the lower level government—so that recipient actions coincide with [desired] national interest."

There are three kinds of categorical grants: formula, project (these make up about 70 percent of all categorical grants, but considerably less than one-half of total categorical outlays), and a hybrid version of project/formula. For the sake of brevity, these will not be discussed here, but the interested reader can consult Mikesell (2018, 659) and the *Catalog of Domestic Federal Assistance* referenced above).

There are three basic criticisms of categorical grants: (1) administrative complexity of the categorical system; (2) the emergence of overlap and duplication; and (3) categorical grants distort state and local government spending and service priorities. For more details, the reader can consult Mikesell (2018, 661–62) and Dye and MacManus (2015, 71–72).

### *Block grants*

Block grants are usually distributed to general-purpose governments (i.e., counties and municipalities and occasionally to townships) for a general government function according to a statutory formula to finance activities in a broad functional area (e.g., health, welfare, law enforcement, education, conservation and community development). Recipient governments usually have fairly wide latitude in how to spend block grant money within a functional area. For example, a city or a county receiving a "community development" block grant can decide for themselves about specific neighborhood development projects, housing projects, and community facilities, as well as having substantial discretion to identify problems, design programs, and allocate grant money. Furthermore, administrative, fiscal reporting, planning, and other federally imposed requirements are limited to those necessary to ensure that national goals are being accomplished. Block grant money is distributed on the basis of a statutory formula with few, if any, matching requirements and spending is capped. This last feature makes block grants a favorite of federal lawmakers because it may encourage recipient agencies to be more efficient in the use of grant resources. For more details on block grant, see Mikesell (2018, 662–63) and Bowman and Kearney (1999, 40, 43, 45, 48–50).

While categorical grants outnumber block grants, some of the more notable block grants fund programs that include health (Community Mental Health Services, Prevention and Treatment of Substance Abuse, Maternal and Child Health Services, Preventative Health and Health Services), crime control (Local Law Enforcement, Juvenile Accountability Incentive), community development (Community Development), social services (Social Services, Child Care and Development, Low-Income Home Energy Assistance, Community Services), aid for the needy (Temporary Assistance to Needy Families), and emergency management (Emergency Management Performance).

***Revenue sharing (general-purpose fiscal assistance)***

A third type of federal grants is revenue sharing, a formula distribution with few or no restrictions on the use of funds provided. The federal general revenue-sharing (FRS) began in 1972 and used a formula to disburse multiyear appropriations to states and general-purpose local governments. The idea for revenue sharing was part and parcel of Richard Nixon's New Federalism initiative. The timing of Nixon's unveiling of his initiative came at the time when both the President and Congress recognized that states and especially local governments were the front line providers of essential public services and the cost of providing these services was rapidly increasing at a time when local governments were finding it more and more difficult to generate the required funds locally to effectively provide them. Moreover, these reasons were echoed in 1976 when Congress extended the FRS program for an additional four years, until 1980. An additional reason stated was that Congress believed that this federal support provided stability to the economy. When Congress extended the FRS for the final time, it did so only for the local governments' portion. The states' portion was discontinued for budgetary reasons.

The funding approach outlined in the State and Local Fiscal Assistance Act of 1972—appropriation rather than a share of certain taxes—provided some greater certainty of federal aid during the appropriation's life (unforeseen changes in federal revenue did not influence distributed shares), but the funds had to be appropriated again when the appropriation period expired. As noted above, the FRS program was initially authorized for four years and was extended three times, in 1976, 1980, and 1983, before expiring in 1986 under President Reagan. FRS grants were distributed one-third to states and two-thirds to local governments.

FRS allocated funds based on a formula that considered population, percentage of urban population, tax effort, income tax effort, and per capita income to determine the appropriate state and local government shares. State governments initially received one-third of revenue-sharing funds, but these governments were gradually eliminated as recipients. The funds were sent by check to eligible governments, without them having to apply for the money and with minimal restrictions as to how they could use it (more specifically, there had to be a publicized appropriation process, there could be no discrimination in hiring or compensation, funds could not be used for grant matching, use had to be subject to external financial audit, etc.).

Although the federal government officially ended revenue sharing at the national level in 1986, similar programs are still in existence in several states (Michigan, Alaska, Louisiana, Maine, and Wisconsin) and constitute a major form of state financial assistance to local governments.[1] Funds are awarded in two principal ways: shares of particular taxes or specific appropriations. Like what was the case with FRS, state revenue-sharing funds are disbursed by a formula, and the money is for general use by recipient governments with few, if any, restrictions. When these funds are distributed on a per capita basis, they potentially can help to reduce fiscal disparity to an extent because the per capita amount provides greater comparable assistance to lower-capacity communities than to higher-capacity ones.

Programs of revenue or tax sharing have a number of other qualities that are emphasized by proponents. First, they can strengthen local spending power while also reducing differences in fiscal capacity across governments. Second, such programs are not as likely to shape the priorities of local governments to make them more consistent with national interests because of the absence of controls placed on the aid. Third, general aid to local governments can possibly improve capacity to provide services or reduce taxes with no change in services. Fourth, and perhaps most appealing, is that revenue sharing is likely to reduce fiscal disparity among governments while strengthening their spending capacity of those governments with limited taxing authority.

It is important to examine the nature and manner of distribution of federal stimulus money flowing to the states and local governments in the wake of several recessions in recent years, but especially since 2000, as much of the financial assistance bears a close resemblance to general revenue sharing of the 1970s and 1980s. For instance, the stated purpose of the American Rescue Plan Act (ARPA) is to permit "recipient government across the country to invest these funds to address the unique needs of their communities and simultaneously create a stronger national economy." Moreover, there are clear reporting requirements and the time period that is required to obligate the funds.

After the early 2000s recession and the beginning of a trend of "jobless recoveries," a Republican lead Senate wanted to make $30 billion available to states over an 18-month period to support economic growth. Congress ended up making $20 billion available, $10 billion to states for Medicaid, and $10 billion was distributed to states by population.

The last recession before the one we are currently in was the Great Recession of 2007–09. That recession was deep and the economic recovery was historically slow. Both Presidents George W. Bush and Barack Obama enacted temporary stimulus measures. However, given the usual sluggishness of the economy's recovery when it comes to fiscal policy efforts and the smallness of the appropriations, the Bush and Obama measures provided very little relief in either the short- or long-run.

More recently, Congressional policymakers on both sides of the isle may be seeing the value of using federal fiscal stimulus tools to spur economic activity and employ more people. Consequently, Congress under President Trump made over $3 trillion in fiscal stimulus available to combat the Coronavirus pandemic and economic downturn (not to mention the large stimulus tax cuts enacted prior to the pandemic) in what was called the CARES Act (CRF) of 2020 (March) and the Consolidated Appropriations Act (CAA) of 2020 (December). Then, Congress under President Biden enacted the ARPA that made $1.9 trillion available to state and local governments. It is significant to mention that under the State and Local Fiscal Recovery Fund Program section of ARPA provided $65 billion to both county governments and municipalities and an additional $165 billion to states. In some cases, states are making a portion of state funds available to local governments. These funds have to be obligated by 2024 and spent by 2026. So these funds are still flowing through to local governments. Once additional data from the Census of Governments becomes available beyond 2020, it will be possible to assess the impact that this money has had on the local government financial picture.[2]

Could ARPA with over $130 billion in local government funds be the beginning of a new federal revenue-sharing effort? Optimists who believe this could be so have offered the following thought: "Imagine what local communities could be like with sustained federal resources!" (Washington Post 2021). According to Rocco and Kass (2022), enactment of the ARPA's Coronavirus State and Local Fiscal Recovery Funds (CSLFRF) program was "a milestone in the history of American fiscal federalism." First, it was the largest financial aid package (in current dollars) for multi-purpose usage targeted to state and local governments since enactment of the GRS program in 1972, which provided over $388 billion to these same governments" (Kass and Rocco 2021). Nevertheless, the CSLRFR is not the GRS program—arguably the only truly "no strings attached "federal aid program in American history—which included only minimal accounting and reporting requirements in the form of a one page report on planned (and actual) use in American history," with the specific purpose to capture fraud (Rocco and Kass 2022, 348). By the same token, the CSLFRF contains very few of the restrictions and "strings attached" like a categorical grant. In fact, the program in some ways looks like earlier block grant programs—like the ones created during the Great Recession—which were purposed to support state and local governments' programmatic spending in broad areas while providing substantial latitude and discretion to recipient governments to determine spending priorities (Rocco and Kass 2022).[3] Additionally, the CSLFRF also substantially increased the number of categories of allowable spending when compared to the CRF (for details, see Rocco and Kass 2022, 251, Table 2).

Suffice it to say that state aid grant systems may contain many elements similar to the federal system, although each state may have its own peculiar mix. State grants to general-purpose local governments (mostly counties and municipalities but occasionally townships) have always been for relatively broad purposes. The grants sometimes distribute earmarked percentages of state taxes (usually referred to as shared revenue). These percentages are almost always determined by the state and not open to negotiation. Good examples are tax proceeds collected by the state on things such as motor fuel, tobacco and alcohol, insurance premium sales, document stamp, intangibles, beverage licenses, mineral or petroleum extractions, and private utilities.

## The dollars and cents of intergovernmental revenue

Over the last 58 years (i.e., 1962–2020), the three types of intergovernmental revenue (IR) derived from the federal and state governments and other local governments have constantly accounted for a substantial part of local governments' total revenues (TRs). From Figure 8.1, it can be seen that IR made up about 29 percent of local governments' TR in 1962. But by 2020, that proportion

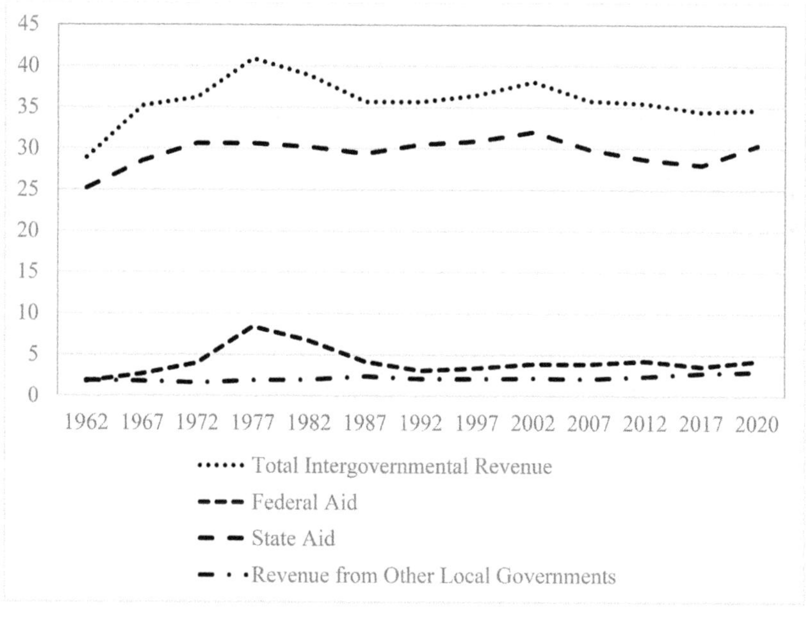


*Figure 8.1* (a and b) Intergovernmental Revenue for All Local Government as a Proportion of Total Revenue (TR), 1962–2020

*Source:* U.S. Bureau of the Census. Census of Governments. Compendium of Government Finances series, 1962–2017 and the 2020 Annual Survey of State and Local Government Finances.

had increased to approximately 35 percent. This means that in recent years, local governments annually have depended on revenue from some other government (but usually from the federal government and their states) to supply approximately one-third of the resources needed to provide services to their citizens. The high water mark for local government IR as a proportion of TR, however, was reached in 1977, when it climbed to just over 41 percent.

As would be expected, local governments' dependency on IR is not the same across the states or even within states. The IR proportion of TR in four states (Vermont, Arkansas, Delaware, and New Mexico) accounted for a least one-half of their TR and thus far exceeded the national average (35 percent) in 2020 (see Table 8.1). That is, local governments in Vermont received 72 percent of their TR from revenues originating from the federal and state governments and other local governments, while local governments in Arkansas obtained 54 percent of their TR from these same sources. In the other two states (Delaware and New Mexico), 50 percent of their TR was obtained from IR. High levels of dependency on IR

*Table 8.1* Total Intergovernmental Revenue (IR) as a Percentage of All Local Governments' Total Revenue (TR) in 1962 and 2020 and Change over Time

| *50-State Mean* | *29* | *35* | | *50-State Mean* | *29* | *35* | |
|---|---|---|---|---|---|---|---|
| *State* | *1962* | *2020* | *Change* | *State* | *1962* | *2020* | *Change* |
| Vermont | 22 | 72 | 50 | Virginia | 33 | 36 | 3 |
| Arkansas | 39 | 54 | 15 | North Carolina | 48 | 35 | −13 |
| Delaware | 49 | 50 | 1 | Massachusetts | 25 | 34 | 9 |
| New Mexico | 50 | 50 | 0 | Tennessee | 31 | 34 | 3 |
| North Dakota | 29 | 48 | 19 | Ohio | 36 | 33 | −3 |
| Mississippi | 41 | 47 | 6 | Oklahoma | 29 | 33 | 4 |
| Michigan | 32 | 44 | 12 | Connecticut | 18 | 32 | 14 |
| Nevada | 27 | 44 | 17 | New York | 16 | 32 | 16 |
| Wisconsin | 34 | 44 | 10 | Rhode Island | 23 | 32 | 9 |
| Minnesota | 32 | 43 | 11 | Utah | 34 | 32 | −2 |
| California | 31 | 42 | 11 | Georgia | 43 | 31 | −12 |
| Idaho | 30 | 42 | 12 | Louisiana | 37 | 31 | −6 |
| Kansas | 26 | 39 | 13 | Maryland | 39 | 31 | −8 |
| Montana | 26 | 39 | 13 | South Carolina | 41 | 29 | −12 |
| Oregon | 31 | 39 | 8 | South Dakota | 18 | 29 | 11 |
| Pennsylvania | 29 | 39 | 10 | Missouri | 42 | 28 | −14 |
| West Virginia | 35 | 39 | 4 | Nebraska | 13 | 27 | 14 |
| Arizona | 32 | 38 | 6 | Texas | 25 | 27 | 2 |
| Wyoming | 33 | 38 | 5 | Colorado | 35 | 26 | −11 |
| Alabama | 40 | 37 | −3 | Florida | 23 | 25 | 2 |
| Alaska | 32 | 37 | 5 | Illinois | 40 | 25 | −15 |
| Kentucky | 33 | 37 | 4 | Maine | 13 | 25 | 11 |
| Washington | 35 | 37 | 2 | New Hampshire | 29 | 25 | −4 |
| Indiana | 28 | 36 | 8 | New Jersey | 16 | 25 | 9 |
| Iowa | 22 | 36 | 14 | Hawaii | 32 | 13 | −19 |

*Source:* U.S. Bureau of the Census. Census of Governments. Compendium of Government Finances series, 1962 and 2017.

(i.e., obtaining 10 percent of more of it above the national mean) were also recorded for local governments in North Dakota and Mississippi (see Table 8.1), while local governments in six states (Florida, Illinois, Maine, New Hampshire, New Jersey, and Hawaii) exhibited a much lower level of dependency on IR (i.e., receiving 10 percent or less of it below the national mean) in 2020 than local governments in the typical state.

Another point worth noting is that local governments, on average, in five states posted significant increases in the IR proportion of their TR of 15 percent or more—Vermont (50 percent), Arkansas (15 percent), North Dakota (19 percent), Nevada (17), and New York (16 percent). Then, local governments, on average, in six states experienced a noticeable decline in the IR proportion of their TR—Hawaii (19 percent), Illinois (15 percent), Missouri (14 percent), North Carolina (13 percent), and Georgia and South Carolina (12 percent for each state) (see again Table 8.1).

To appreciate better the role that IR plays in the finances of U.S. local governments, it is important to examine these three sources of IR (state governments, the federal government, and other local governments) separately and the contribution that each makes to the budgets of counties, municipalities, townships, special districts, and school districts. It is to that analysis that we now turn.

## State transfers: Revenue sharing, grants-in-aid, and payments in lieu of taxes

Looking again at Figure 8.1, it is clear that local governments obtain the greatest amount of their IR from their state governments.[4] IR received from one's state government comes from three primary sources.[5] Since 1962, state aid has accounted for at least one-fourth of local government TR. However, the state aid proportion of TR began to rise after 1962, and by the early part of the first decade of the 21st century, it represented nearly one-third of these governments' TR. This increase—but especially during the 1960s and early 1970s and then again between 1987 and 2002—is likely attributable to the concerted efforts of civic reformers who pushed for larger amounts of state aid while also lobbying for greater fiscal home rule authority for these governments.[6] After 2002, there was a visible decline in the state aid proportion that was likely caused by the fallout from the Great Recession. It is reasonable to conclude that state governments, also left reeling in the aftermath of the sharpest downturn in the economy since the Great Depression, were not in the financial position to provide customary levels of state aid to their local governments. This proposition is validated by data collected by the Washington Post (2021) which showed that a majority (26) of states experienced revenue declines between December 2019 and December 2020. In short, they were having serious difficulties in making ends meet due to experiencing a significant reduction in their own revenue. As a result, local governments found themselves caught in a financial dilemma aptly referred to as "fend-for-yourself federalism" (Shannon 1987; Pagano and Hoene 2003; Benton 2018). But also notice the upward tick in the IR proportion of TR by 2020 which might be accounted for by the receipt of early Trump and Biden administrations' coronavirus assistance money flowing through the states or even to local governments directly after heavy lobbying by NACo and NLC; in addition, there were a few states (e.g., California) that came to the aid of their local governments in the early part of the health pandemic.

### *State fiscal assistance to full-service local government—Counties and municipalities*

Among full-service general-purpose local governments, county governments historically have received a larger proportion of their TR from state aid than have municipalities (see Figure 8.2). This is as anticipated, given the reasoning behind states creating counties and assigning them significant responsibility for the provision of a number of important functions known as traditional services (see Benton 2002, 29–30, 71–113). Legally speaking, counties or their equivalent in Louisiana and Alaska in 48 states (exceptions being Rhode Island and Connecticut) are political and administrative subdivisions or arms of their states. In fact, county governments have often been referred to as "branch" or "satellite" offices" of the states (see Benton 2002, 2019). The primary purpose for their establishment was to carry out or enforce state laws and administer state

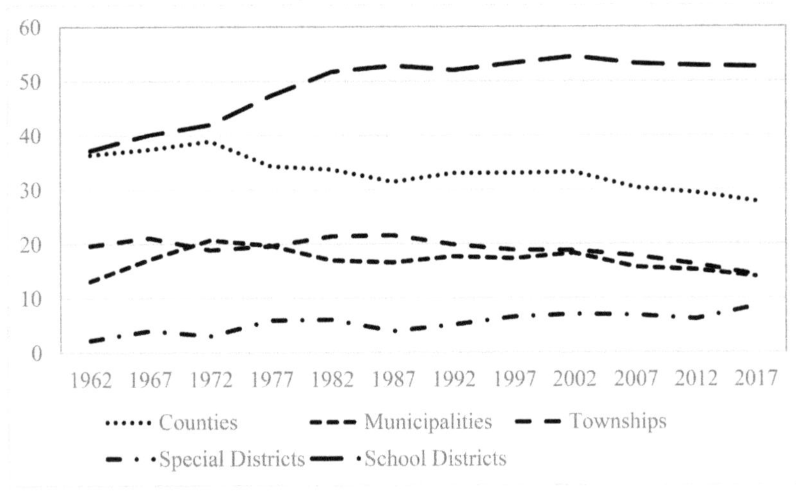


*Figure 8.2* State Aid to Individual Local Governments as a Percentage of Total Revenue (TR), 1962–2017

*Source:* U.S. Bureau of the Census. Census of Governments. Compendium of Government Finances series, 1962–2017.

programs (registering people to vote, keeping track of births and deaths, recording legal documents like titles, deeds, and marriage licenses, and assessing property for tax purposes) or deliver state-level services (health care, public welfare, construction and maintenance of roads and bridges, operation of criminal and civil courts and provision of other judicial services, dissemination of agricultural information, and enforcement of health and safety standards and codes) at the local level. Therefore, it is reasonable to assume that states would supply a considerable proportion of the funds necessary to carry out these service responsibilities that are often mandated (see Fisher and Bristle 2012).

Upon closer inspection of Figure 8.2, it is evident that county governments have received around one-third of their TR from state aid over the last 55 years. In fact, the state aid proportion was actually closer to 40 percent of these governments' TR from the 1960s until about midway through the 1970s before it began tapering off to around the one-third level. For the next 20 years or so, state aid as a proportion of county TR remained fairly stable. But, by the early part of the 21st century, the state aid proportions began to drop again (i.e., to around 30 percent by 2007 and to about 28 percent by 2017).

Two logical factors would seem to account for these decreases in the state aid percent of county government TR. From 1962 going forward, the conspicuous decline in this proportion is probably due to county governments (but especially, medium- to highly populated and rapidly growing ones) spending a smaller proportion of their resources on state-mandated ("arm of the state") services like public welfare, health, highways, and judicial/legal functions and more money on municipal- and urban-type services (see Benton 2002). Evidence supporting this supposition can be found in a comparison of the proportion of county expenditures dedicated to these typically mandated kinds of services in 1962 and 2012. Over this period, the proportion of county government TR spent for "arm of the state" functions declined appreciably from 35 to under 28 percent. Moreover, a Pearson correlation (simple R) of .81 confirms that a reasonably strong relationship exists between a decrease in the proportion of county government money being spent on "arm of the state" services and a precipitous drop in state aid as a proportion of county governments' TR. In spite of this general trend among counties in all states, this is not the case in four states (California, Michigan, North Dakota, and Pennsylvania), as the proportion of TR spent on "arm of the state" services continues to increase, while state aid accounts for a larger percentage of county TR.

The most recent and continuing drops in the state aid proportion of county governments' TR would seem to be explained by counties having to devote smaller parts of their monetary resources to "arm of the state" services and concomitantly larger shares of their budgets to purely local services that are sometimes referred to as municipal- and urban-type services (see Benton 2002). In short, county officials have to be more sensitive to a growing number of vocal and energized residents who live in more urban and densely populated enclaves in the county and expect a different repertoire of services that are normally associated with living in municipalities. This suggests that the service role of counties continues to be shifting from being mere appendages of their state governments and routinely delivering state-level services albeit at the local level for the government (the state) that established them to serve this purpose.

Stated differently, the ongoing decline in the state aid proportion of county governments' TR is likely the result of the continuing transformation of counties from their historical role as deliverers of traditional, "arm of the state" services to what some have called the "modern county," with a compelling, redirected focus on providing municipal- and urban-type services (see Duncombe 1977; Marando and Thomas 1977; Kajfez, Hall, and Karnig 1984; Salant 1988, 1991; DeSantis 1989; Marando and Reeves 1991; Streib and Waugh 1991; Marando and Baker 1993; Berman 1993; Berman and Lehman 1993). In addition, one cannot overlook the possibility that the drop in the state aid component since 2002 was an unfortunate consequence of the deleterious effects of the Great Recession. That is, state governments whose own revenue collections were suffering from the most significant downturn in the economy since the Great Depression of the 1930s were in no position to provide the level of financial assistance to their local governments, including counties, like they had in the past.

Examination of other pertinent data provides an additional perspective on state financial aid to county governments. While counties have been receiving a smaller proportion of their TR over the last 55 years from their state governments, they also have been getting a smaller share of money that states make available to all of their local governments. More specifically, the proportion of state aid allotted to county governments in the 48 states that have these political subdivisions declined from 28 to 22 percent between 1962 and 2017. However, as shown in Table 8.2, this trend is not uniform across these 48 states. On the one hand, county governments in six states (California, Hawaii, Maryland, North Carolina, Tennessee, and Virginia) have always received a much larger share of state aid monies given to local governments since 1962. In Maryland, North Carolina, Tennessee, and Virginia, this is likely due to the state assigning their counties the responsibility for operating K-12 schools. On the other hand, counties in 13 states have usually received a much smaller part of state financial assistance that is distributed to all local governments. This is what one would expect in four New England states (Maine, Massachusetts, New Hampshire, and Vermont) since county governments have always played a minimal role in service delivery compared to municipalities and townships. Delaware's three counties also receive a much smaller share of state aid than is the case in the typical state because there is very little unincorporated area in the state. In another state (Missouri), counties are not as active in the provision of services, as evidenced by the fact that they account for a much smaller percentage of total local government expenditures when compared to the typical county in the United States (11 percent versus 25 percent). As for counties in seven other states (Alabama,

*Table 8.2* Proportion of State Financial Assistance Allocated to County Governments in 1962 and 2017 and Change over Time

| *48-State Mean* | *28* | *22* | | *48-State Mean* | *28* | *22* | |
|---|---|---|---|---|---|---|---|
| *State* | *1962* | *2017* | *Change* | *State* | *1962* | *2017* | *Change* |
| Alabama | 24 | 6 | −18 | Montana | 8 | 10 | 2 |
| Alaska | 0 | 11 | 11 | Nebraska | 76 | 14 | −62 |
| Arizona | 3 | 19 | 16 | Nevada | 21 | 23 | 2 |
| Arkansas | 20 | 4 | −16 | New Hampshire | 3 | 5 | 2 |
| California | 42 | 35 | −7 | New Jersey | 38 | 15 | −23 |
| Colorado | 48 | 14 | −34 | New Mexico | 6 | 6 | 0 |
| Delaware | 2 | 2 | 0 | New York | 14 | 11 | −3 |
| Florida | 12 | 14 | 2 | North Carolina | 96 | 88 | −8 |
| Georgia | 14 | 3 | −11 | North Dakota | 32 | 26 | −6 |
| Hawaii | 50 | 40 | −10 | Ohio | 41 | 24 | −17 |
| Idaho | 30 | 10 | −20 | Oklahoma | 28 | 9 | −19 |
| Illinois | 28 | 13 | −15 | Oregon | 28 | 19 | −9 |
| Indiana | 35 | 10 | −25 | Pennsylvania | 5 | 20 | 15 |
| Iowa | 32 | 12 | −20 | South Carolina | 19 | 9 | −10 |
| Kansas | 50 | 5 | −45 | South Dakota | 27 | 11 | −16 |
| Kentucky | 6 | 12 | 6 | Tennessee | 65 | 76 | 11 |
| Louisiana | 11 | 15 | 4 | Texas | 4 | 13 | 9 |
| Maine | 1 | 1 | 0 | Utah | 7 | 7 | 0 |
| Maryland | 59 | 81 | 22 | Vermont | 0 | * | * |
| Massachusetts | * | * | * | Virginia | 62 | 60 | −2 |
| Michigan | 24 | 20 | −4 | Washington | 61 | 3 | −5 |
| Minnesota | 37 | 17 | −20 | West Virginia | 61 | 3 | −58 |
| Mississippi | 28 | 10 | −18 | Wisconsin | 42 | 16 | −26 |
| Missouri | 3 | 7 | 4 | Wyoming | 25 | 10 | −15 |

* Less than .5 percent.

*Source:* U.S. Bureau of the Census. Census of Governments. Compendium of Government Finances series, 1962 and 2017.

Arkansas, Georgia, Kansas, New Mexico, Utah, and West Virginia), several plausible explanations exist but the more likely ones are that these states contain a large number of counties with sparsely populated unincorporated areas and that county governments are expected to raise more of their own revenue from sources at their disposal. An additional explanation for Alabama, Arkansas, and West Virginia could be that the state is just too poor to be able to aid counties as well as other local governments.

Further inspection of Table 8.2 reveals that county governments in the majority of states were the beneficiaries of much smaller proportions of state aid in 2017 than they were in 1962. So if county governments have experienced a significant drop in their share of state aid money (and as will be discussed later in this chapter, municipality, township, and special district proportions have not appreciably increased), then where is more of state aid (transfers) going? The simple answer is that school districts have been receiving a much larger proportion of state aid than was the case in the past (see Figure 8.2).

The bottom line is that most county governments are increasingly being expected to play different roles. More to the point, it is now incumbent on county governments to provide a much larger number of municipal-type government services (e.g., fire protection, garbage collection, utilities, and sidewalks) and urban-type services to an entire metropolitan area (e.g., solid waste and sewage disposal, 911-emergency dispatch, transit, and environmental protection), in addition to a number of well-known traditional services (welfare, health, highways and roads, judicial/legal, and voter registration and elections). Furthermore, states, more often than not, expect their county governments to provide this larger number and varied repertoire of services with less financial help from them. All of this suggests that county governments in the 21st century are likely functioning as more than traditional administrative service arms of their state governments. This is particularly so in states which have large concentrations of people residing in unincorporated parts of counties that need and expect a larger number of services normally associated with municipalities. A case in point can be seen in the State of Florida. Some of the more populous counties there (e.g., Dade, Broward, Palm Beach, Hillsborough, Pinellas, Orange, and Sarasota) contain many more unincorporated area residents than persons living within cities. As a result, it is not uncommon for the county sheriff to be viewed as the "county police chief."

In looking again at Figure 8.2, one can get a quick sense of the part that state aid plays in the overall revenue picture of municipal governments. In some ways, the pattern depicted for municipalities is different than the one seen for county governments, while in other ways it is similar. In contrast to what is seen for county governments, state aid historically has accounted for a much smaller percentage of municipal governments' TR. In fact, the municipal proportion typically has averaged approximately one-half the size of what it has been for county governments over the last 55 years. It has never risen above about 21 percent (1977) and then even declined somewhat during the remainder of the 1970s and throughout the 1980s and 1990s until it began to increase slightly again to 18 percent by 2002. Similar to what was seen for county governments, the state aid proportion of municipalities' TR also declined visibility after 2002, dropping to 16 percent by 2007 and to 14 percent by 2017. Nevertheless, the municipal state aid proportion of its TR was slightly higher in 2017 than it was in 1962 (i.e., 14 versus 13 percent).

Accounting for the differences in state aid as a proportion of municipal and county governments' TR is to understand the rationale for the establishment of cities in the United States and elsewhere. Upon being granted statehood by the Congress, states immediately saw the need to create political subdivisions (counties or their equivalent) to assist them in providing essential state-level services (public welfare, health care, roads and highways, minimal law enforcement, court and legal systems, archival of public records, elections administration, property assessment and tax collection, and dissemination of agricultural information and advice) to citizens at the local level in what was usually a large, far-flung territorial domain. However, if concentrated groups of citizens wished to receive a larger or higher tier of services, then they could petition the state to grant them a municipal charter for the explicit purpose of being allowed to provide a longer list of services and ones that were believed to be consistent with the needs of people living in a densely populated, urban environment. In short, their new city would be able to provide services such as the following: a level of police protection greater than what was typically provided by the county sheriff; fire protection by a full-time department with professionally trained firefighters; utilities like water, sewer and garbage collection and disposal, electric power and gas; paved streets; sidewalks; street lights; community parks and recreational facilities; and so forth. As part and parcel of being granted a city charter (or being permitted to "incorporate"), new municipalities were allowed to raise most of their own revenue along guidelines established by the state. In many instances, municipalities were granted more latitude in raising their own revenue than were county governments. This included the power to levy taxes, which always included the ability to tax real estate and structures and sometimes to tax other items (sales, income, real estate transactions, vehicles, luxury items, utilities, etc.).

But, in granting municipalities the authority to raise their own revenue came with the understanding that they should not expect to receive the same level of state financial assistance available to county governments. This is because municipalities, for the most part, were neither expected nor required to provide a list of services mentioned above that would have made them administrative arms of the state. Put differently, municipalities were designed to do what the state was not willing to do—provide a number of optional local-type services to their citizens.

As noted above, state aid to municipal governments has basically remained stable over time when compared to counties. This could be due in large measure to the fact that most states have not saddled their municipal governments with more administrative arm of the state functions than they originally gave them at the time of incorporation. In those instances where they have imposed on their cities (or mandated) to act as administrative arms, states have been inclined to grant them greater latitude in raising their own revenues to pay for these additional costs rather than provide them with additional state aid. There are, however, some instances where state aid to municipalities declined, and given the time when they occurred (late 1970s thru early 1980s and after 2007), it is most likely that they were caused by downturns in the U.S. economy. As mentioned earlier with respect to counties, all local governments (including municipalities) usually suffer reductions in state aid (but particularly, shared revenues) when their states are having to deal with recessionary forces that curtail their own revenue intake.

*Table 8.3* State Aid as a Percentage of Total Revenue (TR) of Municipal Governments, 1962 and 2017 and Change over Time

| *Mean* | *13* | *14* | | *Mean* | *13* | *14* | |
|---|---|---|---|---|---|---|---|
| *State* | *1962* | *2017* | *Change* | *State* | *1962* | *2017* | *Change* |
| Alabama | 3 | 3 | 0 | Montana | 2 | 15 | 13 |
| Alaska | 10 | 22 | 22 | Nebraska | 3 | 7 | 4 |
| Arizona | 17 | 25 | 8 | Nevada | 3 | 28 | 25 |
| Arkansas | 22 | 7 | −15 | New Hampshire | 4 | 23 | 19 |
| California | 10 | 4 | −6 | New Jersey | 7 | 19 | 12 |
| Colorado | 17 | 5 | −12 | New Mexico | 5 | 17 | 12 |
| Connecticut | 12 | 37 | 25 | New York | 20 | 28 | 8 |
| Delaware | 25 | 4 | −21 | North Carolina | 8 | 8 | 0 |
| Florida | * | 7 | 7 | North Dakota | 3 | 18 | 15 |
| Georgia | 11 | 1 | −10 | Ohio | 16 | 8 | −8 |
| Hawaii | 17 | 5 | −12 | Oklahoma | 7 | 3 | −4 |
| Idaho | 6 | 11 | 5 | Oregon | 9 | 6 | −3 |
| Illinois | 19 | 19 | 0 | Pennsylvania | 7 | 16 | 9 |
| Indiana | 11 | 13 | 2 | Rhode Island | 17 | 40 | 23 |
| Iowa | 13 | 8 | −5 | South Carolina | 5 | 4 | −1 |
| Kansas | 7 | 7 | 0 | South Dakota | 4 | 3 | −1 |
| Kentucky | 1 | 4 | 3 | Tennessee | 14 | 10 | −.4 |
| Louisiana | 15 | 11 | −4 | Texas | 3 | 3 | 0 |
| Maine | 9 | 25 | 16 | Utah | 6 | 6 | 0 |
| Maryland | 35 | 29 | −6 | Vermont | 7 | 6 | −1 |
| Massachusetts | 24 | 31 | 7 | Virginia | 20 | 29 | 9 |
| Michigan | 16 | 14 | −2 | Washington | 11 | 6 | −5 |
| Minnesota | 8 | 11 | 3 | West Virginia | 1 | 7 | 6 |
| Mississippi | 5 | 17 | 12 | Wisconsin | 27 | 15 | −12 |
| Missouri | 3 | 4 | 1 | Wyoming | 13 | 30 | 17 |

State—this is where state aid as a percentage of TR and state aid as a percentage of all state aid to local governments has always been considerably lower than the 50-state average.

* Less than .5 percent.

*Source:* U.S. Bureau of the Census. Census of Governments. Compendium of Government Finances series, 1962–2017.

A state-by-state examination of state aid to municipalities reveals several distinguishable patterns that warrant some explanation (see Tables 8.3 and 8.4). First, there are 20 states where state aid as a percent of TR and state aid as a percent of all state aid to local governments has always been considerably lower than the average in all 50 states. This would seem to imply that cities in these states have never been expected or counted on to provide very much in the way of customary "administrative arm of the state" functions. Municipalities in these states operate very much like the prototypical city described above that concentrates on the provision of what are usually referred to as "municipal-type services" that are not provided by the state and usually not by counties. Consequently, municipalities are

*Table 8.4* Proportion of State Financial Aid Allocated to Municipal Governments in 1962 and 2017 and Change over Time

| *Mean* | *20* | *16* | | *Mean* | *20* | *16* | |
|---|---|---|---|---|---|---|---|
| *State* | *1962* | *2017* | *Change* | *State* | *1962* | *2017* | *Change* |
| Alabama | 3 | 4 | 1 | Montana | 3 | 10 | 7 |
| Alaska | 21 | 14 | −7 | Nebraska | 6 | 9 | 3 |
| Arizona | 2 | 26 | 24 | Nevada | 2 | 14 | 12 |
| Arkansas | 11 | 5 | −6 | New Hampshire | 24 | 23 | −1 |
| California | 9 | 3 | −6 | New Jersey | 22 | 19 | −3 |
| Colorado | 19 | 9 | −10 | New Mexico | 3 | 14 | 11 |
| Connecticut | 40 | 38 | −2 | New York | 47 | 60 | 13 |
| Delaware | 20 | 2 | −18 | North Carolina | 4 | 7 | 3 |
| Florida | 1 | 8 | 7 | North Dakota | 3 | 12 | 9 |
| Georgia | 1 | 1 | 0 | Ohio | 19 | 7 | −12 |
| Hawaii | 50 | 53 | 3 | Oklahoma | 7 | 5 | −2 |
| Idaho | 6 | 7 | 1 | Oregon | 9 | 6 | −3 |
| Illinois | 19 | 23 | 4 | Pennsylvania | 9 | 9 | 0 |
| Indiana | 11 | 13 | 2 | Rhode Island | 64 | 64 | 0 |
| Iowa | 19 | 10 | −9 | South Carolina | 3 | 3 | 0 |
| Kansas | 9 | 7 | −2 | South Dakota | 11 | 6 | −5 |
| Kentucky | 1 | 4 | −3 | Tennessee | 36 | 23 | 13 |
| Louisiana | 8 | 5 | −3 | Texas | 5 | 3 | −2 |
| Maine | 19 | 25 | 6 | Utah | 5 | 4 | −1 |
| Maryland | 41 | 19 | −22 | Vermont | 12 | 2 | −10 |
| Massachusetts | 60 | 59 | −1 | Virginia | 38 | 35 | −3 |
| Michigan | 20 | 8 | −12 | Washington | 11 | 5 | −6 |
| Minnesota | 9 | 8 | −1 | West Virginia | 30 | 2 | −28 |
| Mississippi | 3 | 14 | 11 | Wisconsin | 33 | 10 | −23 |
| Missouri | 5 | 5 | 0 | Wyoming | 8 | 16 | 8 |

State—this is where state aid as a % of TR and state aid as a % of all state aid to local governments has always been considerably lower than the 50-state average.

* Less than .5 percent.

*Source:* U.S. Bureau of the Census. Census of Governments. Compendium of Government Finances series, 1962 and 2017.

expected to raise more of their own revenue and depend less of state financial assistance.

Another pattern is found in these two tables in six other states (Colorado, Delaware, Hawaii, Iowa, Ohio, and Wisconsin). In these states, it appears as though municipalities may have at one time provided a number of "arm of the state" functions but no longer are expected to do so. This is evidenced by the fact that the percentage of state aid they received in 1962 was either at or exceeded the 50-state average but had dropped noticeably below the mean of all states by 2017 (see Table 8.3). Moreover, the state aid proportion of municipal government TR in these states, which had been at or above the 50-state average in 1962, had also dropped noticeably by 2017 (see Table 8.4). It is reasonable to assume that these states may have relieved their municipalities from some of their mandated "arm of the state" responsibilities so that they can focus more on the delivery of the typical kinds of municipal-type services.

A third pattern detected from Tables 8.3 and 8.4 is seen in seven additional states (Arizona, Florida, Maine, Mississippi, Montana, Nevada, and New Mexico). Here, there are noticeable increases in state aid as a proportion of municipal TR and state aid received as a proportion of state aid to all local governments, suggesting that municipalities are quite likely performing more "arm of the state functions" than they were in earlier years. In the case of Maine, this may be an indication that cities have to be more active in service delivery since county governments are assigned fewer service responsibilities, while municipal governments in New Mexico have been given more functional responsibilities in recent years. As for Florida, this may be a reflection of the expanded "arm of the state" service role of the Cities of Miami (merged with Dade County to form a federated government in 1962) and Jacksonville (consolidated with Duval County in 1968). In another state (Virginia), the state aid proportion of municipal TR and municipal governments' share of total state aid to local governments has always been much higher than the 50-state average. One likely explanation is that the Virginia's 38 independent cities have authority and service responsibilities similar to county governments.

In addition, two other interesting patterns are visible from the data in Table 8.3. Both patterns are characterized by state aid accounting for a higher proportion of municipal TR than the typical state and a municipal share of total state aid to local governments that is higher than the 50-state average. In one pattern that appears in five states (Connecticut, Massachusetts, New Jersey, New York, and Rhode Island), municipalities show a greater dependency on state aid to supply TR and the receipt of a larger share of state aid allocated to all local governments than found in cities in other states over time. This is probably not explained by an expansion of these governments' "arm of the state" functional service assignments but rather as efforts of states to direct larger amounts of state aid to assist large cities that have had a long history of fiscal stress and economic decline. In fact, states have always been viewed as having an important vested interest in ensuring that citizens' health, safety, and "necessities of life" needs are provided for (e.g., clean drinking water, streets and sidewalks, solid waste and sewer collection and disposal, mosquito abatement, rat control, economic development, decent housing, adequate fire and police protection, children and senior daycare, and traffic control). This line of reasoning is also consistent with the reasoning behind an increasing number of federal grant-in-aid programs—financial aid should be directed more toward assisting people and not necessarily to places.

The second of these patterns can be seen in four other states (Alaska, North Dakota, Wyoming, and Nevada). It is like municipalities in these states benefit from a state aid policy approach of "let's share the wealth" that is made possible because of mineral and oil severance tax revenue in Alaska, North Dakota, and Wyoming and gambling tax proceeds in Nevada. While the trend of cities receiving larger proportions of their TR from state aid has been evident for several decades in Alaska and Wyoming, it has been more apparent in North Dakota and Nevada in recent years.

***State fiscal assistance to limited full-service local government—Townships***

While townships may fit the description of more limited types of general-purpose local governments, they however do provide a number of services that are more akin to those provided by both counties and municipalities (see Benton 2002). On the one hand, township governments serve to assist counties in the provision of some state-level services at the local level (e.g., health care, public welfare, roads, and even some administrative and judicial functions). On the other hand, townships, more often than not, resemble municipalities in that they may provide a number of services normally associated with municipalities (e.g., fire and police protection, utilities, libraries, snow removal, protective inspections, parks and recreation). Therefore, it is not surprising to see from Figure 8.2 that the percentage of township TR obtained from their state governments, while falling somewhere between the levels received by municipalities and counties, tends to be closer to the typical county government. The township state aid proportion basically ranged from 19 to 21 percent from 1962 to 2002, but like the proportion for counties and municipalities, it visibly declines after 2002. Here again, it appears that the Great Recession may have been responsible for township states' inability to provide state fiscal assistance to these types of local governments as well.

To gain a better understanding of the importance of state aid to township governments, states with townships were divided into two theoretically relevant categories—those located in more rural areas versus those situated in more urbanized places (see Table 8.5). The left-side of the table indicates the degree to

*Table 8.5* State Aid as a Percentage of Total Revenue (TR) of Rural and Urban Townships and Rural and Urban Township Percentage of Total State Aid, 1962 and 2017

| | *State Aid as % of Township Total Revenue (TR)* | | *Township % of Total State Aid* | |
|---|---|---|---|---|
| *Mean* | *20* | *17* | *7* | *4* |
| | *1962* | *2017* | *1962* | *2017* |
| Rural Townships | 20 | 13 | 2 | 0.6 |
| Urban Townships | 20 | 14 | 9 | 6 |

*Source:* U.S. Bureau of the Census. Census of Governments. Compendium of Government Finances series, 1962 and 2017.

which state aid contributes to the TR of the two different types of township governments. In 1962, state aid accounted for the same proportion of these governments' TR regardless whether they were located in a rural or an urban area. This suggests that their responsibility for "arm of the state" type services (normally associated with county governments) basically stayed the same over the last 55 years. By 2017, however, the data suggest that more urban-type townships may now have less responsibility for those traditional "arm of the state" functions and at the same time are involved in more municipal-type services that are provided by cities. The data on the right-side of the table with respect to the township share of state aid available to all local governments would also support the proposition that townships in more urban settings today may be more pre-occupied with providing services similar to those of municipalities and less so with services offered by counties which typically function as administrative appendages of their state government. Evidence of this can be seen where both kinds of townships experienced a diminution in their share of state aid, but particularly for townships located in an urban setting.

### *Special district minimal reliance on state fiscal assistance*

Further inspection of Figure 8.2 indicates that the state aid proportion of special districts' TR is the lowest among the five kinds of local governments. In 1962, state aid supplied only 2 percent of special districts' TR. This figure had climbed to 7 percent by 2002 and stayed there until 2012 when it dropped to 6 percent, only to rise again to nearly 9 percent by 2017. A similar trend appears for the special district share of all state aid distributed—it rose from .5 percent in 1962 to around 2 percent by 2002 and stayed there until 2017 when it climbed to just over 4 percent (see Figure 8.2). These recent simultaneous trends suggest that state governments may have stepped in to assist special districts that were continuing to suffer from the negative effects of the Great Recession. This is in spite of the fact that special districts have only minimally functioned as administrative arms of state government like counties (and thereby provided very few state-level services). This can explain why they receive so little of their TR from their states and are allocated the smallest part of state aid that is made available to all local governments. In point of fact, special districts are significantly more reliant on charges for services/fees, property taxes, and even federal aid for most of their TR.

While no data are presented here, suffice it to say that there are no revealing differences in the state aid percentage of TR or the proportion of all state aid collected by special districts when a state-by-state analysis is conducted.

### *State fiscal assistance: A vital source of revenue for local school districts*

Compared to other types of local governments, school districts are the most dependent on financial assistance from their states (see Figure 8.2). However, that has not always been the case. From roughly the early 1960s until the mid-1970s, the proportion of school district TR derived from state aid was similar to what it was for county governments. But, as the data in Figure 8.2 reveal, the state aid proportion for school districts had begun to increase noticeably by the middle of the 1970s and then began to take an even sharper upward trajectory by the end of the 1970s and early 1980s and eventually peaking at around 55 percent in 2002. By 2017, state aid still accounted for almost 53 percent of school districts' TR.

These findings are not unexpected, since the provision of K-12 education as well as higher education opportunities has always been a long-standing state-local passion, undertaking, and partnership. As part and parcel of this partnership, states anticipated that they would assist school districts in financing the cost of public education because they had created school districts (like county governments) for the explicit purpose of providing a state-level service to citizens at the local level. Evidence of this is that spending for education has consistently been the highest expenditure priority of most, if not all, state governments. Moreover, the emphasis placed on education by both states and their localities is certainly consistent with the American creed and value system that touts the availability of an affordable education as a fundamental right of every American and a likely pathway to a better life for everyone and his/her family (see Donovan, Mooney, and Smith 2009).

The abrupt rise in the state aid proportion of school districts' TR that occurred in the mid- to late 1970s is not without a plausible explanation. From the outset, the public viewed state aid to education as a positive thing for school districts because it would permit the state to address funding inequities that may often exist between districts. That is, states would be able to devise state aid funding formulas in such a way as to allocate more money to those districts with less ability to generate adequate property tax revenues due to having lower real estate values. In other words, states could provide all districts with a minimum level of fiscal support but could also distribute varying amounts of additional aid to poor districts. Unfortunately, most states, however, did very little over the years to correct the funding inequities—indeed, the gross disparities—that developed from the onset of public education until the 1970s. As a consequence of the unwillingness of most states to take corrective action inevitably led to a number of legal challenges. In the landmark case of *Serrano* v. *Priest* (1971), the California Supreme Court ruled that inequities in school district spending resulting from variations in taxable wealth were unconstitutional. Following *Serrano*, successful lawsuits were filed in most other states by plaintiffs seeking to have their states' own property tax-based systems declared unconstitutional as violating "equal protection" guarantees found in their state constitutions that are analogous to the U.S. Constitution's 14th Amendment. Subsequently, many states by the late 1970s began to substantially increase their financial assistance to school districts and also began to seriously address equity issues in funding.

But as seen in the analysis of state aid to the other four types of local governments, it is also apparent from Figure 8.2 that the Great Recession had a noticeable impact on states' ability to help fund the nation's school districts. While the amount of state aid allocated to school districts was continuing to increase in terms of total dollars in the wake of the Great Recession, state aid as a percentage of school districts' TR was showing signs of declining after 2002 and was continuing to decrease by 2017. In 2002, state aid constituted 55 percent of school districts' TR, but the proportion had dropped to 53 percent in 2007 and to 52.5 percent by 2017. That meant that local school districts were having to make up the difference in needed funding by depending more on their own-source revenue (OSR), which increased from 43 percent in 2002 to 45 percent in 2017. Yet, this was happening in spite of the fact that states were allocating an even larger proportion of their state aid to school districts and subsequently smaller proportions to other local governments. In 2002, school districts' share of state aid amounted to 54 percent but increased to 56 percent in 2007 and stayed at that level through 2012 and even increased further to 57 percent by 2017.

In sum, it is clear that, although state aid was accounting for a smaller proportion of school districts' TR during and after the Great Recession, states were being more generous in their allocation of financial assistance dollars, to the point of providing smaller proportions of state aid to counties, municipalities, townships, and special districts. At the same time, state governments were having to plug the huge holes in their own budgets in a time marked by substantial revenue shortfalls and subsequent fiscal stress they were experiencing. None of this bodes well for local school districts' finances going forward. It will be interesting to see what the effect that the COVID-19-induced recession has had on state aid to school districts once reliable data becomes available.

With the current financial situation and the effects of the Great Recession noted, it is instructive to refocus attention on the important general trends in state aid to school districts that have occurred over the last 55 years. Without doubt, school districts have normally depended on state aid to supply a substantial proportion of the TR needed to operate their schools, while education has always been a major priority of state governments as indicated by the proportion of state aid historically allocated to school districts. As far back as 1962, counties are the only type of local government to receive a share of state aid close to what school districts received. And, as noted above, school districts, on average, were becoming the beneficiaries of a larger proportion of state fiscal assistance. But, have these trends been the same across all states?

While the norm has been that state aid has usually accounted for a significant proportion of school districts' TR and that this percentage increased notably since the mid-1970s, this is not the case in some states (see Table 8.6). On the one hand, school districts in four New England states (Connecticut, Maine, Massachusetts, and New Hampshire) and three Mid-Atlantic states (New Jersey, New York, and Pennsylvania) have never depended on state aid to provide a large portion of their TR; this also true in the last several decades for another state in New England—Rhode Island. In these states, school districts

*Table 8.6* State Aid as a Percentage of Total Revenue (TR) of School Districts, 1962 and 2017 and Change over Time

| *Mean* | *37* | *53* | | *Mean* | *37* | *53* | |
|---|---|---|---|---|---|---|---|
| *State* | *1962* | *2017* | *Change* | *State* | *1962* | *2017* | *Change* |
| Alabama | 60 | 65 | 5 | Montana | 28 | 54 | 26 |
| Alaska | 55 | 91 | 36 | Nebraska | 7 | 38 | 31 |
| Arizona | 34 | 48 | 14 | Nevada | 37 | 72 | 35 |
| Arkansas | 43 | 86 | 43 | New Hampshire | 9 | 14 | 23 |
| California | 38 | 66 | 28 | New Jersey | 18 | 32 | 14 |
| Colorado | 22 | 50 | 28 | New Mexico | 68 | 75 | 7 |
| Connecticut | 10 | 34 | 24 | New York | 47 | 45 | −45 |
| Delaware | 73 | 65 | −8 | North Dakota | 28 | 64 | 36 |
| Florida | 45 | 50 | 5 | Ohio | 29 | 46 | 17 |
| Georgia | 60 | 54 | −6 | Oklahoma | 40 | 55 | 15 |
| Idaho | 32 | 70 | 38 | Oregon | 29 | 56 | 27 |
| Illinois | 20 | 34 | 14 | Pennsylvania | 39 | 44 | 5 |
| Indiana | 21 | 67 | 46 | Rhode Island | 57 | 32 | −25 |
| Iowa | 22 | 58 | 36 | South Carolina | 58 | 55 | −3 |
| Kansas | 20 | 64 | 44 | South Dakota | 11 | 41 | 30 |
| Kentucky | 54 | 61 | 7 | Texas | 46 | 43 | −4 |
| Louisiana | 74 | 53 | −21 | Utah | 47 | 59 | 12 |
| Maine | 41 | 40 | −1 | Vermont | 13 | 96 | 83 |
| Massachusetts | 18 | 39 | 21 | Washington | 57 | 65 | 8 |
| Michigan | 35 | 63 | 28 | West Virginia | * | 57 | 57 |
| Minnesota | 38 | 70 | 32 | Wisconsin | 26 | 59 | 33 |
| Mississippi | 59 | 62 | 3 | Wyoming | 42 | 62 | 20 |
| Missouri | 34 | 49 | 15 | | | | |

*Source:* U.S. Bureau of the Census. Census of Governments. Compendium of Government Finances series, 1962 and 2017.

traditionally receive the largest percentage of their TR from OSR locally derived revenue (OSR) and the proportion received from state aid is considerably below the 50-state mean. Several other states in other parts of the country (Illinois, Nebraska, Ohio, South Dakota, and Texas) are also characterized by this pattern, although not to the same degree. On the other hand, school districts in seven states (Alabama, Delaware, Kentucky, Mississippi, New Mexico, Utah, and Washington) have always relied on state aid to supply a much larger proportion of TR than has been true in the typical state. Another six states (Arkansas, Idaho, Indiana, Minnesota, Nevada, and Vermont) also fit this mold in recent years.

Differences in the degree to which states are willing to supply state aid to school districts and how these variances depart from the average state are also noteworthy and can also be seen in Table 8.7. Four states (Connecticut, Massachusetts, New York, and Rhode Island) have always allocated a much smaller share of their state aid than the 50-state average; note that all of them are also ones where their school districts have a lower dependency of state aid

*Table 8.7* Proportion of State Financial Assistance Allocated to School Districts in 1962 and 2017 and Change over Time

| *Mean* | *48* | *57* | | *Mean* | *48* | *57* | |
|---|---|---|---|---|---|---|---|
| *State* | *1962* | *2017* | *Change* | *State* | *1962* | *2017* | *Change* |
| Alabama | 73 | 85 | 12 | Montana | 89 | 77 | −12 |
| Alaska | 79 | 75 | −4 | Nebraska | 16 | 76 | 60 |
| Arizona | 76 | 54 | −22 | Nevada | 76 | 63 | −13 |
| Arkansas | 69 | 90 | 21 | New Hampshire | 42 | 60 | 18 |
| California | 49 | 53 | 4 | New Jersey | 38 | 58 | 20 |
| Colorado | 33 | 73 | 40 | New Mexico | 91 | 79 | −12 |
| Connecticut | 1 | 6 | 5 | New York | 37 | 29 | −8 |
| Delaware | 78 | 98 | 20 | North Dakota | 64 | 56 | −8 |
| Florida | 85 | 75 | −10 | Ohio | 38 | 67 | 29 |
| Georgia | 84 | 92 | 8 | Oklahoma | 65 | 86 | 21 |
| Idaho | 63 | 77 | 14 | Oregon | 63 | 72 | 9 |
| Illinois | 49 | 56 | 7 | Pennsylvania | 81 | 61 | −20 |
| Indiana | 53 | 75 | 22 | Rhode Island | 2 | 5 | 3 |
| Iowa | 49 | 78 | 29 | South Carolina | 78 | 88 | 10 |
| Kansas | 41 | 88 | 47 | South Dakota | 58 | 80 | 22 |
| Kentucky | 93 | 83 | −10 | Texas | 90 | 80 | −10 |
| Louisiana | 79 | 80 | 1 | Utah | 89 | 88 | −1 |
| Maine | 13 | 50 | 37 | Vermont | 13 | 93 | 80 |
| Massachusetts | 1 | 10 | 9 | Washington | 73 | 78 | 5 |
| Michigan | 52 | 67 | 15 | West Virginia | 9 | 94 | 85 |
| Minnesota | 53 | 72 | 19 | Wisconsin | 17 | 66 | 49 |
| Mississippi | 69 | 75 | 6 | Wyoming | 67 | 72 | 5 |
| Missouri | 91 | 77 | −14 | | | | |

*Source:* U.S. Bureau of the Census. Census of Governments. Compendium of Government Finances series, 1962 and 2017.

compared to districts in the typical state. On the flip side, it is clear that there are 18 states (Alabama, Alaska, Arkansas, Delaware, Georgia, Idaho, Kentucky, Louisiana, Mississippi, Missouri, New Mexico, Oklahoma, Oregon, South Carolina, Texas, Utah, Washington, and Wyoming) that have always been more generous in the proportion of state aid that they allot to their school districts than is the average state.

Other important patterns are also evident from the data in Table 8.7. First, there are seven states (Colorado, Kansas, Maine, Nebraska, Vermont, West Virginia, and Wisconsin) where their school districts in recent years have received a significantly larger share of state aid than the national state mean. Other notable gains were also recorded in Arkansas, Delaware, Indiana, Iowa, Minnesota, New Hampshire, New Jersey, Ohio, Oklahoma, and South Dakota. The conspicuous boost in state aid allotments to school districts in these states is probably reflective of conscious efforts to reduce major gaps in financial resources that existed between poor and more affluent districts.

Another noticeable pattern found in Table 8.7 is where eight states (Florida, Kentucky, Missouri, Montana, Nevada, New Mexico, Pennsylvania, and Texas) experienced a reduction in percentage of financial assistance and shared revenue received from their states over the last 55 years. Upon further analysis (data not shown here), most of this decrease occurred in the last ten years (i.e., 2007–17) and coincides with the Great Recession and its lingering effect.

## Federal grants-in-aid

While fiscal assistance from the federal government has never been a major source of revenue for local governments, generally, or for any particular type of local government, federal aid is still an important source of revenue for these governments as they attempt to balance their budgets while providing staple services to their constituents. Obviously, federal money permits local (like state) governments to do things and provide services that these governments' limited resources would not allow. By contrast, federal aid has been a vital source of revenue for state governments in the post-World War Era. In 2017, federal aid supplied over 25 percent of states' TR, while, at its height in the mid- to late 1970s, it accounted for approximately one-third of states' TR.

Ratification of the 16th Amendment in 1913 forever changed the face of fiscal federalism in the United States and resulted in the federal government being able to run a fairly hefty surplus which was used to create and expand a massive federal grant-in-aid system. As mentioned above, local governments, however, were not initial direct or major recipients of the federal government's newly found largesse. Even 50 years after the creation of the first grant-in-aid programs, local governments still received only a small fraction of the amount of money available from the federal government. This small amount of direct federal aid money accounted for an average of around 2 percent of the TR of all local governments in the early 1960s.

Figure 8.3 breaks down the proportion of TR accounted for by federal aid by type of local government.

These data reveal similar trends in the ups and downs of reliance on federal aid for the two general-purpose local governments (counties and municipalities), although the municipal proportion has always been higher. Federal aid as a proportion of county and municipal TR grew rather slowly until the late 1960s (averaging around 1–2 percent for counties and about 3 percent for municipalities), until it shot upward as rapidly increasing amounts of federal grant money began to flow to state and local governments from the Johnson administration's Great Society programs and the Nixon's administration's general and specific revenue-sharing initiatives. But, by 1977, the federal proportion for counties had risen to around 9 percent, while it had grown to nearly 13 percent for municipalities, only to begin declining steeply as the Reagan administration and Republicans in Congress sought deep cuts in federal aid. They were even

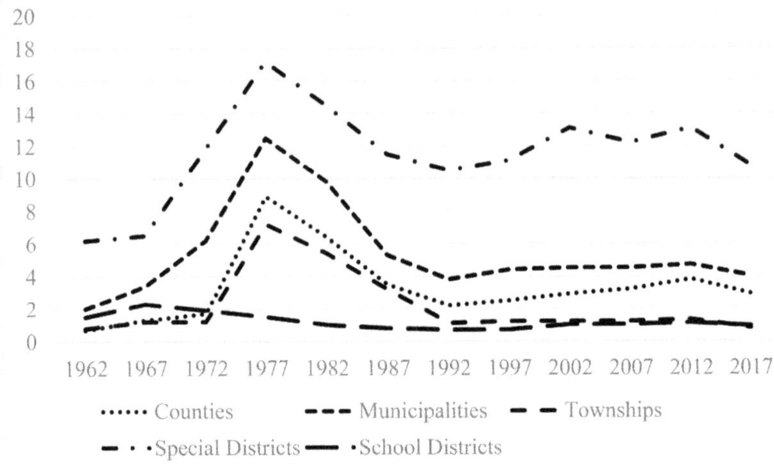


*Figure 8.3* Federal Aid to Individual Local Government as a Percentage of Total Revenue (TR), 1962–2017

*Source:* U.S. Bureau of the Census. Census of Governments. Compendium of Government Finances series, 1962–2017.

joined by some Democrats in Congress when program evaluations of a number of grant-in-aid programs strongly suggested that there was a significant amount of waste and inefficiencies in the spending of federal money and little evidence that programs achieved their goals (i.e., programmatic effectiveness). In addition, many of the recipients of these programs were not effectively organized enough to maintain a consistent lobby presence in Washington. By the early part of the first decade of the 21st century, the federal aid proportion for counties and municipalities had shrunk to around 3 and 4.5 percent, respectively. These proportions did rise only so slightly in the Great Recession with the release of federal stimulus funding under the American Recovery and Reinvestment Act (ARRA) in 2009 to counteract the significant downturn in the economy.

Another look at Figure 8.3 reveals a somewhat similar pattern for limited general-purpose governments—townships—except that the federal aid proportion of these governments' TR is lower and closer to that for county government and even "flat lines" after 1992. Moreover, it is evident from the trend line in the figure that very little federal stimulus money was distributed to townships during the Great Recession.

It is also clear from the data presented in Figure 8.3 that school districts have never counted on federal aid to supply more than a very tiny proportion of the their TR between 1962 and 2017. Since 1982, the federal aid proportion of school districts' TR has been no more than 1 percent and usually less. The only time over the last 55 years that the federal aid proportion rose even slightly was in the aftermath of congressional enactment of the Elementary and Secondary Education Act of 1962 and the beginning of federal funding for the Head Start and free lunch programs during the mid-1960s.

Perhaps the most intriguing finding to emerge from Figure 8.3 is the degree to which special districts depend on federal aid. Even as early as 1962, special districts were receiving a larger proportion of their TR from federal grants-in-aid than were even counties, municipalities, and townships, and, of course, school districts. Similar to what was detected for municipalities, the federal aid proportion of special districts' TR began to steadily increase by the mid-1960s and peaked around the mid-1970s at about 17 percent, thus coinciding with the proliferation of federal grants during the Johnson administration and the advent of revenue sharing during the Nixon administration. But, near the end of the 1970s, this proportion began to decrease due to an economy rocked by double-digit inflation and the Reagan administration's concerted efforts to achieve significant cuts in both the number of and amount of money flowing through federal grants-in-aid. Moreover, revenue sharing came to an end in 1988. By 1992, the federal aid proportion had dropped to close to 10 percent. Nonetheless, the federal aid proportion began to rise again during the George W. Bush administration, and Bush himself has been portrayed as an "uncharacteristic Republican" and "a big spending conservative" (Benton 2007). Finally, it can be seen that there was another slight increase in the federal aid proportion after 2007 which can be accounted for by the infusion of additional federal dollars from the ARRA during the Great Recession.

Given the programmatic purposes for which federal aid usually has been spent by special districts, it is important to take a closer look at the kinds of special districts that receive this money and the circumstances under which these governments were created. The fact of the matter is that quite a number of special districts have been established by states upon the urging of general-purpose local governments—that is, counties and municipalities—and their residents. Why would counties and municipalities want and/or need special districts? The answer is simple. Over the last half a century, municipalities and counties have been greatly challenged in efforts to deal meaningfully with increasing poverty, escalating crime rates, an aging and inadequate housing stock, deteriorating infrastructure and neighborhoods, unavailability of a potable water supply and safe sewage disposal, protection of the environment, and traffic gridlock, among other things. Yet, these governments' needs are greatly surpassed by their monetary resources at their disposal, while their state legislatures historically have not empathized with their sometimes-dire situations and therefore have not been willing to provide sufficient amounts of state aid.

From this perspective, it is reasonable to conclude that much of the federal money that flows to special districts eventually ends up being "additional" federal aid for local governments (but especially counties and municipalities) albeit somewhat through a proverbial "backdoor." It is almost like a "bonus" kind of federal aid to cities and counties that are cash strapped. That is, the federal money helps to finance the provision of services for which residents of counties and municipalities receive (e.g., public housing, urban renewal and redevelopment, crime prevention, safeguarding the environment, looking out for the welfare of children and seniors, replacement of decaying infrastructure, mass transit, safe water supply and sewage disposal, and anti-poverty programs) but for which these governments do not have the resources to directly pay for. In short, the receipt of federal fiscal assistance by special districts can be viewed as an indirect type of federal aid to the nation's two types of general-purpose local governments.

It addition to entertaining the possibility that an indefinite amount of federal aid allotted to special districts is just an indirect form of aid to county and municipal governments, it is also important to keep in mind that an undetermined amount of federal aid received by the states eventually finds its way to local government, as a result of congressional language that stipulates that some of this money must be "passed-through" to the local level (usually economic and community development grants). This inevitably means that Census of Government financial data is likely to over-report the actual amount of purely state aid to local governments while also under-reports the real amount of federal aid to them.

## Revenue derived from other local governments

Strictly speaking, of course, revenue received by one local government from another local government is not the same as federal or state grant-in-aid money, whereby one government (usually higher level) is providing financial assistance to another government (normally lower level). Whenever a government reports the receipt of revenue from another local government, it is usually a payment of sorts for the rendering of services by the former to the latter. For instance, it is not uncommon for local governments (but particularly, cities) to provide water and sewer service, police or fire protection, solid waste collection and disposal, parks and recreation services, maintenance of vehicles, buildings, and other facilities, planning and zoning expertise, payroll and other administrative functions, libraries to another city or to the unincorporated area of a county. In other words, the revenue that one local government derives from another local government potentially serves to augment the fiscal resources of the providing government so that it may become less dependent on revenue received from one's own sources (OSR) as well as federal and state aid.

Figure 8.4 displays data on the degree to which various local governments take advantage of this alternative source of revenue that can be best described as an entrepreneurial venture. These data show that this form of IR supplies, at best, a very small proportion of local governments' TR. This is especially true for four of the five types of local governments (the exception being special districts).

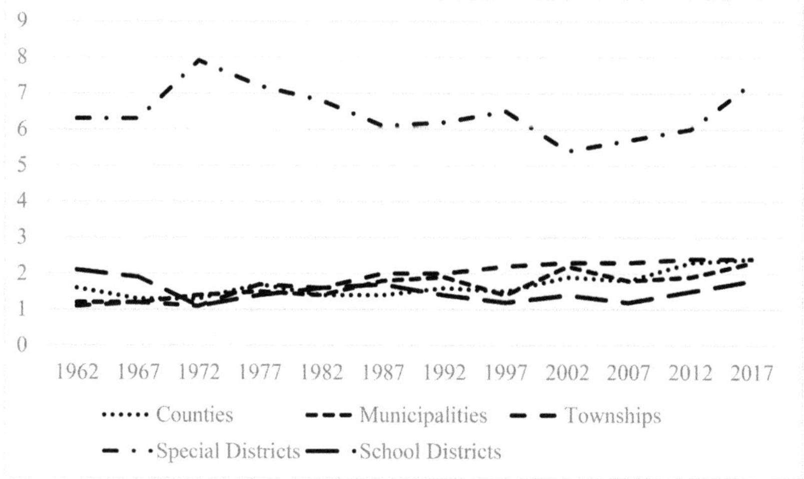


*Figure 8.4* Revenue from Other Local Governments for Individual Local Governments as a Percentage of Total Revenue (TR), 1962–2017

*Source:* U.S. Bureau of the Census. Census of Governments. Compendium of Government Finances series, 1962–2017.

Although varying somewhat, revenue proceeds from other local governments provided anywhere from 1 to 2.5 percent of the TR for counties, municipalities, townships, and school districts between 1962 and 2017. In most cases, the revenue from other local governments was comparable to the proportion that these local governments received in the form of federal aid. Upon closer examination, the other local government revenue proportion was slightly higher for counties, municipalities, and townships.

Again, it was somewhat interesting to find that special districts were receiving a larger proportion of their TR from other local governments. Over time, revenue received from other local governments has constituted around 6 percent of these governments' TR, although this proportion ranged upward to around 8 percent during the late 1960s and early 1970s. Given that counties and especially municipalities have a long history of providing services such as water supply, sewer disposal, fire suppression, police protection, parks and recreation, protective inspections, and various financial and administrative functions, one would think that they would derive a larger proportion of their TR from other local governments. One possible explanation for special districts being more successful in collecting a larger proportion of their TR from revenue from other local governments is that they may possess the expertise or experience to provide a service that a city or county views as a burdensome albeit mandated functional responsibility. Good examples could include managing public housing projects, overseeing urban renewal and redevelopment programs, assuming responsibility for anti-poverty programs, operating airports, transit systems, marinas, and sports facilities, running hospitals and out-patient medical facilities, among others.

One would think that during times of a troubled economy or dwindling revenue due to purely indigenous factors (depressed local economy, increasing levels of poverty, exodus of more affluent and educated residents and lucrative businesses, rising crime rates, undesirable place to live, climate, etc.) local governments would take advantage of any existing opportunities to bring in additional revenue to replace lost dollars from previously reliable revenue sources or even become creative in developing and nurturing money-making opportunities. But, maybe those opportunities do not exist in some areas and therefore is not necessarily a situation of "missing the boat" and "taking advantage of a golden opportunity." Or, it may be the case that opportunities are available to contract with other local governments to provide services, but the ability to make a reasonable profit is not feasible or worth the administrative effort or may pose the possibility of opening up the government to civil liability.

In the end, it is likely that most local governments get involved in providing services to other local governments for a mutually agreed upon fee as a result of trying to help a neighboring jurisdiction to provide a needed service at a cheaper cost than what it would cost the contracting government.

## Summary overview

The receipt of revenue from other governments (i.e., IR) by local governments is no small matter. In fact, it is hard to imagine local governments being able to do what they do and the vast array of services they provide today if they did not receive revenue from the federal government, their states, or other local governments—but especially the first two. As was seen in this chapter, IR has grown noticeably over the years and currently accounts for approximately one-third of the revenue available to local governments. Again, this is no small matter. While the largest proportion of IR comes from state governments, federal grant-in-aid money and even revenue obtained from other local governments is substantial (but more so for the former) and serves to augment a local government's OSR. But, given the unpredictability of politics in Congress and the economic impact of several recent, severe recessions, this vital source of revenue for local governments is not the certainty that it once was.

In the next chapter, the focus will turn to what local governments do when the revenue that they receive from several kinds of taxes (primarily property), charges for services, a host of miscellaneous sources of funding (i.e., special assessment, fines and forfeitures, sale or rental of property, proceeds from the operation of liquor stores and legalized gambling and lotteries, and interest earnings), and intergovernmental sources are insufficient to balance their budgets. While one obvious option would be to scale back projected expenditures to match projected revenue, most local governments choose to do what most people do in this situation. That is, they opt to borrow money on either a short- or long-term basis by selling bonds, with the understanding that they will have to put aside money in future budgets over the life of the "loan" to repay the principal plus interest.

## Notes

1 According to Mikesell (2018, 665), tax- or revenue-sharing programs from central to subnational governments "are a common feature of the finances in a fair number of countries, including both unitary and federal systems." In these programs, the central government levies a tax such as an income tax or a valued added tax (VAT) and determines what share to be allotted to regional and local governments (for instance, 30 percent). In this example, 30 percent of individual income or VAT tax collected by each regional or local government is given to that government. In this type of arrangement, fiscal decisions are made centrally, but a share of the tax is set aside and is earmarked for subnational governments. Shared revenue may also be returned to the region from which it was collected or it may be distributed by a formula in the form of equal per capita shares.

2 There are skeptics who worry that too much money being dumped into the economy with ARPA funds could have serious negative repercussions like runaway inflation and adding to the federal deficit. However, some key Republicans and Democrats in Congress and the Chair of the Federal Reserve, Jerome Powell, argue to the contrary, saying that the strong congressional fiscal support to date has helped the economic recovery progress just to the level of replacing lost income (Washington Post 2021). In order to build productivity over time, Powell has further stated that Congress through fiscal investments can do this, and not the Fed.

3 CSLFRF represents a major change from its 2020 predecessor, the CARES Act's Coronavirus Relief Fund (CRF). In addition to guaranteeing a larger allocation of federal funds to more jurisdictions than the CRF, the 2021 legislation provides for greater discretion in how local governments can use these funds (see Rocco and Kass 2022, 339, Table 1). While only 154 cities received CRF money, tens of thousands of local governments were eligible for CLFRF aid. Moreover, CRF aid to state and local governments turned out to be cumbersome to use because program rules required officials to demonstrate how the funds were used for necessary expenses related directly to COVID's health and economic impacts. Furthermore, the funds could not be used to replace revenue and maintain existing spending levels even though tax collections were negatively impacted by the pandemic (see Rocco and Kass 2022 for more elaboration).

4 Another way to conceptualize the importance of state aid to local governments is to calculate the proportion of IR that is accounted for by revenue received from one's state government. In 1962, state aid amounted to 87 percent of local governments' IR but declined steadily until the early 1980s (it was 78 percent in 1982) perhaps due to the greater availability of federal aid during this period (see Figure A8.1 in the Appendix). By 1987, the state aid proportion of IR had begun to climb again until the early part of the 21st century (when it reached a high of 85 percent in 1997) and likely the result of a robust economy for most of this time. By 2007, there were clear signs of a faltering economy (Great Recession), as the state aid percentage of IR dropped to 83 percent and declined even further to 81 percent by 2012 and remained at that level in 2017.

5 Unfortunately, the Census of Governments series reports state aid to local governments as an aggregated figure ("intergovernmental revenue from state government") and does not break down this figure into three separate categories (i.e., a proceeds from state revenue sharing, state grants-in-aid, and state payments to local governments in lieu of taxes). Therefore, it is not possible to conduct a more refined analysis of these data in this book.

However, we do know that most state aid money is in the form of revenue that states share with their local governments. Good examples are state revenues that are generated from taxes on general sales, intangible property, insurance licenses, mining of natural resources, gasoline, tobacco products, alcoholic beverages, transportation tolls and other user fees, various fines and administrative fees for legal recording purposes, proceeds for lotteries and gambling, etc. But, in all instances, the state determines the distributional formula, although some negotiation may take place.

6 Illinois is a good example of this influence (see Banowitz and Thomas 1983; Banowitz 2002; Benton 2018).

## References

Banowitz, James M. 2002. "Illinois Home Rule: A Case Study in Fiscal Responsibility," *Journal of Regional Analysis & Policy*, 32(1): 79–98.

———. and W. Kelty Thomas. 1983. "The Use (and Misuse?) of Illinois Home Rule," *Illinois Municipal Review*, 14: 11–14.

Benton, J. Edwin. 1985. "Federalism's 'First Principles' and Reagan's New Federalism Policies," *Policy Studies Journal*, 13(March): 568–75.

———. 1986. "Federal Grant-in-Aid Cut-Backs and State and Local Government Spending Policies." In Benton, J. Edwin, and David R. Morgan (eds.), *Intergovernmental Relations and Public Policy*. Westport, CT: Greenwood Press: 1–34.

———. 2002. "*Counties as Service Delivery Agents: Changing Expectations and Roles*." New York: Greenwood Press.

———. 2007. "George W. Bush's Federal Aid Legacy," *Publius: The Journal of Federalism*, 37(Summer): 371–89.

———. 2018. "Intergovernmental Relations in the Early Twentieth-First Century: Lingering Images of Earlier Phases or Emergence of a New Phase?" In Stenberg, Carl, and David Hamilton (eds.), *Intergovernmental Relations in the United States: Reflections and Directions*. New York: Routledge: 15–36.

———. 2019. "Local Government Service Roles in the U.S.: Constancy and Change." In Kerley, Richard, Joyce Liddle, and Pamela Dunning (eds.), *Handbook of International Local Government*. New York: Routledge: 183–202.

Berman, David R. 1993. "Counties, Other Governments, and the Future." In David R. Berman (ed.), *County Governments in an Era of Change*. Westport, CT: Greenwood Press: 135–42.

———. and Katheryn A. Lehman. 1993. "Counties, Change, and Reform: An Overview." In David R. Berman (ed.), *County Governments in an Era of Change*. Westport, CT: Greenwood Press: xi–xix.

Bowman, Ann O'M, and Richard C. Kearney. 1999. "*State and Local Government*." 4th ed. Boston: Houghton Mifflin Company.

DeSantis, Victor S. 1989. "County Government: A Century of Change." In *The Municipal Yearbook, 1989*. Washington, DC: International City/County Management Association): 55–84.

Donovan, Todd, Christopher Z. Mooney, and Daniel A. Smith. 2009. *State and Local Politics: Institutions and Reform*. Belmont, CA: Wadsworth/Cengage Learning.

Duncombe, Herbert S. 1977. *Modern County Government*. Washington, DC: National Association of Counties.

Dye, Thomas R. 1966. *Politics, Economics and the Public: Policy Outcomes in the American States*. Chicago: Rand McNally.

———. and Susan MacManus. 2015. *Politics in States and Communities*. 15th ed. Upper Saddle River, NJ: Pearson.

Easton, David. 1965. *A Systems Analysis of Political Life*. New York: Wiley.

Fisher, Ronald C, and Andrew Bristle. 2012. "State Intergovernmental Grant Programs." In Robert D. Ebel and John E. Petersen (eds.), *The Oxford Handbook of State and Local Government Finances*. New York: Oxford University Press: 213–45.

Kajfez, Laura J., John S. Hall, and Albert K Karnig. 1984. "Counties in the National Context." In John S. Hall and Albert K. Karnig (eds.), *County Government in Arizona: Challenges in the 1980s*. Phoenix, AZ: The Arizona Academy: 1–31.

Kass, Amanda, and Philip Rocco. 2021. "Will Recovery Funds Really Allow State and Local Governments to Build Back Better?" *Notes on the Crisis*, June 25. Accessed at: https://www.crisisnotes.com/will-recovery-funds-really-allow-state-and=local-governments-to-build-back-better?/

Marando, Vincent L., and C. Douglas Baker. 1993. "Metropolitan Counties and Urbanization." In David R. Berman (ed.), *County Governments in an Era of Change*. Westport, CT: Greenwood Press: 71–87.

Marando, Vincent L., and Mavis Mann Reeves. 1991. "Counties as Local Governments: Research Issues and Questions," *Journal of Urban Affairs*, 13: 45–54.

Marando, Vincent L., and Robert D. Thomas. 1977. *The Forgotten Governments: County Commissioners as Policy Makers*. Gainesville, FL: The University Presses of Florida.

Mikesell, John L. 2018. *Fiscal Administration: Analysis and Application for the Public Sector*. 8th ed. Boston: Cengage.

Pagano, Michael A., and Christopher W. Hoene. 2003. "'Fend-For-Yourself' Federalism: The Impact of Federal and State Deficits and American Cities," *Government Finance Review*, 19: 36–42.

Rocco, Philip, and Amanda Kass. 2022. "Flexible Aid in an Uncertain World: The Coronavirus State and Local Government Fiscal Recovery Funds Program," *State and Local Government Review*, 54(December): 346–61.

Salant, Tanis J. 1988. *County Home Rule: Perspectives for Decision Making*. Tucson, AZ: University of Arizona.

———. 1991. "County Governments: An Overview," *Intergovernmental Perspective*, 17(Winter): 5–9.

*Serrano v. Priest*, 487 P. 2d 1241. 1971.

Shannon, John. 1987. "The Return to Fend-For-Yourself Federalism: The Reagan Mark," *Intergovernmental Perspective*, 13(Summer–Fall): 34–37.

Streib, Gregory, and William J. Waugh Jr. 1991. "The Changing Responsibilities of County Governments: Data from a National Survey of County Leaders," *American Review of Public Administration*, 21(June): 139–55.

Washington Post. 2021. "Why Some State and Local Governments Are Desperate for More Stimulus Aid," Accessed at: https://www.washingtonpost.com/business/2021/02/15/biden-stimulus-state-local-aid/?arc404=true

## Appendix

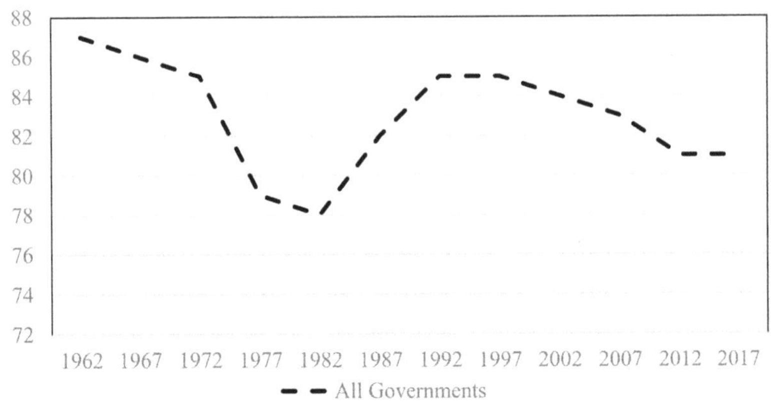


*Figure A8.1* State Aid to All Local Governments as a Proportion of Total Intergovernmental Revenue (IR), 1962–2017

*Source:* U.S. Bureau of the Census. Census of Governments. Compendium of Government Finances series, 1962–2017.

# 9 Borrowing

## The Means to Finance Capital Improvements

Local governments oftentimes act in ways much like the citizens they serve when it comes to financial matters. For instance, both governments and citizens for the most part prefer to follow a "pay-as-you-go" approach to making purchases. However, this is not always possible when there is a big-ticket item they want or need to purchase but do not have the cash readily available to pay for it in their wallet or in a checking or savings account. "Borrowing on time," as some people call it, has become as much of a tradition passed down from one generation to another as it is an American way of life. This is especially so for local government officials who are constantly expected to provide adequate facilities to educate children, house the offices of government employees and equipment, guarantee safe drinking water, dispose of sewage and solid waste, preserve the artifacts of history, offer a range of recreational and cultural amenities, construct and maintain streets and roads and install traffic signals for travel and safety purposes, or otherwise provide a large and varied menu of services. Without having the necessary financial resources in hand to pay for these things (typically referred to as "infrastructure" or "capital improvements") at the time of purchase or upon taking delivery of them, local governments usually borrow money so that their citizens can enjoy the benefits of services made possible by these facilities, equipment, materials, supplies, etc., on a daily basis while they simultaneously pay for them over a period of time.

While there are certainly similarities between private- and public-sector borrowing, there are also some important differences. Perhaps the biggest difference between public- and private-sector borrowing is the method or process each uses to borrow money. When individuals decide to borrow money, they usually go to a bank or savings and loan institution and apply for a loan. Upon obtaining personal and financial information from the person(s) seeking a loan as well as how much he/she/they wish to borrow, the lending institution conducts a credit check. If the credit check indicates that the person(s) applying for a loan is "credit-worthy," then the lending institution is likely to offer him/her/them a loan for a certain amount of money at an agreed upon interest rate with the principal plus interest to be paid back over a specific period of time. Once such

DOI: 10.4324/9781032640389-9

an agreement is reached, the lender provides the borrower with the loan money so that a desired purchase can be made and the lender begins making monthly payments.

For the most part, however, local governments are not accustomed to borrowing money in the manner described above.[1] Instead, local governments normally borrow money for an extended period of time (typically 5, 10, 15, 20, 25, or 30 years or so) through the sale of bonds. The process of selling local government bonds consists of several steps. First, the local government decides that it needs to borrow a specific sum of money for a particular capital improvement like a new city hall, fire station, water or sewer treatment plant, solid waste facility, library, civic center, school building, among other things. The next step is to find someone who is willing to buy the local government's proposed bond. Since the dollar amount of most bond issues are too large to be bought by a single investor and the issuer cannot effectively market the issue to large numbers of individuals.[2] The process of selecting an underwriter (the lender) is done either by negotiation or by competitive bidding (most likely method for full-faith and credit bonds and for many revenue bonds). Once the local government and underwriter agree to a maturity structure and schedule to repay the principal and interest, call provisions, and other required legal details, the local government (borrower) typically receives the entire proceeds quickly so that it can begin spending the money for the planned capital improvement. Meanwhile, the investor (underwriting firm) usually resells all or part of the bond issue to investors (i.e., individuals with readily available cash, life insurance companies, public and private pension funds, commercial banks, savings and loans institutions, mutual savings banks, nonfinancial corporate businesses, mutual and money market funds, and brokers). Normally, underwriters find it easy to identify willing investors, in that the interest earned from local government bonds can still be tax exempt under certain circumstances.[3]

Although not discussed here, local governments increasingly have been able to purchase much-needed infrastructure/facilities and acquire vital capital equipment through plans known as lease-purchase financing and certificates of participation.[4]

## Appropriate bond policy and bond guarantees

Borrowing is an acceptable and reasonable financial tool for local governments to acquire funds for public use. Of course, the debt from the borrowing must be repaid, with interest, in the future. Therefore, borrowing commits future budgets in the form of another encumbrance and the necessity of having to set aside future revenues to satisfy the debt normally over a number of years. This may also mean that local governments will be limited in the use of new revenue for other needs and desires of their citizens. For these reasons and the obvious contractual rigidity that comes with borrowing, debt must be issued with care. Succinctly stated, irresponsible use of debt can disrupt the lives of those paying taxes and expecting services in the future because debt service costs can impair the ability of the borrower to operate as it usually would.

Financial experts consistently remind local governments of several fundamental rules of borrowing policy. Perhaps the most well-known rule is that a government should not issue debt for a maturity (time period to repay it) longer than the financed project's useful life. Simply put, if, on the one hand, the debt life extends beyond the useful life of a project, then its real annual cost has been understated and citizens will continue to pay for the project after it is gone—bad thing that some would consider foolish (Mikesell 2018). If, on the other hand, the useful life exceeds the debt period, the annual cost has been overstated, and citizens will receive benefits without payment—good thing and desirable (Mikesell 2018). The timing-of-payment question is especially important across generations and, at the local level, across a local citizenry that is constantly changing.

A second, while related, fundamental rule is that long-term borrowing is an appropriate way for local governments to acquire long-life capital facilities. It is reasonable to assume that a community experiencing economic growth will normally require an expansion in publicly provided capital infrastructure like streets, sidewalks, streetlights, traffic signals, water supply, wastewater, and sewer facilities, government office buildings (fire/rescue and police stations), jails, new or expanded school facilities, libraries, parks, recreational, and cultural amenities, more courtrooms and offices for judicial personnel, for example. In such a scenario, a strong case can be made for borrowing money for infrastructure needs since future revenue streams should be adequate to service debt expansion. While some local governments may choose to use a pay-as-you-go financing approach (paying for capital facilities from current-year operating surpluses), most financial experts warn that such a policy can lead to both inefficiency and inequity (Mikesell 2018). Moreover, these same experts point out the virtue of debt financing producing annual debt service charges that are fixed by contract—that is, as an area's tax base grows, the tax rate required for debt service for a project will decline over time.[5]

While it is acceptable for local governments to borrow over the long-term for capital or infrastructure improvements, it is not appropriate to do so for normal day-to-day or reoccurring operating expenses. In fact, to do so would be an almost sure recipe for financial disaster for either individuals or governments. Even if a bank or savings and loan were to lend money to people (not very likely) to pay for common daily, weekly, or monthly expenses (food, clothing, housing, medical needs, insurance, entertainment, transportation, utilities, and so forth), such an unwise strategy would eventually catch up with them, as they would be unable to make regular payments without receiving any additional income. If such a financial strategy would not work for individuals or private-sector businesses, it certainly would not be a feasible financial game plan for governments. That is, governments, like individuals, must be able to meet their regular financial obligations—make payroll for their employees, set aside money for employee fringe benefits and pensions, remit federal and state (and sometimes local) income taxes, make mandatory contributions to Social Security, workman's compensation, Medicare, etc.—or bankruptcy is all but a certainty. In short, even the thought—much less the reality—of long-term borrowing for reoccurring expenses would be a doomsday financial approach that would turn out to be a certain "dead end street" for a government and its citizens.

Another essential rule of borrowing for local governments is to exercise caution so not to jeopardize their credit status (i.e., bond rating) as usually determined by Moody's Investor's Service, Standard & Poor's Investor's Company, and Fitch Investor's Service. Creditworthiness opinions issued by these three highly regarded services are critical in determining the interest rate paid by borrowing governments. Even a slight movement up or down in one's credit rating report can easily result in significantly less or greater amounts of interest money paid by a local government on a long-term bond issue. Perhaps the most important thing that governments can do to protect their credit rating (as it would be for individuals) is to make sure that payments are paid on time (like clockwork, as some would say). Nothing makes an investor (bond holder) nervous more than habitually late payments, and such behavior is always reported to these three credit rating companies and further disseminated to the investment community. Another "red flag" to avoid (or if experienced) is a reduction in the receipt of pledged revenues to repay the debt. This can occur in two ways. For most full-faith and credit bond issues, this would be the projected revenue from new taxes or increase in the rate of a current tax (usually a property tax). For revenue bonds, revenue shortfalls typically are the result of the failure of local governments to raise rates or prices charged to users of a service made possible by the construction of a facility to provide it (e.g., water or sewer treatment plant, electric power facility, sports stadium, and civic center). Credit ratings may also be lowered because a local government may not keep enough money in their "rainy day" or "contingency" fund to cover unexpected expenses/repairs or necessary maintenance costs to keep the facility functioning satisfactorily so as to maximize revenue yields. Regardless of the reason for any shortfall in pledged revenue to cover bond payments or keeping enough funds on hand for infrastructure repairs and maintenance, local governments must move quickly to make adjustments to the satisfaction of the bondholders and the credit rating service or run the risk of hurting their government's rating—or even worse—having their loan "called in." To provide further protection against a credit rating reduction or foreclosure on the debt, local governments in recent years have been able to do several things including but not limited to several forms of third-party guarantees such as state-credit guarantees, bank letters of credit, and buying bond insurance.[6] In addition, these kinds of guarantees, which reduce the risk associated with a bond, can even enable the borrower to obtain a lower interest rate.

In sum, while borrowing or incurring debt is a normal and often necessary part of local government financial operations, great care and sound judgment should be exercised at all times.

## Local government borrowing: An overview

All levels of government—federal, state, and local—have a long tradition of borrowing, but governments borrow for different reasons. While the federal government debt historically has been the result of war finance and efforts to stabilize the country's macro-economy (i.e., to deal with the twin challenges of unemployment and inflation), state and local governments typically have borrowed to finance capital-project construction (infrastructure[7]) and cover short periods within a fiscal year in which costs exceed cash on hand. While it is important to mention that government borrowing should never be misconstrued as evidence of poor fiscal management, it is equally important to remember that the borrower (governments) must always be mindful of the moral and legal obligation to the repay the resulting debt.

Given the enormous growth in the public's expectations of government over time (but especially since the end of World War II), it should not come as a surprise that all three levels of government have amassed huge amounts of debt and that this debt has grown significantly over the last three-quarters of a century. From the data in Table 9.1, it can be seen that total government debt outstanding in 2019 amounted to nearly $26 trillion, with the bulk of it—$22.8 trillion or 87.8 percent—belonging to the federal (national) government.[8] When total government debt is apportioned across the total U.S. population in 2019 (328.3 million people), it amounted to $79,031 per capita. Again, the bulk of per capita debt ($69,374) was attributable to the borrowing of the national government.

Total debt outstanding owned by state and local governments, while relatively small in comparison to the national government, is still substantial. The latest available data shown in Table 9.1 indicates that debt outstanding of states and their local governments—the product of borrowing by states, counties, municipalities, townships, special districts, and school districts—is approximately

*Table 9.1* Revenue Obtained by Borrowing of Federal, State, and Local Governments, 2019

| *Government Type* | *Amount (in millions)* | *Per Capita* | *% of Total* |
|---|---|---|---|
| Federal Governments | $22,775,547 | $69,374 | 87.8 |
| State and Local Governments | 3,170,325 | 9,657 | 12.2 |
| State Governments | (1,174,375) | (3,577) | (37.0) |
| Local Governments | (1,995,950) | (6,080) | (63.0) |
| TOTAL | 25,945,872 | 79,031 | 100.0 |

*Source:* U.S. Bureau of the Census. 2019 State & Local Government Finance Historical Datasets and Tables. Compendium of Government Finances (Washington, DC: Government Printing Office).

$3.2 trillion. These data also reveal that total local government debts are larger than are total state government debts (63 percent versus 37 percent). A significant proportion of this debt is long-term. This differs markedly from the federal government debt. Moreover, state and local government debt (but more so for the latter than for the former government) is usually issued for construction of identifiable life-long assets. Much of this debt is for education, transportation, public-utility infrastructure, and general government buildings. The borrowing results from the need to finance a discernible and particular kind of structure. Such an identification of purposes typically would be almost impossible for federal debt.

Examination of state and local government borrowing activity for the 1962–2017 period reveals that debt accumulation, for the most part, increased significantly for both governments (see Table 9.2). Local government debt, on average, increased by around 44 percent over every five-year period or by nearly 9 percent annually, while state government debt increased at a somewhat higher rate (about 55 percent during every five-year interval or approximately 11 percent on an annual basis). However, there have been three pauses in the growth rate of state and local governments' borrowing in recent years. One occurred between 1987 and 1992 when an economic downturn occurred toward the end of the George Herbert Walker Bush's presidency, while another reduction in borrowing happened between 1997 and 2002 that coincides with the 9/11 attack and a recession in the early part of the George W. Bush administration. The latest decline in the growth rate of borrowing by both state and local governments was recorded after 2007, as state and local officials apparently became more cautious about accumulating additional debt, given the economic uncertainty

*Table 9.2* State and Local Government Debt Outstanding, 1962–2017 (in millions of dollars)

| *Year* | *State and Local Governments* | *State Governments* | *Percent Change* | *Local Governments* | *Percent Change* |
|---|---|---|---|---|---|
| 1962 | 80,802 | 22,023 | — | 58,779 | — |
| 1967 | 113,659 | 32,472 | 47.4 | 81,187 | 38.1 |
| 1972 | 175,158 | 54,453 | 67.7 | 120,705 | 48.7 |
| 1977 | 259,658 | 90,300 | 65.8 | 169,458 | 40.4 |
| 1982 | 403,621 | 140,326 | 55.4 | 263,295 | 55.4 |
| 1987 | 732,131 | 265,551 | 89.4 | 461,580 | 75.3 |
| 1992 | 975,610 | 372,319 | 40.2 | 603,291 | 30.7 |
| 1997 | 1,421,501 | 456,657 | 22.7 | 464,844 | 59.9 |
| 2002 | 1,681,378 | 636,796 | 39.4 | 1,044,582 | 8.3 |
| 2007 | 2,408,620 | 937,109 | 47.2 | 1,471,511 | 40.9 |
| 2012 | 2,950,468 | 1,146,720 | 22.4 | 1,803,748 | 18.4 |
| 2017 | 3,068,055 | 1,159,804 | 1.1 | 1,908,251 | 5.8 |

*Source:* U.S. Bureau of the Census. Census of Governments. Compendium of Government Finances series, 1962–2017.

caused by the Great Recession and its aftermath.[9] More recent data for 2018 and 2019, along with anecdotal reports and information emanating from state and local public officials and the media, indicate that both governments still appear to be reluctant to incur additional debt because the much-anticipated full recovery from the Great Recession has yet to happen. Although we are still awaiting data for 2020 and 2021, it is reasonable to speculate that both state and local governments probably have continued to be reticent about taking on new debt, given the grave uncertainties about the economy during the COVID-19 pandemic.

Other summary data on state and local government borrowing activity provides further perspective on these government's debt profile. As can be seen from the data in Table 9.3, local governments, like their state governments, borrow substantial amounts of money on both a long- and short-term basis. Additionally, it is evident that both governments borrow significantly more money on a long-term rather than on a short-term basis. These data also show that local governments borrow more in both the long-term (about 63 percent more) and short-term (about 360 percent more) than do state governments. As explained earlier in this chapter, local governments historically have been more prone to encounter cash flow problems near the end of the fiscal year, as they are heavily reliant on property tax proceeds to make ends meet. As is usually the case in most local government jurisdictions, property tax payments trickle in slowly during the year (with most of them being remitted very close to the payment deadline). As a result, local governments commonly find it necessary to secure short-term "tax anticipation" loans to continue

*Table 9.3* State and Local Government Debt Outstanding, 1962–2017 (in millions of dollars)

| *Year* | *State Governments* | | | *Local Governments* | | |
|---|---|---|---|---|---|---|
| | *Long-Term* | *Short-Term* | *Short-Term Debt % of Total* | *Long-Term* | *Short-Term* | *Short-Term Debt % of Total* |
| 1962 | 21,612 | 411 | 1.9 | 55,455 | 3,324 | 5.7 |
| 1967 | 31,185 | 1,287 | 4.0 | 75,462 | 5,723 | 7.0 |
| 1972 | 50,542 | 3,912 | 7.2 | 108,556 | 12,607 | 10.4 |
| 1977 | 87,184 | 3,016 | 3.3 | 159,632 | 9,826 | 6.0 |
| 1982 | 175,565 | 2,311 | 1.3 | 248,200 | 15,904 | 6.0 |
| 1987 | 263,946 | 1,606 | .6 | 447,279 | 14,307 | 3.1 |
| 1992 | 369,370 | 2,949 | .8 | 584,774 | 18,516 | 3.1 |
| 1997 | 453,515 | 2,142 | .5 | 750,427 | 14,417 | 1.5 |
| 2002 | 618,152 | 18,644 | 2.9 | 1,019,984 | 24,598 | 2.4 |
| 2007 | 930,532 | 6,577 | .7 | 1,445,627 | 25,883 | 1.8 |
| 2012 | 1,131,253 | 15,468 | 1.3 | 1,975,585 | 28,163 | 1.6 |
| 2017 | 1,151,936 | 7,868 | .7 | 1,880,001 | 28,251 | 1.5 |

*Source:* U.S. Bureau of the Census. Census of Governments. Compendium of Government Finances series, 1962–2017.

to operate and thus be able to "pay the invoiced bills" on time as well as ensure that they can responsibly make expected employee payroll payments (along with obligatory federal and state government payments and employee fringe benefits contributions) at periodic intervals.

Another way of getting a better handle on local government debt and understanding the implications of local government borrowing (and perhaps, more importantly) how its plays into the overall picture of local government finances is to consider the amount of long-term debt issued as a proportion of the amount of long-term debt retired over time. This is particularly important since most local and state government debt is in the form of long-term borrowing. These data are presented in Table 9.4 and are especially enlightening and tell us a lot about the prudence that these governments exercised during periods of economic uncertainty. Two similar patterns for both states and their local governments are plainly evident. First, the ratio of the issuance of new debt to the retirement of old debt drops noticeably between 1977 and 1982. This is probably due to the back-to-back effects of a period of unprecedented double-digit inflation during the late 1970s and the early signs of the start of a recession in the early 1980s, as these governments were likely uneasy about increasing their debt load in these uncertain economic times. A similar trend that also suggests that states and their local governments were again exercising budgetary caution can be seen with the further decline in "the issuance of new debt to the retirement of old debt" ratio after 2007.

*Table 9.4* State and Local Government Long-Term Debt Issued and Retired, 1962–2019 (in millions)

| *Year* | *State Governments* | | | *Local Governments* | | |
|---|---|---|---|---|---|---|
| | *Long-Term Debt Issued* | *Long-Term Debt Retired* | *Ratio of Issued to Retired* | *Long-Term Debt Issued* | *Long-Term Debt Retired* | *Ratio of Issued to Retired* |
| 1962 | 3,122 | 1,065 | 2.931 | 6,440 | 3,149 | 2.045 |
| 1967 | 4,244 | 1,419 | 2.991 | 7.867 | 4,275 | 1.840 |
| 1972 | 8,495 | 2,225 | 3.818 | 13,609 | 5,949 | 2.288 |
| 1977 | 12,377 | 4,016 | 3.082 | 21,981 | 9,543 | 2.303 |
| 1982 | 32,333 | 21,888 | 1.477 | 30,114 | 13,641 | 2.208 |
| 1987 | 50,225 | 33,259 | 1.510 | 84,132 | 49,778 | 1.690 |
| 1992 | 70,081 | 44,966 | 1.551 | 87,866 | 55,578 | 1.581 |
| 1997 | 54,431 | 41,136 | 1.323 | 97,166 | 68,010 | 1.429 |
| 2002 | 104,150 | 64,906 | 1.605 | 158,533 | 96,979 | 1.635 |
| 2007 | 162,280 | 93,606 | 1.734 | 217,407 | 134,268 | 1.619 |
| 2012 | 137,075 | 138,552 | .989 | 204,731 | 194,453 | 1.053 |
| 2017 | 154,493 | 153,750 | 1.005 | 253,208 | 237,378 | 1.067 |
| 2018 | 149,861 | 136,765 | 1.096 | 244,321 | 211,444 | 1.155 |
| 2019 | 124,302 | 107,885 | 1.152 | 218,129 | 185,506 | 1.176 |

*Source:* U.S. Bureau of the Census. Census of Governments. Compendium of Government Finances series, 1962–2017 and the 2019 Annual Survey of State and Local Government Finances.

As noted earlier, this is likely to be another consequence of the Great Recession and the lingering effects of it that continued long after economists and financial experts had officially declared that the Great Recession had ended. Although there is no data yet available beyond 2019, it is reasonable to speculate from anecdotal comments from state and local public officials that the COVID-19-induced recession has caused their governments to continue their cautionary approach with respect to accumulating more long-term debt than they are paying off in the immediate future (see Benton, Rissler, and Wagner 2020).

Perhaps the most insightful information (data) that demonstrates the importance of the revenue local governments obtain through borrowing as well as the continuous need for local officials to exercise caution and practice sound fiscal principles is to calculate the borrowed-revenue proportion of total, overall revenue for these governments. These data are displayed in Table 9.5. As these data indicate, revenue obtained by counties, municipalities, townships, special districts, and school district through borrowing constitute a sizable percentage of all funds available to them. When considered as a percent of total local government revenues, borrowed money represents around 10 percent of all money available to these governments since the late 1980s. However, if intergovernmental revenue is excluded, borrowed money makes up a larger proportion of those funds (around

*Table 9.5* Borrowed Revenue of Local Governments as a Proportion of Total Revenue and Preliminary Revenue, 1962–2019

| *Year* | *Total Revenue*[1] | *Preliminary Revenue*[2] |
|---|---|---|
| 1962 | 13.6 | 19.5 |
| 1967 | 13.4 | 18.7 |
| 1972 | 10.5 | 16.5 |
| 1977 | 8.6 | 14.5 |
| 1982 | 8.3 | 13.6 |
| 1987 | 9.9 | 15.4 |
| 1992 | 9.2 | 14.1 |
| 1997 | 11.5 | 18.1 |
| 2002 | 9.4 | 15.2 |
| 2007 | 9.8 | 15.3 |
| 2012 | 11.0 | 17.0 |
| 2017 | 10.0 | 15.3 |
| 2018 | 11.1 | 13.5 |
| 2019 | 9.7 | 16.4 |

1 Includes own-source revenue, total intergovernmental revenue, and borrowed money.
2 Includes only own-source revenue and borrowed money.

*Source:* U.S. Bureau of the Census. 2017 Census of Governments. Compendium of Government Finances series, 196–2017 (Washington, DC: Government Printing Office) and the 2019 Annual Survey of State and Local Government Finances.

15-18 percent) that local governments can spend. These statistics underscore the importance of intergovernmental revenue (but particularly financial assistance from the states and, to a lesser extent, monetary aid from the federal government) in helping local governments carry out their varied functions and provide a host of services. This becomes even more evident in looking at the debt owed as a proportion of own-source revenue (OSR) since the Great Recession, ranging from 13.5 to 17.0 percent. If local government did not receive intergovernmental revenue or even smaller amounts of it, they would have tough options to make like cutting back what they do or raise taxes and/or fees and charges for services.

What we do not know as this book goes to press is the extent to which the COVID-19-driven recession has impacted the borrowing behavior of local governments. At this point, based on survey data collected by the ICMA, PEW, National League of Cities, National Association of Counties (NACo) and even some preliminary statistics compiled by the U.S. Bureau of the Census, we have learned that traditional revenues of local governments have dropped significantly since the spring of 2019. Moreover, according to a recent article (Benton, Rissler, and Wagner 2020), a representative sample of city and county leaders indicated that revenue receipts from a number of usually reliable sources (property and local option sales and income taxes, user fees/charges, shared state revenues, and even a number of miscellaneous proceeds) were down significantly. In addition, most of these same officials worried about how their governments were going to maintain current services levels and make regular bond payments unless the federal government came to the rescue sooner rather than later (Benton, Rissler, and Wagner 2020).

As we know, the Trump administration and Congress did provide some financial assistance in late 2019 and early 2020, but many medium-sized and small city and county officials criticized the funding scheme because it funneled most of the money to the states who, in turn, were to allocate it to their local governments (only cities with populations over 500,000 received a direct allocation). Many of these officials also voiced concerns that their states might keep most of the money to balance their own budgets, while a host of other officials in "red" states (where there was a Republican governor or Republican-controlled legislature or both) feared that the state would withhold funds from "blue" cities and counties" with a significant number of registered Democratic voters (see Benton, Rissler, and Wagner 2020). The early federal aid provided under the Trump administration was subsequently bolstered under the Biden administration in April 2021 when Congress enacted the American Rescue Plan Act (a $1.9 trillion stimulus package) and followed up with a $1.2 trillion Instructure Investment and Jobs Act in November. We will have to wait to see if these landmark pieces of federal legislation were able to provide local governments enough time to "get on their feet" and "make ends meet" until their traditional sources of revenue are able to recover from the blows of not one, but two recessions—that is, the Great Recession and the COVID-19-induced one. Lurking ominously in the background as this book goes to press, however, is a double-digit inflationary spiral that the country has not seen since the late 1970s that is wreaking havoc with the economy and threatens the prospects for a full recovery and a rebounding of historically reliable and bountiful local government revenue sources.

As the information presented thus far shows, local governments depend to a considerable extent on funds that are derived from sources other than taxes, fees, charges, and an assortment of miscellaneous revenues to balance their budgets and pay for a wide variety of infrastructure needs. Without this significant amount of additional revenue, local government would not be able to provide a large menu of services that are either mandated by their states and/or expected from their citizens. In short, borrowing is an important—indeed, critical—component of the overall picture of local government budgeting and efforts to "make ends meet." While local governments (like individuals) may prefer to operate on a pay-as-you-go budgetary approach, the necessity of borrowing as a means to bridge the gap between the traditional monetary resources that they have in hand and the funds that are required to perform vital requisite functions and provide expected services is a reality that local officials must live with on a daily basis.

## Dependency levels among different types of local governments

Now that we have seen the importance for local governments being able to augment the amount of money available to them from traditional revenue sources by borrowing money on a long-term basis to finance the cost of "big ticket" infrastructure costs, it is worth investigating the extent to which there are noticeable differences among the five types of local governments, as to the degree each type government relies on money received through long-term borrowing. Likewise, it is equally important that we also speculate as to those factors that may explain why some local governments seem to depend more on borrowed money than do their local government counterparts.

### *Borrowed money (outstanding debt): Differences among individual governments?*

One simple way to learn more about local governments' dependency on borrowing as a means to make ends meet and balance their budgets is to examine the proportion of total local government debt owned by counties, municipalities, townships, special districts, and school districts. These data are located in Figure 9.1. Here, we see that municipalities have historically accounted for the largest percentage of all local government debt. This is due to the fact that cities provide a wide range of services (public works, water supply, electric power, sewage collection and disposal, fire and police protection, parks and recreation activities, the arts and other cultural amenities, in addition to government administrative functions) that require huge investments in infrastructure and equipment (fire stations and

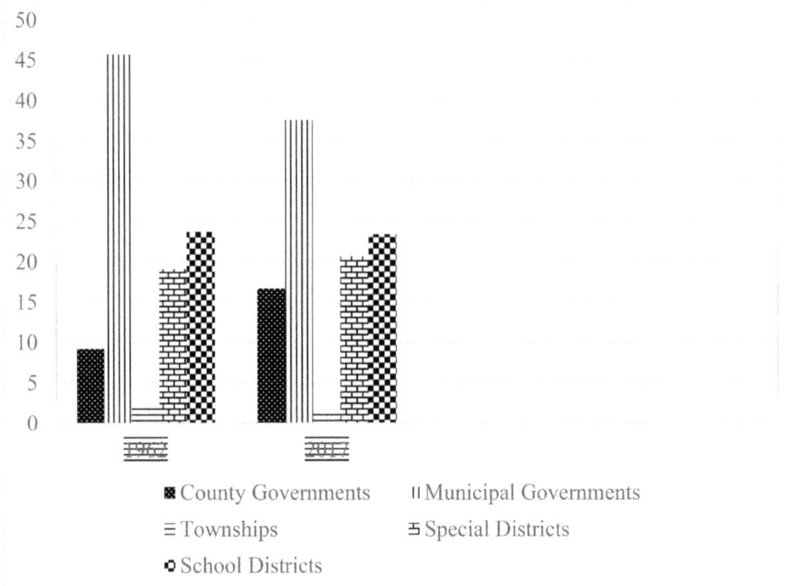


*Figure 9.1* County, Municipal, Township, Special District, and School District Proportions of Local Government Debt Outstanding, 1962 and 2017

*Source:* U.S. Bureau of the Census. Census of Governments. Compendium of Government Finances series, 1962–2017.

firefighting apparatus; officer's work space and detention facilities for police departments, along with police vehicles and equipment; water and sewage treatment plants and supply lines; heavy equipment, vehicles, office and storage facilities for public works functions, office buildings/facilities for administrative and support operations, museums, sports and civic facilities; streets and curbing; sidewalks; street lighting; traffic signals, just to mention a few). In 1962, nearly one-half of the total local government debt (46 percent) belonged to cities. By 2017, however, the municipal government share of local government debt had declined visibly to around 38 percent. A likely explanation for this decline, as discussed below, is the significant increase in the borrowing activity of county governments.

The next two largest users of borrowed money are special districts and school districts, with each accounting for around one-fifth of all local government debt. Oftentimes, special districts are created when citizens living in densely populated unincorporated areas demand the availability of municipal-type services even if they do not live in a municipality. In providing these type services, special districts would be expected to spend large sums of money (although not as much as cities do) to build requisite infrastructure and purchase equipment and supplies much like municipalities. Likewise, school districts must spend significant sums of money on infrastructure (primarily for acquiring property and constructing school buildings), as well as for purchasing instructional material, teaching equipment, and books and related materials for a school library. Therefore, special and school districts, like municipalities, normally find it necessary to borrow money to pay for these things that represent fixed costs since they do not have sufficient cash on hand or are able to generate enough revenue in one fiscal year. As a result, these governments' proportions changed very little over time.

Figure 9.1 also indicates that, as would be expected, townships (located in only 20 states and having a more limited service role) own the smallest amount of all local government debt.

The borrowing behavior of county governments, however, is an interesting case for a more detailed analysis. While these governments account for a smaller proportion of all local government outstanding debt than is true of municipalities and even school and special districts, their proportion nearly doubled between 1962 and 2017 (i.e., from 9 to 17 percent) and was similar to the proportion of special districts as of 2017. Is it plausible that this information is reflective of the changing service role of county governments as noted by several scholars who have studied counties for a long time (Schneider and Park 1989; Berman 1993; Benton 2002a, 2002b, 2003a, 2003b, 2022) have noted? These scholars' findings, along with several comprehensive longitudinal reports issued by the NACo and the former U.S. Advisory Commission on Intergovernmental Relations (ACIR) (Duncombe 1977; ACIR 1977), indicate that county governments, in general, and rapid growth counties, in particular, increasingly have had to play a much greater role in the delivery of a larger menu of municipal-type services (e.g., water supply, sewer collection and disposal, solid waste management, civic centers, sports stadiums/arenas, government buildings that provide public safety, transportation, administrative, and support functions, sidewalks, parks, and street lights) that require significant infrastructure investments.[10]

An examination of data for county governments from selective states provides a good test of the possible effect that population changes have on these governments' borrowing activity (see Table 9.6). Initially, let's compare the

*Table 9.6* County Government Percentage of Total Local Government Debt in Selective States with Different Levels of Population Growth Rates, 2017

| *National Average: 17 Percent* | | |
|---|---|---|
| *Rapid Growth* | *Moderate Growth* | *Slow/Negative Growth* |
| 7.8 (CA) | 26.9 (SC) | 9.3 (KS) |
| 12.9 (TX) | 20.6 GA) | 7.2 (IL) |
| 37.8 (FL) | 14.1 (AZ) | 25.3 (NJ) |

*Source:* U.S. Bureau of the Census. Census of Governments. Compendium of Government Finances series, 2017.

proportion of total local government borrowing accounted for by counties in the Nation's fastest growing states—California, Texas, and Florida. County governments in only one of these states (Florida) fit the hypothesized scenario whereby they would potentially need to make major investments in infrastructure due to significant surges in their population over a sustained period of time (see Benton 2002a). More specifically, county governments in Florida accounted for over one-third (38 percent) of total local government debt in 2017 compared to county governments in California and Texas (8 and 13 percent, respectively). In fact, Florida counties accounted for a much larger proportion of total local government debt than did the State's municipalities (38 versus 28 percent) and is also comparable to the proportion for all municipalities in the United States.

So, what sets apart county governments in Florida from counties in California and Texas and helps explain the apparent greater need for counties in the Sunshine State to rely on borrowing to balance their budgets? Simply stated, much of the significant population growth that Florida has experienced since the end of World War II has occurred in the unincorporated areas of the state and not in its cities (like what happened in California and Texas). This means that many county governments in Florida have increasingly been expected to provide a much larger and diverse set of municipal-type services than heretofore had been the case (see Benton 2002a). At the same time, counties were still required (in many instances, mandated) to provide costly staple services in the areas of health care, welfare, judicial/law enforcement, and voting administration that are part and parcel of their role as administrative arms and political subdivisions of the state.

Still, it is important to keep in mind that not all fast growth counties in Florida have large or rapidly expanding populations in their unincorporated areas. For example, Broward County with a population of nearly 2 million has only about 17,000 people living in unincorporated areas or less than 3 percent of its total population. Similar cases can be found in St. Lucie and Volusia Counties, although they have somewhat more people residing in unincorporated areas (77,000 and 117,000, respectively). However, 21 of Florida's 67 counties that have populations over 200,000 people also have over one-half of their residents living in the unincorporated area. In nine of these counties, the unincorporated area population makes up over 80 percent of the total county population. In several of the state's most populous counties—Hillsborough, Orange, Pinellas, Pasco, Polk, and Sarasota—around two-thirds of all county residents live in the unincorporated part of the county and expect the county government to provide many municipal-type services for which the county must borrow money to finance the construction of costly related infrastructure. And, even in some counties where the unincorporated area proportion of the population is smaller, there are still a substantial number of people that need municipal-type services (e.g., 1.2 million in Dade, 650,000 in Palm Beach, and 290,000 in Pinellas).

This information about Florida counties notwithstanding, several caveats need to be noted about the effects of population growth or the lack thereof after examining the data from other states (see Table 9.6). First, note that county governments in two of the three states listed in the "slow/negative growth" category (Illinois and Kansas) accounted for a significantly smaller proportions of total local government borrowing (7.2 and 9.3 percent, respectively) than did counties in Florida that had undergone major growth in their unincorporated areas. In fact, the county proportion in these states was much lower than that national average (16.7 percent). Yet, county governments in general in a third state in the same category (New Jersey) were responsible for the largest proportion of all local government debt. This may be explained by the out-migration of city residents to the unincorporated parts of some New Jersey counties over time, thus producing pressure on these county governments to provide a greater number of municipal-type services. Second, observe that county governments in two of the three states (South Carolina and Georgia) experience greater growth in their populations than the states in the "slow/negative growth" category and even the national average for counties but less than what the case is in the three rapid growth states accounted for a noteworthy proportion of all local government borrowing (26.9 and 20.6, respectively). This is undoubtedly due to the growth in the size of the unincorporated population in counties like Charleston, Dorchester, Horry, Lexington, and Greenville in South Carolina and Gwinnett, DeKalb, Cobb, Cherokee, and Bibb in Georgia. The fairly small proportion of total local government borrowing seen for county governments in Arizona is likely the result of a significant surge in the number of people moving there but have chosen to live in large- and medium-size cities like Phoenix, Tucson, Mesa, Flagstaff, Chandler, Gilbert, Glendale, and Scottsdale.

While there is certainly variability among local governments as to their reliance on borrowing to augment revenue derived from their own sources and intergovernmental fiscal assistance from their states and the federal government, all local governments, however, are most likely to borrow on a long-term as opposed to a short-term basis. As the data in Figure 9.2 indicate, most debt owned by each of the five types of local governments is long-term. In 2017, the long-term portion of all debt obligations ranged from 91 percent for townships to 99 percent for municipalities and special districts. From these data, it can also be inferred that, while local governments may continue to resort to short-term (tax anticipation) loans because of occasional shortfalls in revenue, most borrowing is for massive infrastructure needs where large sums of money can be paid off over a more convenient long-term period of time. A comparison of data for 1962 and 2017 shows that long-term debt as a proportion of total debt increased for four of our five types of local governments (the exception being townships), but especially for county governments and special districts. The higher proportions for counties and special districts are additional indicators of the expanding role that these two governments have had to assume in the provision of

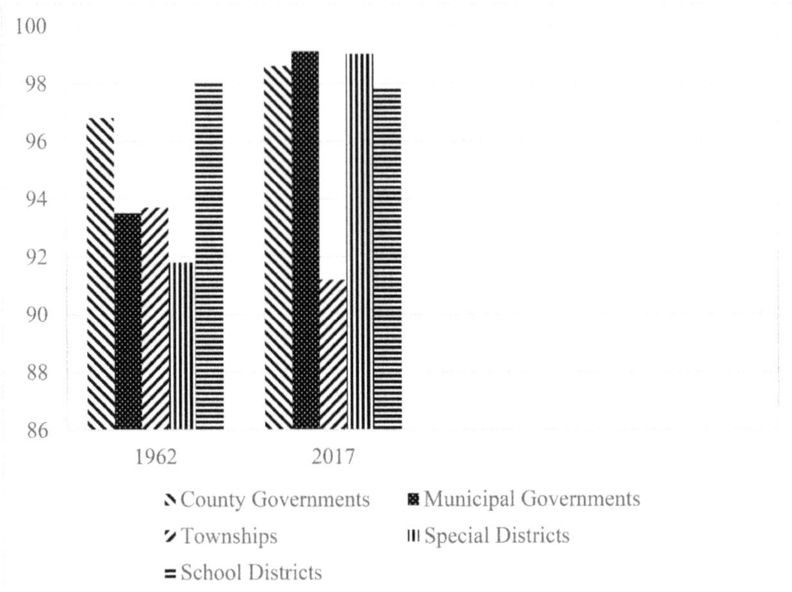


*Figure 9.2* County, Municipal, Township, Special District, and School District Proportions of Long-Term Debt, 1962 and 2017

*Source:* U.S. Bureau of the Census. Census of Governments. Compendium of Government Finances series, 1962–2017.

expensive, large-scale municipal-type services to unincorporated area residents and businesses.

### *Long-term debt issued and retired: A comparison of five governments*

Another way to differentiate between various local governments on the basis of their borrowing/debt patterns is to examine the amount of new debt issued and old debt retired over time. These data can tell us a lot about how counties, municipalities, townships, special districts, and school districts manage their need to borrow money in the long-term. It will be particularly important to see how these governments are able to balance the obligation to pay off old debt while simultaneously acquiring new debt.

First, let's look at their history of the issuance of new debt. From these data, which are presented in Figure 9.3, several patterns are noteworthy. One general observation is that there has been an overall upswing in incurring more debt since around 1982 (even if actual dollars are converted to constant dollars) for four of our five types of local governments (townships being the exception). This has especially been the case for municipalities and school districts (nearly

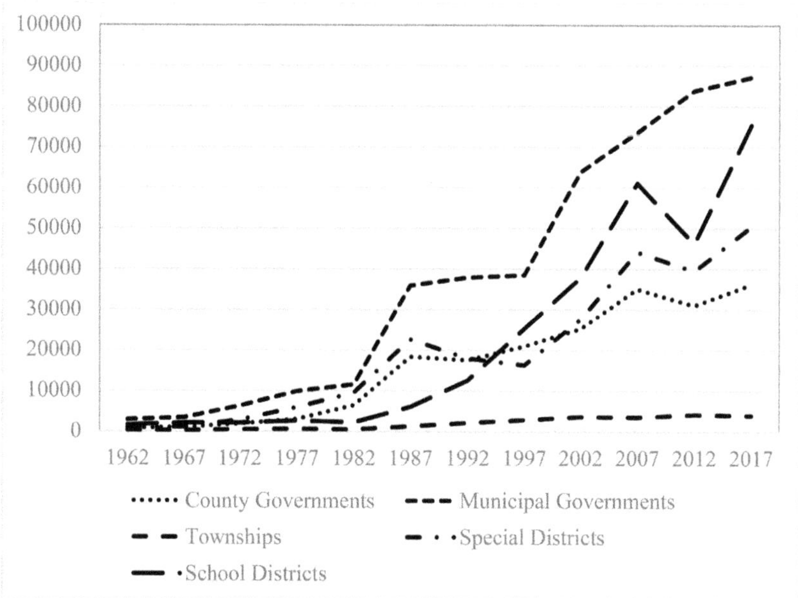


*Figure 9.3* Long-Term Debt Issued by Counties, Municipalities, Townships, Special Districts, and School Districts, 1962–2017 (in millions of dollars)

an eight and seven-fold increase, respectively). It is also clear from the figure that there was a slowdown in the issuance of new debt by counties, municipalities, and special districts between the late 1980s and the early 1990s that probably can be attributed to the recession that coincided with this period of time. Notice, however, that a pause in issuing new debt did not happen for school districts. This aberration is likely explained by the fact that education historically has been the chief policy priority of state and local governments and citizens have always been willing to spend more (even if sacrificially) to provide for a quality educational experience to prepare future generations for life, in general, and workforce needs, in particular. Once this recession was over by the early 1990s, the issuance of new debt began to increase noticeably for counties and special districts but even much more so for municipalities, while the upward spiral continued for school districts.

But, with the U.S. economy beginning to suffer from the effects of the Great Recession by 2007, the borrowing behavior of counties, school districts, and special districts curtailed significantly (overall declines compared to 2002), while municipal government borrowing continued its upward trend unabated. Nonetheless, the issuance of new debt by municipalities did slow down considerably with the onset of the Great Recession (i.e., the growth rate declined from 66 percent in the 2002–07 period to 14 percent in the 2007–12 period and decreased further to 4 percent) in the 2012–17 period as the Recession's lingering effects were causing municipal governments to be more cautious about incurring more debt. At the same time (2012–17), counties and special districts, while still exercising a fair amount of caution about taking on additional debt, did begin to borrow more during the 2012–17 period than they had in the previous five-year period that coincided with the Great Recession (2007–12). School districts, also apparently more confident in the economy after 2012, began to borrow at a higher level than even counties and special districts in the 2012–17 period.

What this analysis indicates is that local governments, for the most part, have become leery and indeed more cautious in accumulating more debt during recent downturns in the economy and are inclined to borrow less money with the end result having to delay or postpone infrastructure projects that are on their "to do" list. Is the same thing happening now because of the local governments' concerns about double-digit inflation? It will be interesting to find out once more recent financial data becomes available beyond the current endpoint (2017) of our analysis in this book.

Examining local governments' history of retiring old debt provides additional insightful information about their borrowing activity. At the same time, local governments are borrowing money for important infrastructure needs; they are also paying off old debt obligations. Data on the retirement of old debt is shown in Figure 9.4 and reveals some interesting patterns and trends.

Initially, it is plainly evident that there has been a consistent uptick in the amount of debt retired by for all five types of local governments (although somewhat less for townships) over time. Moreover, this trend seems to have accelerated just before the onset of the Great Recession and continued during the Recession itself and even for a considerable time after economists declared that the Recession had ended in 2009. It should also be noted that these trends hold when actual dollars are converted to constant dollars (data not shown here). Further inspection of Figure 9.4 indicates that the greatest increase in the retirement of old debt was recorded for municipalities. This finding would seem reasonable since municipalities have always been responsible for the largest proportion of all local government debt. Much smaller increases were found for school districts and special districts, while county governments were not too far behind. Given that townships have historically accounted for the smallest proportion of total retired local government debt, it was to be expected that they would have recorded the smallest amount of retired debt and an even smaller increases in debt retirement over the years. In light of these findings, it is will be important to find out if the current period of double-digit inflation and other negative economic indicators will have led to the same or greater efforts of local governments to pay off old debt at a quicker pace.

The picture that we have of net long-term debt comes into much sharper focus by jointly considering the net effect of both new debt issued and old net retired. To do this, we simply subtract the amount of debt retired from the amount of

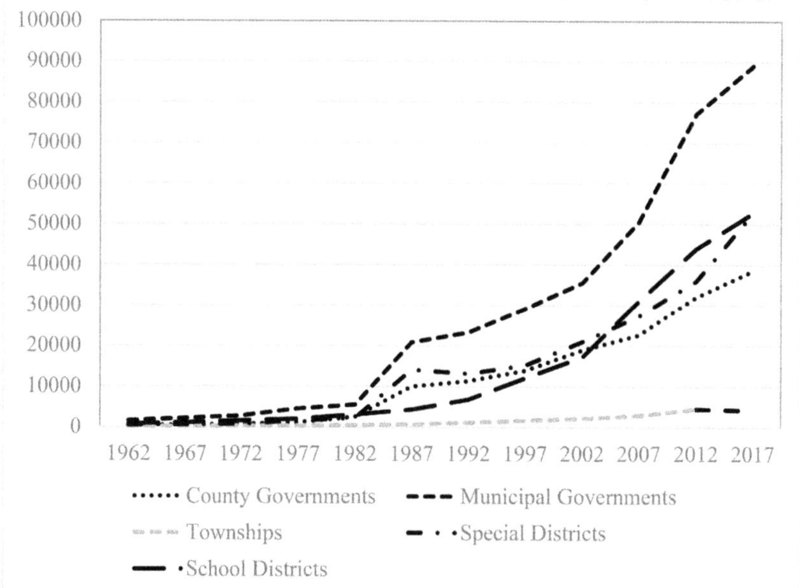


*Figure 9.4* Long-Term Debt Retired by Counties, Municipalities, Townships, Special Districts, and School Districts, 1962–2017 (in millions of dollars)

*Source:* U.S. Bureau of the Census. Census of Governments. Compendium of Government Finances series, 1962–2017.

newly issued debt at any given period in of time. The difference that is obtained should be especially helpful in determining the extent to which local government officials are mindful of and responsive to the likely negative fiscal impact of borrowing for their jurisdiction in times of a rapidly deteriorating economy. These data, which can be thought of as the "net increase/decrease in long-term debt," are found in Figure 9.5.

As we know, local governments in the last 30 years or so have had to deal with more than their fair share of unstable, poorly performing economies and the most significant downturn in the U.S. economy since the Great Depression of the 1930s (Great Recession of 2007–09). Upon initial examination of the figure, it can be seen that an earlier period of double-digit inflation that occurred in the late 1970s had a discernable effect on the borrowing behavior of three of five local governments. For school districts, the dollar amount gap between the issuance of new debt and the retirement of old debt shrank significantly. In fact, the dollar amount for the retirement of old debt actually exceeded the dollar amount for the issuance of net debt. From the figure, it is also apparent that the net long-term gap dropped sharply for townships, while the gap for municipalities continued to grow albeit at a noticeably much slower pace.

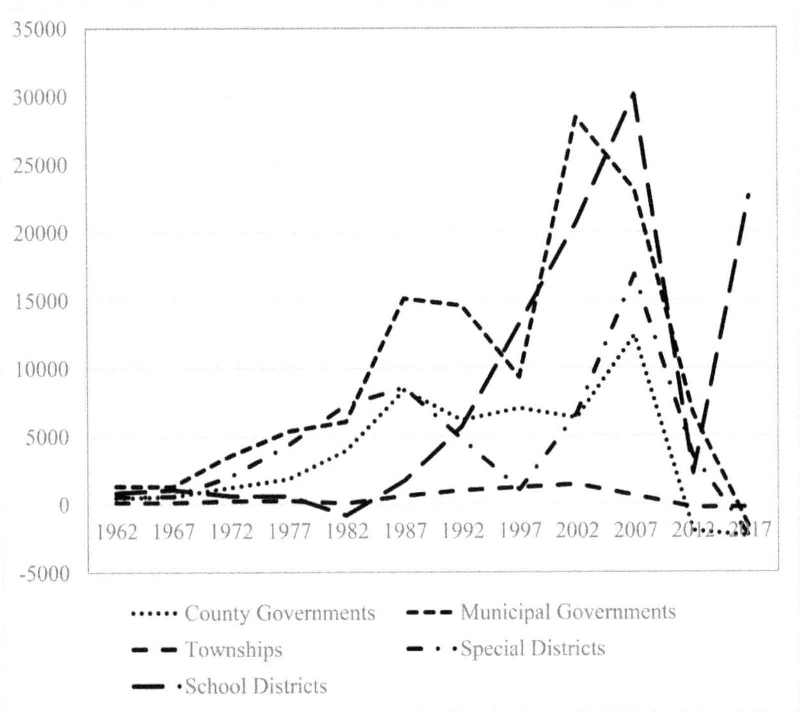


*Figure 9.5* Net Long-Term Increases/Decreases in Debt of Counties, Municipalities, Townships, Special Districts, and School Districts, 1962–2017 (in millions of dollars)

*Source:* U.S. Bureau of the Census. Census of Governments. Compendium of Government Finances series, 1962–2017.

Further inspection of Figure 9.5 suggests that the recession of the late 1980s likely had a considerable effect on the debt management behavior of three of five local governments. Specifically, noticeable declines in the new debt issued/old debt retired dollar amount differences were reported by counties and special districts, whereas the differences for municipalities were somewhat smaller but still an important departure from patterns of previous years. Furthermore, these patterns continued for special districts and municipalities until 1997 with differences shrinking even more, as differences for county governments rose only slightly.

Then, the Great Recession occurred and appears to have had a longer-lasting influence on local government debt management practices. This is unusual, as local governments typically will "tighten their belts" with spending and exercise a bit more caution when borrowing until a recession ends and will then resume a "business as usual" approach to spending and debt management soon thereafter.[11] However, based on further inspection of Figure 9.5, this does not seem to have happened after the Great Recession had been officially declared "over." More specifically, it appears that four of five local governments continued to maintain a very cautious posture with respect to how they managed their debt activities long after economists and Wall Street had declared that the Great Recession had ended. This conclusion is clearly supported by Figure 9.5 which reveals that the dollar amount gap between the issuance of new debt and the retirement of old debt dropped sharply for counties, municipalities, special districts, and school districts between 2007 and 2012, but, perhaps more importantly, by the fact that the gap continued to decrease markedly for three of the four governments from 2012 to 2017. The gap also closed for townships, but it was not nearly to the degree as seen for counties, municipalities, and special districts. In sum, these data strongly suggest that the dislocation suffered by most local governments (the exception may be school districts) may be long-term if not permanent.

Notwithstanding and before the Nation could recover fully from the Great Recession, another recession caused by the COVID-19 health pandemic was in the making by the middle of 2019 and resulted in massive involuntary unemployment and underemployment. And, if that were not enough, the U.S. economy by mid-2021 was beset with spiraling double-digit inflation that was likely triggered by supply chain problems for most essential domestic consumer products.[12] Unfortunately, to some degree, the inflationary spiral could have also been made worse by an over-saturation of the economy with federal stimulus money that was intended as relief for the American public, medical facilities, and cash-strapped state and local governments.

It may be a decade or longer before we are able to assess completely the impact that the COVID-19-induced recession coupled with a prolonged period of double-digit inflation will have had on local government borrowing behavior. With that said, it is fair to infer that the art and practice of debt management are currently in a state of turmoil or "uncharted waters," as most local government officials find themselves in the unenviable position of trying to chart a course of action with respect to debt management that permits them to balance the infrastructure and service needs of their jurisdiction for today without doing harm to their long-term finances. It is, to say the least, a tricky business to make these kinds of decisions in an uncertain economy. In fact, there are reports (see Chapman 2021 and Lofton and Kioko 2021) that some local governments have engaged in short-term borrowing to reduce or postpone annual expenses, raise operating capital, and restructure otherwise damaged finances, and, in essence, paying for projects that previously were paid for with cash. Other observers (McNamee 2004; Benton 2009, 2012, and 2018 and Benton, Rissler, and Wagner 2020) have speculated that the above-mentioned twin nemeses could result in a "new normal" for local government debt management and borrowing policy.

### *Ratio of outstanding debt to revenue: Differences among types of local governments?*

If we accept that borrowing is an integral part of what local governments must do in order to "make ends meet" and to satisfy the service expectations and needs of their citizens, then it is important that local officials determine an optimal level of debt for their jurisdiction to carry relative to their normal expected revenue. Simply put, local governments must wisely use their capability to borrow money so as to be able to build and maintain adequate infrastructure while also at the same time be mindful as to what their citizens can afford in the way of paying off the debt. Over the years, most local officials have been responsible stewards of the public's money and exercised good judgment when they believed it necessary to borrow. In the end, it must be remembered, that responsible and successful debt management just doesn't happen…it must be carefully planned, nurtured, and constantly monitored.

How have our five types of local governments fared in this regard? Data on the ratio of outstanding long-term debt to both OSR and total revenue (TR) from 1962 to 2017 for each type government local government (see Figures 9.6 and 9.7, respectively) assists in answering this question.

Looking first at the "debt to OSR" ratio (Figure 9.6), one sees that the ratios are quite similar for four of the five local governments (the exception being special districts), but particularly for counties, townships, and school districts. This observation is reinforced by the mean ratios shown below the graph. The mean ratio for municipalities is a little higher but expected since these governments typically are more likely to have to invest in expensive capital improvements like water treatment plants, sewer disposal facilities, civic and sports centers and arenas, streets and public transit, storm water management infrastructure, and government buildings. Based on both a visual inspection of Figure 9.6 and the range statistics, it should also be noted that there has been very little fluctuation in the ratios for these four governments over the 1962–2017 period.

In looking again at Figure 9.6, it is very clear that the necessity to borrow large sums of money for capital improvements is markedly greater for special districts, as is evident by the much higher "debt to OSR" mean ratio. Like municipalities, special districts must also construct some of the same kinds of costly capital improvements, plus things like hospitals, airports, mass transit, public housing, and conservation needs. In fact, it is not unusual for the capital outlay portion of most special district budgets to contain a much larger proportion of district funds than is the case for the operating side of these governments' budgets. This means that a large part of the charges for services collected by special districts are used to repay debt obligations and not to pay for salaries and fringe benefits of district employees. It is also important to note that in spite of the very large range in the "debt to OSR" ratios for special districts over time, it

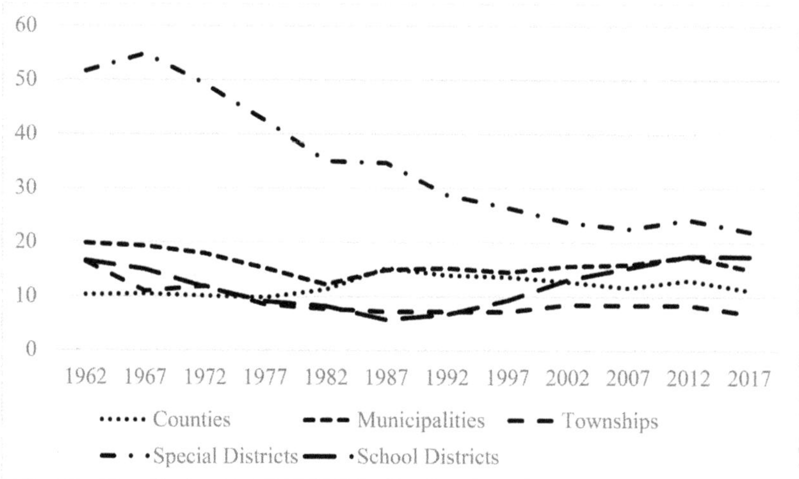


| | County Gov'ts | Municipal Gov'ts | Townships | Special Districts | School Districts |
|---|---|---|---|---|---|
| Range | 5.4 | 7.6 | 5.1 | 32.8 | 9.9 |
| Mean | 11.9 | 16.9 | 11.1 | 34.6 | 12.1 |

*Figure 9.6* Ratio of Long-Term Outstanding Debt to Own-Source Revenue (OSR) for Individual Local Governments, 1962–2017

*Source:* U.S. Bureau of the Census. Census of Governments. Compendium of Government Finances series, 1962–2017.

is nonetheless evident that the ratio has declined substantially over time, but especially in recent years. In 2017, the ratio was 16.1 percent and not much higher than what is was for municipalities (12.0 percent).

A clearer (and perhaps more discerning or realistic) picture of local government debt as a proportion of these governments' revenue can be obtained if we consider a broader definition of "local government revenue." Instead, it might make more sense to substitute "total revenue" for "own source revenue." In this way, we can conceptualize the "debt to revenue" ratio to take into consideration all of the monetary resources at the disposal of local governments. After all, many federal and state grants contain specifically designated funds for local government infrastructure projects like water, sewer, storm-water facilities, police, fire, library, public works, and similar type public buildings, cultural, recreational, and sports complexes, housing construction and rehabilitation, public transportation, airports, and hospitals. Therefore, it will be instructive to view the "debt to revenue" ratio through a sharper lens when conceptualized as total outstanding debt as a percentage of TR.

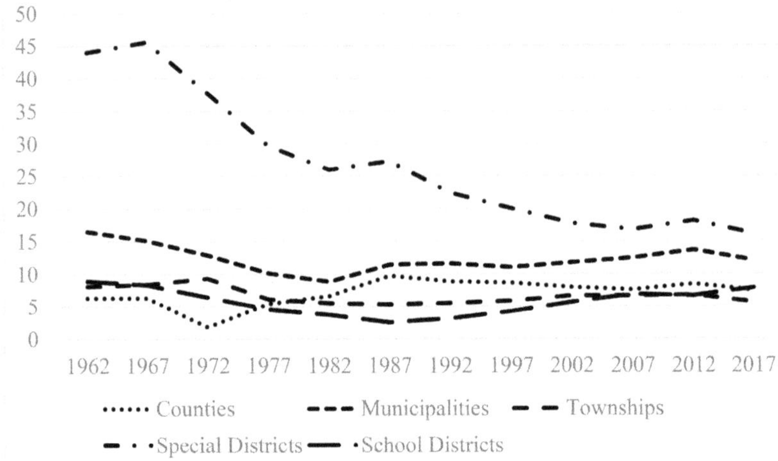


| | County Gov'ts | Municipal Gov'ts | Townships | Special Districts | School Districts |
|---|---|---|---|---|---|
| Range | 4.3 | 7.7 | 4.0 | 29.5 | 7.4 |
| Mean | 7.4 | 12.3 | 6.6 | 26.8 | 5.8 |

*Figure 9.7* Ratio of Long-Term Outstanding Debt to Total Revenue (TR) for Individual Local Governments, 1962–2017

*Source:* U.S. Bureau of the Census. Census of Governments. Compendium of Government Finances series, 1962–2017.

In examining Figure 9.7 and the accompanying statistics, very similar patterns and trends are visible when using the reformulated measure of the "debt to revenue" ratio. That is, there were very small differences in the means (and even ranges) for counties, townships, and school districts, while the mean for municipalities was a little larger and likely due to these governments having to make greater investments in multi-million dollar infrastructure projects and facilities. A comparable pattern was also found for special districts whereby the "debt to TR" ratio was much larger than what was the case for the other four types of local governments.

Again, it was apparent that the "debt to revenue" ratio for special districts has dropped noticeably over the last 55 years, and more so since the mid-1980s.

When comparing these two different sets of "debt to revenue" ratios (one where revenue is measured as OSR and the other measured as TR) that are plotted in Figures 9.6 and 9.7, it become readily evident that the availability of generous amounts of intergovernmental fiscal assistance means that the burden of borrowing money to pay for necessary infrastructure is made lighter for local governments. The largest proportion of this intergovernmental assistance, as documented in other chapters of this book, comes from the "parent" of local governments—state governments. This is as would be expected since local governments are creatures of their states and were established to assist them in the provision of basically state-level services albeit at the local level. This is yet another of the many decentralized features found in the American federal system of government.

## Conclusions, summary observations, and thoughts

Based on a reading of this chapter, it is reasonable to conclude that local governments would be hard-pressed, if not find it impossible, to provide their current wide array of important (many times, mandated) services, along with the necessary infrastructure, without the ability to borrow large amounts of money. In short, being able to borrow enables local governments to close the gap between the sum total of expected OSR and intergovernmental funds so that they can satisfy citizen needs and expectations. As noted at the outset of this chapter, borrowing to "make ends meet" has become a "settled institution" or even a "necessary evil" in the real world of local government finances.

As everyone knows, borrowing money to help pay for part of the cost of government operations is nothing new. While the federal government overshadows all governments by the use of borrowing, local governments borrow substantial sums of money (even more than their states) to "stretch" their financial resources in order to satisfy their citizens' appetite for a long list of services and programs. Most of the debt that local governments incur when borrowing is in the form of long-term obligations with most of the proceeds going to finance a wide variety of infrastructure projects, usually referred to as "capital improvements." Since 1982, there has been a significant increase in long-term debt for four of the five types of local governments (the exception being townships), with the largest increases recorded for municipalities and school districts. While not as great, the increase in borrowing among county governments is noteworthy and is likely reflective of the greater expectations of these governments (but especially ones with a large proportion of unincorporated area residents) to provide a number of new municipal-type services. In spite of borrowing larger amounts of money over time, the ratio of borrowed money to both OSR and TR has remained remarkably steady. In addition, it is important to mention that local government borrowing activity has tended to slow down during downturns in the economy, which was particularly obvious during the Great Recession and its lingering aftermath. Could the COVID-19 pandemic-driven recession and ensuing double-digit inflation cause local government officials to continue their much more cautious approach to borrowing in the foreseeable future?

## Notes

1 Under certain kinds of circumstances, local governments sometimes may borrow money in a similar manner. These types of loans are usually in the form of what are referred to as short-term "tax anticipation" loans. Such loans are often necessary because of the uneven flow of money being spent and collected by local governments during the fiscal year. Local governments (like individuals) must satisfy financial obligations when they incur expenses and receive an invoice. Many times, however, expenses accrue faster than local governments can collect the revenue that is due to them (this is especially the case for the receipt of property tax revenue that is usually not due until near the end of the fiscal year). This, of course, creates a cash flow problem. Simply put, bills are due, and local governments do not have enough money on hand to pay them. It is then that local governments "shop around" for the cheapest interest rate to borrow enough money to pay their bills and "make payroll" over the next few months (normally two to four) until citizens and businesses pay their property taxes for which they have been billed and the local government "anticipates" it will receive. In fact, it is not unusual for an overwhelming proportion of property tax payments to be made close to the payment deadline. Upon receiving what many local officials refer to as "an avalanche of property tax money" that eases the cash flow problem, the local government repays the balance of the money they have borrowed, aptly called a "tax anticipation loan."

From time to time, local governments have also found it necessary to borrow money on a short-term basis from conventional lending institutions to cover unanticipated expenses due to emergencies such as hurricanes, flooding, or other types of natural disasters. This money is typically paid back when adjustments are made to the budget of the current fiscal year or additional funds are added the next year's budget.

2 For more details, see Mikesell (2018, 702).

3 See Mikesell (2018, 686–88) for the impact of the Tax Reform Act of 1986. For more specific information about local government borrowing, consult Chapter 15 in Mikesell (2018).

4 Additional information about these alternatives to the sale of long-term bonds by local governments is provided by Mikesell (2018, 708–09).

5 Among the concerns expressed by local government financial experts, three are mentioned most often according to Mikesell (2018). Given the inevitability of population mobility, users of capital infrastructure facilities would not pay a fair charge fee (those in taxing range would pay when the facility is built but may not be there when the facility for which they have paid for is actually providing services). Then, an excessive high single-year price tag for a major project may discourage construction, regardless of the soundness and practicality of the project. In addition, significant tax-rate unpredictability (artificially high rates during the construction phase and artificially low rates during operation) is not likely to promote the healthy and stable development of the local economy.

6 For fuller discussion and details about these three types of bond guarantees, see Mikesell (2018, 700–02).

7 For an excellent discussion of the intricacies of and challenges to crafting infrastructure financing plans, see Chen and Bartle (2017).

8 It should be noted that there is no meaningful linkage of borrowing to particular capital expenditure projects since federal debt levels are the accumulated totals of deficit outcomes.
9 It is important to mention that the growth rate in local government borrowing also decreased noticeably between 1997 and 2002. It is likely explained by local leaders' uneasiness about the impending recession that began to appear in the late 1990s and continued into the first decade of the 21st century.
10 Added to this list would be public school buildings in three states (Maryland, North Carolina, and Tennessee) where county governments provide K-12 education and community colleges and technical education schools.
11 The cutback management literature contains countless studies that describe the typical local government response to recessions (Levine 1978; Levine, Rubin, and Wolohojian 1981; MacManus 1993; Hoene and Pagano 2003; LaPlant 2012).
12 As this book goes to press, current levels of double-digit inflation (reaching as high as 14–15 percent beginning in late summer 2021) brought on by supply chain slowdowns and interruptions due to lagging effects of the COVID-19 health pandemic could also result in a similar drop in the ratio of the issuance of new debt to the retirement of old debt.

## References

Benton, J. Edwin. 2002a. "*Counties as Services Delivery Agents: Changing Expectations and Roles*." Westport, CT: Praeger.

———. 2002b. "County Service Delivery: Does Structure Matter?" *Public Administration Review*, 62: 423–31.

———. 2003a. "County Government Structure and County Revenue Policy: What's the Connection?" *State and Local Government Review*, 35(Spring): 78–89.

———. 2003b. "The Impact of Structural Reform on County Government Service Provision," *Social Science Quarterly*, 84: 858–74.

———. 2009. "Coping with Forclosures." In Miller, Gerald J., and James H. Svara (eds.), *Navigating the Fiscal Crisis: Tested Strategies for Local Leaders*. Washington, DC: ICMA/Alliance for Innovation: 49–51.

———. 2012. "State-City and State-County Fiscal Relations: A Look at the Past and Present and a Glimpse at the Future." In Meek, Jack W., and Kurt Thurmaier (eds.), *Networked Governance: The Future of Intergovernmental Management*. Washington, DC: Sage/CQ Press: 39–63.

———. 2018. "Intergovernmental Relations in the Early Twentieth-First Century: Lingering Images of Earlier Phases or Emergence of a New Phase?" In Stenberg, Carl, and David Hamilton (eds.), *Intergovernmental Relations in the United States: Reflections and Directions*. New York: Routledge: 15–36.

———. 2022. "USA: Intra-State Governments in the United States: Powers and Authority, Elections, Finances, and Intergovernmental Relations." In Kerley, Richard, Colin Copas, and Alistair Jones (eds.), *Intra-State Governments: National, Local and Intermediate Governments in 24 Countries*. Cheltenham Gros, UK: Edward Elgar Publishing: 81–99.

Benton, J. Edwin, Grant Rissler, and Spencer Wagner. 2020. "City and County Governments in the Time of COVID-19: The Long and Winding Road," *State and Local Government Review*, 51: 28–52.

Berman, David R. (ed.). 1993. "*County Governments in an Era of Change*." Westport, CT: Greenwood Press.

Chapman, Jeff. 2021. "State and Locals Relied on Debt for Budgetary Help in 2021." PEW Institute. January 28, 2021. Accessed at: https://www.pewtrusts.org/en/research-and-analysis/articles/2021/01/28/state-and-local-governments-relied-on-debt-for-budgetary-help-in-2020

Chen, Can, and John R Bartle. 2017. "*Infrastructure Financing: A Guide for Local Government Managers*." Washington, DC: International City/County Management Association and Government Finance Officers Association.

Duncombe, Sidney. 1977. "*Modern County Government*." Washington, DC: National Association of Counties.

Hoene, Christopher W, and Michael A Pagano. 2003. "Fend-for-Yourself Federalism: The Impact of Federal and State Deficits on America's Cities," *Public Finance Review*, 19(5): 36–42.

LaPlant, Josephine M. 2012. "A Framework for Deciphering and Managing the Fiscal Environment." In Helisse Levine, Eric Scorsone and Jonathan Justice (eds.), *Handbook in Local Government Fiscal Health*. Burlington, MA: Jones & Bartlett Learning: 285–320.

Levine, Charles H. 1978. "Organizational Decline and Cutback Management," *Public Administration Review*, 38: 316–25.

Levine, Charles, Irene Rubin, and George G Wolohojian. 1981. "*The Politics of Retrenchment: How Local Governments Manage Fiscal Stress*." Beverly Hills, CA: Sage.

Lofton, Michelle L, and Sharon N Kioko. 2021. "The Use of Short-Term Debt by General-Purpose Governments," *Public Budgeting & Finance*, 41(Winter): 71–93.

McNamee, Roger. 2004. "*The New Normal: Great Opportunities in a Time of Risk*." New York: Penguin Books.

MacManus, Susan A. 1993. "Budget Battles: Strategies of Local Government Officers during Recession," *Journal of Urban Affairs*, 15(3): 293–307.

Mikesell, John L. 2018. "*Fiscal Administration: Analysis and Applications for the Public Sector*." 10th ed. Boston: Cengage.

Schneider, Mark, and Kee Ok Park. 1989. "Metropolitan Counties as Service Delivery Agents: The Still Forgotten Government," *Public Administration Review*, 49: 345–52.

U.S. Advisory Commission on Intergovernmental Relations (ACIR). 1977. "*Profiles of County Government*." Washington, DC: Government Printing Office.

# 10 The Ever-Present Challenge to Fund Local Government Operations

## The 21st Century and Beyond

In reminiscing about and reflecting on their long journey through life or just taking stock of the reality of the world they have lived in and where it seems to be heading, senior adults often say to their children, grandchildren, and even great-grandchildren that "times are changing and you must be ready to adapt to it!" I still vividly remember both of my grandfathers who were born in the late 1800s and lived through the profound shock of the Great Depression offering these words of wisdom and encouragement to me as a young boy in the late 1950s. Surely, this perspective they shared with me about the world they had seen and experienced, while not new, is filled with a certain truism that heralds the necessity of keeping up with the times and being able to successfully respond to the day-to-day challenges that await every new generation. Indeed, time certainly does not stand still for anyone and history will judge every new generation accordingly.

The same holds true for governments, including local governments, as they endeavor to dutifully respond to the service needs and demands of their residents. In so doing, local officials must always be mindful of the simultaneous responsibility to provide quality services at a reasonable cost to their citizen customers. This is no easy task to accomplish in a world where recessions, inflation, and other intangibles raise the cost of providing services, while local officials must also be keenly aware of what their residents are able to afford. Other factors also loom on the horizon that can thwart the most well-meaning and well-planned attempts of local officials to make ends meet in crafting a budget for their jurisdiction. Any unforeseen jolt to the economy—be it a debilitating recession with a tremendous loss of jobs or rampant inflation that erodes the purchasing power of the dollar and a health pandemic like COVID-19—can throw a huge "monkey-wrench" in the delicate job of balancing the local government budget. Such are the times we live in now as we are trying to deal with the impact of the COVID-19 pandemic and the ensuing economic uncertainty. How does a nation endure and emerge from this pandemic that continues to exact its toll on the health of the U.S. (and world) population (serious illness and over a million deaths as this book goes to press) and result in the temporary, if not permanent shuttering of businesses with attendant high levels of unemployment?

DOI: 10.4324/9781032640389-10

Certainly, history will record how our governments responded, and most importantly, how we fared.

Given this context, the purpose of this book has been to provide a detailed account as to how local governments have endeavored to satisfy citizenry service expectations with the focus primarily being on the revenue side of the budget. Succinctly put, this book has sought to present the reader with an "upfront and close," general to minute, and exhaustive account of the awesome task of raising sufficient revenues to fund adequately the cost of providing myriad local government services. To that end, this book has been purposively organized to examine local government revenue patterns and trends since 1962 for the following major sources of money: property, sales, income, and other types of taxes; charges for services/user fees; miscellaneous sources; intergovernmental funding, and borrowing money through the sale of bonds.

The remainder of this concluding chapter will be divided into two primary sections. The first section will be retrospective in scope in that it will present a brief summary and review of local government revenue patterns and trends since 1962 or "the road already taken." Here, the numbers will tell the story of how local governments have chosen to fund the cost of the services and programs they have provided to this point. The second section ("the road lying ahead") will be prospective or forward looking at ways in which revenue patterns/trends and approaches may or should change in the future due to revenue inadequacies in the past, criticism of the rationale behind certain revenue sources, unfair inequitable impact of various revenue sources, or changes in the public's thinking of local governments' role in providing specific services/programs.

## The road already taken: Revenue patterns and trends of the last 55 years or so

As would be expected, the total amount of revenue collected by all local governments in the United States from 1962 to 2017 has increased many fold, even when the amount is measured in constant dollars. Moreover, this trend is plainly evident for each of the five types of local governments—counties, municipalities, townships, special districts, and school districts. Like any other enterprise, the cost of running local governments, over time, has risen as a result of the citizenry's increasing appetite for more services and, of course, inflationary forces. In 1962, all local governments raised $43.2 billion in revenue; by 2017, this amount had skyrocketed to $1.7 trillion, and based on the latest estimates by the U.S. Census Bureau, it had risen to $1.9 trillion by 2020. And, there is no reason to expect that the revenue needs of local governments will ever decline, barring any unforeseeable catastrophic event(s). Nonetheless, there was a conspicuous slowdown in the growth rate of local government revenues beginning with the Great Recession and continuing during the post-Great Recession period (roughly 2009–18) and the COVID-19 health pandemic (2019–the present). As this book goes to press, it is reasonable to believe that the decline in the growth rate in total local government revenues could persist during a sustained period of double-digit inflation and chronic supply chain issues, although the federal government has unleashed a huge amount of money to both state and local governments with the enactment of American Rescue Plan Act (ARPA).

One related trend that warrants watching closely is the decline in recent years of the local government proportion of total state-local revenues. This was not something that was stressed in either Chapter 3 or other analytical chapters (Chapters 4–9) since it may be a short-term trend that can be explained by several innocuous factors that do not necessarily portend a permanent or long-term slowdown in local government revenues going forward. For example, some states or the federal government may have assumed greater or total responsibility for both the provision and cost of certain kinds of local government services (e.g., health care, welfare, roads, conservation of natural resources, and others), thereby relieving local governments of the financial responsibility for them. Another possibility could be that local governments may need less revenue going forward to fund various services, as these governments have found more efficient, cheaper, and cost-effective ways to pay for a large variety of staple services like fire and police protection, water and sewer, parks and recreation, libraries, utilities, among others. In other service areas, local governments may have turned to outsourcing as a means to cut costs and thereby have been able to trim the size of their budgets. Nevertheless, there could be other factors at work that could have jeopardized the viability of various revenue sources (e.g., reductions in federal and state aid, substantial increase in online purchasing by the public and the loss of potential sales tax revenue, declining property values and hence reduced property tax yields, outmigration of more affluent citizens and businesses who pay large amounts of income taxes, areas in economic decline with low quality of life, high crime rates, and high poverty levels that could discourage new economic development and thwart much-needed sustainable growth and job opportunities). Again, the decrease in the local proportion of state-local revenues warrants close monitoring in the years ahead.

Another constant of local government revenue collections plainly evident from the data presented in this book is that own-source revenues (OSRs) constitute the much greater part of total revenues (TRs), although this proportion did drop from 71 percent in 1962 to 65 percent in 2017. This means that local governments have been obtaining a smaller part of their TR from internal sources under their control and subsequently receiving a larger proportion of their funds from intergovernmental financial assistance (IR) provided by their states, the national government, and even other local governments (35 percent in 2017 versus 29 percent in 1962). However, there is a fair amount of variability among the five types of local governments as to the proportion of TR that comes from OSR (i.e., 61.6 percent in 1962 compared to 66.3 percent in 2017). In comparison to other type local governments, municipalities (84 and 76 percent in 1962 and 2017, respectively) and townships (79 and 82 percent in 1962 and 2017, respectively) have always collected the largest proportion of their revenue from internally generated sources

(OSR). While the township proportion increased slightly over time, the municipal percentage declined by 8 percentage points and is likely the result of receiving larger amounts of federal and state aid over the last 55 years. In spite of continuing to receive substantial amounts of fiscal assistance from their states, county governments were also collecting a noticeably larger proportion of their TR from OSR. Receipt of more money from this source may be explained by states granting their county governments more latitude in taxing not only property (real estate and construction on it) but also personal and corporate income, gasoline, natural resources, utilities (phones, cable, Internet, etc.), and general sales. In addition, it is reasonable to speculate that county governments in highly populated urban areas could be obtaining more money from utility charges for services and construction fees and charges associated with new population growth.

Special districts and school districts, while still deriving a considerable proportion of their TR from OSR, have increased their reliance on IR since the 1960s. Specifically, the OSR proportion of special district TR fell from 85 to 66 percent (a 19-percentage point drop) from 1962 to 2017, whereas the OSR proportion for school districts declined from 59 to 45 percent (a 14-percentage point reduction) over the same time period. Stated differently, this means that special districts now receive 34 percent of their total funds from IR as opposed to 15 percent in 1962, and school districts now count on IR to supply 55 percent of their TR compared to 41 percent in 1962. The growing reliance of special districts on IR is undoubtedly related to the increasing availability of large amounts of federal funds for a myriad of projects related to urban renewal, economic development/redevelopment, public housing, transportation, transit, and environmental protection/conservation and, more recently, health and welfare programs. As for school districts, many states since the late 1970s have been under constant pressure to increase substantially the amount of money available to local schools, given the push back by parents, education reform groups, and even school districts themselves with regard to the significant inequities in funding between school districts that have continued to increase over the years. Furthermore, there have been some instances of large infusions of money coming from the federal governments in landmark legislation like various Elementary and Secondary Education Acts and the No Child Left Behind Initiatives.

When breaking down OSR into the various streams of revenue that compose it, one is quickly reminded of what has become a "given" among local government budget personnel, elected officials, and the public alike. Simply put, the largest proportion of local government OSR money is derived from some form of taxation. (This is also the case for four of the five types of local governments, with the exception being special districts.) This reality is perhaps best underscored by an old adage which simply says that "…in this world, nothing is certain except death and taxes."[1] In 1962, total tax revenue accounted for 68 percent of OSR (or approximately $2 out of every $3 raised by local governments): by 2017, however, the tax proportion of local government OSR had dropped somewhat to 64 percent. The only way for this to happen would be that local governments were deriving a greater proportion of their OSR from other revenue streams, namely charges for services and a variety of miscellaneous sources. According to the data presented in Chapter 6, a significant increase in the receipt of more money from charges for services helped to offset the smaller proportion of OSR attributable to some form of tax-generated revenue. Looking back at the numbers from Chapter 6, one sees that the proportion of local government OSR collected from non-utility charges for services almost doubled from 15 to 29 percent between 1962 and 2017. Again, by reviewing the numbers from Chapter 7, it is also evident that the smaller contribution of tax revenue to OSR was partially offset by a smaller yet discernible increase in the proportion accounted for by miscellaneous revenue that rose from 6 to 8 percent.

Another long-standing familiar feature of the local government revenue picture has been the preponderance of the property tax as the major producer of tax revenue. (Again, this is also true for four of the five types of local governments, with special districts being the exception.) However, even before 1962, grassroots efforts across the country had already prompted state governments to provide relief for overburdened property owners who had to pay for the bulk of the costs associated with providing most local government services. Evidence of the success of such social movements can be seen from the declining proportion of tax revenue that was being derived from the property tax between 1962 and 2017. As the data analysis in Chapter 4 clearly corroborates, property tax revenue, which had accounted for 60 percent of OSR in 1962, had steadily spiraled downward to 41 percent by 2017 (a 19-percentage point drop). A similar trend is noteworthy as property taxes as a proportion of all taxes tumbled from 88 to 72 percent over the same time frame. Long-time critics of the overuse of the property tax were hopeful these figures indicated that the owners of property were enjoying some measure of relief as the burden of paying for the cost of providing local government services was being spread out among a larger number of people who availed themselves of services but were able to escape paying the full cost of them since they owned no property (sometimes alluded to as the "freeloader problem"). This assessment is supported by the numbers presented in Chapter 5 which shows that the burden of paying taxes to fund local government services was beginning to shift decidedly away from property owners to a broader spectrum of the actual users (consumers) of services with these governments (mostly municipalities and counties, and to a lesser extent, townships) being empowered to impose local option sales and individual and corporate income taxes. More specifically, the proportion of tax revenue accounted for by these newer types of taxes increased noticeably between 1962 and 2017 as follows: sales tax (7–17 percent); individual income tax (1–6 percent), and corporate income tax (negligible proportion to 1 percent).

As mentioned above, the proportion of local governments' TR received from some form of intergovernmental fiscal assistance or IR also increased over the 1962–2017 period from 29 to 35.0 percent). Historically, the largest part of local government IR has always been obtained from their states either through grants-in-aid or shared revenues, and this amount has also increased over time (i.e., 31 out of 35 percent in 2017 versus to 25 out of 29 percent in 1962). With all of the fanfare usually associated with fiscal assistance provided by the federal government to state and local governments since the Great Depression of the 1930s, it is instructive to point out that local governments receive a much smaller proportion of their IR from Washington than from their states. In 1962, federal aid accounted for 1.8 percent of all their local government IR, but by 2017, this figure had increased five-fold to 8.8 percent. Nevertheless, the amount of money that local governments receive directly from the national government does not truly represent what these governments ultimately get from Washington, as it is estimated that there are billions of dollars of federal aid that are funneled to local governments due to "pass through" provisions built into federal aid legislation.[2] The remaining portion of local government IR normally is derived from other local governments (4.1 versus 7.3 percent, respectively, in 1962 and 2017). Note, however, that the portion received from other local governments in 1962 was actually higher than it was for federal aid (4.1 percent compared to 1.8 percent).

A final set of trends highlighted in this book pertains to how counties, municipalities, townships, special districts, and school districts close the revenue gaps in their budgets when traditional sources of revenues are not enough to cover projected or desirable expenditures. If paring down the proposed budget is not something that local officials and their constituents wish to consider, then a viable and often-chosen option usually is to borrow money through the sale of bonds with the understanding that the bonds must be paid off over time in future budgets. From the analysis in Chapter 9, we see that it is still commonplace for local governments to borrow in both the short-and long-terms to make ends meet. This is evidenced from the fact that the issuance of long-term debt for all local governments has continued to increase over time. Yet, it is also clear that local governments (both collectively and individually) have been noticeably diligent in retiring old debt at a faster pace than incurring new debt, particularly in recent years that have been marred by an unstable economy. Moreover, it is obvious that local governments have shown signs of exercising fiscal prudence and steadfastly holding the line in making sure that they have not encumbered more debt than their citizens could afford. This is seen from data that measures incurred debt as a proportion of both total and own-source revenues for all (i.e., TR and OSR) and individual local governments. In fact, the latest figures indicate that this proportion is smaller than what it was at the start point of the analysis in this book (16.4 percent in 2017 compared to 19.5 percent in 1962).

As would be expected, there was a fair amount of variability in trends and patterns among the states, within states, and across regions of the country than is presented here and is likely explainable by historical, cultural, economic, and political factors. These discussions and explanations can be found in more detail in the analytical chapters (Chapters 3–9). To assist the reader, a thumbnail synopsis of the primary revenue trends and patterns of local governments is provided in Tables 10.1 and 10.2.

*Table 10.1* Summary of the Main Revenue Trends and Patterns of Local Governments

| *Revenue Source* | *% of Total Revenue (TR) Change, 1962–2017* | *% of Own-Source Revenue (OSR)Change, 1962–2017* |
|---|---|---|
| **Own-Source Revenue (All Local Governments)** | **decrease (71.0 % to 65.0 %)** | ------------------------------------ |
| Counties | increase (61.6 % to 66.3 %) | ------------------------------------ |
| *Municipalities* | decrease (83.6 % to 75.9 %) | ------------------------------------ |
| *Townships* | increase (78.5 % to 81.7 %) | ------------------------------------ |
| *Special Districts* | decrease (85.3 % to 66.2 %) | ------------------------------------ |
| *School Districts* | decrease (59.2 % to 44.8 %) | ------------------------------------ |
| **Intergovernmental Revenue (All Local Governments)** | **increase (29.0 % to 35.0 %)** | ------------------------------------ |
| *Counties* | decrease (38.4 % to 33.1 %) | ------------------------------------ |
| *Municipalities* | increase (16.4 % to 24.1 %) | ------------------------------------ |
| *Townships* | decrease (21.5 % to 18.3 %) | ------------------------------------ |
| *Special Districts* | increase (14.7 % to 33.8 %) | ------------------------------------ |
| *School Districts* | increase (40.8 % to 55.2 %) | ------------------------------------ |
| **Tax Revenue (All Local Governments)** | **decrease (48.5% to 37.1%)** | **decrease (68.3 % to 64.1%)** |
| *Counties* | decrease (48.3 % to 39.8 %) | decrease (80.0 % to 66.1 %) |
| *Municipalities* | decrease (48.8 % to 40.5 %) | decrease (75.9 % to 63.3 %) |
| *Townships* | increase (67.0 % to 64.6 %) | decrease (90.4 % to 82.6 %) |
| *Special Districts* | decrease (17.5 % to 14.2 %) | decrease (81.7 % to 17.2 %) |
| *School Districts* | decrease (51.8% to 38.6 %) | decrease (87.4 % to 86.2 %) |
| **Property Tax Revenue (All Local Governments)** | **decrease (42.7 % to 26.9 %)** | **decrease (60.0 % to 40.8 %)** |
| *Counties* | decrease (45.7 % to 28.1 %) | decrease (79.7 % to 43.2 %) |
| *Municipalities* | decrease (35.7 % to 20.2 %) | decrease (55.6 % to 36.6 %) |
| *Townships* | decrease (62.5 % to 59.2 %) | decrease (84.4 % to 75.7 %) |
| *Special Districts* | decrease (17.5 % to 9.0 %) | decrease (36.7 % to 17.2 %) |
| *School Districts* | decrease (51.0 % to 37.0 %) | decrease (86.2 % to 82.5 %) |
| **Other Tax Revenue (All Local Governments)** | **increase (5.9 % to 10.4 %)** | **increase (9.5 % to 18.1 %)** |
| *Counties* | increase (2.6 % to 11.7 %) | increase (3.9 % to 12.9 %) |
| *Municipalities* | increase (13.1 % to 20.3 %) | increase (20.3 % to 31.8 %) |
| *Townships* | increase (4.5 % to 5.4 %) | increase (6.6 % to 6.9 %) |
| *Special Districts* | increase (0.0 % to 5.3 %) | increase (0.0 % to 18.1 %) |
| *School Districts* | increase (0.7 % to 1.7 %) | increase (1.2 % to 3.7 %) |

(*Continued*)

*Table 10.1* (Continued)

| *Revenue Source* | *% of Total Revenue (TR) Change, 1962–2017* | *% of Own-Source Revenue (OSR)Change, 1962–2017* |
|---|---|---|
| **Revenue Source** | **% of Total Revenue (TR) Change 1962–2017** | **% of Own-Source Revenue (OSR) Change 1962–2017** |
| **Charges for Services-Non-Utility (All Local Governments)** | **increase (9.4 % to 15.8 %)** | **increase (15.3 % to.29.4 %)** |
| *Counties* | increase (9.6 % to 20.5 %) | increase (15.6 % to 31.5 %) |
| *Municipalities* | increase (9.3 % to 17.6 %) | increase (14.5 % to 27.5 %) |
| *Townships* | increase (3.6 % to 9.3 %) | increase (4.8 % to 11.9 %) |
| *Special Districts* | increase (31.5 % to 33.1 %) | increase (57.2 % to 63.5 %) |
| *School Districts* | decrease (6.2 % to 3.5 %) | decrease (10.5 to 7.9 %) |
| **Miscellaneous Revenue-(All Local Governments)** | **increase (3.8 % to 4.4 %)** | **decrease (6.1 % to 7.8 %)** |
| *Counties* | increase (2.8 % to 4.8 %) | increase (4.6 % to 7.4 %) |
| *Municipalities* | decrease (6.2 % to 5.8 %) | decrease (9.6 % to 9.1%) |
| *Townships* | increase (3.5 % to 4.3 %) | increase (4.7 % to 5.5 %) |
| *Special Districts* | decrease (6.1 % to 4.7 %) | increase (6.1 % to 9.0 %) |
| *School Districts* | increase (1.2 % to 2.6 %) | increase (2.1 % to 5.9%) |
| **Revenue Source** | **% of Tax Revenue (TTR) Change 1962–2017** | |
| **Property Tax Revenue (All Local Governments)** | **decrease (88.0 % to 72.1 %)** | |
| *Counties* | decrease (94.7 % to 70.6 %) | |
| *Municipalities* | decrease (73.2 % to 49.8%) | |
| *Townships* | decrease (93.3 % to 91.7 %) | |
| *Special Districts* | decrease (100 % to 63.0 %) | |
| *School Districts* | decrease (87.4 % to 72.1 %) | |
| **Charges for Services/ Fees-Utilities (All Local Governments)** | **increase (0.5 % to 0.6 %)** | **decrease (0.9 % to 0.8 %)** |
| *Counties* | decrease (2.8 % to 1.5 %) | decrease (4.5 % to 2.3 %) |
| *Municipalities* | decrease 19.3 % to 15.6 % | decrease (23.1 % to 19.6 %) |
| *Townships* | decrease (4.4 % to 4.2 %) | decrease (5.6 % to 5.1 %) |
| *Special Districts* | increase (30.2 % to 63.3 %) | increase (35.4 % to 86.2 %) |
| *School Districts* | ---------------------------------- | ---------------------------------- |

*Table 10.2* Summary of Local Government Revenue from Sale of Bonds (Debt) and Main Debt Trends and Patterns

| *Government* | *Total Outstanding Debt (in millions of dollars), 2017* |
|---|---|
| **All Local Governments** | $1,909,257 |
| *Counties* | 317,975 |
| *Municipalities* | 716,717 |
| *Townships* | 32,046 |
| *Special Districts* | 394,594 |
| *School Districts* | 446,560 |
| | **% Change in Debt Outstanding (Borrowing), 1962–2017** |
| *Counties* | increase (9.2 % to 16.7 %) |
| *Municipalities* | decrease (45.7 % to 37.6 %) |
| *Townships* | decrease (2.4 % to 1.7 %) |
| *Special Districts* | increase (19.1 % to 20.7 %) |
| *School Districts* | decrease 23.7 % to 23.4 %) |
| | **Long-Term % of Outstanding Debt, 2017** |
| **All Local Governments** | **98.5 %** |
| *Counties* | 98.6 % |
| *Municipalities* | 99.0 % |
| *Townships* | 91.2 % |
| *Special Districts* | 99.0 % |
| *School Districts* | 97.8 % |
| | **% Change in Long-Term Debt (Borrowing), 1962–2017** |
| **All Local Governments** | **increase (94.4 % to 98.5 %)** |
| *Counties* | decrease (96.8 % to 98.6%) |
| *Municipalities* | increase (93.5% to 99.1 %) |
| *Townships* | decrease (93.7 % to 91.2%) |
| *Special Districts* | increase (91.8 % to 99.0 %) |
| *School Districts* | decrease 98.0 % to 97.8 %) |
| | **% Change in Long-Term Debt (Borrowing) Issued, 1962–2017** |
| **All Local Governments** | **increase (94.4 % to 98.5 %)** |
| *Counties* | decrease (96.8 % to 98.6%) |
| *Municipalities* | increase (93.5% to 99.1 %) |
| *Townships* | decrease (93.7 % to 91.2%) |
| *Special Districts* | increase (91.8 % to 99.0 %) |
| *School Districts* | decrease 98.0 % to 97.8 %) |
| **Ratio of Issued to Retired Debt (All Local Governments), 1962–2017—Decreased (2.045 to 1.176)** | |
| | **Ratio of Long-Term Outstanding Debt to Total Revenue (TR), 1962 to 2017** |
| **All Local Governments** | (1.23 to .99) |
| *Counties* | increase (6.3 to 7.4) |
| *Municipalities* | decrease (16.5 to 12.4 |
| *Townships* | decrease 8.1 to 5.6 |
| *Special Districts* | decrease (44.0 to 16.1) |
| *School Districts* | decrease (8.9 to 7.8) |

(*Continued*)

*Table 10.2* (Continued)

| *Government* | *Total Outstanding Debt (in millions of dollars), 2017* |
|---|---|
| | **Ratio of Long-Term Outstanding Debt to Own-Source Revenue (OSR), 1962 to 2017** |
| *Counties* | increase (10.3 to 11.1) |
| *Municipalities* | decrease (19.8 to 15.9) |
| *Townships* | decrease (16.4 to 6.8) |
| *Special Districts* | decrease (51.6 to 22.0) |
| *School Districts* | decrease (16.6 to 17.4) |
| Borrowed Revenue of Local Governments as a Proportion of Total Revenue and Preliminary Revenue, 1962–2019 | |
| Year | Total Revenue |
| 1962 | 13.6 |
| 1967 | 13.4 |
| 1972 | 10.5 |
| 1977 | 8.6 |
| 1982 | 8.3 |
| 1987 | 9.9 |
| 1992 | 9.2 |
| 1997 | 11.5 |
| 2002 | 9.4 |
| 2007 | 9.8 |
| 2012 | 11.0 |
| 2017 | 10.0 |
| 2018 | 11.1 |
| 2019 | 9.7 |

## The road lying ahead: Trends into the future

Any discussion of the direction that local governments should follow in the future with respect to what type of revenues they should tap (or rely on) must, of necessity, also carefully consider projected future expenditures. Stated differently, each side of the local government budget is inextricably connected to the other side of the budget—that is, there must be sufficient revenues to fund expected or desired expenditures so that the budget balances. Therefore, we must look at the entire budgetary process and the practical as well as legal interdependency of revenues and expenditures, even if the primary focus of interest is on revenues.

Given this perspective, it is imperative that we begin to critically rethink how local budgeting has and continues to be done. Such an effort began in earnest a few years ago with the International City/County Management Association (ICMA), the Government Finance Officers Association (GFOA), and a large group of partners deciding to work together in what has been called the Rethinking Budgeting Initiative. Participants in this initiative, like those who study and write about government budgeting, understand that local governments typically adhere to an age-old approach in developing their budgets as they usually accept that the budget is fundamentally incremental. This basically means that "last year's budget becomes next year's budget with changes at the margin" (Kavanagh and Agarunova 2022). In his seminal work, *The Politics of the Budgetary Process*, Aaron Wildavsky succinctly states that the budgetary process is in fact incremental by its nature[3] and is involved with "relatively small increments to an existing base" (1964, 15).[4] Wildavsky elaborates on this compelling point when concluding that the analysis of the budget is therefore limited to "only those parts of the budget within the control of the participants" (Wildavsky 1964, 123). This shortsightedness of the incremental approach is complicated further as it results in a budget built around line-items (i.e., categories of spending like personnel, commodities, and contractual services), which are then grouped into departments and funds (Kavanagh and Agarunova 2022). As such, the budget focuses simply on outputs and not the important outcomes that can be used to measure the extent to which policy goals have been realized.

Even a cursory review of the political science and public administration literature reveals that scholars are nearly unanimous in their view that incrementalism is neither an acceptable nor preferred way to create (or as some might say, "cobble together") a budget. In short, while many scholars may agree that incrementalism is a useful analytical concept in studying the budgetary process as it reflects the reality of budgeting, most would be unlikely to view it as a prescribed, or productive way to formulate a budget. Again, the same literature, along with anecdotal information, has reported a similar perspective among both elected officials and practitioners. Further still, incrementalism, probably at its best, can be viewed as nothing more than what Charles Lindbloom (1959) referred to as "muddling through" a critical process in the execution of an indispensable government responsibility, with a likely outcome that could be described as mere "satisficing" (see Simon 1955; Lindbloom 1959). But, is this acceptable and the best that we can do, given Harold Lasswell's description of the budget as the "most important political document" that any government will adopt?

This rather tepid assessment of the incremental approach to budgeting has been linked to three main criticisms that underscore its shortcomings and the less than desirable outcomes for local governments and their citizens. Kavanagh and Agarunova (2022) succinctly summarize these criticisms as follows:

- Previous decisions "are frozen" in time beyond the point at which they are reasonable or pertinent. After a change is made in the budget, the change is carried over to the next budget. A good example would be to make things made possible by one-time money from federal or state grants like additional staffing a permanent fixture in future budgets after the grant ends. This kind of "layering effect" produced by such a situation adds to financial distress and is a suboptimal allocation of resources.

- The traditional incremental budget is not strategic. Since money is apportioned to line-items related to day-to-day governmental operations (e.g., equipment, supplies, salaries and benefits, training, etc.), it is difficult to gauge accurately how spending affects critical policy responsibilities like economic development, housing, public safety, health, and education. This is a backward-looking approach to budgeting when governments should be forward-thinking and thereby makes them less able to effectively and efficiently respond to current policy issues or new issues on the horizon.
- The traditional incremental budget is a "zero-sum game." In such a scenario, one group of stakeholders wins, while another group(s) must lose. That is, in order for one government department (as well as those vested interests that benefit from its programs) to get additional funding, another department must get less. As such, a zero-sum game promotes power dynamics that favor maintaining the status quo and encourages self-interested decision-making.

Suffice it to say that these and similar problems normally associated with incremental budgeting also have direct and critical implications for local governments' ability to raise sufficient revenue to support their operations. Moreover, incremental budgeting hinders local governments in the expenditure of already scarce revenue in more prudent, efficient, and cost-effective ways.[5] But, local governments also may face other obstacles in raising enough revenue to balance their budgets such as being creatures of their states, thereby having their revenue raising ability and debt-capacity options limited and micro-managed by the state government. In addition, states and the federal government may impose unfunded mandates that create financial hardships for local governments, while the national government suddenly decreases the amount of federal aid to both local governments and their states. Then, there is the ever-present possibility that the public has an aversion to new or higher taxes or charges for services and hold the belief that their local governments are wasteful with what they think are adequate resources they already have at their disposal—or worst still, money has been siphoned off due to political corruption. And, of course, local governments typically find themselves in dire straits whenever there are natural disasters and significant downturns in the economy, whether it be a recession, exorbitant inflation, or a health pandemic like COVID-19. Who would have dreamed ten years ago that something like a health pandemic would virtually bring the United States and world economy to a standstill and cause great havoc in local, as well as state, governments in meeting the constitutional and/or statutory requirement to balance their respective budgets?

With these and other possible challenges posed to local governments' revenue raising abilities, what viable and reasonable alternatives are available to these governments that are often considered to be the "workhorses" of all governments in the United States and operate at a critical level "where the rubber meets the road"? While there will always be naysayers, there are still many plausible ways for local governments to generate ample revenues to pay for vital services and programs deemed worthy by their citizens. Some of the possibilities presented here will be ones already experimented with but have not produced desirable results in the past, while other idea/suggestions are ones that have been kicked around for years but never adopted. Still, other alternatives will be novel (perhaps even risky) or represent "outside the box" thinking. It is important to mention that some of the alternatives and ideas discussed below are ones that have been identified by the study group known as the Rethinking Local Government Revenues Initiative, which is a spin-off of sorts of the Rethinking Budgetary Initiative mentioned earlier and is also spearheaded by the ICMA and GFOA and many of the same large grouping of partners.

### *New non-tax types of OSR*

Although not entirely novel suggestions to those who are already familiar with the local government budgetary process, several of these proposals/strategies have gained significant currency in the last decade or so. They include ideas such as urban wealth funds (UWFs), entrepreneurial thinking in local government, legal financing, and payment in lieu of taxes. All of them have received a considerable amount of attention in reports issued through the Rethinking Budgetary Initiative, as well as the ICMA and GFOA.

#### *Urban wealth funds (UWFs)*

According to Shayne Kavanagh, the senior manager of research for the GFOA, "local governments might be sitting on a metaphorical gold mine" that could potentially result in [local] governments being able to generate billions or trillions of new revenue annually for their jurisdictions (Kavanagh 2022a, 2). What he is referring to are UWFs whereby local governments have the same potential to make money like private individuals or corporations by taking advantage of assets (i.e., land, buildings, machinery, location, etc.) that they own or are under their control. Under such a scenario, UWFs are entrusted with government assets with moneymaking "value under unified, professional management who own and manage these assets for the betterment of the local community" (Kavanagh, 2022a, 2).

This can be illustrated with a simple example. Let's assume that a city either owns or has the means to purchase an undeveloped or underutilized piece of property that is located along a navigable deep-water river or bay in a scenic community with national historical significance where waterfront property is presently a hot commodity. Given the large size of the property, it could easily accommodate several 8–10 story high-end condominium buildings, a large number of upscale restaurants, bars, and shops, 2–3 cruise ship terminals with berths, a research/business incubator facility, parking garage, public park, some mid-size (4–5 story) office buildings, a branch office of city hall, a fire station, police sub-station, and perhaps a public meeting hall or small- to mid-size auditorium. Without giving much thought to the matter other than increasing the city's property tax base, most city leaders would probably sell the property to a private developer while missing out on "once-in-a lifetime" opportunity to significantly increase the city's revenue. If instead, however, city leaders decide to maintain ownership of all of this large parcel of property and lease parts of the land not dedicated for public benefit (i.e., parking garage, park, city hall branch office, fire station, police substation, and meeting hall or auditorium) to private developers, they would then assign its asset (the property) to the UWF so that it could tract the true market value of it and then promote the development of the property to generate resources for the public benefit commensurate with its true market value. Not only will the city obtain revenue from the lease of some parcels of the land to private developers, but it will also be able to collect property tax and utility revenue from structures and facilities build on the leased property. Moreover, the bonus in all of this for the city is that, with the UWF retaining ownership interest in the property, the public will be able to enjoy a substantial portion of the financial benefit.

UWFs have been utilized by local (and even regional) governments in Europe and East Asia to generate billions of dollars to pay for infrastructure while keeping public control of their assets. To date, only a few local governments in North America have begun to experiment with UWFs. In fact, the Rethinking Revenue Initiative is currently working with Schmidt Futures, the Lincoln Institute of Land Policy, and the Sorenson Impact Center to launch an UWF incubator program as a first step at harnessing the power of UWF on a large scale in the United States (Kavanagh 2022a, 2).[6]

*Entrepreneurial thinking in local government*

Another possible source of new money for local governments could be derived from these governments' willingness to engage in what has been called "entrepreneurial thinking." Here, local governments have the potential to avail themselves of huge amounts of untapped additional income if they are willing to be innovative and skillful in their search for new revenue sources beyond what they usually relied on in the past. This does not mean that they abandon reliable revenue streams like taxes, fees, charges, etc., but rather they become more creative by considering other means of generating the resources their governments need to keep pace with citizen needs and expectations. One good way to do this is to begin to think *entrepreneurially*—in short, think from a private-sector perspective as to how one can make money by producing a desirable commodity that people will buy. If private-sector businesses can do it, why can't local governments? It is just a matter of resetting one's mindset in thinking about different ways of obtaining money since governments (like people) sometimes limit themselves by believing that there is only one way to think about approaching a financial challenge.

With a little brainstorming, one can think of many opportunities that local governments have to engage in entrepreneurial activities that permit them to take advantage of their assets to create more value for the community and to financially strengthen the local government. In some ways, entrepreneurial thinking is similar to the logic behind the creation of UWFs by utilizing the government's assets. But it differs in that the local government will be producing a marketable product to sell and make money through the use of its assets rather than letting private developers create a product or service to make money with the government receiving just a small share of the profit through lease payments, taxes, and fees/charges for services. It is important to understand, however, that innovation along the lines of entrepreneurialism is only successful when there is efficient execution of the carefully crafted plan-of-action to create new value for the public (Kavanagh 2021).

Unlike UWF which typically works best in larger metropolitan areas, entrepreneurial thinking can happen at any scale, from the very small to the largest governments. A good real-world example as to how entrepreneurial thinking can help a local government to generate additional but heretofore untapped revenue is clearly evident from the experience of the City of Lancaster, California. The City, with a population of 150,000, is located in the Mojave Desert in northern Los Angeles County but is separated from the main population center of the county by a large area of forests and mountains. With the abundance of sun, the City was an ideal location to capture solar energy and sell it. While exercising due caution, the City started its solar project on a small scale by installing solar panels on unutilized city property. Early success at generating and selling excess to the energy grid led the City to partner with the local school district to install more panels at school sites. From there, the City was able to permit community members to buy energy directly from the City. At present, over 90 percent of eligible accounts participate in the City's energy program (Kavanagh 2021). The best news, however, is that the City's energy program accounts for \$40 million of the City's total budget of \$234 million (or 19 percent), and the energy program more than covers its costs (Kavanagh 2021). While it is not realistic that every local government can have the success with in a solar energy project like the City of Lancaster, we do know that "every local government has assets, physical or otherwise, that have the potential to be unlocked with entrepreneurial thinking" (Kavanagh 2021).

Let's consider some possibilities in other areas besides the production and sale of solar energy. Most local governments operate their own utilities like water service, sewage collection and treatment, storm water management, solid waste management, and sometimes electric power and natural gas supply. Moreover, local governments may have excess or unlimited capacity in their utility operations to take on additional customers (users) and thereby be able to achieve even better economies of scale in their own operations.[7] Local governments with these kinds of additional capacity are in a particularly enviable position to "sell" these services to neighboring jurisdictions or private-sector entities that find it more costly to continue to construct and operate their own utility facilities. Another opportunity to exercise entrepreneurial thinking would be in the leasing of unused office building or storage space to the private-sector or to other governmental entities (local, state, and even federal). In fact, some governments consciously construct buildings with this intent in mind, knowing that they will not need the extra space themselves in the immediate future and see it as "a smart business decision" to generate additional revenue for their government in the meantime. Such was the case for the City of Temple Terrace, Florida in the early 1980s when it constructed a new city hall/police department complex. Over the course of 25 years, the City leased the third floor of this facility to the Florida Department of Law Enforcement, with the lease payment covering the extra cost of the bond note used to pay for the structure. In the end, Temple Terrace was able to acquire future office space at no cost to the City and even made additional money to augment the City's revenues for 25 years. In 2005, at the end of the lease, the City eventually occupied the third floor.

There are plenty of other examples. For example, a county in South Carolina is exploring the possibility of constructing a new jail complex which would contain much more space than what the county is projected to need in the next 30 years. If the county can secure a lease commitment from state and federal prison authorities to house excess prisoners for which they currently do not have space for and are willing to agree to an acceptable per diem charge, the county is likely to go ahead with plans to build such a facility and thereby will be able to generate an estimated additional $5 million in revenue.

In yet another example, a large hospital in central Florida, which is an independent state-created hospital authority, significantly expanded its facilities and services a few years ago in order to provide medical care beyond its traditional clientele to people in neighboring counties so as to take advantage of a new and abundant source of revenue. It turned out to be a win-win scenario for everyone. That is, people living outside the county where the hospital was located whose own local medical centers did not provide more advanced types of medical services avail themselves of superior medical care while resident in the county where the hospital is situated also benefitted from the same type of more sophisticated medical care previously not available at the hospital.

In a similar vein, local official may want to explore some new and innovative ideas and opportunities as a means to collect more revenue. For example, see some new wrinkles in taxation and property taxes reported by Brunner and Schwegman (2022) and Larson and Carroll (2023).

*Payment in lieu of taxes*

A third likely source of new revenue for local governments are payments in lieu of taxes. It is not unusual for many local governments to have a number of tax-exempt properties within their boundaries. For those governments that heavily depend on property tax revenue (and most do), tax-exempt properties present an ever-present challenge to obtain enough revenue to balance the budget. These properties pay no taxes but still must be served by local governments. Take the City of Boston as an example. The City has 16 colleges and universities/universities and 12 hospitals, and the most recent estimates indicate that they have total property values of $7.0 and $5.7 billion, respectively (Kavanagh 2022b). If these properties had been taxed at the commercial rate, it is estimated that they would have produced $345 million in additional revenue for a variety of local governments in the Boston metropolitan area (Kavanagh 2022b). By comparison, the commercial sector produced $764.5 in the same period (Kavanagh 2022b).

Make no mistake about it, convincing tax-exempt entities like those in Boston to make financial contributions (i.e., payments in lieu of taxes) to the local governments in which they are located is a tricky business. Simply put, local governments must use a well-crafted strategy to get these entities to "buy into" something that they are not legally required to do—pay money to their local governments for services received. Such a strategy or method must be able to assist local governments successfully work through an age-old conundrum. This conundrum basically boils down to how to balance the following:

- "the contributions that tax-exempt properties make to the local government budget and community well-being by virtue of their pro-social missions versus
- the resources these properties consume from the local budget" (Kavanagh 2002b).

Economists refer to the conundrum as the "common pool resource" problem. In its simplest terms, Kavanagh (2022b) explains it this way: "The local government budget is 'owned' by everyone in the community, but any single person has the incentive to avoid contributing to the pool (budget) while still using resources from the pool (services)." Local governments hoping to augment their revenues with money obtained through the payment in lieu of taxes idea are lucky in that there is a ready-made method ("Financial Foundations for Thriving Communities"[8]) to deal with the "common pool resource" conundrum. It was developed a few years ago by the GFOA and used successfully in Boston, with the City being able to obtain $67 million in additional revenue (i.e., $17 million in new cash payments in lieu of taxes from tax-exempt properties *annually* and $50 million in new in-kind contributions *annually*) (Kavanagh 2002b).

As an aside, it should be mentioned that local governments in some states (but especially cities and counties) have been accustomed to obtaining revenue from other governments who have substantial land and real estate holdings located in their borders. Think of the City of Tallahassee, Florida where over half of all real estate is not on the property tax rolls, since it is the county seat for Leon County, the Florida state capital, home to two major universities and one community college, as well as having a large number of religious, charitable, and non-profits organizations there. The city is fortunate that the state government has long recognized that it impacts the City's budget and has been making voluntary contributions to the city since the 1970s. But, is the amount that the state and other tax-exempt entities are currently paying sufficient in light of the services used by them? And, there are states where the state government or other tax-exempt entities make no payments in lieu of taxes to their local governments. Then, there is the matter of the federal government with tax immunity which contributes as it may will for local services that it consumes. Perhaps, there is some opportunity for local governments to negotiate with their states and the federal government for some kind of payments in lieu of taxes or a larger payment or contribution.

In addition, is it too far-fetched for local governments to approach other tax-exempt entities (e.g., religious and charitable organizations and large non-profits) that own substantial property about making payments in lieu of taxes? After all, these entities avail themselves of local government services while paying nothing for them, meaning that property owners, wage earners and business owners paying an income tax, and consumers paying a local option sales tax subsidize these groups' use of services provided by local governments in the area.

### *Legal financing*

A rather intriguing yet much riskier idea for raising new or additional revenue is something called legal financing. Legal financing basically is venture capital for litigation, where private funders back legal action they believe have a good chance of succeeding in exchange for a portion of the eventual judgment or settlement. Most local governments, until recently, knowing that they are not likely to be able to realize the full potential, have shied away from it, especially given the huge cost of litigation and greater legal resources available to well-funded defendants Local governments, however, are more likely to pursue this kind of opportunity to generate more revenue if they are able to reduce the risks. This can happen when a well-funded and well-established law firm is willing to step up to the plate and take on the "big powerhouse evil-doers" (e.g., when several state governments along with several high-profile law firms took on "Big Tobacco" in the late 1990s).

Just like a private-sector entity, state and local governments retain the right to sue in state and federal courts. In many instances, this can lead to a financial award to the government by a court-ordered judgment or an out-of-court settlement between the parties. Examples include the tobacco (mentioned above) and the current opioid litigation. While these cases represent a broader public interest and not the local government's corporate interest, these actions are known as "public sector affirmative litigation."[9] It is important to mention that the tobacco litigation produced over $200 billion in revenue for state and local governments. Based on some early estimates, there is the possibility that the current pending opioid litigation could result in an even larger payout for these governments. In some instances, these have already been settled for hundreds of millions of dollars (Farrar, Eiselt, and Kavanagh 2022). This is indicative of the potentially huge monetary impact of public-sector affirmative litigation[10]

### *New and more revenue with greater home rule*

Greater home rule authority in fiscal matters would provide more opportunities for local governments to generate additional or new revenue.[11] Owing to the fact that local governments are creatures of their states and also subject to Dillion's rule, they have been historically limited in their revenue options and ability to increase the rates of current taxes and fees/charges for services. Presently, 40 states permit some form of local government home rule, with greater authority typically given to municipalities. However, states (even ones with some type of home rule) historically have been less inclined to give their local governments' widespread authority in financial matters while at the same time being more willing to grant them more latitude in other areas such as functions (powers), structure, and personnel. Consequently, local governments have had to forgo a large amount of potential revenue estimated to be in the range of hundreds of millions of dollars.

The debate over greater home rule authority for local governments has been an enduring one and is not likely to go away in the foreseeable future. On the one hand, states argue that they have a legal and moral responsibility to protect the financial interests of citizens living within local government jurisdictions from unduly burdensome taxes and fees/charges since these individuals are also citizens of the state (Krane, Rigos, and Hill 2001; Benton 2012). In addition, states and opponents of expanding home rule make the point that the states created local governments and therefore have the sovereign authority to act in local governments' and their citizens' best interest. On the other hand, advocates of greater home rule counter by saying that local officials are in a better (closer) position to know and understand the service needs and expectations of their citizens, as well as their willingness/ability to pay more to provide them (Krane, Rigos, and Hill 2001). Moreover, home rule proponents make the point that those people who reside in local jurisdictions are in a better position to hold their local officials fiscally accountable at regular intervals via the ballot box.

Given that states have shown a greater willingness to grant more home rule authority, generally, and for fiscal matters, specifically, lately, this could bode well for local governments going forward in efforts to capture additional revenue to assist in balancing their budgets.

## Additional state aid and/or shared revenue

If states, however, are not willing to give local government greater latitude in raising their own revenue, then they should be amenable to providing greater amounts of financial assistance to them. At least, that is the argument of home rule proponents and an ever-growing chorus of local officials and their citizens. More specifically, they want either a "bigger piece of the action" when it comes to state shared revenues derived from things like the fuel, excise, sales, income, severance, and other types of taxes and larger amounts of money awarded through grants-in-aid. Local government requests in this regard would seem reasonable and are based on several important premises. First, state governments are better at raising revenue than are local governments and also equipped with the constitutional (legal) authority to do so. As a result, they are in a strategic position to share this money. That is, revenue collected by the state is collected from people who live in counties, municipalities, townships, special districts, and school districts. Therefore, is it not fair that the money should be sent back to these local governments to be spent by those people who paid it into the state treasury? Second, since service needs differ from one community to another, does it not make more sense for one's local government to be better suited to make prudent and informed decisions as to how state-collected revenue can be best spent for the welfare of their citizens who are also citizens of the state? Third, Americans have always preferred a decentralized government to a centralized one, where local governments, which are supposedly closer to the people and know more about their constituents' service needs should be given more authority to spend government-collected money for the greatest public good.

Based on the data analysis in Chapter 8, however, there is little evidence that states have become more receptive to persistent pleas from their local governments for greater financial assistance, While state aid as a proportion of total local revenues increased from 29 to 34 percent between 1962 and 2017, this was not the case for all types of local governments. Counties, municipalities, and townships actually saw the state aid portion of their TR decline noticeably over this same time frame. Only school districts and special districts experienced an increase in the proportion of TR coming from their state governments—that is, from 37 to 53 percent and from 2 to 8 percent, respectively. The likely explanation for greater state aid to school districts is that a "legal cloud" was hanging over states where they could potentially be held in violation of the Equal Protection Clause of the 14th Amendment of the U.S. Constitution or similar protections in state constitutions for not trying to reduce significant disparities in funding available to less- and more-affluent local school districts. But, even this trend slowed considerably when the Great Recession hit. From 1962 until 2002, state aid as a proportion on TR of school districts increased from 37 to 55 percent. Then it dropped back down to 53 percent by 2017. As for special districts, the increase in the state aid proportion of TR is likely the result of several idiosyncratic factors in different states where the state has a strong vested and/or legal interest in the services provided by a certain type special district.

At the same time that local governments have been lobbying for a larger cut of shared revenues and more grant-in-aid money, they have also intensified efforts to convince their states that they should be willing to share money that they receive from the federal government (i.e., funds not designated by Congress as pass-through" money). In short, local governments are constantly pushing their states to adopt a benevolent policy of" share and share alike," much like what a parent would or should do for one's children. This issue came to a head recently when Congress enacted the first financial package to assist states and their communities in economic recovery efforts in the aftermath of the COVID-19 pandemic—the $2 trillion Coronavirus Aid Relief Economic Security (CARES) Act of 2020. To the dismay of and outcry of many local government officials, the National League of Cities (NLC) and the National Association of Counties (NACo), most of this money was allocated to the states with total discretion to share or not share with their local governments (only cities over 500,000 population were allocated money directly from the U.S. Treasury). This led to a massive outcry from local government officials (especially cities and counties) that their states withheld money from them for purely "political" and "ideological" reasons (Benton, Rissler, and Wagner 2020). This backlash led Congress to change the distribution method of similar funds when adopting the ARPA in 2021. Under ARPA, counties and municipalities received direct allocations of "flexible aid" from Washington under a non-politicalized formula that objectively estimated their financial needs.[12] This action by the federal government represents a partial victory for local governments. Only time will tell if states will demonstrate a greater willingness to share more of their federal aid funds with their local governments in the future or if federal prodding or mandating will be necessary. Another important feature of the ARPA is that it permits local governments to use this money to "replace lost revenue" due to COVID-19.

### *More federal aid*

Federal aid has never been a major annual source of revenue for local governments like it has been for states. In 1962, federal aid accounted for a paltry 1.8 percent of total local government revenue; by 2017, federal aid proportion had risen somewhat but still amounted for only 3.8 percent of these governments' total receipts. Significant spurts in federal aid to local governments have usually occurred during and after major recessions when the federal government sought to assist cash-strapped local governments to continue to provide essential services to their constituents. There were a few other times when federal money became a larger source of local governments revenue receipt. Examples include the early 1960s through the late 1960s when the Congress and Presidents Kennedy and Johnson specifically targeted large, impoverished inner cities or highly urbanized counties for large sums of money through model cities, urban redevelopment/renewal, housing and infrastructure repair and replacement and crime control projects. Federal aid also became a larger share of local revenue receipts from 1972–89 under the Federal Revenue Sharing Program (GRS).[13]

While local governments should always be mindful of the way in which they should treat federal aid (i.e., not counting on it in future years to balance the budget) and also being fully aware of the conditions that normally accompany the receipt of this kind of money. This does, in no way, imply that they should stop chasing federal grant dollars or even turning it down, as this kind of otherwise" free money" can produce substantial additional, much-needed money to do things that local governments and their residents probably could not otherwise afford.

Federal funding that came to local government through the ARPA in 2021–24, as mentioned above, was a God-send due to these governments having to spend for unanticipated and unbudgeted items and services and much smaller monetary yields from historically reliable revenue sources due to COVID-19 and the resulting pandemic-induced recession. Specifically, counties, cities, townships, and even school districts had to shift funds from pre-planned budgeted items to pay for facemasks, coronavirus testing, protective clothing and other gear, decontamination of facilities, sick leave and overtime pay for employees, unemployment compensation, staff training, and public education. Furthermore, many local governments report that property tax revenue collections were down as a result of people losing their jobs or missing paychecks after contracting the Coronavirus, while they also indicated that traditional yields from other normally reliable OSR like local option sales and income taxes, user fees and charges for services, special assessments, and miscellaneous revenues were also down substantially (Benton, Rissler, and Wagner). In fact, Zoom interviews with city mayors from Kodiak, Alaska to Athens, Ohio to Oklahoma City, Oklahoma to Pittsburgh, Pennsylvania indicated that they were very worried about being able to "make ends meet" in their current and future budgets if the federal government "did not come to the rescue" (Benton, Rissler, and Wagner). In fact, it is not far-fetched to suggest that it may take several more years—indeed decades—for local governments to recuperate from the deleterious fiscal effects of COVID, unless they continue to receive large amount of federal financial assistance, given the persistence of unprecedented double-digit inflation that is currently plaguing the U.S. economy as of 2024.

While the ARPA relief funds were certainly welcomed by local governments, the big question going forward is as follows: Have local governments, but especially full-service local governments (i.e., counties and municipalities), limited full-service governments (townships), and even special and school districts spent this money wisely, knowing that this money like GRS in the 1970s and 1980s as going to be *a one*-shot deal and would end in 2024? While a definitive answer to this question probably will not be known until a few years after 2024 or even perhaps for a decade, financial experts warned local governments about the perils of ignoring the one-shot nature of this money. In fact, the Government Finance Officers Association (GFOA) in June 2021 and coinciding with the release of ARPA funds issued the following piece of important guidance: "Use of ARPA funds to cover operating deficits caused by COVID-19 should be considered temporary and additional budgetary restraint may be necessary to achieve/maintain structural balance in future budgets" (Kleine 2023). However, according to Kleine (2023), a senior Government & Planning Director at EY-Parthenon, Ernst & Young LLP and the former Budget Director for the City of Baltimore, indicates in an article in *PA Times* (2023) that local governments seemingly have not followed the astute advice of a highly respected entity like GFOA:

> "Nearly two years…later [after the aforementioned statement from GFOA], many local governments have ignored the GFOA's advice and continue to rely on ARPA funds to make ends meet. The operating deficits they are covering at this point were not caused by COVID-19. They predate the pandemic, and ARPA's generous revenue loss provisions allow counties, cities, and towns to defer tough budget choices until the clock runs out on December 31, 2024."

What Kleine is saying is that these local governments are setting themselves up for an ARPA fiscal cliff as they appear to have relegated this serious and ominously looming "hard and fast" deadline" as nothing more than a minor distant concern. Stated differently, the clock is ticking and ARPA funds will end soon. With this though in mind, this means that local government leaders have a relatively short period of time to wean themselves off ARPA dependency and chart a new and more practical long-term approach to the spending ARPA money that would hopefully help them make all-important progress toward fiscal sustainability.[14]

With this said, it would seem that prudent utilization of federal fiscal assistance (i.e., ARPA money) could be indispensable for local governments to continue to meet the service expectations of their citizens and may be necessary to save them from insolvency in both the short- and long-terms, (see Brachman and Haskins 2023).

Other economic experts have also sounded the alarm about what could happen in the post-ARPA period. In a recent virtual meeting on municipal distress held by the Volcker Alliance, one participant (Harvard law professor David Schleicher) made the following statement:

> "We're at a moment of inflection right now. We have been living though this period of flush state and local budgets, and we're about to see a real turn"
>
> (Vock 2023)

What he and others at this gathering were concerned about was the imminent end of ARPA funds, uncertainty about the economy, inflation, and demands for expensive local government programs (principally, social services) not only for full-service local governments (i.e., municipalities and counties) but also townships and even special and school districts (Vock 2023). Another meeting participant (Stephanie Miner, a former mayor of Syracuse, New York), expressed the concern that, once ARPA funding ends, "local leaders will be forced to make difficult choices at the same time when their revenues are unstable, at best, or may be going down because the model of how we go to work and how we pay taxes and how we think about that is changing" (Vock 2023). And like Klein, this group was also very worried about local governments "falling off the fiscal cliff" (Vock 2023). And also like Klein, this gathering of the fiscal experts and local government officials proffered that we are certain to find out quite soon once ARPA money goes away if local government used the boom of free-flowing federal dollars responsibly or not (Vock 2023). That is, did they use this huge surge in money to fund one-time investments that match the fact that the revenue was volatile? Or alternately, did they spend the last few years cutting taxes and creating new spending policy programs that will be hard to reverse in the future?

***New revenue from gifts and donations***

Local governments (from municipalities to counties to school districts) have always been blessed by and benefitted from the willingness of generous and civic-spirited philanthropists and well-endowed businesses and corporations to donate large sums of money for the welfare and good of their communities. The names of people like Henry Ford, John D. Rockerfeller, Andrew Carnegie, Cornelius Vanderbilt, E.I DuPont, Robert Mellon, George Steinbrenner, Thomas A. Yawkey, Walt Disney, Samuel Walton, Bill Gates, and many other less known individuals in smaller communities (where they are still revered figures there for their good works and willingness to share their wealth) makes their names synonymous with philanthropy in the United States. They have helped to finance the creation and construction of everything from libraries and other public buildings to civic centers, to roads and highways to auditoriums for the arts to sports facilities to parks to hospitals, to living facilities for the poor to paying for utilities and infrastructure for their businesses. Their generosity does not stop there, as they also make in-kind donations in the form of state of the art medical equipment in hospitals, classroom and library computers and books and other educational supplies and materials to local districts to sports equipment for local government recreational departments to orphanages for children without parents to real estate and buildings for public use.

Therefore, it is very important for local officials to establish and nurture relationships with individuals and business who have the ability and willingness to donate whether it is monetary or in-kind contributions. Money obviously can be used to augment what always seems to be not enough revenue from traditional sources, while in-kind gifts can free up funds obtained from normal revenue streams so as to enable local governments to stretch their limited resources to provide additional services and programs or expand and/or improve the quality of existing ones.

## Revenue savings due to reduced expenditures

While not technically "new revenue" per se, any money that local governments can avoid spending, in essence, can be redirected to the cost of providing current services or future new services and programs. Another way to think about this scenario is that, whenever local governments are able to realize any kind of "revenue savings," it usually means that they can reallocate current funds in different ways so as to achieve the "end-game goal" (if not, state constitutional mandate) to balance the budget. Revenue savings can result from several kinds of possibilities.

One way that this can happen would be for one's state or possibly the federal government being agreeable to assuming total or partial financial responsibility for a service or program currently provided either in part or full by a local government. Many times, this is referred to as the transference of a service or program responsibility from a lower to a higher level of government. Although there are many possibilities here, but shifting the service responsibility (and attendant costs) of services in the areas like health care, welfare, and transportation would undoubtedly result in substantial cost savings for local governments.

The relaxation or elimination of unfunded state and federal mandates would be another important way for local governments to realize cost savings and redirect these funds to services and programs more valued by their constituents. If we have learned nothing else in recent years from local government officials, it is that they have become greatly overburdened with onerous state and federal mandates that are consuming a greater portion of their limited financial resources. Many estimates have placed the costs of these unfunded mandates in the billions of dollars, while citizens complain that their local governments are not able to spend more of their own money on fixing potholes, hiring more police officers or firefighters, expanding roads snared with traffic, building more schools, economic development, etc.

Another strategy for reducing local government expenditures that has received a lot of attention in the last several decades has been the outsourcing of services to either private-sector vendors, non-profit organizations, or other local governments. While these plans are not necessarily suitable for all type services and not able to produce appreciable cost savings,[15] they have been popular among local governments, especially since the 1980s when cutback management became a necessity.[16] Therefore, it is still important for local governments to continue to employ these means to cut direct service costs and even expand their use of them where feasible so as to permit them to more judiciously utilize limited current revenues, as long as there is no appreciable diminution in the quality of service delivery.

A closely related cost savings idea is the co-production of services with neighboring jurisdictions. For example, two or more local governments may decide to jointly finance, build, and cooperate in the operating of a facility such as a water filtration complex, sewage treatment plant, electric generating station, 911 emergency call center, storage building or share a computing system, equipment, or personnel. At a cheaper cost to all parties, each government is able to realize a cost savings unlike if they were to "go it alone" and therefore either need less revenue in their budget than in previous years or be able to spend some current revenue for other service needs.

Greater reliance on non-profits and/or volunteerism is yet another means of achieving spending reductions and thereby freeing up current revenues for other purposes. Sometimes, these tactics are closely associated with outsourcing because they can in either part or fully relieve local governments from current financial commitments. At any rate, it is worth the effort of local governments to continue, if not expand, their usage of these means to close the gap in their budgets and while also being able to redirect vital resources to the delivery of other services that are not amenable to turning over to non-profits entities or using volunteer workers.

The adoption of more or better cost-efficient measures in the production and provision of services is another alternative to having to raise more revenue (e.g., through "right-sizing" or some form of "reinventing government"[17] strategies"). These means of ferreting out operating inefficiencies[18] that can lower spending needs while also making better use of one's revenue for other services can be accomplished by also adopting different approaches to allocating limited resources such as Zero-Based Budgeting (ZBB), Planning, Programming, and Budgeting System (PPBS), Priority-Based Budgeting (PBB), or Management by Objectives, or some form of performance budgeting techniques that are designed to promote cost savings, efficiency, effectiveness, and responsiveness. In the end, local governments will be better prepared to rank order service priorities and then allocate available revenue in a logical, consistent, and effective manner.

In addition, it is important for local governments to rethink the pricing and collection of certain fines and fees that are onerous for the poor and people who are habitually late with utility and fee payments or rack up a lot of civil offenses and ultimately are not able to pay the original fine/fee plus late/add-on charges and penalties. In fact, some studies (e.g., see Dube, Glenn, and Kavanagh 2022) have found out that local governments practicing something known as "segmented pricing" actually collect more revenue while reducing expensive administrative and collection costs. At the same time, they are also able to ensure greater fairness and equity for all members of their community. Simply put, given the inequity and unfairness of some forms of taxation, fines, and assessment and penalties on the poor and minorities and also the fact that continuing this practice can be counterproductive (i.e., local governments end up "throwing good money after bad" by spending precious, limited resources to collect delinquent payments for utilities and traffic fines and other penalties), it would be prudent for these governments to just write off the debt and move on!

Finally, it is incumbent on local government officials to connect regularly with their constituents to determine if there is still support for certain kinds of services that they may no longer want to receive and instead would prefer for the monetary savings be allocated to improving current services or providing new kinds of services. It would be unfortunate to continue to waste money on services that are neither used nor desired when the local government is being challenged by shrinking revenues and even experiencing shortfalls in its budget. Excellent ways for local governments to keep an open dialogue with their constituents are through regular usage of professionally administered citizen surveys and having citizens participate in carefully constructed virtual budgeting exercises. The latter suggestion is especially important as it permits citizens to "walk a mile in the shoes" of the elected local representatives and thus be able to appreciate the dilemmas and political cross-currents that these officials confront when constructing the annual budget.

## Conclusions and thoughts to ponder

Someone picking up this book a hundred or two hundred years from now will likely be able to affirm that local governments are still in existence. That is, one will probably be able to locate and testify to the real world, day-to-day functioning of local governments like San Bernardino County California, Clarke County Nevada, City of Georgetown, South Carolina, City of Winchester, Virginia, City of Cleveland, Ohio, Town of Rockland in Maine, Town of Bridgeport, Connecticut, Bear Creek Township in Michigan, Grandview Township in Illinois, Evangeline Parish Solid Waste Disposal District in Louisiana, Southwest Florida Water Management District in Florida, Maries County R-II School District in Missouri, and Northeast Bradford School District in Pennsylvania. Moreover, it is conceivable that these governments will be continuing to do what their states had originally intended for them to do—essentially providing "local" type services to local residents and even delivering "state" services (many of them mandated) at the local level much as if they were "branch" or "satellite" offices of their state governments. Counties, municipalities, and townships will undoubtedly be providing many of their large menus of the same services that they have provided for many decades with some new services added and some no longer available, while special districts are most likely to exist in their capacity to fill the service gaps left by county and municipal governments. And, school districts will still be providing the one service for which they have always been responsible for—education—with perhaps some tweaks here and there.

But, would a person a hundred or two hundred years from now find from an inspection of county, municipal, township, special district, or school district budgets that these governments are funding the provision of services and programs in the same way that they had in the past? In other words, would such an analysis indicate that revenue patterns of local governments have mainly remained the same over time or had they changed either moderately or even appreciably in predictable or unpredictable ways? Based on the discussion above about "the road lying ahead," it is conceivable that revenue patterns of some or all local governments could change over time given the increasing and sometimes unpredictable challenges facing these governments as well as taking advantage of novel and even unknown or previously unthinkable opportunities available to them. Will local governments become more creative and innovative in crafting their revenue systems or be willing to take calculated gambles by "thinking outside of the box"? Will local governments rethink how they tax or determine various types of fees or charges for services to ensure their fairness and sensitivity to citizens' income or ability to pay? Only time will tell if they do so and the degree to which they were successful. In the meantime, however, it will be imperative for political science and public administrative scholars who study and write about local government finances to continue to closely monitor the revenue side of county, municipal, township, special district, and school district budgets (i.e., how local officials decide how to pay the bills) and especially those internal and external factors that can prompt or necessitate changes in various funding alternatives.

## Notes

1 While some attribute the adage to a quote make by Benjamin Franklin in a letter to Jean-Baptiste Le Roy in 1789, others claim that it was first used by Daniel Defoe (*The Political History of the Devil*, 1726) or Christopher Bullock (*The Cobbler of Preston*, 1716).

2 Simply stated, federal aid provided to states that is subsequently "passed on" to their local governments is officially recorded as federal aid to local governments, for to do so would amount to what is referred to as "double counting."

3 Wildavsky's notion about the incremental approach to budgeting is closely related to the concept of incremental change developed by Dahl and Lindbloom in *Politics, Economics, and Welfare* (1953, especially pp. 82–85).

4 This critical depiction of the budgetary process should be as accurate for state and local governments as it is for the national government, although Wildavsky's chief focus in his book was the federal budgetary process.

5 Because of these and other inadequacies associated with the age-old and antiquated incremental approach to local government budgeting, a growing number of practitioners and scholars have begun to embrace a new, refreshing way to go about devising the local government budget referred to as priority-based budgeting or PBB. In fact, over 200 North American local governments have implemented this relatively new approach to the budgeting process. In its simplest terms, PBB reflects a contemporary attempt to systematically determine and implement the budgetary allocation or reallocation of resources. PBB is a spin-off of sorts of Zero-Based Budgeting (ZBB) that, according to Zhang and Nguyen-Hoang (2022, 4), "requires an organization to identify its service delivery programs and their associated costs, determine organizational priorities, rate the programs according to their alignment with said priorities, and then reallocate budgetary resources from lower-priority programs to higher-priority ones." Proponents of the PBB reform process believe that it will inevitably result in budgetary winners and losers, and, most importantly, bring about significant benefits that both local official and their citizens have desired for many years—that is, enhanced governmental effectiveness, efficiency, and equity. For more details about this fairly novel budgetary approach, the interested reader may want to consult the article by Zhang and Nguyen-Hoang, along with some other sources like Natchez and Bupp 1973; Ho, 2011; Kavanagh, Johnson, and Fabian 2011; Kavanagh 2012; Mitchell and Thurmaier 2016; Mitchell 2023.

6 For more details on how UWF works, see Detter and Kavanagh 2021.

7 Most local governments also have the ability to expand their utilities' capacity if there is a surge in new users within their jurisdiction and if there is money to be made from contracting with other governments to provide sundry utility services.

8 See Kavanagh (2022b) for a fuller description of the "Financial Foundations for Thriving Communities" method and the five "pillars" that undergird it (establishing a long-term vision, build trust and open communication, use collective decision-making, create clear rules, and treat everyone fairly).

9 For more specific details about private-sector affirmative litigation, see Farrar, Eiselt, and Kavanagh (2022).

10 In addition, to opioids, private-sector affirmative action litigation subject matter has included the following: revenue recovery, vaping, environmental matters, false actions claims, data breach/electronic privacy, antitrust and anticompetitive conduct, consumer protection, and medical services. For more detailed information, see Farrar, Eiselt, and Kavanagh (2022).

11 When given the opportunity to do so, local governments have been creative in utilizing the ability to tap new sources of revenue. Some recent examples include taxing windfarms and assisted living facilities (e.g., see Brunner and Schwegman 2022; Larson and Carroll 2023).

12 Under the ARPA legislation, townships may apply for these funds, while several pools of money were set aside by Congress for specific federal departments and agencies (e.g., Departments of Education, Housing and Urban Development, Interior, and Transportation) so they could provide financial assistance to school districts and special districts.

13 This program, which was part and parcel of Richard Nixon's New Federalism election campaign platform in 1972, took advantage of a large federal government budget surplus and was touted as a means of sharing this "windfall" kind of money with the citizens at the local level who had paid it into the federal treasury as taxes. In short,

it was "sold" to the public and Congress as a noble gesture of retuning this money back to its source ("hard-working taxpayers") and their governments to be spent in a way in which as they thought best. In fact, local (and state) governments were given wide latitude in how they could spend the money. As would be expected, revenue sharing was strongly supported by state and local government officials as well as their residents.

14 According to Kleine (2023), local government officials could start this process by asking themselves several key questions, including: (1) Are we using ARPA funds to reduce future operation costs? (2) Could we save money through competition? (3) Can we better leverage our assets? (4) Are we giving away too much in tax incentives? (5) Are we recovering the full cost of our services? (6) Are our pension and medical plans fair to both employer and employees? (7) Can we go big with bots? Kleine is absolutely correct, in that there is no better time than the immediate present for local government leaders to ask these tough questions and possibly some others and decisively take concrete steps to bring their budgets into structural balance so that they can hopefully avoid the fast approaching ARPA fiscal cliff.

15 For a good explanation of the motives behind local governments' interest in and practicalities of contracting out, see Benton and Menzel (1992).

16 See Levine (1978, 1979, 1980, 1999) for excellent overviews of cutback management in both theory and practice.

17 In the 1990s, former Vice-President Al Gore's National Performance Review movement (NPR) started a much-needed, earnest dialogue about the overdue need to candidly and boldly assess what governments and the public were getting for what they were spending. Although NPR was initially meant to focus on the national or federal government, the merits of this new way of thinking about budgeting spread to state and local governments as well. The NPR movement was inspired by Osborne and Gaebler's (1993) classic book on reinventing government.

18 This could also include things like bureaucratic reorganization, multi-tasking and/or retooling employees, use of emerging technology, and cutting back by holding the line on employee wages and fringe benefits (especially exorbitant or unreasonable pensions).

## References


Benton, J. Edwin. 2012. "State-City and State-County Fiscal Relations: A Look at the Past and Present and a Glimpse at the Future." In Jack W. Meek and Kurt Thurmaier (eds.), *Networked Governance: The Future of Intergovernmental Management*. Washington, DC: Sage/CQ Press: 39–63.

———. and. 1992. "Contracting and Franchising County Services in Florida," *Urban Affairs Quarterly*, 27 (March): 436–56.

———. Grant Rissler, and Spencer Wagner. 2020. "City and County Governments in the Time of COVID-19: The Long and Winding Road," *State and Local Government Review*, 51(March): 28–52.

Brachman, Levea, and Glencora Haskins. 2023. "*The American Rescue Plan, Two Years Later: Analyzing Local Governments' Efforts at Equitable, Transformative Change*." Washington, D.C." Brookings Institution. March. https://www.brookings.edu/articles/the-american-rescue-plan-two-years-later-analyzing-local-governments-efforts-at-equitable-transformative-change/. Accessed on October, 1, 2023.

Brunner, Eric J., and David J. Schwegman. 2022. "Windfall Revenues from Windfarms. How Do County Government Respond to Increases in the Local Tax Base Induced by Wind Energy Installations," *Public Budgeting & Finance*, 42(Fall): 93–113.

Dahl, Robert A., and Charles E. Lindbloom. 1953. *Politics, Economics, and Welfare*. New York: Harper and Brothers.

Detter, Dag, and Shayne Kavanagh. 2021. *Putting Public Assets to Work: Examining the Potential of Urban Wealth Funds for North American Cities*. Chicago: Government Finance Officers' Association.

Dube, Jean–Pierre, Bryan Glenn, and Shayne Kavanagh. 2022. *Segmenting Prices for Fines and Fees: Increasing Revenues and Fairness at the Same Time*. Washington, DC: International City/County Management Association. https://www.gfoa.org/materials/putting-public-assets-to-work

Farrar, W. Grant, Erich Eiselt, and Shayne Kavanagh. 2022. *Legal Financing: Can Private Capital Unlock the Hidden Asset of Local Government Affirmative Litigation?* Chicago: Government Finance Officers' Association. https://www.gfoa.org/materials/legal-financing

Ho, Affred T. 2011. "PBB in American Local Governments: It Is More Than a Management Tool," *Public Administration Review*, 71(May/June): 391–401.

Kavanagh, Shayne. 2012. "Zero-Based Budgeting: Modern Experiences and/Current Perspectives," *Public Finance Review*, 26(2): 8–14.

———. 2021. *Entrepreneurial Thinking in Local Government: Unlocking the Revenue-Creating Potential of Community Assets without Privatization?* Chicago: Government Finance Officers' Association.

———. 2022a. "Rethinking Local Government Revenue: Why the Time is Now and What Can Be Done." *Public Management (PM) Magazine*, 104 Number 4): April 1.

———. 2022b. *Rethinking Revenue: Boston's Pilot (Payment In Lieu of Taxes) Project*. Chicago: Government Finance Officers' Association.

———. C. Jon Johnson, and Chris Fabian. 2011. *Anatomy of Priority-Driven Budget Process*. Chicago, Il: Government Finance Officers Association.

———. and Sabrina Agarunova. 2022. "Rethinking Budgeting: Are We Ready for a New Approach?" *Public Management (PM) Magazine*, 104 Number 4): March 21.

Kleine, Andrew. 2023. "Questions From the Edge: The End of the American Rescue Plan Act Is Not Far Off. Is Your Local Government Ready?" *PA Times*, May 26. Accessed at: https://patimes.org/questions-from-the-edge-the-end-of-the-american-rescue-plan-act-is-not-far-off-is-your-local-government-ready/

Krane, Dale, Platon N. Rigos, and Melvin B. Hill. Jr. 2001. *Home Rule in America: A Fifty-State Handbook*. Washington, DC: CQ Press.

Larson, Sarah E., and Deborah A. Carroll. 2023. "Now You're Tax Exempt, Now You're Not: Property Tax of Assisted Living Facilities," *Public Budgeting & Finance*, 43(Spring): 3–20.

Lasswell, Harold. 1936. *Politics: Who Get What, When, How?* New York: McGraw-Hill Company.

Levine, Charles H. 1978. "Organizational Decline and Cutback Management," *Public Administration Review*, 38(March/April): 316–25.

———. 1979. "More on Cutback Management: Hard Questions for Hard Times," *Public Administration Review*, 39(July/August): 179–83.

———. ed. 1980. *Managing Fiscal Stress: The Crisis in the Public Sector*. Chatham NJ: Chatham House Publishers.

———. 1999. *Organizational Decline and Cutback Management*. New York: Routledge.

Lindbloom, Charles E. 1959. "The Science of 'Muddling Though'," *Public Administration Review*, 19(Spring): 79–88.

Mitchell, David. 2023. "Priority-Based Budgeting: An Honest Broker among Municipal Functions," *Public Budgeting & Finance*, 43(Spring): 21–37.

———. and Kurt Thurmaier. 2016. "Currents and Undercurrents in Budgeting Theory: Exploring the Swirls, Heading Upstream." In Jos C. N. Raadschelders and Richard J. Stillman. (eds.), *Foundations of Public Administration*. Irvine, CA: Melvin & Leheigh Publishers: 192–211.

Natchez, Peter B., and Irvin C. Bupp. 1973. "Policy and Priority in the Budgetary Process," *American Political Science Review*, 67(September): 951–63.

Osborne, David, and Ted Gaebler. 1993. *Reinventing Government: How the Entrepreneurial Spirit Is Transforming the Public Sector*. New York: The Penguin Group.

Simon, Herbert A. 1955. "A Behavioral Model of Rational Choice," *Quarterly Journal of Economics*, 69(February): 99–118.

Vock, Daniel C. 2023. "Cities Facing Mounting Financial Pressures," *Route Fifty*. May 19. Accessed at: https://www.route-fifty.com/finance/2023/05/cities-face-mounting-financial-pressures/386604/

Wildavsky, Aaron. 1964. *The Politics of the Budgetary Process*. Boston: Little, Brown and Company.

Zhang, Pengru, and Phuong Nguyen-Hoang, 2022. "Home Rule and Municipal Revenue Stability: New Evidence from Texas," *Public Budgeting & Finance*, 43 (Spring): 38–60.

# Index

*Note:* Page numbers followed by *n* represent endnote.